Orientation to
Professional
Counseling
Past, Present, and Future Trends

edited by **Sylvia C. Nassar** and **Spencer G. Niles**

AMERICAN COUNSELING
ASSOCIATION
6101 Stevenson Avenue • Suite 600
Alexandria, VA 22304
www.counseling.org

Orientation to
Professional
Counseling
Past, Present, and Future Trends

American Counseling Association

6101 Stevenson Avenue, Suite 600 • Alexandria, VA 22304

Associate Publisher • Carolyn C. Baker

Digital and Print Development Editor • Nancy Driver

Senior Production Manager • Bonny E. Gaston

Copy Editor • Beth Ciha

Cover and text design by Bonny E. Gaston

Library of Congress Cataloging-in-Publication Data

Names: Nassar, Sylvia C., editor. | Niles, Spencer G., editor.
Title: Orientation to professional counseling: past, present, and future
    trends / [edited by] Sylvia C. Nassar, Spencer G. Niles.
Description: Alexandria, VA : American Counseling Association, [2017] |
    Includes bibliographical references and index.
Identifiers: LCCN 2017015994 | ISBN 9781556203664 (pbk. : alk. paper)
Subjects: LCSH: Counseling.
Classification: LCC BF637.C6 O687 2017 | DDC 158.3—dc23 LC record
    available at https://lccn.loc.gov/2017015994

Table of Contents

SECTION III Current Issues for Personal and Professional Development

Foreword

Courtland C. Lee[1]

I have been a counselor educator for 38 years. I have seen and used a number of orientation to the counseling profession books in my preparation of counselors at several leading universities. These books have always served a useful purpose in helping give students an overview of the profession as they prepare for their counseling careers. When introducing beginning students to the profession of counseling, I ask myself the following: What is it that I want them to know? How do I begin the socialization process that will ultimately result in knowledgeable professional counselors? The answers to these questions usually focus on ensuring that students get an understanding of the foundations of the profession, an overview of the specialties that make up the profession, and an examination of current issues that impact the personal and professional development of a counselor. Over the years I have observed that an understanding of these three areas provides a solid professional foundation in the training and development of counseling students.

This book, edited by Sylvia C. Nassar and Spencer G. Niles, colleagues of long standing whose careers I have watched grow in stature over the years, hits the mark in all three of these areas. For me, this book represents the next generation in the introduction to the counseling profession text genre. With *Orientation to Professional Counseling: Past, Present, and Future Trends,* the editors have enlisted an impressive collection of individuals to introduce readers to the foundations of counseling, the specialties that enrich the profession, and current issues that impact counselors both professionally and personally. I know and have worked closely with many of the contributors to this

---

[1]Courtland C. Lee is a professor in the Counselor Education Program at The Chicago School of Professional Psychology, Washington, DC, and served as American Counseling Association President, 1997–1998.

book over the years and can attest to the fact that they are scholarly leaders in the counseling profession and provide keen insight into their respective subject areas.

The contents of this book also reflect issues that professional counselors will confront in the highly technical, culturally diverse, globally interconnected world of the second decade of the 21st century. The chapters in each of the three sections of the book reflect the realities of this contemporary world as they relate to the profession of counseling.

Section I explores the foundational elements of professional counseling, including ethics, multicultural competency, individual and group counseling, and assessment and research in counseling. Any individual beginning a career as a professional counselor must be anchored in these elements, and the chapters in this section provide this foundational framework.

Section II looks at a number of the counseling specialties that form crucial pieces of the broad quilt that can be considered the counseling profession. Although each chapter makes a cogent case for the significance of the specialty, the overarching theme throughout this section of the book is that counseling is in reality a unified profession.

Section III places the book in its place in time—the end of the second decade of the 21st century. The chapter contributors in this section do this by examining current issues that impact the evolution of the profession and the ongoing development of counselors.

As I reflect on the excellent work that Nassar, Niles, and the contributors to this book have done, I am struck by the myriad issues and trends that swirl around the profession of counseling, for example, multiculturalism and social justice, licensure and certification, accreditation, health care legislation, counselor advocacy, best practice, just to name a few. These issues and trends present those of us who prepare counselors with the challenge of orienting our students to the profession within the context of the questions I posed earlier. I am pleased that the American Counseling Association took up this challenge by publishing this book and entrusting its completion to two preeminent leaders in the field.

Preface

How This Book Came About

This book was years in the making. Really, when we think about it in retrospect, we can recount our very earliest conversations about the counseling profession and our unique and distinct perspectives, which evolved in tandem with the profession itself.

For Sylvia, this included perspectives gained over several terms on the National Board for Certified Counselors, over several terms on the state licensure board and as state board ethics chair, as a section and then senior associate editor of the *Journal of Counseling & Development,* as a member of the Council for Accreditation of Counseling and Related Educational Programs (CACREP) 2016 Standards Revision Committee, and most recently as an appointee to an Association for Multicultural Counseling and Development committee to revise the Multicultural Counseling Competencies.

For Spencer, it included his roles and perspectives as a several-term journal editor (of the *Journal of Counseling & Development* and *The Career Development Quarterly*), a several-term president of the National Career Development Association, and president of Chi Sigma Iota.

Both of us were professional counselors and subsequently career academicians. Both of us have been in roles as administrators of counselor education programs. Both of us have received numerous awards and distinctions throughout our careers, and both of us have published extensively in the counseling literature. Both of us have consulted nationally and internationally on professional counseling, credentialing, and competency development.

In our combined and overlapping tenures, we have witnessed the emergence and development of professional counseling—from the early battles for state licensure and other professional recognitions to competency and standards development, to the quickly emerging need for and implications of policy work at the national and international levels.

The rationale for, and relevance of, this text is that it provides both a historical perspective as well as—and more important—a comprehensive overview of the critical current issues for contemporary counselors-in-training. Fully aligned with 2016 CACREP Standards, it introduces all of the content areas identified as being practiced by counselors in the United States today. It also orients beginning counselors to the range of specialty areas currently encompassed by the counseling profession and underscores the core content and expertise common within a unified counseling identity. We believe that this perspective is critical in fostering and strengthening a unified identity among all counselors and essential to ensuring the success of the counseling profession, both nationally and globally.

Overview of the Book

Early on in the development of this project, we made two key decisions. First, we decided that the book would be an edited volume—that is, chapter authors would be identified and invited based on their expertise and prominence regarding the particular content of the chapter. Although both of us, as textbook editors, have expansive experience and perspectives, we decided that it was important that the voices of experts in specific content areas be represented throughout the text. Thus, the array of chapter authors and their historical contributions to the field, both individually and collectively, are daunting. These authors are truly the leaders of the profession as we now know it!

Second, we made the commitment to align the text as fully as possible with the 2016 CACREP Standards. Other texts may incorporate and cite the standards, but they reflect the authors' or editors' perspectives on key topics and content within the field. Although our perspectives and those of the chapter authors are certainly represented, we defer to the current CACREP Standards as representing those of the counseling profession, and it is our intent to fully support them in our orientation to professional counseling as well as to support past, present, and future trends.

We believe that you will find our textbook both stimulating and engaging. The chapters are generally written in the first person and speak directly to their counselor-in-training audience. Each chapter includes learning objectives, learning activities, review questions, and supplementary resources. Section I (Foundational Elements of Professional Counseling) chapters intersperse thought questions, brief case examples, and implications for practice throughout. Section II (Counseling Specialties) chapters incorporate both the contextual and practice dimensions to reflect those same dimensions in the 2016 CACREP Standards. These chapters additionally include voices from the field (perspectives from practicing professional counselors in their respective areas of expertise) as well as special considerations. Finally, Section III (Current Issues for Personal and Professional Development) chapters incorporate, again, voices from the field as well as rich opportunities for self-reflection for counselors-in-training.

Acknowledgments

We acknowledge the wealth of information we have gained from each of the professional counselors who have crossed our paths daily over the past three decades and dedicate this book to all of the future counselors who aspire to join our profession. Furthermore, we thank the Council for Accreditation of Counseling and Related Educational Programs for its visionary leadership and the professional standards it promulgates for and on behalf of the counseling profession and thus for providing the basis for the current text. We also thank the American Counseling Association, Chi Sigma Iota, the National Board for Certified Counselors, and the myriad other counseling organizations that promote the professionalization of counseling. Last but in no way least, we give our unending thanks to Aisha Al-Qimlass, who served tirelessly as the editorial project manager for this text, and to the American Counseling Association editorial staff for its gentle patience and support throughout the project.

About the Editors

Sylvia C. Nasser, PhD, is currently a professor and doctoral program coordinator of counselor education at North Carolina State University. She earned her doctorate in counseling and counselor education from the University of North Carolina at Greensboro in 1994 and her master's degree in guidance and counseling in 1984. She has served in a variety of clinical mental health, school, and college settings over the past 30 years, and her initiatives have included promoting the professionalism of counseling and counselor education. Her scholarship spans multicultural, gender, and career development issues, with a special focus on Arab American acculturation and ethnic identity development. She has published nearly 90 books, refereed articles, and other instructional materials and delivered more than 100 conference presentations. Dr. Nassar recently served on the Association for Multicultural Counseling and Development's Multicultural Counseling Competencies Revision Committee and on the Council for Accreditation of Counseling and Related Educational Programs 2016 Standards Revision Committee. She has served as board member for the Census Information Center Advisory Board to the Arab American Institute, the National Board for Certified Counselors, and the North Carolina Board of Licensed Professional Counselors. She is past associate editor for multicultural issues for the *Journal of Counseling & Development*, for which she currently serves as senior associate editor. Her recent National Science Foundation and National Aeronautics and Space Administration–funded projects have examined career stereotyping and evaluated curriculum tools. Dr. Nassar's undergirding areas of scholarship and consulting include acculturation, advocacy, career development and underrepresentation issues, program evaluation, clinical supervision, and internationalization. She has provided training and consultation on such issues to international colleagues at institutional and governmental levels in Canada, Finland, Germany,

Lebanon, Mexico, and Qatar. She received the Extended Research Award from the American Counseling Association in 2013 and the Distinguished Service Award from the Association for Counselor Education and Supervision in 2016. She was named the Michael G. Morris Endowed Chair in Eastern Michigan University's College of Education for 2014–2015 and Research Triangle Institute International University Scholar for 2016–2017.

Spencer G. Niles, PhD, serves as dean of and professor in the School of Education at the College of William and Mary in Williamsburg, Virginia. Previously he served as distinguished professor and department head for the Department of Educational Psychology, Counseling, and Special Education at The Pennsylvania State University and professor and assistant dean in the Curry School of Education at the University of Virginia. Dr. Niles is the recipient of the National Career Development Association's (NCDA) Eminent Career Award; an NCDA Fellow; a Fellow of the American Counseling Association (ACA); a recipient of ACA's Thomas J. Sweeney Award for Visionary Leadership and Advocacy, President's Award, David K. Brooks, Jr., Distinguished Mentor Award, and Extended Research Award; and a recipient of the University of British Columbia Noted Scholar Award. He has served as president of NCDA (2003–2004), president-elect of NCDA (2017–2018), and president of Chi Sigma Iota (2016–2017); is a board member of the International Centre for Career Development and Public Policy; was a two-term editor of *The Career Development Quarterly* and the *Journal of Counseling & Development*; and currently serves on numerous journal editorial boards. He has authored or coauthored approximately 130 publications and delivered more than 150 presentations on career development theory and practice.

Dr. Niles is an honorary member of the Japanese Career Development Association, an honorary member of the Italian Association for Educational and Vocational Guidance, and a lifetime honorary member of the Ohio Career Development Association. He has conducted career counseling training in Argentina, Australia, Belgium, Canada, Denmark, England, Estonia, Finland, Germany, India, Ireland, Italy, Japan, New Zealand, Portugal, Qatar, Rwanda, Singapore, South Africa, Spain, and the United Arab Emirates. His current research addresses creating and sustaining hope in career and life planning among marginalized populations.

About the Contributors

Carla Adkison-Johnson, PhD, is a professor in the Department of Counselor Education and Counseling Psychology at Western Michigan University. She has published extensively in the areas of counselor preparation, clinical mental health counseling, and child-rearing practices in African American families. Her research has garnered attention in the legal, child welfare, and counselor education literature.

Aisha Al-Qimlass, MS, LPCA, CRC, LCASA, is a doctoral candidate in counseling and counselor education at North Carolina State University. Her primary areas of clinical and research interest include chemical dependency, co-occurring disorders, Islamic feminism, and career development.

Richard S. Balkin, PhD, LPC, NCC, is a professor at the University of Mississippi. He is editor of the *Journal of Counseling & Development,* a Fellow of the American Counseling Association, and past president of the Association for Assessment and Research in Counseling. His primary areas of interest include client-centered outcomes, assessment, research methods and statistics, and religious diversity.

Shanita Brown, PhD, LPCA, NCC, ACS, is a visiting assistant professor of counselor education at Wake Forest University. She has more than 15 years of clinical mental health experience in various work settings. Her research and service focuses on emerging contexts of intimate partner violence, multicultural counseling, social justice advocacy, and adolescence.

Rick Bruhn, EdD, LPC-S, LMT, is a professor and doctoral program director in the Department of Counselor Education at Sam Houston State University.

Craig S. Cashwell, PhD, LPC, NCC, ACS, is a professor in the Department of Counseling and Educational Development at the University of North Carolina at Greensboro and maintains a part-time private practice specializing in addiction and couples counseling.

He has served as chair of the Council for Accreditation of Counseling and Related Educational Programs board; president of Chi Sigma Iota International; president of the Association for Spiritual, Ethical, and Religious Values in Counseling; and Association for Counselor Education and Supervision representative to the American Counseling Association Governing Council.

Annemarie Connor, PhD, is an assistant professor of rehabilitation sciences at Florida Gulf Coast University. She has a doctorate in rehabilitation counselor education from Michigan State University and nearly 15 years of clinical experience as a licensed occupational therapist. Her research and scholarly interests include the working alliance, psychological wellness, social participation, and vocational rehabilitation.

Darcie Davis-Gage, PhD, is an associate professor and mental health clinical counseling coordinator at the University of Northern Iowa. Her current research interests include the effectiveness of career construction groups, creative interventions in counseling and supervision, and counselor wellness and self-care.

Thelma Duffey, PhD, is a professor in and chair of the Department of Counseling at the University of Texas at San Antonio and immediate past president of the American Counseling Association (ACA). Dr. Duffey was the founding president of the Association for Creativity in Counseling, a division within the ACA, and is editor of the *Journal of Creativity in Mental Health*. Dr. Duffey served as guest coeditor of the *Journal of Counseling & Development* special issue on counseling men and the *Journal of Counseling & Development* special section on relational-cultural theory. Dr. Duffey, an ACA Fellow, has received numerous leadership and research awards from professional organizations, such as the Association for Counselor Education and Supervision; the ACA; the Texas Counseling Association; the Southern Association for Counselor Education and Supervision; the Association for Creativity in Counseling; the Texas Association for Counselor Education and Supervision; and the Association for Assessment, Research, and Counseling. She has more than 60 peer-reviewed publications and three edited and coedited books: *Creative Interventions in Grief and Loss Therapy: When the Music Stops, a Dream Dies*; *A Counselor's Guide to Working With Men*; and *Child and Adolescent Counseling Case Studies: Developmental, Relational, Multicultural, and Systemic Perspectives*.

Perry C. Francis, EdD, LPC, NCC, ACS, is a professor of counseling at Eastern Michigan University, where he also manages the College of Education Counseling Training Clinic. He has been involved in the leadership of the American College Counseling Association for more than 20 years. He has written and presented in the area of ethics and college counseling for more than 20 years and manages the college counseling program at Eastern Michigan University.

Shane Haberstroh, EdD, is an associate professor and doctoral program director in the Department of Counseling at the University of Texas at San Antonio. He is a past president of the Association for Creativity in Counseling and served on its founding board. He is currently the Association for Creativity in Counseling representative to the American Counseling Association Governing Council and the Governing Council liaison to the Research and Knowledge Committee of the American Counseling Association. Dr. Haberstroh serves as associate editor of the *Journal of Creativity in Mental Health.* He has published a coedited book and numerous articles and book chapters primarily focused on developmental relational counseling, online counseling, creativity in counseling, and addiction treatment and recovery. His collaborative research project on relational competencies won the 2010 Texas Counseling Association Research Award, and his collaborative publication on assessment practices in counselor education programs was recognized with the 2014 Association for Assessment and Research in Counseling/Counseling Outcome Research and Evaluation Outstanding Outcome Research Award. Dr. Haberstroh began his career in 1992 as a residential technician in a 28-day drug treatment program and has worked as a counselor and supervisor in addiction treatment centers, private practice, and criminal justice settings. He has been a counselor educator since 2003, and he joined the faculty at the University of Texas at San Antonio in 2004.

Barbara Herlihy, PhD, NCC, LPC, LPC-S, is professor emeritus in the Counselor Education Program, Department of Educational Leadership, Counseling, and Foundations, at the University of New Orleans. She has published numerous articles and book chapters on the topics of ethics, feminist therapy, social justice, and international perspectives on counseling and is the coauthor of three current textbooks on counselor ethics. She is currently engaged in efforts to further the internationalization of the counseling profession.

Cheryl Holcomb-McCoy, PhD, is dean of the School of Education and a professor of education at American University in Washington, DC. Previously she held appointments as vice provost for faculty affairs and vice dean of academic affairs at Johns Hopkins University. In counselor education, she served as associate professor of counselor education at the University of Maryland, College Park, and assistant professor and director of the School Counseling Program at Brooklyn College of the City University of New York. Dr. Holcomb-McCoy earned a doctorate in counseling and educational development from the University of North Carolina at Greensboro and a master of education in school counseling and bachelor of science in early childhood education, both from the University of Virginia. Her areas of research specialization include the measurement of multicultural self-efficacy and the examination of school counselors' influence on low-income students' college and career readiness. Dr. Holcomb-McCoy, a Fellow of the American Counseling Association, is the author of the best-selling book *School Counseling to Close the Achievement Gap: A Social Justice Framework for Success.*

Virginia A. Kelly, PhD, LPC, is a professor at Fairfield University in Fairfield, Connecticut. Her primary area of scholarly interest is addictions, specifically the ways in which addiction impacts families. She teaches classes in research, assessment, and addiction in the family.

Trenton Landon, PhD, is a graduate of Michigan State University with a doctorate in rehabilitation counselor education. Prior to working in academia, Dr. Landon worked for 7 years as a rehabilitation counselor. During that time, he had the opportunity to work with transition-age youth, participate in the mental health and drug courts programs, and work with the state psychiatric hospital. Currently, Dr. Landon teaches master's-level coursework in the rehabilitation counseling program at Utah State University. His research interests include the professional development of counselors, clinical supervision, ethics and ethical decision making, rural rehabilitation, and the social inclusion of individuals with disabilities.

Michael J. Leahy, PhD, LPC, CRC, is a university distinguished professor of rehabilitation counseling and director of the Office of Rehabilitation and Disability Studies at Michigan State University. He has a doctorate in rehabilitation psychology from the University of Wisconsin–Madison and more than 40 years of experience in rehabilitation as a counselor, administrator, researcher, and educator. Dr. Leahy is a licensed professional counselor and a certified rehabilitation counselor.

Matthew Lyons, PhD, is a faculty member at Central Michigan University in Mt. Pleasant, Michigan. His primary areas of interest include spirituality, human development, and leadership in the counseling profession.

W. Bradley McKibben, PhD, NCC, ACS, is an assistant professor of counselor education at Nova Southeastern University in Davie, Florida, where he teaches master's-level courses in clinical mental health counseling. His research interests in clinical supervision focus on relational issues, counselor development, and multicultural considerations.

Amy Milsom, DEd, LPC-S, NCC, is a certified kindergarten-through-Grade 12 school counselor, a professor at Clemson University, and coordinator of the school counseling program at Clemson University. Her primary areas of research include students with disabilities, postsecondary transition planning, and counselor preparation. She is coauthor of *Career and College Readiness Counseling in P-12 Schools.*

Judith Nelson, PhD, LMT, is an associate professor (retired) in the Department of Counselor Education at Sam Houston State University.

Mary Nichter, PhD, LMT, is a professor in and chair of the Department of Counselor Education at Sam Houston State University.

Mark Pope, EdD, NCC, MCC, MAC, ACS, is the curators' distinguished professor in the Counseling and Family Therapy Program at the University of Missouri–Saint Louis. He is a former president of the American Counseling Association; National Career Development Association; Association for Lesbian, Gay, Bisexual, and Transgender Issues in Counseling; and Society for the Psychological Study of Lesbian, Gay, Bisexual, and Transgender Issues. Dr. Pope is widely considered to be one of the founders of and leading authors in the field of cultural diversity issues in career counseling, especially gay and lesbian career development. His major publications have focused on counseling with sexual, racial, and ethnic minorities; the history of and public policy issues in counseling; and professional identity. He has also served as editor of *The Career Development Quarterly.*

Jeffrey Strozier, MA, LCPC, is a doctoral candidate at the University of New Orleans. His research interests include experiential trainings, empathy development, and serious mental illness. He has extensive experience providing community-based counseling to persons with serious mental illness.

Vilia M. Tarvydas, PhD, is a university professor emerita of rehabilitation and counselor education and faculty director of the Iowa—Support, Education, and Resources for Veterans and Enlisted program at the University of Iowa. She has a doctorate in rehabilitation psychology from the University of Wisconsin–Madison and more than 40 years of experience in rehabilitation and mental health counseling as a direct service provider, scholar, and educator. Dr. Tarvydas is a licensed mental health counselor (retired) and a certified rehabilitation counselor.

Ann Vernon, PhD, LPC, is professor emerita at the University of Northern Iowa and is the author of many books, chapters, and articles. She conducts training programs in the United States and abroad on rational emotive and cognitive behavior therapy as well as other workshops focusing on counseling children, adolescents, and couples.

Richard E. Watts, PhD, LPC, is distinguished professor of counseling at Sam Houston State University in Huntsville, Texas, and a Texas State University System regents' professor.

Section I

Foundational Elements of
Professional
Counseling

Chapter 1

Professional Counseling and Ethical Practice

Barbara Herlihy, Matthew Lyons, and Jeffrey Strozier

Learning Objectives

1. Understand the history and core values of the counseling profession.
2. Gain knowledge of major professional organizations and understand how they serve individual counselors and the profession as a whole.
3. Understand the primary activities of professional counselors and the importance of ethical practice.
4. Understand what it means to be a professional counselor.

• • •

Counselors make a unique contribution to promoting mental health and wellness for individuals, families, groups, and communities in contemporary society. This is an exciting time to be entering the counseling profession. If you are like most counselors, you will derive a strong sense of fulfillment from your work and from knowing that you have made a difference in the lives of others (Remley & Herlihy, 2016). You will find opportunities to practice counseling in schools, universities, community agencies, psychiatric hospitals, substance abuse treatment facilities, juvenile and adult justice programs, private practice offices, and other diverse settings. The job market for professional counselors is promising. The *Occupational Outlook Handbook* (Bureau of Labor Statistics, 2016a) projects a positive growth of 19% for mental health counselors and marriage and family therapists over the next decade. This means the addition of 31,400 jobs. The median annual salary was $41,880 in 2014, and the top 10% earned $68,790. The projected growth for school and career counselors, who are listed separately in the *Occupational Outlook Handbook,* is not as high at 8%; however, the median annual salary is higher at $53,660, with the top 10% earning $87,640 (Bureau of Labor Statistics, 2016b).

You should understand that these employment opportunities have been hard won. Counselors are relative newcomers to the field of mental health care compared to other mental health professionals (such as psychologists, social workers, and psychiatrists), and it has taken many years of sustained effort in the professional, political, and legislative arenas for counseling to establish itself as a separate profession. Having a sense of our origins will help you gain an appreciation for the current status enjoyed by counselors in the United States. We begin this chapter with a brief history of the counseling profession, and then we explain our unique philosophy. We discuss the importance of professional organizations and of credentialing. We introduce the ethical standards in which our profession is grounded. Finally, we describe the work of the counselor by highlighting some of the major professional activities in which counselors engage.

A History of the Counseling Profession

No two descriptions of the origins of the counseling profession are alike; various writers have emphasized different historical events and have interpreted them through their own lenses. It is difficult to identify a distinct starting place for our profession because counseling evolved from several diverse fields. Most historians suggest that early ideas about the need for counseling emerged in the climate of the early 20th century, when U.S. society was undergoing a number of changes due to industrialization, social reform, population growth, a burgeoning immigrant population, and realization of the ideal of education for all citizens. Three social movements that occurred at that time can be identified as forerunners of counseling as we understand it today: vocational guidance, school guidance and counseling, and the mental hygiene/mental health movement. Several decades later, counseling psychology emerged as a specialty within the field of psychology; this development had an equally strong influence on the counseling profession.

Frank Parsons, who is often acknowledged as the father of the vocational guidance movement, was one of many social reformers in the early 20th century who sought to make the United States a better place to live and work. He founded, directed, and served as a counselor at the Vocational Bureau in Boston, which opened in 1908 with the purpose of helping the burgeoning population of immigrants who were looking for work (Glosoff & Schwarz-Whittaker, 2013). In his book *Choosing a Vocation* (1909), he proposed that people must consider their interests, skills, and qualifications if they are to be happy and successful in a particular career.

Whereas some historians see vocational guidance as the earliest impetus for the development of counseling, others see the school setting as the first home for the profession (e.g., Sweeney, 2001). An early pioneer in school guidance and counseling was Jesse B. Davis, a progressive school superintendent in Grand Rapids, Michigan, who incorporated vocational guidance into the high school curriculum in 1907. Similar vocational guidance services were created at much the same time in other regions of the country (Glosoff & Schwarz-Whittaker, 2013). Throughout the 1920s, organized secondary school guidance programs, which were usually modeled after college student personnel programs, emerged with increasing frequency.

At much the same time that the vocational and educational guidance movements were taking root, a dramatic shift took place in society's view of mental illness (Erford, 2014), which led to the mental hygiene movement. The catalyst was the publication of an autobiography titled *A Mind That Found Itself* (1908) by Clifford Beers, who had been treated for mental illness under deplorable conditions in psychiatric institutions. His reform efforts led to more humane treatment for people suffering from mental illnesses.

The Great Depression of the 1930s created an impetus for further development of vocational guidance, as there was a clear need for vocational and career counseling to assist the millions of adults and youth who had suffered loss of employment (Ohlsen, 1983). E. G. Williamson and his colleagues, working with university students, developed what is thought to be the first theory of career counseling, which came to be known as the *Minnesota model* (Gladding, 2013). In this model, traits of individuals were matched with those of various occupations in a directive, counselor-centered approach.

The two world wars provided an impetus for the development of both psychological testing and mental health treatment (Glosoff & Schwarz-Whittaker, 2013). At the onset of World War I, the Army commissioned the development of psychological tests in response to the need to screen large numbers of personnel. After World War I, psychological testing became pervasive in personnel work in business and industry and in education, to the extent that testing and counseling were often considered synonymous (Glosoff & Schwarz-Whittaker, 2013). After World War II, it became evident that returning soldiers needed help dealing with what was called *battle fatigue* or *shell shock* (now termed *posttraumatic stress disorder*). The War Department

5

established a counseling program, and the Veterans Administration also established counseling centers within their hospitals (Shertzer & Stone, 1981). As a result of increased recognition of the need to treat mental health problems, the National Mental Health Act of 1948 was enacted.

Another seminal development during this era was a growing awareness in the United States of Sigmund Freud's theory of psychoanalysis, which was the first systematic and comprehensive approach to psychotherapy. Freud's theory ushered in a new way of thinking about mental health and mental illness.

The decade of the 1950s saw a number of significant developments that advanced the counseling profession. Recognition of the value of school counseling increased after the Soviets launched Sputnik, the first satellite (Erford, 2014). U.S. politicians feared that their country was losing the space race, which led to legislation that funded substantial programs aimed at encouraging high school students to seek careers in math and science. Title V of the National Defense Education Act of 1958 provided grants to offer counseling services in high schools and to train school and career counselors. As a result, the number of school counselors increased dramatically.

In 1951, Carl Rogers published *Client-Centered Therapy,* in which he proposed his theory of nondirective counseling (now called *person-centered counseling*). Rogers's ideas that clients, rather than their therapists, were the experts on their lives and that clients would move in a positive direction in a counseling relationship that conveyed certain therapeutic conditions offered an alternative to the then-existing approaches of directive vocational counseling and psychoanalysis. Perhaps more than any other person, Rogers influenced how counselors interact with clients (Gibson & Mitchell, 2008).

Also during the 1950s, Thorazine, a medication that alleviates symptoms of severe mental disorders, was discovered, enabling the release into the community of large numbers of individuals who had been institutionalized in state hospitals. The continuing deinstitutionalization of persons with mental illness provided the impetus for the enactment a decade later of the Community Mental Health Act of 1963, which called for establishing comprehensive community mental health centers across the country (Fuenfhausen, Young, Cashwell, & Musangali, 2016). This act was expanded in 1975, creating an increased need for community mental health counselors.

The later decades of the 20th century were marked by the expansion, diversification, and professionalization of counseling. Whereas the three main approaches to counseling had been psychodynamic (Freudian), directive, and client centered (Gladding, 2013), many new approaches emerged during the 1960s, including cognitive behavior, rational emotive, gestalt, reality, and existential therapies (Neukrug, 2011). In 1964, the National Defense Education Act was expanded to include training counselors to serve clients from elementary school through junior colleges. By 1967, almost 20,000 school counselors had been trained as a result of this act (Tolbert, 1982). The Rehabilitation Act of 1973 ensured that vocational rehabilitation services would be available to individuals with disabilities, increasing the need for counselors trained in the specialty of rehabilitation counseling.

Several events occurred during the second half of the 20th century that furthered the professionalization of counseling. In 1952, four existing professional organizations merged into the American Personnel and Guidance Association (APGA), now the American Counseling Association (ACA). The association grew in the ensuing decades to reach a membership of 40,000 (Neukrug, 2011), and several new divisions were formed. One division, the Association for Counselor Education and Supervision, began to offer suggested training standards for master's-level counseling programs. The Council for Accreditation of Counseling and Related Educational Programs (CACREP) was formed in 1981 to continue to define standards for education and training. National credentialing was initiated with the establishment of the Council on Rehabilitation Education (CORE) in 1973 and the National Board for Certified Counselors (NBCC) in 1981. State licensure began in 1976, when Virginia became the first state to license counselors. The state licensure movement continued to gain momentum, moving toward the goal of achieving counselor licensure in every state.

Before we conclude our history tour, it is important to acknowledge the profound influence of counseling psychology on the development of the counseling profession. From the mid-20th century onward, our profession basically shares its history with the emergence of counseling psychology as a specialty within the psychology profession (Goodyear, 2000). At the same time that APGA was being formed in 1952, counseling psychology was emerging as Division 17 of the American Psychological Association (APA). Counseling psychology distinguished itself as a specialty concerned with addressing the normal adjustment needs of clients, in contrast to clinical psychology, which focused on individuals with chronic and severe mental disorders. For many years, it was not uncommon for therapists to affiliate with both APGA and Division 17 of APA, and counselor trainees studied much of the same literature as counseling psychology trainees. Although many similarities still exist, an important difference between counselors and counseling psychologists is that a doctorate was established as the required degree to practice as a psychologist, whereas counselors practice with a master's degree. Unfortunately, in the 1970s, marketplace politics led APA to launch an initiative to establish state legislation that would limit the practice of counseling to doctoral-level psychologists or those working under their supervision (Sweeney, 2001). Of course, counselor organizations opposed such

7

efforts. This generated a great deal of tension between counseling and counseling psychology, which is ongoing.

Today, people seeking mental health services can choose from a variety of providers—not only counselors and psychologists but also clinical social workers, psychiatrists, marriage and family therapists, and other specialists. Practitioners of all of these professions are similar in that all are trained at the master's degree level or higher and all provide mental health services for clients (Remley & Herlihy, 2016). Important differences exist, however, and when you become a counselor, it will be vital that you understand the differences among mental health professionals and are able to articulate the unique identity and services of counselors. The primary difference is that counselors espouse the wellness model, a philosophy described in some detail in the next section. In addition, differences among the various mental health professionals are reflected in their training and preparation. The psychology curriculum reflects a focus on understanding human behavior and emphasizes assessment and research. Social work training focuses on improving clients' lives by advocating for social justice and the eradication of poverty and emphasizes linking clients to social services. Counselor training emphasizes the learning of counseling skills. Most counselor training programs are located in schools or colleges of education, and the requirements for a master's degree are substantial compared to those in other degree programs. Your program of study entails 48 to 60 credit hours or more and prepares you in eight essential areas of knowledge and skill. It includes an extensive field experience during which you will practice counseling under close supervision. Your professors are counselor educators who promote a strong professional counselor identity (Gladding, 2013) that is grounded in the wellness model. Throughout your training program, your professors aim to ensure that you also will have a strong professional identity and take pride in your profession (Remley & Herlihy, 2016).

In the 21st century, counseling has continued to make advances on many fronts to establish itself as a unique profession. Counselor licensure is now a reality in all 50 states, the District of Columbia, Puerto Rico, and the Virgin Islands. The American Association of State Counseling Boards, founded in 1985, is working to achieve license portability, so that counselors who are licensed in one state can be licensed in other states as well. ACA (originally APGA) remains the largest association representing counselors, with more than 53,000 members and 20 divisions as of 2017. A task for the future is to find a way to unify counselors who identify with diverse specialties under a shared umbrella organization. An important step toward unification was taken recently with the merger of ACA and CORE, the organization that credentials rehabilitation counselors. CACREP and NBCC continue to provide leadership in the setting of training standards and in national testing and certification, and both of these organizations as well as ACA are providing leadership as counseling becomes more globalized.

The Philosophy of the Counseling Profession

Although there are similarities between counseling and other mental health professions, the values and beliefs underlying our profession are what set us apart (Neukrug, 2011). Key concepts in understanding the philosophy of the counseling profession are wellness, developmental perspective, prevention, and empowerment (Remley & Herlihy, 2016).

If you are to be an effective advocate for the counseling profession, you will need to understand and be able to explain the differences between the wellness model and the medical or illness model of mental health. The medical model was created by physicians to guide them in treating people with physical illnesses. Older mental health professions such as clinical psychology, psychiatry, and social work came into existence when the medical model was prevalent, so they have their roots in this model. Although we are oversimplifying here, it can be said that mental health professionals who operate from the medical model begin by diagnosing a mental disorder, and then they apply scientific knowledge to cure the disorder or reduce its symptoms. Underlying assumptions of this approach are that the client is ill or diminished in some way and that the mental health professional is the expert in ameliorating or eliminating the client's symptoms. Counseling, a newer profession, is grounded in the wellness model. Rather than focusing on the mental illness, counselors take a more holistic perspective and recognize that mental health exists along a continuum: At one end are individuals with severe and chronic mental illnesses, and at the other end are self-actualizing people who practice wellness in their lives. We encourage you to learn more about the wellness wheel of counseling (Myers, Sweeney, & Witmer, 2000), which is holistic and takes into consideration multiple areas of a person's life, such as relationships, spirituality, career or job, and leisure activities. We also encourage you to personally apply what you are learning about wellness by considering the questions in Sidebar 1.1.

Sidebar 1.1   Reflection

As a counselor who espouses the wellness model, how important is it that you practice wellness in your own personal and professional lives?

Make a list of good self-care habits that you can cultivate while you are in graduate school. Which of these habits will you commit to starting or improving on today?

• • •

Another thing that distinguishes counselors from other mental health professionals is a developmental perspective. Counseling psychologists who are trained in the medical model tend to focus on diagnosing a mental disorder and view clients' problems as pathological. By contrast, counselors believe that many of these problems are better understood as developmental in nature and as natural and normal responses to life's challenges. Some examples are a 4-year-old crying and clinging to her parent during the first weeks of kindergarten, a teenager being defiant and rebellious toward his parents, a woman in her 40s having an affair with a younger man after 20 years in a committed marriage, and a 63-year-old feeling depressed as retirement approaches. Counselors avoid pathologizing behaviors such as these by viewing them through a developmental lens and focus on helping clients understand that life transitions can be difficult but are transitory.

Some counseling psychologists and other mental health professionals who subscribe to the medical model work primarily to assist clients whose problems are severe enough to be diagnosable. Counselors, in contrast, are committed not only to remediation (helping clients resolve existing mental health issues) but also to the prevention of mental illness to the extent possible. We as counselors often say that "counseling is for everyone," which is a way to convey our hope that people will seek counseling long before their problems become serious or chronic. Counselors encourage people to seek counseling when they first begin to experience discomfort or distress rather than to wait until the distress becomes severe. Early intervention can help prevent problems from escalating, and counselors can teach clients skills to manage their concerns and prevent future occurrences.

A final cornerstone of the counseling philosophy is empowerment. Unlike the medical model of illness, which can encourage a pattern of lifelong dependence on a professional expert, counselors aim to empower clients to problem-solve independently in the future. As Remley and Herlihy (2016) stated, counselors "encourage clients to assume responsibility for their lives and learn to live in a manner that allows them autonomy and independence as those concepts are understood in the clients' cultures" (p. 30).

In summary, counselors are guided by the wellness model, which takes a holistic view of clients in all areas of functioning in their environments. Counselors understand clients from a developmental perspective, advocate for prevention, and work to empower clients to be able to resolve problems on their own in the future.

Professional Organizations

Professional organizations play an important role in the counseling profession. As previously noted, ACA is the largest organization representing professional counselors. The organization connects professional counselors, serves as the primary vehicle for continuing education (Spurgeon, 2012), and promotes our professional identity. The ACA mission statement reads as follows:

> The mission of the American Counseling Association is to enhance the quality of life in society by promoting the development of professional counselors, advancing the counseling profession, and using the profession and practice of counseling to promote respect for human dignity and diversity. (ACA, 2017)

ACA consists of 20 divisions, 56 chartered branches, and four regional organizations. ACA offers discounted membership dues for students, and we urge you to join now as a means of connecting with your intended profession and developing your professional identity. We hope you will visit the ACA website (www.counseling.org) to see the benefits of membership and get a sense of which divisions you would like to join. Some divisions represent counseling specialties by work setting (such as the American College Counseling Association and the American School Counselor Association [ASCA]), and other divisions serve counselors who are interested in specialty areas of practice (such as the Association for Creativity in Counseling and Association for Specialists in Group Work). The divisions do important work in promoting professional identity and advancing areas of the professions. For example, in 2005, ASCA published the ASCA National Model, which provides the design and delivery roadmap for comprehensive school counseling programs.

Also under the ACA umbrella are 56 branches, most of which are state associations, although divisions also exist in Europe and Latin America. Each branch is geographically specific and has its own membership, conferences, and in most cases, publication. Most state divisions hold annual conferences that are a significant source of continuing education hours and local networking.

Other organizations that are not connected to ACA play a significant role in the counseling profession. A particularly important organization is NBCC. You can visit their website (www.nbcc.org) to learn more. NBCC provides continuing education opportunities and is the primary source of certification resources for counselors. NBCC manages the National Counselor Examination and the National Clinical Mental Health Counseling Examination. In many states, counseling program graduates who intend to practice independently in the community are required to take one of these exams to become eligible for a license.

Other important organizations include CACREP and CORE. Historically, CACREP was the accrediting body for counselor education programs and CORE was the accrediting body for rehabilitation counseling programs. The two organizations set an official merger date of July 1, 2017 (CACREP, 2016). The importance of this merged organization in our profession cannot be understated, as it accredits counselor training programs, funds research on best practices, and helps to unify our profession.

A discussion of professional organizations would not be complete without a mention of Chi Sigma Iota (CSI). CSI is an international honor society serving the counseling profession. CSI supports scholarship and provides numerous resources, including leadership training, mentoring opportunities, and community service events. You are eligible to join CSI once you have completed one full-time semester of graduate-level coursework with a grade point average of 3.5 or higher (CSI, 2016).

You will want to peruse the websites of ACA, NBCC, CACREP, CSI, and any of the ACA divisions that you find interesting to further understand their mission, purpose, and role in the profession. Joining professional organizations helps you connect with mentors and solidify your identity in the profession. The specializations represented in each of the ACA divisions afford you the opportunity to spend time with professionals with similar interests and gain exposure to cutting-edge research. In addition, you will have access to educational resources and professional liability insurance. Our professional organizations have played a key role in the development of our professional identity, and your participation will help solidify your place in the profession as well.

Credentialing

Credentialing is important because it serves to identify members of an occupational group and provides credibility to the profession as a whole (Forster, 1978; Sweeney, 1995). The master's degree is a credential that all professional counselors hold. Counselors may acquire other credentials that vary according to their specialization areas and work settings. Three primary terms used to describe these other credentials are *licensure, accreditation,* and *certification* (Adams, 2006; Forster, 1978; Sweeney, 1995). These credentials can be confusing both to counselors and to consumers because the terminology is not used consistently (Remley & Herlihy, 2016).

Licensure is granted by the state in which a counselor practices. Virginia adopted the first licensure law in 1976 (Mascari & Webber, 2013), and a significant achievement for the profession is that all 50 states, the District of Columbia, Puerto Rico, and the Virgin Islands now have counseling licensure laws. Licensure laws provide legal sanction for a profession and help define the scope of practice (Adams, 2006). State licensing boards help determine codes that regulate practice, ensure professional conduct, and remediate misconduct. You should be aware that state licensure laws have different titles in different states, and counselors may be licensed, certified, or even registered. A true state licensure law, no matter what it is called, is a practice law, which means that the counselor must be licensed to be able to practice in that state. Counselor licensure continues to evolve and requirements often change, so it is important that you know how to access current information. Information on licensure requirements can be found on the ACA website at https://www.counseling.org/knowledge-center/licensure-requirements.

One type of certification is granted by state agencies to ensure that individuals are qualified to hold certain state jobs (Remley & Herlihy, 2016). Certification does not grant you the legal right to practice, but it assures the public and employers that you have met standards determined by the profession. Types of counselors for whom state certification is usually required include school counselors, substance abuse counselors, and rehabilitation counselors. Another type of certification is national voluntary certification. Two national certification agencies important to counselors are NBCC and the Commission on Rehabilitation Counselor Certification. To earn the NCC (National Certified Counselor) credential, you must hold a master's degree, have 2 years of post-master's supervised experience, and pass the National Counselor Examination. We hope you will consider acquiring this credential, even though it is not required, as it conveys to clients, the public, and employers that you have met the highest standards developed by the profession (Remley & Herlihy, 2016).

The various types of credentialing described here may appear complicated. The ongoing need to ensure the credibility of our work, however, depends on the connections forged from the accreditation of training programs to certification and/or licensure. The future of credentialing lies in work on licensure portability and continuing to unify around common standards that define the profession.

Ethical Practice

Clients come to counseling in a vulnerable position. They need to feel safe to discuss intimate and personal aspects of their lives, to trust that their counselor is competent to help them, and to be confident that the counselor places their welfare foremost in their relationship (Remley & Herlihy, 2016). Because counselors often work with clients with little oversight and behind closed doors in confidential circumstances (Neukrug, 2011), it is essential that counselors uphold the highest standards of ethical practice.

Counselors are frequently faced with ethical questions and dilemmas and are challenged to know how to appropriately handle these situations. A primary resource for guidance on ethical questions is the *ACA Code of Ethics* (ACA, 2014). Both counseling practitioners who are ACA members and counseling students are bound to adhere to this code; therefore, you should be knowledgeable about its provisions from the very beginning of your studies. In this section of the chapter, we familiarize you with the ethics codes of counseling organizations

13

and with the underlying principles and major sections of the *ACA Code of Ethics* in particular. We also describe the relationship between law and ethics and discuss ethical decision making.

The *ACA Code of Ethics* (ACA, 2014) enumerates six fundamental principles on which ethical behavior is based. *Autonomy* refers to the counselor's obligations to respect the right of clients to make their own decisions and to avoid imposing his or her own values and beliefs onto clients. *Nonmaleficence,* which is based on the Hippocratic oath in medicine, means to do no harm to clients, even inadvertently. *Beneficence* is the flip side of the coin from nonmaleficence and means that the counselor actively works for the good of clients and society by promoting mental health and well-being. *Justice* means that the counselor treats individuals fairly and without prejudice. *Fidelity* refers to the counselor's pledge to keep promises in the service of upholding trust in the professional relationship. *Veracity* means that the counselor deals truthfully with clients and others with whom he or she comes into professional contact. All of the standards in the *Code* are grounded in these six principles.

The *ACA Code of Ethics* (ACA, 2014) is a lengthy document that contains specific standards for practice in nine areas:

- **Section A: The Counseling Relationship** provides guidelines on forming, maintaining, and ending the counseling relationship; securing the client's informed consent; avoiding imposition of personal values; maintaining professional boundaries; advocacy; fees and business practices; and working with multiple clients and clients served by other professionals.
- **Section B: Confidentiality and Privacy** offers standards related to upholding the client's right to privacy in counseling sessions and records and explains exceptions to confidentiality.
- **Section C: Professional Responsibility** gives guidance on developing and maintaining competence, advertising services and qualifications, and fulfilling responsibilities to the public and other professionals.
- **Section D: Relationships With Other Professionals** addresses relationships with fellow counselors and other professionals, employers, employees, and consultees; and respecting and maintaining good working relationships with colleagues in other mental health professions.
- **Section E: Evaluation, Assessment, and Interpretation** contains standards regarding how to select, use, and interpret assessment instruments; client rights in testing, test security, and proper testing conditions; and diagnosis and forensic evaluations.
- **Section F: Supervision, Training, and Teaching** offers standards delineating the responsibilities of supervisors and counselor educators to maintain boundaries, evaluate and remediate fairly, endorse students to enter the profession, and safeguard student and supervisee welfare.

- **Section G: Research and Publication** contains standards related to researcher responsibilities, the rights of research participants, the reporting of research results, and the ethical procedures in seeking publication.
- **Section H: Distance Counseling, Technology, and Social Media** is a newly expanded section offering ethical guidelines for the use of new and emerging technologies and for distance counseling.
- **Section I: Resolving Ethical Issues** addresses the responsibilities of counselors and counseling students to know ethical and legal standards and procedures for resolving and reporting suspected ethical violations.

Throughout your career as a counseling practitioner, you will be expected to adhere to the *ACA Code of Ethics* (ACA, 2014) as well as the ethical standards of other professional organizations to which you belong. For instance, if you become a National Certified Counselor, you will be bound to the NBCC's ethics code. In addition, if you become licensed as a professional counselor, you will need to be familiar with and adhere to the ethical standards of your state's counselor licensure board. You will need to be knowledgeable about all of the ethics codes that pertain to your practice. Adding to the complexity created by multiple codes is the need to keep current. Codes of ethics are living documents that change over time. The *ACA Code of Ethics* has been revised six times since it was first adopted in 1961; the present (2014) code is the seventh version. If you were to review previous versions, you would easily discern how the code has changed in response to our growing knowledge base and to our having reached consensus about new ethical issues. For example, earlier versions contained no guidance regarding the need for multicultural competence or the proper uses of technology.

In addition to being knowledgeable about ethics, counselors need to have a basic understanding of the law. Most areas of counseling practice are affected in some way by the law. Federal and state legislatures continually enact laws that affect counselors, and sometimes courts hand down decisions that have an impact on counselors (Neukrug, 2011). Most counselors view the law as intimidating, threatening, and antithetical to the goals of counseling. In a sense this is true: In legal proceedings, one side wins at the cost of making the other side lose, whereas counselors aim to resolve issues in a nonadversarial win–win manner. Because counselors are uncomfortable and unfamiliar with legal proceedings, they should seek legal advice when they have a legal question or issue. Remley and Herlihy (2016) explained that a legal issue is involved when (a) legal proceedings have been initiated, (b) an attorney is on the scene, or (c) you are vulnerable to having a misconduct complaint filed against you. As you gain experience, you may encounter a legal issue, seek legal advice, and then feel conflicted because following that legal advice does not seem to entail best ethical practice. Fortunately, the *ACA Code of Ethics* (ACA, 2014) recognizes that such conflicts may occur and contains guidelines for handling these situations (e.g., Standard I.1.c.).

It is important to keep in mind that the *ACA Code of Ethics* (ACA, 2014) and other codes, despite their specificity, will not contain answers to all ethical issues that will arise for you in your work. Counseling is fraught with ethical ambiguities. Fortunately, we can suggest several steps you can take when you are (inevitably) faced with an ethical dilemma. First, counselors "are expected to use a credible model of decision making" (p. 3), so you will need to study ethical decision-making models and select one that works for you when you encounter difficult issues. Second, it is good practice to collaborate with your client (and the parents/guardians of minor clients) to work out a resolution whenever possible. Counselors sometimes mistakenly think that they must resolve dilemmas *for* the client rather than *with* the client. Third, while you are working under supervision, we encourage you to bring your ethical questions to your supervision sessions so that a more seasoned professional can help you grapple with them. Fourth, ACA offers a range of resources on ethics that can be accessed at www.counseling.org/knowledge-center/ethics. Finally, advice that has become almost a mantra for dealing with ethical dilemmas is "When in doubt, consult, consult, consult." You can consult with colleagues or former professors who taught you about ethics, and ACA has an ethics specialist with whom you can consult. However, be sure that your dilemma is an ethical rather than a legal issue. When you have a legal issue, you do not want to consult with nonlawyers. Instead, you will want to contact your professional liability insurance carrier or the risk management consultant for the ACA Ethics Department.

You should be aware that even after you have collaborated and consulted in search of a solution to an ethical dilemma, there is rarely one clearly right answer (Herlihy & Corey, 2015). In the final analysis, ethical decision making requires professional judgment and the courage to make the best decision you can and act on it. You will become more comfortable with these ambiguities as you gain professional experience. You will find that your sense of ethical selfhood remains intact and grows stronger as long as you keep client welfare first and foremost, are willing to engage in reflection about how your own needs and values might be influencing your decision-making process, remember to consult (and follow the consensus of the advice you are given), keep current through reading and attending professional development workshops and conferences, and constantly aspire to maintain the highest level of ethical practice.

Professional Activities of Counselors

In this section of the chapter, we introduce you to some of the most important activities in which professional counselors engage. The primary professional activity for counselors is counseling. The consensus definition of *counseling* is that it is "a professional relationship that empowers diverse individuals, families, and groups to accomplish mental health, wellness, education, and career goals" (Kaplan, Tarvydas, & Gladding, 2014, p. 368). Despite the primary importance of counseling, we do not elaborate on it here, as an extensive discussion is presented in Chapter 3. Although the work of the counselor is complex and varied, and your work setting may emphasize activities not discussed here, almost all counselors engage in supervision, collaboration and consultation, advocacy, and the use of technology. We discuss each of these activities in turn.

Supervision

Acquiring any of the credentials discussed earlier entails completing not only formal coursework but also the vital process of practicing under supervision both while and after completing the master's degree. Because many counseling students find the idea of supervision daunting, anxiety producing, and challenging, we discuss supervision in some detail. The thought of being evaluated by a senior clinician produces apprehension, and the mystery of the process does little to help calm the fears of beginning students. These feelings are understandable considering the vulnerability needed to engage in the supervision process. Effective supervision asks counselors-in-training to open themselves up to assessment of their still-developing skills by senior clinicians. Fortunately, once counselors-in-training learn about the process, what is expected, and how they will be evaluated, these fears abate, and most tend to appreciate and even look forward to supervision.

Broadly defined, *supervision* is a collaborative process in which you will be observed by an advanced clinician while working with clients. The goal of supervision is to develop your counseling skills and ensure that clients are cared for in a competent way (American Association of State Counseling Boards, 2007). Basic counseling skills, theoretical orientation, ethics, cultural factors, and professional development are just a few of the areas that you can expect to be explored during the supervision process. Throughout the supervision process, your supervisor will provide you with feedback that is meant to facilitate your growth as a professional.

You can expect your supervisor to be a senior clinician with specialized training in clinical supervision. Requirements for qualifying as a clinical supervisor vary from state to state, and some states require supervisors to obtain an additional licensure credential. Your initial experiences with counseling under supervision will occur during your field experiences late in your master's degree program. Later, after you graduate, you will need to work under supervision if you want to pursue counselor licensure in your state. It should be noted that not all counselors need a license to practice; for example, school counselors typically are exempt from the requirement to be licensed.

The counseling profession also trains supervisors at the doctoral level. These doctoral programs, typically called counselor education and supervision programs, are open to experienced counselors and prepare students to teach and supervise counselors-in-training. During a doctoral counselor education and supervision program students are given the opportunity to practice supervision. This means that a doctoral student, under the supervision of faculty, may supervise you during your practicum and internship. This layered supervision process helps doctoral students develop their competencies as supervisors and strengthen their professional identity.

The exact structure of and approach to supervision will depend on the supervision model your supervisor chooses to follow. Supervision approaches and models are numerous and varied. To give you a sense of the variety, we briefly describe four of the most common models you may encounter during supervision: cognitive behavioral, person-centered, discrimination, and integrated developmental models.

Supervisors who operate from a cognitive behavioral model in their work with clients may gravitate toward the cognitive behavioral supervision model. A supervisor using this model will focus on exploring distressing thoughts you have while counseling a client. The supervisor will help you examine these thoughts, understand how they affect your mood and the counseling process, and assist you with modifying these thoughts (Kindsvatter, 2008).

Person-centered supervision is a truly collaborative approach in which there is no expert in the room. A supervisor using this model, which is based on Carl Rogers's person-centered counseling, will rely on his or her relationship with you, avoiding giving directions and analyses, to develop an atmosphere that contributes to your growth and change as a counselor (Lambers, 2000).

The discrimination model is an atheoretical model that describes the areas of focus or clinical skills to be addressed in supervision. It also describes three roles in which your supervisor can function (Bernard, 1979). A supervisor using this model may choose to focus on your intervention, conceptualization, or personalization skills. In working with you to develop these skills your supervisor will function as a teacher, consultant, or counselor.

The integrated developmental model describes how counselors grow over time and identifies four stages that counselors move through as they develop (Stoltenberg & McNeill, 2010). Each of these four stages is characterized by three elements, including self-awareness, motivation, and autonomy. The stages are fluid, which means that a supervisee may move back and forth through the stages as new challenges are presented. The model also outlines strategies and interventions that a supervisor might use depending on the developmental stage of the supervisee.

Whichever model your supervisor utilizes, it is important to keep in mind that supervision is a collaborative process. It may be useful to ask your supervisor about his or her supervision model as a way to gain further understanding of the process and what will be expected of you. Now that you have read about the process of supervision, we invite you to personally apply what you have learned by considering the questions in Sidebar 1.2.

Collaboration and Consultation

Counselors view development, prevention, and wellness as key components of their professional identity (Mellin, 2011). It is this unique, refined professional identity that makes counselors vital contributors in mental health care settings. It is likely that in your work as a counselor, you will be called on to address complex issues that will require collaboration with mental health professionals who are not counselors. It is necessary to acknowledge and understand the strengths of other mental health professionals and recognize that no one profession alone can resolve multifaceted client issues (Lopez-Baez & Paylo, 2009). Among the wide variety of mental health professionals with whom you may collaborate and consult are psychologists, psychiatrists, nurse practitioners, social workers, and community support specialists.

Professional collaboration and consultation are important components in facilitating client care, and the variety of professionals with whom you work and the dynamics of the collaboration and consultation will depend on the setting in which you are employed. Whether you are working in a school, university, community agency, psychiatric hospital, substance abuse treatment facility, juvenile and adult justice program, or private practice, you should understand how collaboration and consultation are utilized within your particular setting.

Multidisciplinary community outreach teams are increasingly being used to provide mental health care to clients (Moser, Monroe-DeVita,

Sidebar 1.2   Thought Questions

What do you foresee as some of the benefits of supervision?
What concerns do you have about supervision?
How can you resolve these concerns?
What is your role as a supervisee in the supervision process?

• • •

& Teague, 2013). Community outreach teams provide the majority of their services within the client's natural setting. This setting may be the client's home, a Social Security office, a physician's office, public transportation, a coffee shop, or any environment where a client would like to develop skills or requires support. Teams are typically composed of a variety of different mental health professionals, each practicing within their discipline. Teams may be composed of counselors, social workers, community support specialists, psychiatrists, and nurses who function as a unified team under the direction of a senior clinician, typically referred to as the *team leader*. Each of these professionals brings unique skills and perspectives that in combination provide for effective treatment.

Community outreach teams are a good example to consider to understand how interdisciplinary collaboration occurs. Professionals on the team come to rely on one another to develop comprehensive treatment approaches and fill in the gaps for one another. For example, the team psychiatrist may consult with counselors to understand how a client is responding to medication in his or her natural setting. Social workers may consult with counselors to understand systemic issues facing a client, and counselors may consult with nurses to understand how physical health issues might be affecting the counseling process. Collaboration is client focused, with client well-being and progress paramount to the process.

Earlier in the chapter, we noted that counselors and other mental health professionals may find themselves in an adversarial position with each other. For instance, you may be testifying before your state legislature to advocate for the inclusion of counselors as approved providers for the company that provides health insurance for state employees, and a psychologist with whom you consult and collaborate may be testifying against that same proposed legislation. It is important for you to understand that these kinds of political differences are always set aside in the work environment to best serve shared clients.

Advocacy

The history of the counseling profession demonstrates how important it is that both individuals and organizations assume the role of advocate. Lee and Walz (1998) defined *advocacy* as the "process or act of pleading for a cause or a proposal" (p. 8). Assuming the role of an advocate involves both recognizing "a need or problem and having the necessary motivation to take action" (Myers, Sweeney, & White, 2002, p. 398).

As you learned earlier in the chapter, counseling is still a relatively new profession, and our history is rich with examples of those who have advocated specifically for the establishment and advancement of our profession and the clients we serve. Likewise, you will be presented with opportunities to advocate for the profession and increase our representation alongside other mental health providers.

Our understanding of advocacy has developed in parallel with the development of the counseling profession. As we increasingly embrace the philosophies that make our profession unique, we understand the developmental barriers that impact the wellness of individuals, groups, and entire cultures. Professional counselors actively seek ways to advocate with and for individuals and groups to eliminate barriers and encourage the development of and access to resources (Lee & Rodgers, 2009; Lewis, Lewis, Daniels, & D'Andrea, 1998).

In 2003, the ACA Governing Council endorsed the ACA Advocacy Competencies (Toporek, Lewis, & Crethar, 2009). These competencies, which describe the complex and multilevel nature of advocacy, can be found at https://www.counseling.org/Resources/Competencies/Advocacy_Competencies.pdf. You will be presented frequently with opportunities to advocate for and with individual clients who face specific barriers and have not been able to identify resources or allies to promote their own growth.

However, the profession increasingly recognizes that barriers are systemic and that macrolevel factors affect human development and well-being. Professional counselors are becoming more involved in systemic and macrolevel change that challenges social, economic, and cultural barriers and influences public opinion and legislation (Lee & Rodgers, 2009). The globalization of counseling means that professional borders are expanding. The development of the counseling profession around the world brings with it opportunities to advocate in the geopolitical arena and to participate in conversations on conflict resolution, peace, and global citizenship.

ACA's (2011) *20/20: A Vision for the Future of Counseling* describes advocacy priorities for our future. According to this document, the counseling profession should:

- Promote client welfare and advocacy;
- Offer ongoing education and training for counselors on client and student advocacy;
- Identify one advocacy project that will be completed annually within a selected community as a way to strengthen our counseling identity, present ourselves as one profession, and improve public perception;
- Promote optimum health and wellness for those served as the ultimate goals of all counseling interventions; and
- Encourage evidence-based, ethical practice as the foundation for counselors-in-training and professional counselors' interventions across settings and populations served.

In addition, in 2015, ACA and the Association for Multicultural Counseling and Development endorsed the Multicultural and Social

Justice Counseling Competencies, which are based on an ecological approach to counseling and advocacy. You can find these competencies at https://www.counseling.org/docs/default-source/competencies/multicultural-and-social-justice-counseling-competencies.pdf?sfvrsn=20. These competencies are addressed more thoroughly in Chapter 2. However, it is safe to say that advocacy is and will continue to be an important part of your work as a professional counselor. Advocating with and for clients, communities, and societies to eliminate individual and systemic barriers and to develop and provide access to resources is at the heart of our professional counselor identity. Some questions regarding how you might begin to advocate are offered in Sidebar 1.3.

The Use of Technology

Fascinating areas of development in the counseling profession are the integration of technology and the delivery of online counseling services. We know that the commercialization of the Internet and the availability of personal computers and other technologies have changed the world in which we live and work (Ozcelik, 2008). You can now sit in the comfort of your home and connect with counselors across the country and even the world using e-mail, instant messaging, text messaging, or one of the many available videoconferencing platforms. In addition, professional counselors are using platforms such as YouTube, Facebook, and Twitter and are developing therapeutic apps to assist them in their work. In fact, the Internet is its own toolkit and provides an "infinite series of applications, each with its own use" (Greenfield & Yan, 2006, p. 393).

Technological advances have progressed to the point that recent revisions of the *ACA Code of Ethics* (ACA, 2014) have addressed the use of technology. The introduction to the relatively new Section H: Distance Counseling, Technology, and Social Media reads as follows:

Sidebar 1.3   Reflection

It is possible for you to advocate for many important issues and/or populations?

How has your life experience prepared you to be an advocate?

For what mental health issues, populations, or causes might you advocate in the future?

Are there steps you need to take now to gain additional knowledge and experience to advocate effectively?

• • •

Counselors understand that the profession of counseling may no longer be limited to in-person, face-to-face interactions. Counselors actively attempt to understand the evolving nature of the profession with regard to distance counseling, technology, and social media and how such resources may be used to better serve their clients. Counselors strive to become knowledgeable about these resources. Counselors understand the additional concerns related to the use of distance counseling, technology, and social media and make every attempt to protect confidentiality and meet any legal and ethical requirements for the use of such resources. (p. 17)

Discussion regarding technology in counseling has centered primarily around ethical considerations in the delivery of online counseling services. Online counseling is becoming more widespread, but it is still controversial (Baker & Ray, 2011). Questions remain regarding the use of online therapies in cases in which clients are experiencing debilitating distress or homicidal or suicidal intent (Corey, Corey, & Corey, 2019). Especially important in urgent situations when there is imminent danger or threat of harm to self or others is the ability to verify both the identity and location of clients to provide for their safety. Working through virtual platforms or electronic media makes this task more challenging (Corey et al., 2019).

In addition, lingering concerns remain concerning confidentiality. Conducting counseling online, whether using e-mail, instant messages, or videoconferencing platforms, makes it hard to guarantee clients' confidentiality. Transmitted data may be accessible by hacking e-mail accounts or instant messenger records (Bradley, Hendricks, Lock, Whiting, & Parr, 2011). Another significant concern has to do with state licensure laws. The profession continues to debate the legality of a counselor in one state providing therapy for a client in another state using either the Internet or a telephone (Baker & Ray, 2011; Corey et al., 2019).

Despite the concerns, more state licensure boards are allowing the delivery of therapy online (Haberstroh, Barney, Foster, & Duffey, 2014). Some evidence suggests that clients who have participated in online therapy have found it to be beneficial (Haberstroh et al., 2014; Haberstroh, Parr, Bradley, Morgan-Fleming, & Gee, 2008). However, the delivery of online counseling is still in the development stage, and more outcome research is needed.

We are only beginning to see how the counseling profession will change as we adopt and incorporate technology. Advancing the counseling profession will require that we embrace technological advances. To be sure, every conversation about the use of technology must include a discussion of ethics, and applications of technology must be developed in a way that remains rooted in the philosophy that makes us unique.

Chapter Summary

We began this chapter by observing that this is an exciting time to be joining the counseling profession. Counseling has been evolving for more than a century and is now a firmly established profession with its own identity, training, and skills. It is unique among mental health professions in that it is grounded in the wellness model. Counseling has a code of ethics that is updated periodically to reflect its growing knowledge base. Counselors who practice in the community are licensed in every state, and counselors who work in other settings (such as schools, substance abuse treatment facilities, and rehabilitation counseling) hold certification credentials. Our professional associations, such as ACA and NBCC, are strong advocates for the counseling profession. Although our primary function is counseling, we are also involved in supervision, consultation, and collaboration to better serve our clients. We are making creative use of new technologies.

Indeed, counseling has come a long way as a profession, yet work remains to be done. Political battles and turf wars are ongoing, as psychologists and other mental health providers continue to challenge the qualifications of counselors to perform functions such as testing and diagnosis and to be employed in certain job classifications. ACA and other counseling organizations are advocating for the inclusion of counselors among insurance providers, health maintenance organizations, and the federal government (Guindon, 2011). A recent success was the inclusion in the Veterans Administration of mental health counselors as approved providers of services to veterans. However, the Affordable Health Care for America Act, which was enacted in 2009 and provided for mental as well as medical health care, did not include counselors as approved providers for Medicare patients. On an ongoing basis, health care coverage is legislated and relegislated for political reasons; thus, it is difficult to predict future developments.

Although challenges remain, counselors continue to work to improve services and expand them to clients in diverse settings. Changing demographics and societal developments have created new opportunities to work with clients not traditionally served by counselors, such as individuals suffering from addictions, the elderly, immigrants, and people who have experienced disasters or other trauma-inducing events in the United States and across the world. Today's counselors have unprecedented opportunities to serve individuals and society. You can begin to contribute in important ways while you are still a student. You can advocate for counseling by using every opportunity to explain our unique professional identity and the services we provide. You can engage in advocacy in the political arena by joining the efforts of our professional associations to lobby for legislation that will allow counselors to serve more clients. We urge you to get involved with your chosen profession and begin to make a difference.

Learning Activities

1. Suppose you have been invited to be a panelist at a career fair in your community. Although a variety of professions are represented among the panelists, you are the only mental health professional. Panelists are instructed to answer questions from audience members in 2 minutes or less. Your first question is "Why did you choose to pursue a graduate degree in counseling, and what attracts you to the profession?" How will you answer? Try this with a classmate or a friend, and ask him or her to time your response.

2. A friend has recently gone through the breakup of a romantic relationship and tells you that she is "miserable." She says that she knows you are studying to be a counselor and asks whether you will counsel her. She adds, "It would help me and would be a great opportunity for you to practice what you're learning." Visit www.counseling.org to find and review the *ACA Code of Ethics* (ACA, 2014) for guidance on how to respond in an ethically appropriate way.

3. Consider the type of setting (e.g., school, community agency, residential treatment facility) in which you hope to work as well as your intended client population. Describe some advocacy needs that your clients in that context might have, and consider how you might work within your setting's system to address those needs.

4. Investigate the type of credential (e.g., license, certification) that you will be required to hold to practice in your intended setting in your state. Access the credentialing body's website and note the steps you will need to take to acquire that credential.

Review Questions

1. How do the philosophy of the profession and the activities of counselors fit with your own values and make counseling a good professional fit for you?

2. You have read about many people who have been influential in the profession because of their advocacy. How important do think the work of advocacy is, and in what professional areas might you advocate to help advance the profession?

3. Technology is developing rapidly, and alternatives to face-to-face counseling sessions now exist. How do you see technology continuing to shape the profession? What ideas do you have for ensuring ethical practices while continuing to embrace technological developments?

4. If a friend or family member asked you, "Why do you want to be a professional counselor?" how would you answer based on your reading of this chapter?

Further Resources

American Counseling Association
www.counseling.org
American School Counselor Association
www.schoolcounselor.org
Association for Specialists in Group Work
www.asgw.org
Chi Sigma Iota Counseling Academic and Professional Honor Society International
www.csi-net.org
Council for Accreditation of Counseling and Related Educational Programs
www.cacrep.org
National Board for Certified Counselors
www.nbcc.org

References

Adams, S. A. (2006). Does CACREP accreditation make a difference? A look at NCE results and answers. *Journal of Professional Counseling Practice, Theory, and Research, 33*(2), 60–76.

American Association of State Counseling Boards. (2007). *Approved supervisor model*. Retrieved from www.aascb.org/aws/AASCB/asset_manager/get_file/37297

American Counseling Association. (2011). *20/20: A vision for the future of counseling*. Retrieved from https://www.counseling.org/knowledge-center/20-20-a-vision-for-the-future-of-counseling

American Counseling Association. (2014). *ACA code of ethics*. Retrieved from www.counseling.org/Resources/aca-code-of-ethics.pdf

American Counseling Association. (2017). *Our mission*. Retrieved from https://www.counseling.org/about-us/about-aca/our-mission

American School Counselor Association. (2005). *The ASCA national model: A framework for school counseling programs*. Alexandria, VA: Author.

Baker, K. D., & Ray, M. (2011). Online counseling: The good, the bad, and the possibilities. *Counseling Psychology Quarterly, 24*(4), 341–346.

Beers, C. W. (1908). *A mind that found itself*. New York, NY: Doubleday.

Bernard, J. M. (1979). Supervisor training: A discrimination model. *Counselor Education and Supervision, 19,* 60–68.

Bradley, L. J., Hendricks, B., Lock, R., Whiting, P. P., & Parr, G. (2011). E-mail communication: Issues for mental health counselors. *Journal of Mental Health Counseling, 33,* 67–79.

Bureau of Labor Statistics. (2016a). *Occupational Outlook Handbook: Mental health counselors and marriage and family therapists.* Retrieved from www.bls.gov/ooh/community-and-social-service/mental-health-counsclors-and-marriage-and-family-therapists.htm

Bureau of Labor Statistics. (2016b). *Occupational Outlook Handbook: School and career counselors.* Retrieved from www.bls.gov/ooh/community-and-social-service/school-and-career-counselors.htm

Chi Sigma Iota. (2016). *Member FAQ.* Retrieved from www.csi-net.org/?page=Member_FAQ

Corey, G., Corey, M. S., & Corey, C. (2019). *Issues and ethics in the helping professions* (10th ed.). Pacific Grove, CA: Cengage Learning.

Council for Accreditation of Counseling and Related Educational Programs. (2016). *Extending CACREP accreditation to doctoral rehabilitation counselor education programs under the CACREP 2016 accreditation standards for doctoral programs.* Retrieved from www.cacrep.org/wp-content/uploads/2012/10/Accrediting-PhD-RCE-Programs-Policy-document-10-22-15.pdf

Erford, B. T. (2014). *Orientation to the counseling profession* (2nd ed.). Upper Saddle River, NJ: Pearson.

Forster, J. (1978). Counselor credentialing revisited. *Personnel and Guidance Journal, 56,* 593–598.

Fuenfhausen, K. K., Young, S., Cashwell, C., & Musangali, M. (2016). History and evolution of clinical mental health counseling. In J. S. Young & C. S. Cashwell (Eds.), *Clinical mental health counseling: Elements of effective practice* (pp. 3–30). Thousand Oaks, CA: Sage.

Gibson, R. L., & Mitchell, M. H. (2008). *Introduction to counseling and guidance* (7th ed.). Upper Saddle River, NJ: Pearson.

Gladding, S. (2013). *Counseling: A comprehensive profession* (7th ed.). Upper Saddle River, NJ: Pearson.

Glosoff, H. L., & Schwarz-Whittaker, J. E. (2013). The counseling profession: Historical perspectives and current issues and trends. In D. Capuzzi & D. R. Gross (Eds.), *Introduction to the counseling profession* (6th ed., pp. 30–76). New York, NY: Routledge.

Goodyear, R. K. (2000). An unwarranted escalation of counselor-counseling psychologist conflict: Comments on Weinrach, Lustig, Chan, and Thomas (1998). *Journal of Counseling & Development, 78,* 103–106.

Greenfield, P., & Yan, Z. (2006). Children, adolescents, and the Internet: A new field of inquiry in developmental psychology. *Developmental Psychology, 42*(3), 391–394.

Guindon, M. H. (2011). *A counseling primer: An introduction to the profession.* New York, NY: Routledge.

Haberstroh, S., Barney, L., Foster, N., & Duffey, T. (2014). The ethical and legal practice of online counseling and psychotherapy: A review of mental health professions. *Journal of Technology in Human Services, 32*(3), 149–157.

Haberstroh, S., Parr, G., Bradley, L., Morgan-Fleming, B., & Gee, R. (2008). Facilitating online counseling: Perspectives from counselors in training. *Journal of Counseling & Development, 86,* 460–470.

Herlihy, B., & Corey, G. (2015). *ACA ethical standards casebook* (7th ed.). Alexandria, VA: American Counseling Association.

Kaplan, D. M., Tarvydas, V. M., & Gladding, S. T. (2014). 20/20: A vision for the future of counseling: The new consensus definition of counseling. *Journal of Counseling & Development, 92,* 366–372. doi:10.1002/j.1556-6676.2014.00164.x

Kindsvatter, A. J. (2008). Cognitive techniques as a means for facilitating supervisee development. *Counselor Education and Supervision, 47,* 179–192.

Lambers, E. (2000). Supervision in person-centered therapy: Facilitating congruence. In E. Mearns & B. Thorne (Eds.), *Person-centered therapy today: New frontiers in theory and practice* (pp. 196–211). London, UK: Sage.

Lee, C. C., & Rodgers, R. A. (2009). Counselor advocacy: Affecting systemic change in the public arena. *Journal of Counseling & Development, 87,* 284–287.

Lee, C. C., & Walz, G. R. (1998). *Social action: A mandate for counselors.* Alexandria, VA: American Counseling Association.

Lewis, J. A., Lewis, M. D., Daniels, J. A., & D'Andrea, M. J. (1998). *Community counseling: A multicultural social justice perspective* (4th ed.). Belmont, CA: Brooks/Cole Cengage.

Lopez-Baez, S. I., & Paylo, M. J. (2009). Social justice advocacy: Community collaboration and systems advocacy. *Journal of Counseling & Development, 87,* 276–283.

Mascari, J. B., & Webber, J. (2013). CACREP accreditation: A solution to license portability and counselor identity problems. *Journal of Counseling & Development, 91,* 15–25.

Mellin, E. M. (2011). Counselor professional identity: Findings and implications for counseling and interprofessional collaboration. *Journal of Counseling & Development, 89,* 140–147.

Moser, L. L., Monroe-DeVita, M., & Teague, G. B. (2013). Evaluating integrated treatment within assertive community treatment programs: A new measure. *Journal of Dual Diagnosis, 9*(2), 187–194. doi:10.1080/15504263.2013.779480

Myers, J. E., Sweeney, T. J., & White, V. E. (2002). Advocacy for counseling and counselors: A professional imperative. *Journal of Counseling & Development, 80,* 394–402.

Myers, J. E., Sweeney, T. J., & Witmer, J. M. (2000). The wheel of wellness counseling for wellness: A holistic model for treatment planning. *Journal of Counseling & Development, 78,* 251–266.

Neukrug, E. (2011). *The world of the counselor: An introduction to the counseling profession* (4th ed.). Boston, MA: Cengage.

Ohlsen, M. M. (1983). *Introduction to counseling.* Itasca, IL: Peacock.

Ozcelik, Y. (2008). Globalization and the Internet: Digitizing the nonprofit sector. *Journal of Global Business Issues, 2*(1), 149–152.

Parsons, F. (1909). *Choosing a vocation.* Boston, MA: Houghton-Mifflin.

Remley, T. P., & Herlihy, B. (2016). *Ethical, legal, and professional issues in counseling* (5th ed.). Columbus, OH: Pearson.

Rogers, C. R. (1951). *Client-centered therapy.* Boston, MA: Houghton-Mifflin.

Shertzer, B., & Stone, S. C. (1981). *Fundamentals of guidance* (2nd ed.). Boston, MA: Houghton-Mifflin.

Spurgeon, S. L. (2012). Counselor identity—A national imperative. *Professional Counseling Practice, Theory, and Research, 39*(1), 3–16.

Stoltenberg, C. D., & McNeill, B. W. (2010). *IDM supervision: An integrative developmental model for supervision of counselors and therapists.* New York, NY: Routledge.

Sweeney, T. J. (1995). Accreditation, credentialing, professionalization: The role of specialties. *Journal of Counseling & Development, 74,* 117–125.

Sweeney, T. J. (2001). Counseling: Historical origins and philosophical roots. In D. C. Locke, J. E. Myers, & E. L. Herr (Eds.), *Handbook of counseling* (pp. 3–26). Thousand Oaks, CA: Sage.

Tolbert, E. L. (1982). *An introduction to guidance: The professional counselor* (2nd ed.). Boston, MA: Little, Brown.

Toporek, R. L., Lewis, J. A., & Crethar, H. C. (2009). Promoting systemic change through the ACA Advocacy Competencies. *Journal of Counseling & Development, 87,* 260–268.

Chapter 2

Human Growth and Development in a Multicultural Context

Cheryl Holcomb-McCoy, Shanita Brown, and Aisha Al-Qimlass

Learning Objectives

1. Describe the differences between age-graded, history-graded, and nonnormative influences.
2. Explain how power and privilege related to multicultural contexts can impact human development.
3. Define and explain the role of resilience in human development.
4. Differentiate among the four major human development theories.
5. Describe how intersecting identities reflect diversity and multi-culturalism.

• • •

How does bias develop in children? What do we know about the impact of context (e.g., poverty, substandard education and housing, over-stressed guardians) on development? How do race, ethnicity, religion, and ability levels influence human development? How do individuals typically change physically and mentally as they age? How does being a person of color influence one's development in a sociocultural context? These are among the fascinating questions that arise when studying human development. As professional counselors, we want to better understand how our clients' development and experiences shape their lives. We want to further understand how issues such as race, gender, ethnicity, religion, privilege, and oppression affect their development. More important, we want to know how we can help our clients be more successful and live productive lives.

Human growth and development has been a significant element in the counseling profession, in our training and our research, for decades. More than 20 years ago, Myers (1992) wrote that development is at the core of the counseling profession and overall human wellness. Ivey (1991), in a classic article, also proposed that development is concerned with positive human change and is actually the goal of counseling interventions. For decades, developmental psychologists and researchers studied infant and child development as a means of examining and understanding human development. However, after more extensive empirical study, researchers determined that humans develop over the span of their lifetime rather than solely in the earliest stages of their lives (Baltes, Staudinger, & Lindenberger, 1999). Therefore, it is important for counselors to study and understand development from the point of conception until the time when life (as we know it) ends.

Building from the traditional biological and psychological milestones of development, experts created the Multicultural Counseling Competencies (MCC) in the early 1990s in response to the diversification of the United States. The MCC aimed to address the social and cultural implications of development as well. The MCC were created to focus on multicultural awareness, knowledge, and skills and provided the counseling profession with guidance on interpersonal counseling interactions, with special attention to culture, ethnicity, and race (Arredondo et al., 1996; Sue, Arredondo, & McDavis, 1992). To keep up with increased diversity and change, the MCC were revised and renamed the Multicultural and Social Justice Counseling Competencies (MSJCC) in 2015. This revision sought to incorporate the overlapping of identities of a more modern society (particularly in regard to social identities such as race, gender, sexual orientation, and class), which in turn creates multiple experiences of privilege, oppression, and discrimination for any one individual. The recent development of the MSJCC provides a framework for the variety of identities counselors and clients bring to the therapeutic relationship (Ratts, Singh, Nassar-McMillan, Butler, & McCullough, 2016). The salience of the MSJCC is the belief that multiculturalism and social justice should be the core of all counseling.

This chapter assumes that humans develop within a cultural context (in which development is affected by culture and vice versa) and seeks to provide a window into the journey of how humans develop over time. Together, we explore what it means to take a multicultural life-span perspective on development. We briefly review major theories of human development and identity while incorporating those socio-cultural aspects that lead to experiences of privilege and oppression. Finally, we discuss how professional counseling is enriched through an understanding of how people change over time.

Counseling Within a Multicultural and Life-Span Development Approach

Recently, as part of *20/20: A Vision for the Future of Counseling* (American Counseling Association [ACA], 2017a), delegates from 31 counseling organizations agreed on a unified definition of *counseling:* "a professional relationship that empowers diverse individuals, families, and groups to accomplish mental health, wellness, education, and career goals" (ACA, 2017b). In accordance with this definition of professional counseling, the following core professional values are important to counselors' professional commitment:

1. Enhancing *human development* throughout the life span;
2. Honoring *diversity* and embracing a *multicultural* approach in support of the worth, dignity, potential, and uniqueness of people within their social and cultural contexts;
3. Promoting social justice;
4. Safeguarding the integrity of the counselor–client relationship; and
5. Practicing in a competent and ethical manner. (ACA, 2014, p. 3, emphasis added)

In regard to the enhancement of clients' human development, the *ACA Code of Ethics* (ACA, 2014) further states that professional counselors, when appropriate, advocate for clients to address potential barriers and obstacles that might inhibit clients' access and/or growth and development. Furthermore, the *Code* sets forth standards within each of its nine main sections pertaining specifically to diversity within both clients and counselors.

A life-span human development perspective recognizes periods and/or stages of a person's life with distinct characteristics and tasks. In Table 2.1, you will find a list of the periods that many of today's developmental psychologists regard as important. Note, however, that the ages given are approximate and that the periods represent but one view of the life span. Age, like gender, race, and other significant human characteristics, means different things in different cultures and societies. Each culture divides the life span and treats people within each age group according to its own cultural norms.

Table 2.1   Major Periods in Life-Span Human Development

Period	Age Range
Prenatal	Conception to birth
Infancy	Birth to 2 years
Preschool	2–6 years
Middle childhood	6–11 years
Adolescence	12–20 years
Early adulthood	20–40 years
Middle adulthood	40–65 years
Late adulthood	65 years to death

While reviewing the table, take a moment to think about what each age range may mean, and how it may be experienced, for individuals of intersecting or blended identities (e.g., a homosexual immigrant from a majority Buddhist country, a Black female with a disability from a high socioeconomic background).

It is impossible to discuss human development without considering the increasingly diverse and global context in which people live. The United States, for instance, is undergoing a rapid demographic shift unlike anything it has ever experienced. In 2014, the U.S. Census Bureau indicated that by 2044 White/Euro-Americans will no longer make up a racial majority in the United States. By then, the nation will be made up of a kaleidoscope of racial groups, including Latinos, Blacks, Asians, Native Americans, and multiracial Americans. The U.S. Census Bureau also indicated that, in 2014, more than 20 million children younger than the age of 5 were living in the United States, of whom 50.2% identified as a racial minority. It is predicted that, by 2050, there will be no racial or ethnic majority in the United States and that new immigrants and their children will account for 83% of the growth in the working-age population (U.S. Census Bureau, 2014).

In addition, the United States is diverse in terms of age. Approximately 10,000 Americans turn 65 every day (Passel & Cohn, 2008). Meanwhile, the average life span in the United States has increased to approximately 81 years for women and 76 years for men, with a significant number of people living well beyond those ages (Xu, Murphy, Kochanek, & Arias, 2016). Demographers project that, by 2030, 70 million people, or about 20% of the U.S. population, will be 65 or older (Passel & Cohn, 2008). Industries ranging from health care to technology to real estate have taken note of this emerging trend and are identifying how best to respond to the needs of an older population. Although a great deal has been written about how an aging population will affect the need for biomedical services, the story of how older people maintain optimal mental health throughout the life span has received far less attention.

The recognition of diversity in relation to gender identity and sexual orientation has increased as well. In the first large-scale government survey measuring Americans' sexual orientation, the National Health Interview Survey reported in July 2014 that 1.6% of Americans identify as gay or lesbian and 0.7% identify as bisexual (National Center for Health Statistics, 2014). According to a Williams Institute review based on a June–September 2012 Gallup poll, approximately 3.4% of American adults identify as lesbian, gay, bisexual, or transgender (LGBT; Gates & Newport, 2012). An earlier report published in April 2011 by the Williams Institute estimated that 3.8% of Americans identified as LGBT: 1.7% as lesbian or gay, 1.8% as bisexual, and 0.3% as transgender (Gates, 2011). Studies from several nations, including the United States, conducted at varying time periods have produced a statistical range of 1.2% to 6.8% of the adult population identifying as LGBT.

A culture-centered perspective on the psychological understanding of human development is therefore critical to effective counseling. When examining the cultural influences of various forms of discrimination on human development, it is important to keep in mind the intersection of identities. The development of both MCC and MSJCC corroborates the importance of multicultural awareness and social justice advocacy. Furthermore, the MCC and MSJCC were endorsed by ACA and the Association for Multicultural Counseling and Development. This endorsement speaks volumes about the need to integrate multiculturalism and social justice competencies throughout the counseling profession.

An Overview of Life-Span Human Development

Human development research is a relatively recent endeavor. Whereas studies of children's development began in the late 19th and early 20th centuries, investigations involving adult development, aging, and change over the life span emerged in the 1960s and 1970s. Over time, these studies inspired the construction of human development theories. A *theory* is an orderly, integrated set of statements that describe, explain, and predict behavior (Sigelman & Rider, 2014). For example, a theory of adolescent identity development would (a) describe the behaviors of adolescents as they determine their identities, (b) explain how and why adolescents develop their identities, and (c) predict the consequences of adolescent identity development (or lack of development) throughout life. Theories are important because they provide an organizing framework for our observations of people. They guide and give meaning to what we observe and provide a sound basis for practice and/or action. In short, theories help us understand development and thus help us improve the welfare and treatment of children, adults, and families.

Given the vast cultural differences across the globe, theories of development are influenced by the cultural norms of people and the times in which people live. Rogoff (2003) gave a perfect example of how culture influences development:

> Three-year-old children in Oceania take care of younger children. But, in the US, babysitters are expected to be at least 10 years older than that. And Efe infants safely use machetes, but American middle class adults often do not trust 5 year olds with knives. (p. 5)

What accounts for such marked differences in development? For the most part, human development is significantly influenced by biological, cultural, and environmental factors. One's biological development (e.g., puberty) tends to be the same across cultures, whereas social development tends to be based on one's environment or cultural influences. For instance, one's parenting style may be influenced by cultural expectations and the environment in which one lives. Developmental theorists and writers (e.g., Berk, 2014) have categorized influences on development into three broad areas: age-graded influences, history-graded influences, and nonnormative influences. Each is briefly discussed below.

Age-Graded Influences

Development can be influenced by those events that are significantly related to age and are fairly predictable as to when they occur and how long they last. For instance, most humans walk shortly after their first birthday, acquire their native language during the preschool years, and reach puberty around ages 12 to 14. These milestones are influenced by biology, but social customs can create age-graded influences as well. For instance, starting school around 5 or 6 and entering college around 18 are examples of social norms that drive age-graded events.

History-Graded Influences

Development can also be influenced by events or experiences connected to a particular historical era. Examples include epidemics, wars and/or other traumatic events, periods of economic depression, technological advances (e.g., the Internet, social media), and changing cultural values (e.g., racial integration of schools, revised attitudes toward same-sex marriage). These history-graded influences explain why people born around the same time tend to be alike or different depending on the period in which they were born or came of age.

Nonnormative Influences

Finally, development is influenced by events that happen randomly to one person or a few people. These influences can have a major impact on the direction of one's life and are often more powerful than age-graded influences in contemporary adult development. Examples might include interactions with inspiring teachers, marriages and divorces, parenthood, family deaths, career entry, illnesses, and experiences with privilege and oppression. Because these influences happen haphazardly, nonnormative events are difficult for researchers to capture and study, yet they affect people in powerful ways and are often the source of problems that bring people to a counselor for assistance. Applying the MSJCC model in our counseling work, we are encouraged to constantly take these nonnormative influences into consideration when working with our clients. For example, although we may take for granted some age-graded and/or history-graded influences, we cannot assume to understand anyone's individual experience of these influences.

Neuroplasticity

Incorporating all of those age-graded, history-graded, and nonnormative influences into one individual's life, life-span development can be characterized by lifelong neuroplasticity. *Neuroplasticity* refers to the brain's ability to change and adapt to positive or negative environmental influences. Developmental researchers have long known that child development can be damaged by a deprived environment and optimized by an enriched one. Negative environmental influences such as oppression and discrimination affect how the brain develops and forms neurons (Gee, Walsemann, & Brondolo, 2012). For instance, children who experience racism and discrimination may become self-conscious, may perceive negative feelings toward their ethnicity, and may develop low self-esteem. It is now understood that this plasticity continues into later life. The aging process is not fixed but rather can be altered considerably depending on the individual's experiences. Reflect on Sidebar 2.1 to see how age-graded, history-graded, and nonnormative influences have been a part of your life.

Basic Issues in Human Development

The field of human development contains many theories that offer different ideas about what people are like and how they change.

Sidebar 2.1   Thought Question

Think of a life event that is directly tied to a cultural norm or expectation. Is there an expected age at which this life event occurs?

• • •

Developmental psychologists have varying views of the way in which development progresses throughout the life span and the way in which human behavior is influenced by culture. Researchers and developmental theorists have attempted to determine the pathway or factors in human development. Overall, three basic questions about the nature of development characterize more traditional human development theories:

- Is the course of development continuous or discontinuous?
- Are genetic or environmental factors more important in influencing development (nature vs. nurture)?
- Does one course of development characterize all people, or are there many possible courses?

Making sure to consider multicultural context, we as counselors also need to ask ourselves the following questions when assessing an individual's development:

- How have power and privilege affected this person's development?
- How does this individual experience his or her intersecting identities?

Continuous or Discontinuous Development

Proponents of the continuity view of development (e.g., Bandura, 1977) say that development is a continuous process that is gradual and cumulative. For example, children learn to crawl, then to stand, and then to walk. They are gradually learning how to walk. It is just like hiking up a mountain path: a slow, steady ascent that leads to the top. In contrast, some people see development as consisting of different stages. Adherents to the discontinuity view of development (e.g., Piaget, 1970) believe that people pass through stages of life that are qualitatively different from one another. For example, children go from only being able to think in very concrete terms to being able to think abstractly. They have moved into the abstract thinking phase of their lives. As you can imagine, discontinuous development is like walking up the stairs: a series of stages or steps that get you to the top of the mountain.

Nature Versus Nurture

Nature versus nurture is the popular debate over whether environmental influences or genetics plays the major role in the development of the human being (Moore, 2003; Plomin, 1996). Most researchers today see the two forces as interacting to affect human behaviors, thoughts, and temperament. Studies in which monozygotic (identical) twins are compared with fraternal (nonidentical) twins are cited by those who hold that genetics plays the major role. Other factors have been used to discount the deterministic role of genetics in favor of a more interactive environment–genetics model.

Universality Versus Context Specificity

Many developmental psychologists purport that all people follow the same sequence of development. Stage theorists, for instance, believe that their proposed stages of development (e.g., Piaget's stages) are universal and proceed in the same sequence or direction. At the same time, the field of human development is becoming aware that children and adults experience and live in diverse and varying contexts. For example, children and adults in rural, non-Western countries have experiences in their families and communities that differ from those of children and adults who live in large, urban Western cities. Within a single culture, developmental change may differ from subculture to subculture, from family to family, or from individual to individual (Sigelman & Rider, 2014). Rather than envisioning a single line of stage wise or continuous change, most life-span theorists conceive of development as having many potential pathways depending on the contexts that influence the individual's life course.

Power and Privilege

Social inequalities such as power and privilege influence who people are and how they behave (Cole, 2009; Tappan, 2000). These in-equalities have always been a part of society and can be experienced from the individual level to the institutional level. With the emerging diversification of society, they are more prevalent than ever. In this same context, children and adults from marginalized communities experience injustices that affect their development. For example, children in impoverished regions experience educational disparities based on their race, ethnicity, religion, and socioeconomic statuses, whereas children and adults who have privilege do not have such detrimental experiences.

Intersecting Identities

Intersectionality is the notion that social identities such as race, ethnicity, gender, age, sexual orientation, religion, and so on overlap and create various forms of oppression and discrimination (Carbado, Crenshaw, Mays, & Tomlinson, 2013; Crenshaw, 1991). Given the complexity of the world, people have multiple identities and are members of multiple groups simultaneously. For example, although a heterosexual Japanese American male and a homosexual Japanese American female have similar ethnic identities, the intersection of their ethnic identities and both their gender and sexual orientation identities creates a unique individual identity for each. From a multi-cultural human development context, identity development is fluid and influenced by culture. Recent conceptualizations in both psychology and other disciplines resist the belief that identity is developmental and linear, instead highlighting the fluid, dynamic, and performative nature of identity (Abes, Jones, & McEwen, 2007; Torres, Jones, & Renn, 2009). Thus, intersecting identities are challenging and hard to balance.

Reflect on Sidebar 2.2 to see how these basic issues in human development may arise in your future counseling settings.

Major Human Development Theories

Now that you have an overview of life-span human development, this section includes a brief description of the major human development theories that have informed the work of professional counselors and other helping professionals. As you read about these theories, you will see a developing interest in and inclusion of (over time) the world in which the individual lives as well as his or her own internal development. Although these theories include a range of sociocultural perspectives, it is important for you as a practicing counselor to reflect on the theory being used and apply it using the most up to date and appropriate multicultural approach possible.

Psychoanalytic Theories

Psychoanalytic theories (e.g., Erikson, 1982; Freud, 1933) propose that people move through a series of stages in which they confront conflicts between biological drives and social expectations. The way in which these conflicts are resolved determines the individual's ability to learn, to get along with others, and to cope with anxiety (Austrian, 2008). As you read about these psychoanalytic theories, think of the ways in which social expectations differ from person to person based on sociocultural context and how this affects one's ability to resolve conflicts between biological drives and social expectations. Sigmund Freud (1856–1939) and Erik Erikson (1902–1994) are two of the most significant theorists of the psychoanalytic movement.

Sidebar 2.2   Thought Questions

What are your thoughts on the nature-versus-nurture debate?
How does each of the three human development questions discussed here influence counseling practice?

• • •

Freud's Theory

A central component of Freud's theory is the belief that humans have basic biological urges or drives that must be satisfied. Freud also believed that humans, especially newborns, are driven by instincts or inborn biological forces that motivate behavior—unconscious motivation. For example, an adolescent boy may not realize that his drug behavior is a way of channeling his sexual urges.

According to Freud (1930), the personality has three parts: id, ego, and superego. The id is the largest portion of the mind and is the source of basic biological needs and desires. The ego consists of the conscious, rational part of the personality and emerges in early infancy to redirect the id's impulses. For example, an infant is hungry and cries (id) but stops crying when he sees his mother preparing to feed him (ego).

The last part of the Freudian personality is the superego, the individual's conscience or internalized moral/value standard. For example, a child wants a toy that another child is playing with (id) and thinks about grabbing the toy from the other child (ego) but stops because grabbing the toy is not the acceptable or right behavior. Some have referred to the superego as the *parental voice* in an individual's head. Conflict among the id, ego, and superego is inevitable, according to Freud. His theory purports that psychological problems in humans arise when a person's supply of psychic energy is unevenly distributed among the id, ego, and superego. For instance, an adult male who has an antisocial personality and who consistently cheats to get his way may have a weak superego.

Freud's psychosexual development theory suggests that during childhood, sexual impulses shift their focus from the oral to the anal to the genital regions of the body. He called the psychic energy of the sex instinct the *libido*. Parents must therefore strike an appropriate balance between permitting too much or too little gratification of their child's basic needs (Crews, 1996).

Freud was the first theorist to emphasize the influence of the early parent–child relationship on development. Nevertheless, many developmental psychologists and researchers criticize Freud's theory because it is difficult to test or research, it is ambiguous, and it is inconsistent (e.g., Fonagy & Target, 2000). In addition, Freud did not consider his theory's application to children's development across cultures.

In relation to counseling, Freud transferred his theory of development to the practice of therapy or psychoanalysis. Clients undergoing psychoanalysis are helped to uncover how their early childhood experiences influenced their development and continue to influence their daily lives. Freudian therapeutic strategies include dream analysis, word associations, and projective tests.

Neo-Freudian Theories

Although difficult to test, Freud's theory had an immense influence on understanding of human development, and his writings inspired others to continue his early hypotheses (Mitchell & Black, 1995). Among the well-known neo-Freudians are Alfred Adler, who suggested that siblings are significant in one's development; Carl Jung, a pioneer in the study of adult development who claimed that adults experience a kind of midlife crisis and then become freer to express both the masculine and feminine sides of their personalities; Karen Horney, who challenged Freud's ideas about sex or gender differences; and Harry Stack Sullivan, who suggested that close friendships in childhood set the stage for intimate relationships later in life.

Erik Erikson was one of the most influential neo-Freudians. Erikson proposed that personality development evolves through systematic stages. Less concerned than Freud with sexual urges and instincts, Erikson focused on social influences, such as peers, teachers, schools, and the broader culture. His theory emphasized that the ego not only mediates between id impulses and superego demands but at each stage also encounters conflicts that when solved make the individual an active member of society. In other words, whether the conflict of a particular stage is resolved successfully or not, the individual is pushed by both biological maturation and social demands into the next stage. The unsuccessful resolution of a conflict will influence subsequent stages. See Table 2.2 for Erikson's psychosocial stages.

Unlike Freud, Erikson examined the relationship between normal development and an individual's cultural life situation. In the 1940s, he began to take an interest in cultural anthropology. Influenced by both the work of cultural anthropologists like Franz Boas, Ruth Benedict, and Margaret Mead and his own experience with psychoanalysis, Erikson researched childhood and child-rearing practices among the Lakota and Yurok Indians of the northwestern coast of the United States. Through his observations of these Native American tribes, Erikson became aware of the influence that culture and external events have on behavior and development (Friedman, 1999).

Table 2.2 Erikson's Psychosocial Stages

Psychosocial Stage	Period of Development
Basic Trust vs. Mistrust	Birth to 1 year
Autonomy vs. Shame and Doubt	1–3 years
Imitative vs. Guilt	3–8 years
Industry vs. Inferiority	6–11 years
Identity vs. Role Confusion	Adolescence
Intimacy vs. Isolation	Early adulthood
Generativity vs. Stagnation	Middle adulthood
Ego Integrity vs. Despair	Late adulthood

Behaviorism and Social Learning Theory

Give me a dozen healthy infants, well-formed, and my own specified world to bring them up in, and I'll guarantee to take any one at random and train him to become any type of specialist I might select—doctor, lawyer, artist, merchant, chief, and yes, even beggar-man and thief, regardless of his talents, penchants, tendencies, abilities, vocations, and race of his ancestors. (Watson, 1924, p. 104)

John Watson, a behaviorist and pioneer of learning theory perspective on human development, made this statement illustrating his strong belief in nurturing as the most significant factor in one's development. Inspired by Ivan Pavlov's studies of animal learning, early learning theorists emphasized that human behavior changes in direct response to environmental stimuli (classical conditioning). After many studies with children using classical conditioning (Watson & Rayner, 1920), Watson concluded that environment is the supreme force in development. Adults can mold children's behavior, he thought, by carefully controlling stimulus–response associations. He also believed that development is a continuous process consisting of a gradual increase in the number and strength of these associations.

B. F. Skinner, another behaviorist, developed operant conditioning theory (Skinner, 1953, 1976). Skinner, like Watson, believed that the course of human development depends on the individual's learning experiences. Aggressive behavior in children may be reinforced over time because they get their way with other children. According to Skinner, the frequency of a behavior can be increased by following it with reinforcers such as food, praise, or a friendly smile. The frequency of a behavior can also be decreased through punishment such as disapproval or withdrawal of privileges. As a result of Skinner's theory, operant conditioning became a broadly applied learning principle and theory. Skinner's operant conditioning principles can explain many aspects of human development and are still studied by psychologists (e.g., Staddon & Cerutti, 2003). Nevertheless, some researchers believe that Skinner placed too much emphasis on a single type of learning and gave too little attention to cognitive processes such as memory and reflection in learning.

Social Learning Theory

As a result of the work of Watson and Skinner, many researchers wanted to know more about the connection between social behavior and cognition. Several theories of social learning (currently called *social cognitive theories*) emerged. The most influential, developed by Albert Bandura, emphasizes modeling, also known as *imitation* or *observational learning,* as a powerful source of development. Bandura (1977, 2006) claimed that humans are cognitive beings whose active processing of information plays a critical role in their learning, behavior, and development. Bandura argued that human learning is very different from animal (e.g., rat) learning because humans have more sophisticated cognitive capabilities.

A baby who claps her hands after her mother does so, a child who hits others when angry in the same way that he has been punished at home, and an adolescent who wears the same styles as his friends are all displaying observational learning. The famous Bobo doll experiment showed that children observe the behavior of those around them (Bandura, Ross, & Ross, 1961). Adults, peers, and even television characters model behavior that the children observe and later may imitate (McLeod, 2016). According to McLeod (2016, "Observational Learning," para. 3), "A number of processes … make it more likely that a child will reproduce the behavior that its society deems appropriate" for its sex, racial/ethnic group, or any other group the child identifies with (see also Buchanan & Selmon, 2008).

Unlike Skinner, Bandura (1977) believed that humans take in and process information before blindly imitating the behavior of a model. These cognitive processes, called *mediational processes,* "mediate (i.e. intervene) in the learning process to determine whether a new response is acquired" (McLeod, 2016, "Mediational Processes," para. 2). Bandura proposed four mediational processes.

1. *Attention:* The extent to which we are exposed [to]/notice the behavior. For a behavior to be imitated it has to grab our attention. We observe many behaviors on a daily basis and many of these are not noteworthy. Attention is therefore extremely important in whether a behavior has an influence in others imitating it.
2. *Retention:* How well the behavior is remembered. The behavior may be noticed, but [it is] not always remembered which obviously prevents imitation. It is important therefore that a memory of the behavior is formed to be performed later by the observer. Much of social learning is not immediate so this process is especially vital in those cases. Even if the behavior is reproduced shortly after seeing it, there needs to be a memory to refer to.
3. *Reproduction:* This is the ability to perform the behavior that the model has just demonstrated. We see much behavior on a daily basis that we would like to be able to imitate but . . . this not always possible. We are limited by our physical ability and for that reason, even if we wish to reproduce the behavior, we cannot. This influences our decisions whether to try and imitate it or not. . . .
4. *Motivation:* The will to perform the behavior. The rewards and punishment that follow a behavior will be considered by the observer. If the perceived rewards outweighs [*sic*] the perceived costs (if there are any) then the behavior will be more likely to be imitated by the observer. If the vicarious reinforcement is not seen to be important enough to the observer then they will not imitate the behavior. (McLeod, 2016, "Mediational Processes")

More recently, Bandura (2006) explored the concept of human agency, or ways in which people deliberately exercise cognitive control over themselves, their environments, and their lives. Bandura believed that self-efficacy determines one's motivation, affect, and action. He asserted that whether an individual undertakes an action, such as going on a diet or studying for a test, and whether that individual succeeds depend greatly on his or her sense of self-efficacy with respect to that behavior or action. Bandura's theory of self-efficacy has been linked to constructs such as academic performance, career development, teacher performance, and counselor cultural competence in counseling.

Sociocultural Theory

Sociocultural theory is an emerging theory in psychology that looks at the important contributions that society makes to individual development. Sociocultural theory grew from the work of seminal psychologist Lev Vygotsky (1896–1934), who believed that parents, caregivers, peers, and the culture at large were responsible for people developing higher order functions. The theory focuses on how culture—the values, beliefs, customs, and skills of a social group—is transmitted to the next generation.

According to Vygotsky (1978),

> Every function in the child's cultural development appears twice: first, on the social level, and later, on the individual level; first, between people (interpsychological) and then inside the child (intrapsychological). This applies equally to voluntary attention, to logical memory, and to the formation of concepts. All the higher functions originate as actual relationships between individuals. (p. 57)

According to Cherry (2017),

> Sociocultural theory focuses not only [on] how adults and peers influence individual learning, but also on how cultural beliefs and attitudes impact how instruction and learning take place. According to Vygotsky, children are born with basic biological constraints on their minds. Each culture, however, provides what he referred to as "tools of intellectual adaptation." These tools allow children to use their basic mental abilities in a way that is adaptive to the culture in which they live. ("An Introduction to Sociocultural Theory," paras. 4–5)

Development of Prejudices

The development of prejudiced beliefs among humans has been studied by psychologists for many years. *Prejudice* can be defined as preconceived ideas about people "perceived as being different, due to race, religion, culture, gender, disabilities, appearance, language, sexual orientation, or social status" (Byrnes, 1995, p. 3). Research has documented that prejudiced beliefs can develop early in life (e.g.,

McGlothlin & Killen, 2006; Milner, 1975; Williams, Best, & Boswell, 1975), possibly resulting in long-term negative and faulty stereotypes held by adults.

This section describes the larger systemic influence on an individual's development of prejudiced beliefs over the course of his or her life span. As a counselor-in-training, it is important to be able to understand prejudice and how it manifests in client behavior, client problems, and, more important, the context in which clients live.

For many years, psychologists have studied factors influencing the development of prejudiced beliefs (Minard, 1952; Pettigrew, 1959). These factors include comfort with ambiguity (e.g., Roets & Van Hiel, 2011), social perspective-taking skills (Smetana, 2006), group norm understanding (Abrams & Rutland, 2008), and ethnic awareness and identity development (Nesdale, 1999). Other studies have revealed relationships among prejudiced beliefs and sociocultural factors such as friendships with ethnically dissimilar individuals (Feddes, Noack, & Rutland, 2009), parents with negative intergroup attitudes (White & Gleitzman, 2006), and intergroup contact (Pettigrew & Tropp, 2011). Also, some psychologists believe that social learning theory is the basis for understanding the origins of prejudice—that it is learned in the same way that other attitudes and values are learned (Bandura et al., 1961).

Ecological Systems Theory

How is people's development affected by their social relationships and the world around them? According to Bronfenbrenner's (1979) ecological systems theory (a systems theory that greatly influenced the MSJCC), individuals develop in the context of relationships at multiple levels of the environment: microsystem, mesosystem, exosystem, macrosystem, and chronosystem.

The microsystem has the most direct and immediate impact on the individual. It is the closest system to the individual and might include family members, teachers, caregivers, and friends/peers. Relationships within one's microsystem are bidirectional, which means that each party in the relationship has an impact or effect on the other and vice versa. For instance, a student's reaction to or relationship with his or her teacher influences the teacher's reaction to that student. These bidirectional interactions may have long-term effects on one's development (Crokenbberg & Leerkes, 2003). For this reason, the microsystem can be the most influential level in ecological systems theory (Moen, Elder, Luscher, & Bronfenbrenner, 1995).

The mesosystem encompasses connections between microsystems. In other words, a mesosystem is a system of microsystems. For instance, a child's parents' relationship with his or her teachers and school can significantly impact the student's educational outcomes (Epstein & Sanders, 2002); or how well an adult functions as spouse and parent at home is affected by relationships in the workplace and vice versa (Gottfried, Gottfried, & Bathurst, 2002).

The exosystem is composed of the linkages and processes between two or more settings, one of which does not contain the developing person. In essence, the exosystem contains environmental elements—such as policies and laws, social unrest, or financial upheaval—that have a profound influence on an individual's development, even though the individual is not directly involved with them. This effect can occur over the short term (e.g., a temporary change in a parent's work hours) or the long term (e.g., growing up in a community enduring consistent social unrest or during economic recession).

The macrosystem consists of the beliefs, knowledge, customs, and lifestyles that are part of a culture's micro-, meso-, and exosystems. The macrosystem evolves over time in responses to each successive generation.

Finally, the chronosystem is made up of the environmental events and transitions that occur throughout an individual's life, including sociohistorical events. The specific events tend to change how the individual interacts with others. Moving to another city is one example, as is electing the first Black or first woman president of the United States.

Bronfenbrenner's theory of development has directly influenced the development of the ecological counseling approach (e.g., Conyne & Mazza, 2007). In 2013, *Counseling Today* ran a cover story titled "Building a More Complete Client Picture" by Lynne Shallcross. In this article, Shallcross delineated the foci of ecological counseling. First, ecological counseling focuses on examining individuals or clients within contexts or social systems. Persons and environments are not separate but interrelated, and these interactions are where professional counselors should look to understand their clients. Second, ecological counseling holds that human beings are neither entirely determined by nor radically independent of their environments. The two are interwoven: Using the resources and opportunities provided by their environments, clients seek to live meaningful lives, and in doing so, they change their environments. Thus, change in either person or environment will affect the other. Finally, ecological counseling takes a pragmatic and eclectic view of counseling theory, borrowing tools from different theories to effect change.

Identity Development Theories

Along with these human development theories, theories of identity development have been created that reflect the multitude of sociocultural experiences within society and how individuals create their identities over their life span. There are three forms of identity to consider: identity, social identity, and cultural identity (Baruth & Manning, 2016). The

47

broadest form of identity is understood as the experience of understanding and becoming aware of the values, beliefs, behaviors, and so on that combine into one person. *Social identity* is defined as a part of a person's concept of self that stems from his or her membership within a group. Finally, *cultural identity* is defined as a person's self-concept as it relates to his or her culture, including those beliefs, attitudes, and so on that are unique to that person's cultural heritage.

Although a number of identity models have been developed (including one for White counselors), we briefly review five here:

- The racial/cultural identity development model, created by Sue and Sue (2016), focuses on those individuals who come from a nondominant (or nonmajority) culture. It aims to describe the experience individuals have navigating their culture, the dominant culture surrounding them, and the relationship between the two.
- The biracial identity development model was put forth by Poston (1990) and aims to address the identity of those individuals who are born with more than one race or ethnicity. In particular, this model focuses on how individuals experience the process and integration of two races or ethnicities. This model has spurred the development of more encompassing multiracial models (Baruth & Manning, 2012).
- The feminist identity model was developed by Downing and Roush (1985) and aims to explain the experience of women coming to terms with a (hopefully) positive feminist identity despite societal oppression. Although this theory was originally meant to be all encompassing, it focused on the issues of White women. A number of feminist theories now incorporate gender with other sociocultural factors, for example, Islamic feminism, Black feminism, or Latina feminism.
- Although there is no one distinct identity model for gay and lesbian individuals, a number of models capture the experience for some. For example, van Wormer, Wells, and Boes (2000) focused on the coming-out process, the Falco model (Falco, 1991) and the McCarn and Fassinger model (McCarn & Fassinger, 1996) focus on lesbian identity development, and the Troiden model (Troiden, 1989) looks at both gay and lesbian individuals. Continued research and development for bisexual, transgender, and other LGBT identity models is still needed (Baruth & Manning, 2012).
- Gibson's (2006) disability identity model aims to address the identity development process of individuals with varying forms of disabilities. In particular, this model views disability as an identity instead of a medical, social, or minority issue, as it is more commonly viewed.

As a counselor-in-training and future practicing counselor, your knowledge of how individuals develop over their life span must also coincide with your client's current understanding of self and the world around him or her (i.e., his or her own identity and self-concept).

Resilience and Development

According to Southwick, Bonanno, Masten, Panter-Brick, and Yehuda (2014), stress is a reality of our daily lives. At some point in their lives, almost everyone will experience a life-threatening, traumatic, or stressful event (Karam et al., 2014; Lupien, McEwen, Gunnar, & Heim, 2009). These events, which include interpersonal violence, war, the death of a loved one, natural disasters, serious accidents, and terrorism (e.g., Dimitry, 2012), can affect a person's mental health. Some stressors, such as bullying, dysfunctional relationships, or poverty may be experienced over a lengthy period of time (Arnold, Mearns, Oshima, & Prasad, 2014; G. W. Evans, Li, & Whipple, 2013).

Another ongoing stressor, racial microaggressions, a modern form of racism composed of subtle daily racial slights and insults, has received increased empirical attention (Sue et al., 2007). There are three forms of racial microaggressions: microinsults, microassaults, and microinvalidations. *Microinsults* are behavioral or verbal comments that convey rudeness and demean a person's racial identity or heritage (e.g., saying to a person of color "How did you get your job?"). *Microassaults* are explicit racist verbal or nonverbal attacks intended to harm someone (e.g., referring to Asian Americans as "oriental"). *Microinvalidations* are verbal statements that negate the thoughts, actions, and experiences of people of color (e.g., when White people say they don't see color). Microaggressions first focused on race and racism; however, the term (including the three subforms) is now also applied to other groups marginalized because of their gender, sexual orientation, ethnicity, religion, and so on. Whether intentionally or unintentionally, these everyday brief verbal indignities send derogatory messages to marginalized populations and do more severe psychological damage than overt discrimination. Review Sidebar 2.3 to see how microaggressions can impact your counseling relationship.

Sidebar 2.3   Implication for Counseling Case Example

Tracey is a 42-year-old African American wife and mother of two young children. Tracey presents to counseling with concerns about high blood pressure resulting from discrimination at work. She comes from a line of women who believed that enduring psychological pain was part of their role as "strong Black women." Tracey tells you that prior to counseling, she utilized prayer and faith to assist in coping with challenges. You reply that maybe she was not mistreated because of racism but because of her strong personality.

• • •

Intense levels of stress can give rise to many physiological, psychological, and physical conditions, such as depression, anxiety, or cardiovascular illness (Schneiderman, Ironson, & Siegel, 2005). Some research has even indicated that ongoing stressors related to racism result in high blood pressure, depression, anger, and anxiety (Brewer et al., 2013); yet just as there is concern about the effects of stress exposure, there is also unprecedented interest in people's ability to be resilient (Karatsoreos & McEwen, 2013).

The American Psychological Association (2017) defines *resilience* as "the process of adapting well in the face of adversity, trauma, tragedy, threats or significant sources of stress" ("What Is Resilience?" para. 1); yet according to Southwick, Bonanno, et al. (2014), "Determinants of resilience include a host of biological, psychological, social and cultural factors that interact with one another to determine how one responds to stressful experiences" ("Dr. Steven Southwick: The Evolving Definitions of Resilience," para. 1; see also Southwick, Douglas-Palumberi, & Pietrzak, 2014). Because resilience includes "behaviors, thoughts and actions that can be learned and developed in anyone" (American Psychological Association, 2017, "What Is Resilience?" para. 4), it can be reflected in any stressor or developmental challenge over an individual's lifetime. Furthermore, taken within a multicultural context, resilience can be developed and expressed differently from person to person. For instance, African American boys who witnessed police shootings of African American teens by White police officers experienced insurmountable anxiety, fear, and resilience (Watkins, Desmond, & Miller, 2016). Such negative images about the police acquired during childhood and adolescence had a detrimental effect as they transitioned to adulthood (Patton & Gabarino, 2014; Watkins et al., 2016). Therefore, as they transitioned from adolescence to adulthood, their process of resilience changed and they were socially conditioned (e.g., being respectful, anger management, engaging in self-defense) on how to interact with the police and how to cope with racism and discrimination (Thomas & Blackmon, 2015).

The American Psychological Association (2017) lists 10 ways in which individuals can build resilience:

- Make connections
- Avoid seeing crises as insurmountable problems
- Accept that change is a part of living
- Move toward your goals
- Take decisive actions
- Look for opportunities for self-discovery
- Nurture a positive view of yourself
- Keep things in perspective
- Maintain a hopeful outlook
- Take care of yourself ("10 Ways to Build Resilience")

In many cases, resilience is thought of as a binary trait—one is either resilient or not. However, recent research has indicated that resilience can be conceptualized on a continuum due to the stress or environmental factors affecting individuals or entire communities (Fleming & Ledogar, 2008; Kim-Cohen & Turkewitz, 2012; Pietrzak & Southwick, 2011). An individual's response to stress and/or trauma can occur in the context of interactions with others, available resources, specific cultures and religions, organizations, communities, and societies (Sherrieb, Norris, & Galea, 2010). Each of these contexts may affect the individual's resilience. Therefore, one's resilience or ability to bounce back might vary depending on the context and the resources available to support that individual.

The more we can learn about resilience, the more potential there is for integrating salient concepts of resilience into counseling practice. This integration is beginning to foster an important and much-needed paradigm shift. For example, the new MSJCC is a socioecological model implemented within the counseling profession. Key tenets such as the dynamics of power, privilege and oppression, intersectionality, and social justice competencies are interwoven into counseling theories, practices, and research. Thus, rather than spending the vast majority of their time and energy examining the negative consequences of trauma, counselors can learn to simultaneously evaluate and teach methods to enhance resilience through a lens of multiculturalism and social advocacy. Such an approach moves the field away from a purely deficit-based model of mental health toward the inclusion of strengths- and competence-based models that focus on multiculturalism, prevention, and strength building.

Psychopathology and Development

Developmental psychologists and social scientists are intrigued by the study of the origins and course of maladaptive behavior. A more developmental approach to psychological disorders considers sociocultural experiences, age norms in diagnosis, and the charting of developmental pathways that lead to adaptive or maladaptive developmental outcomes. Refer to Sidebar 2.4 to see how culture may affect diagnosis.

Sidebar 2.4   Brief Case Example

Joseph is a 54-year-old male living and working productively in his community. Joseph has come to you seeking counseling because of job-related stress. Joseph tells you that he is new to counseling and that what he did in the past, with great help, was to ingest drugs and communicate with spirits. Joseph does not see a problem with his drug use or hallucinations. Joseph is Native American and proudly continues the traditions of his forefathers.

• • •

We must still answer questions about nature and nurture and continuity and discontinuity before we can truly understand the development of psychological disorders. Coyne and Whiffen (1995) found that a diathesis–stress model is useful for conceptualizing psychopathology. This model proposes that psychopathology results from the interaction over time of a predisposition or vulnerability to psychological disorders and the experience of stressful events. So for a vulnerable individual, even mild stress may result in disorder, whereas for an individual who is resilient and does not have a vulnerability or diathesis to disorder, it would take extremely high levels of stress to cause disorder (Ingram & Price, 2009).

Socioemotional development is pivotal in the understanding of psychopathology in general and developmental psychopathology in particular. A component of one's socioemotional development is the quality of one's interpersonal relationships. Relationships are key to understanding psychopathology at multiple levels of analysis, from defining psychopathology to describing preconditions and contexts, to understanding its origins and nature. For example, relationship problems are often markers of possible pathology, and the diagnosis of disorder often centers on relationship considerations. From social phobias to conduct problems, across the range of problems in childhood and adulthood, disturbances in social development are prominent criteria for classification in psychopathology.

Social relationships also are viewed by many theorists as important contexts within which psychopathology emerges and persists or desists (Forgas & Fitness, 2008; Sroufe, Duggal, Weinfield, & Carlson, 2000). Psychogenic positions on pathology all focus on relationships, whether social learning experiences, the isolation and anomie emphasized by sociological models, or the emphasis on vital close relationships in psychodynamic and evolutionary positions. Research on risk and protective factors in psychopathology, as well as process-oriented research involving moderator and mediator variables, commonly grants a prominent role to relationship variables.

Implications for the Counseling Profession

Counseling as a profession is distinct and differentiated from other helping professions because of its roots in developmental science and theory (Eriksen & Kress, 2006; Guindon, 2010). Since the field's origins in vocational psychology, counseling professionals have emphasized developmental and preventive services rather than the traditional medical model (i.e., curing and treating; McAuliffe & Eriksen, 1999). Counselors view client problems as developmental tasks and their own role as assisting a wide range of clients in the general population via interventions and strategies that facilitate optimum development (Mellin, Hunt, & Nichols, 2011).

Myers and Sweeney (2008) introduced the notion of counseling as a wellness paradigm in which counselors integrate the mind, body, and spirit to promote the holistic well-being of clients. Remley and Herlihy (2015) expanded on the paradigm by describing counseling as a wellness-based approach to clinical practice that conceptualizes clients' problems from a developmental perspective.

Researchers have examined counselor development and counseling outcomes for many years (e.g., Borders et al., 1991; Ronnestad & Skovholt, 2013; Stoltenberg & McNeill, 2010). Links have been found between counselor development and several other factors, such as empathic responses (DePue & Lambie, 2014), cultural relativism (McAuliffe, Grothaus, Jensen, & Michel, 2012), and overall awareness (Stark & Frels, 2014). These theoretical frameworks for counselor development and studies indicate that counselors' development spans from their preservice experiences through advanced training and involves learning, cognition, and emotion as well as direct, effective supervision (Stoltenberg & McNeill, 2010; Stoltenberg, McNeill, & Delworth, 1998). Likewise, current research is promising in that there is growing evidence of increased and enhanced counselor development after training and professional development (K. M. Evans & Foster, 2000; D. L. Lee & Tracey, 2008). However, little research supports or links increased counselor development with human development theories and trends.

Over the past two decades, there have been calls for counseling professionals to be change agents and advocates for social justice (Chung & Bemak, 2012; Holcomb-McCoy, 2007; Lewis, Ratts, Paladino, & Toporek, 2011) and for the field of counseling to embrace social justice advocacy as a knowledge base and skill area. These calls are primarily a response to the need to more adequately address the systemic oppression experienced by a growing number of counseling clients. For this reason, counselors need to expand their roles to include social justice advocacy (C. Lee & Walz, 1998). The ACA Advocacy Competencies (Lewis, Arnold, House, & Toporek, 2002) have been utilized as a framework for executing social justice advocacy strategies and include the following competencies:

- Advocacy-oriented counselors recognize the impact of social, political, economic, and cultural factors on *human development.*
- They also help their clients and students understand their own lives in context. This lays the groundwork for self-advocacy. (p. 1, emphasis added)

The MCC and MSJCC allude to counselor preparation and practices that integrate multicultural and culture-specific awareness, knowledge, and skills into counseling interactions. Unique to the MSJCC model is that interventions addressing intrapersonal, interpersonal, institutional,

53

community, and public policy levels are provided in an effort to help both beginning and seasoned clinicians continue to work toward a multicultural and social justice model of practice.

Chapter Summary

This chapter reviewed the various components of human life-span development while at the same time taking into consideration the multicultural aspects of any given person, community, or society. Basic components of human development theories and viewpoints were reviewed, as was the role that both resilience and psychopathology can play in an individual's development. Although much attention has been paid to each of these topics individually, it is important and necessary that you take the time to weave them together in your understanding of your clients' worldviews. Diversity includes a multitude of perspectives (age, ability level, gender, sexual orientation, race, religion, ethnicity, and socioeconomic status, to name a few), yet with the MSJCC model, the use of the terms *privilege* and *marginalization* helps to incorporate all aspects of diversity from both the client and counselor points of view.

Learning Activities

1. Ask at least five adults of different ages to describe age-graded, history-graded, and nonnormative influences in their lives thus far. Compile your results and analyze differences, similarities, and themes.
2. Ami, a 7-year-old female, has become quiet and withdrawn in her classroom. Her teacher is concerned about her change in attitude and slip in grades. Three months ago, Ami's parents separated. From the perspective of each of the four different theoretical approaches (psychoanalytic theories, behaviorism and social learning theory, sociocultural theory, and ecological systems theory), explain what may be happening with Ami and identify at least one intervention to use with Ami.
3. Watch "The Complexities of Being a Multiple Minority" (https://www.youtube.com/watch?v=qZR_PO8NtJc) and write a reflection. What multiple identities do you hold?
4. List three biases or assumptions that you hold about different groups of people. Reflect on where those assumptions came from and how they affect your day-to-day life.
5. Watch "Unequal Opportunity Race" (https://www.youtube.com/watch?v=eBb5TgOXgNY). What privileges and marginalizations stand out in the video? In what ways have similar status issues played out in counseling experiences? In what ways could they play out? In what ways can you adjust your current work to be mindful of the implication of statuses?

6. Review all of the development theories discussed. List sociocultural factors (e.g., population of interest, time period) that could have influenced how each came about. Finally, identify ways in which each theory could be applied within a multicultural context.

Review Questions

1. What is the difference between Freudian and Neo-Freudian theories?
2. How are the theories developed by Albert Bandura, John Watson, and B. F. Skinner similar? How are they different?
3. Summarize the nature-versus-nurture question.
4. Define *microaggression,* and explain the three subsets.

Further Resources

American Counseling Association Divisions
   https://www.counseling.org/about-us/divisions-regions-and-branches/divisions
Microaggressions in Everyday Life
   https://www.youtube.com/watch?v=BJL2P0JsAS4
Microaggressions: Power, Privilege, and Everyday Life
   www.microaggressions.com/
Multicultural and Social Justice Counseling Competencies
   https://www.counseling.org/docs/default-source/competencies/multicultural-and-social-justice-counseling-competencies.pdf?sfvrsn=20
National Disability Employment Awareness Month
   https://www.dol.gov/odep/topics/ndeam/
StirFry Seminars and Consulting
   diversity training films, including *The Color of Fear* and *If These Halls Could Talk;* www.stirfryseminars.com/store/

References

Abes, E. S., Jones, S. R., & McEwen, M. K. (2007). Reconceptualizing the model of multiple dimensions of identity: The role of meaning-making capacity in the construction of multiple identities. *Journal of College Student Development, 48,* 1–22.

Abrams, D., & Rutland, A. (2008). The development of subjective group dynamics. In S. R. Levy & M. Killen (Eds.), *Intergroup relations and attitudes in childhood through adulthood* (pp. 4–65). Oxford, UK: Oxford University Press.

American Counseling Association. (2014). *ACA code of ethics.* Retrieved from www.counseling.org/docs/ethics/2014-aca-code-of-ethics.pdf?sfvrsn=4

American Counseling Association. (2017a). *20/20: A vision for the future of counseling*. Retrieved from https://www.counseling.org/knowledge-center/20-20-a-vision-for-the-future-of-counseling

American Counseling Association. (2017b). *20/20: Consensus definition of counseling*. Retrieved from https://www.counseling.org/knowledge-center/20-20-a-vision-for-the-future-of-counseling/consensus-definition-of-counseling

American Psychological Association. (2017). *The road to resilience*. Retrieved from www.apa.org/helpcenter/road-resilience.aspx

Arnold, M., Mearns, R., Oshima, K., & Prasad, V. (2014). *Climate and disaster resilience: The role for community-driven development (CDD)*. Washington, DC: World Bank Group.

Arredondo, P., Toporek, R., Brown, S., Jones, J., Locke, D. C., Sanchez, J., & Stadler, H. (1996). Operationalization of the Multicultural Counseling Competencies. *Journal of Multicultural Counseling and Development, 24,* 42–78.

Austrian, S. G. (Ed.). (2008). *Developmental theories through the life cycle*. New York, NY: Columbia University Press.

Baltes, P. B., Staudinger, U. M., & Lindenberger, U. (1999). Lifespan psychology: Theory and application to intellectual functioning. *Annual Review of Psychology, 50,* 471–507.

Bandura, A. (1977). *Social learning theory*. Englewood Cliffs, NJ: Prentice Hall.

Bandura, A. (2006). Toward a psychology of human agency. *Perspectives on Psychological Science, 1,* 164–180.

Bandura, A., Ross, D., & Ross, S. A. (1961). Transmission of aggression through imitation of aggressive models. *Journal of Abnormal and Social Psychology, 63,* 575–582.

Baruth, L. G., & Manning, M. L. (2012). *Multicultural counseling and psychotherapy: A lifespan approach* (5th ed.). Hoboken, NJ: Pearson Education.

Baruth, L. G., & Manning, M. L. (2016). *Multicultural counseling and psychotherapy: A lifespan approach* (6th ed.). New York, NY: Routledge.

Berk, L. E. (2006). History, theory, and applied directions. In *Child development* (7th ed., pp. 3–39). Boston, MA: Allyn & Bacon.

Borders, L. D., Bernard, J. M., Dye, H. A., Fong, M. L., Henderson, P., & Nance, D. W. (1991). Curriculum guide for training counseling supervisors: Rationale, development, and implementation. *Counselor Education and Supervision, 31,* 58–80.

Brewer, L. C., Carson, K. A., Williams, D. R., Allen, A., Jones, C. P., & Cooper, L. A. (2013). Association of race consciousness with the patient-physician relationship, medication adherence, and blood pressure in urban primary care patients. *American Journal of Hypertension, 26,* 1346–1352.

Bronfenbrenner, U. (1979). *The ecology of human development: Experiments by nature and design*. Cambridge, MA: Harvard University Press.

Buchanan, T., & Selmon, N. (2008). Race and gender differences in self-efficacy: Assessing the role of gender role attitudes and family background. *Sex Roles, 58,* 822–836.

Byrnes, D. (1995). *"Teacher, they called me a ___!" Confronting prejudice and discrimination in the classroom.* New York, NY: Anti-Defamation League of B'nai B'rith.

Carbado, D., Crenshaw, K., Mays, V., & Tomlinson, B. (2013). Intersectionality: Mapping the movements of a theory. *Du Bois Review: Social Science Research on Race, 10*(2), 303–312.

Cherry, K. (2017). *What is sociocultural theory?* Retrieved from https://www.verywell.com/what-is-sociocultural-theory-2795088

Chung, R. C., & Bemak, F. P. (2012). *Social justice counseling: The next steps beyond multiculturalism.* Thousand Oaks, CA: Sage.

Cole, E. (2009). Intersectionality and psychology. *The American Psychologist, 64*(3), 170–180.

Conyne, R., & Mazza, J. (2007). Ecological group work applied to schools. *Journal for Specialists in Group Work, 32,* 19–29.

Coyne, J. C., & Whiffen, V. E. (1995). Issues in personality as diathesis for depression: The case of sociotropy-dependency and autonomy-self-criticism. *Psychological Bulletin, 118*(3), 358–378.

Crenshaw, K. (1991). Mapping the margins: Intersectionality, identity politics, and violence against women of color. *Stanford Law Review, 43,* 1241–1299.

Crews, F. (1996). The verdict on Freud. *Psychological Science, 7,* 63–68.

Crokenbberg, S., & Leerkes, E. M. (2003). Negative infant emotionality and the development of family relationships in infancy and early childhood. In A. C. Crouter & A. Booth (Eds.), *Children's influence on family dynamics: The neglected side of family relationships* (pp. 57–78). Mahwah, NJ: Erlbaum.

DePue, M. K., & Lambie, G. W. (2014). Impact of a university-based practicum experience on counseling students' levels of empathy and assessed counseling competencies. *Counseling Outcome Research and Evaluation, 5,* 89–101.

Dimitry, L. (2012). A systematic review on the mental health of children and adolescents in areas of armed conflict in the Middle East. *Child Care Health Development, 38,* 153–161.

Downing, N. E., & Roush, K. L. (1985). From passive acceptance to active commitment: A model of feminist identity for women. *The Counseling Psychologist, 13,* 695–709.

Epstein, J. L., & Sanders, M. G. (2002). Family, school, and community partnerships. In M. H. Bornstein (Ed.), *Handbook of parenting: Practical issues in parenting* (pp. 407–437). Mahwah, NJ: Erlbaum.

Eriksen, K., & Kress, V. (2006). The *DSM* and the professional counseling identity: Bridging the gap. *Journal of Mental Health Counseling, 28,* 202–217.

Erikson, E. H. (1982). *The life cycle completed: A review.* New York, NY: Norton.

Evans, G. W., Li, D., & Whipple, S. S. (2013). Cumulative risk and child development. *Psychological Bulletin, 139,* 1342–1396.

Evans, K. M., & Foster, V. A. (2000). Relationships among multicultural training, moral development, and racial identity development of White counseling students. *Counseling and Values, 45,* 39–48.

Falco, K. (1991). *Psychotherapy with lesbian clients: Theory into practice.* New York, NY: Brunner/Mazel.

Feddes, A., Noack, P., & Rutland, A. (2009). Direct and extended friendship effects on minority and majority children's interethnic attitudes: A longitudinal study. *Child Development, 80,* 377–390.

Fleming, J., & Ledogar, R. J. (2008). Resilience and indigenous spirituality: A literature review. *Pimatisiwin, 6,* 47–64.

Fonagy, P., & Target, M. (2000). Playing with reality: III. The persistence of dual psychic reality in borderline patients. *International Journal of Psychoanalysis, 81,* 853–874.

Forgas, J. P., & Fitness, J. (2008). *Social relationships: Cognitive, affective and motivational processes.* New York, NY: Routledge.

Freud, S. (1930). *Three contributions to the theory of sex.* New York, NY: Newvous and Mental Disease.

Freud, S. (1933). *New introductory lectures in psychoanalysis.* New York, NY: Norton.

Friedman, L. (1999). *Identity's architect: A biography of Erik H. Erikson.* New York, NY: Scribner.

Gates, G. J. (2011). *How many people are lesbian, gay, bisexual, and transgender?* Retrieved from https://williamsinstitute.law.ucla.edu/wp-content/uploads/Gates-How-Many-People-LGBT-Apr-2011.pdf

Gates, G. J., & Newport, F. (2012). *Special report: 3.4% of U.S. adults identify as LGBT.* Retrieved from http://news.gallup.com/poll/158066/special-report-adults-identify-lgbt.aspx

Gee, G. C., Walsemann, K. M., & Brondolo, E. (2012). A life course perspective on how racism may be related to health inequities. *American Journal of Public Health, 102,* 967–974.

Gibson, J. (2006). Disability and clinical competency: An introduction. *The California Psychologist, 39,* 6–10.

Gottfried, A. E., Gottfried, A. W., & Bathurst, K. (2002). Maternal and dual-earner employment status and parenting. In M. H. Bornstein (Ed.), *Handbook of parenting* (2nd ed., Vol. 2, pp. 207–229). Mahwah, NJ: Erlbaum.

Guindon, M. H. (2010). *A counseling primer: An introduction to the profession.* New York, NY: Routledge.

Holcomb-McCoy, C. (2007). *School counseling to close the achievement gap: A social justice framework for success.* Thousand Oaks, CA: Sage.

Ingram, R. E, & Price, J. M. (Eds.). (2009). Understanding psychopathology: The role of vulnerability. In *Vulnerability to psychopathology: Risk across the lifespan* (pp. 3–17). New York, NY: Guilford Press.

Ivey, A. (1991). *Developmental strategies for helpers.* Pacific Grove, CA: Brooks/Cole.

Karam, E. G., Friedman, M. J., Hill, E. D., Kessler, R. C., McLaughlin, K. A., Petukhova, M., … Koenen, K. C. (2014). Cumulative traumas and risk thresholds: 12-month PTSD in the World Mental Health (WMH) Surveys. *Depression and Anxiety. 31,* 130–142.

Karatsoreos, I. N., & McEwen, B. S. (2013). The neurology and physiology of resilience and adaptation across the life course. *Journal of Child Psychology and Psychiatry, 54,* 337–347.

Kim-Cohen, J., & Turkewitz, R. (2012). Resilience and measured gene-environment interactions. *Development & Psychopathology, 24,* 1297–1306.

Lee, C., & Walz, G. (1998). *Social action: A mandate for counselors.* Alexandria, VA: American Counseling Association.

Lee, D. L., & Tracey, T. J. (2008). General and multicultural case conceptualization skills: A cross-sectional analysis of psychotherapy trainees. *Psychotherapy: Theory, Research, Practice, Training, 45,* 507–522.

Lewis, J. A., Arnold, M. S., House, R., & Toporek, R. L. (2002). *ACA advocacy competencies.* Retrieved from www.counseling.org/Resources/Competencies/Advocacy_Competencies.pdf

Lewis, J. A., Ratts, M. J., Paladino, D. A., & Toporek, R. L. (2011). Social justice counseling and advocacy: Developing new leadership roles and competencies. *Journal for Social Action in Counseling and Psychology, 3,* 5–16.

Lupien, S. J., McEwen, B. S., Gunnar, M. R., & Heim, C. (2009). Effects of stress throughout the lifespan on the brain, behavior, and cognition. *Nature Reviews Neuroscience, 10,* 434–445.

McAuliffe, G. J., & Eriksen, K. P. (1999). Toward a constructivist and developmental identity for the counseling profession: The context-phrase-stage-style model. *Journal of Counseling & Development, 77,* 267–280.

McAuliffe, G. J., Grothaus, T., Jensen, M., & Michel, R. (2012). Assessing and promoting cultural relativism in students of counseling. *International Journal for the Advancement of Counseling, 34,* 118–135.

McCarn, S. R., & Fassinger, R. E. (1996). Revisioning sexual minority identity formation: A new model of lesbian identity and its implications for counseling and research. *The Counseling Psychologist, 24,* 508–534.

McGlothlin, H., & Killen, M. (2006). Intergroup attitudes of European American children attending ethnically homogeneous schools. *Child Development, 77,* 1375–1386.

McLeod, S. A. (2016). *Bandura—Social learning theory.* Retrieved from www.simplypsychology.org/bandura.html_

Mellin, E. A., Hunt, B., & Nichols, L. M. (2011). Counselor professional identity: Findings and implications for counseling and interprofessional collaboration. *Journal of Counseling & Development, 89,* 140–147.

Milner, D. (1975). *Children and race.* Baltimore, MD: Penguin Books.

Minard, R. D. (1952). Race relationships in the Pocahontas coal field. *Journal of Social Issues, 8,* 29–44.

Mitchell, S. A., & Black, M. J. (1995). *Freud and beyond: A history of modern psychoanalytic thought.* New York, NY: Basic Books.

Moen, P., Elder, G. H., Luscher, K., & Bronfenbrenner, U. (1995). *Examining lives in context: Perspectives on the ecology of human development.* Washington, DC: American Psychological Association.

Moore, D. S. (2003). *The dependent gene: The fallacy of nature vs. nurture.* New York, NY: Henry Holt.

Myers, J. E. (1992). Wellness, prevention, development: The cornerstone of the profession. *Journal of Counseling & Development, 71,* 136–139.

Myers, J. E., & Sweeney, T. J. (2008). Wellness counseling: The evidence base for practice. *Journal of Counseling & Development, 86,* 482–493.

National Center for Health Statistics. (2014). *NHIS data, questionnaires and related documentation.* Retrieved from https://www.cdc.gov/nchs/nhis/data-questionnaires-documentation.htm

Nesdale, D. (1999). Developmental changes in children's ethnic preferences and social cognitions. *Journal of Applied Developmental Psychology, 20,* 501–519.

Passel, J. S., & Cohn, D. (2008). *U.S. population projections: 2005-2050.* Washington, DC: Pew Research Center.

Patton, D. U., & Gabarino, J. (2014). The hurting child inside the young Black male. In K. Vaughans & W. Spielberg (Eds.), *The psychology of Black boys and adolescents* (pp. 541–552). Westport, CT: Praeger.

Pettigrew, T. F. (1959). Regional differences in anti-Negro prejudice. *Journal of Abnormal Psychology, 59,* 28–36.

Pettigrew, T. F., & Tropp, L. R. (2011). *When groups meet: The dynamics of intergroup contact.* New York, NY: Psychology Press.

Piaget, J. (1970). Piaget's theory. In P. H. Mussen (Ed.), *Carmichael's manual of child psychology* (Vol. 1, pp. 703–732). New York, NY: Wiley.

Pietrzak, R. H., & Southwick, S. M. (2011). Psychological resilience in OEF-OIF veterans: Application of a novel classification approach and examination of demographic and psychosocial correlates. *Journal of Affective Disorders, 133,* 560–568.

Plomin, R. (1996). *Nature and nurture: An introduction to human behavioral genetics.* New York, NY: Wadsworth.

Poston, W. S. C. (1990). The biracial identity development model: A needed addition. *Journal of Counseling & Development, 69,* 152–155.

Ratts, M. J., Singh, A. A., Nassar-McMillan, S., Butler, S. K., & McCullough, J. R. (2016). Multicultural and social justice counseling competencies: Guidelines for the counseling profession. *Journal of Multicultural Counseling and Development, 44,* 28–48.

Remley, T. P., & Herlihy, B. (2016). *Ethical, legal, and professional issues in counseling* (5th ed.). Upper Saddle River, NJ: Prentice Hall.

Roets, A., & Van Hiel, A. (2011). Allport's prejudiced personality today: Need for closure as the motivated cognitive basis of prejudice. *Current Directions in Psychological Science, 26,* 349–354.

Rogoff, B. (2003). *The cultural nature of human development.* New York, NY: Oxford University Press.

Ronnestad, M. H., & Skovholt, T. M. (2013). *The developing practitioner: Growth and stagnation of therapists and counselors.* New York, NY: Routledge.

Schneiderman, N., Ironson, G., & Siegel, S. D. (2005). Stress and health: Psychological, behavioral, and biological determinants. *Annual Review of Clinical Psychology, 1,* 607–628.

Shallcross, L. (2013). Building a more complete client picture. *Counseling Today, 55,* 30–39.

Sherrieb, K., Norris, F. H., & Galea, S. (2010). Measuring capacities for community resilience. *Social Indicators Research, 99,* 227–247.

Sigelman, C. K., & Rider, E. (2014). *Lifespan human development* (8th ed.). New York, NY: Wadsworth.

Skinner, B. F. (1953). *Science and human behavior.* New York, NY: Macmillan.

Skinner, B. F. (1976). *About behaviorism.* New York, NY: Vintage.

Smetana, J. G. (2006). Social domain theory: Consistencies and variations in children's moral and social judgements. In M. Killen & J. G Smetana (Eds.), *Handbook of moral development* (pp. 119–154). Mahwah, NJ: Erlbaum.

Southwick, S. M., Bonanno, G. A., Masten, A. S., Panter-Brick, C., & Yehuda, R. (2014). Resilience definitions, theory, and challenges: Interdisciplinary perspectives. *European Journal of Psychotraumatology, 5,* Article 25338. doi:10.3402/ejpt.v5.25338

Southwick, S. M., Douglas-Palumberi, H., & Pietrzak, R. H. (2014). Resilience. In M. J. Friedman, P. A. Resick, & T. M. Keane (Eds.), *Handbook of PTSD: Science and practice* (pp. 590–606). New York, NY: Guilford Press.

Sroufe, L. A., Duggal, S., Weinfield, N., & Carlson, E. (2000). Relationships, development, and psychopathology. In A. J. Sameroff, M. Lewis, & S. M. Miller (Eds.), *Handbook of developmental psychopathology* (2nd ed., pp. 75–91). New York, NY: Kluwer Academic.

Staddon, J. E. R., & Cerutti, D. T. (2003). Operant conditioning. *Annual Review of Psychology, 54,* 115–144.

Stark, M. D., & Frels, R. K. (2014). Using sandtray as a collaborative assessment tool for counselor development. *Journal of Creativity in Mental Health, 9,* 468–482.

Stoltenberg, C. D., & McNeill, B. W. (2010). *IDM supervision: An integrated developmental model for supervising counselors and therapists* (3rd ed.). New York, NY: Routledge.

Stoltenberg, C. D., McNeill, B. W., & Delworth, U. (1998). *IDM supervision: An integrated developmental model for supervising counselors and therapists.* San Francisco, CA: Jossey-Bass.

Sue, D. W., Arredondo, P., & McDavis, R. J. (1992). Multicultural counseling competencies and standards: A call to the profession. *Journal of Counseling & Development, 70,* 477–486.

Sue, D., Capodilupo, C., Torino, G., Bucceri, J., Holder, A., Nada, K., & Esquilin, M. (2007). Racial microaggressions in everyday life. *American Psychologist, 62,* 271–286.

Sue, D. W., & Sue, D. (2016). *Counseling the culturally different* (7th ed.). New York, NY: Wiley.

Tappan, M. (2000). Power, privilege and critique in the study of moral development. *Human Development, 43*(3), 164–169.

Thomas, A., & Blackmon, S. (2015). The influence of the Trayvon Martin shooting on racial socialization practices of African American parents. *Journal of Black Psychology, 41*(1), 75–89.

Torres, V., Jones, S., & Renn, K. (2009). Identity development theories. *Journal of College Student Development, 50,* 577–596.

Troiden, R. R. (1989). *Gay and lesbian identity: A sociological analysis.* New York, NY: General Hall.

U.S. Census Bureau. (2014). *ACS demographic and housing estimates: 2010-2014 American Community Survey 5-year estimates.* Retrieved from https://factfinder.census.gov/faces/tableservices/jsf/pages/productview.xhtml?pid=ACS_14_5YR_DP05&src=pt

van Wormer, K., Wells, J., & Boes, M. (2000). *Social work with lesbians, gays, and bisexuals: A strengths perspective.* New York, NY: Pearson.

Vygotsky, L. S. (1978). *Mind in society: The development of higher psychological processes* (M. Cole, V. John-Steiner, S. Scribner, & E. Souberman, Eds.) (A. R. Luria, M. Lopez-Morillas, & M. Cole [with J. V. Wertsch], Trans.). Cambridge, MA: Harvard University Press.

Watkins, D., Desmond, U., & Miller, R. (2016). Introduction to the special issue on the intersection of race, gender and class in the wake of national crisis: The state of Black boys and men post-Ferguson. *Journal of Men's Studies, 24*(2), 119–129.

Watson, J. B. (1924). *Behaviorism.* New York, NY: People's Institute.

Watson, J. B., & Rayner, R. (1920). Conditioned emotional reaction. *Journal of Experimental Psychology, 3,* 1–14.

White, F. A., & Gleitzman, M. (2006). An examination of family socialization processes as moderators of racial prejudice transmission between adolescents and their parents. *Journal of Family Studies, 12,* 247–260.

Williams, J. E., Best, D. L., & Boswell, D. A. (1975). The measurement of children's racial attitudes in the early school years. *Child Development, 46,* 494–500.

Xu, J., Murphy, S. L., Kochanek, K. D., & Arias, E. (2016, December). *Mortality in the United States, 2015* (NCHS Data Brief No. 267). Washington, DC: Centers for Disease Control and Prevention.

Chapter 3

Individual and Group Helping Relationships

Ann Vernon and Darcie Davis-Gage

Learning Objectives

1. Identify characteristics of effective individual and group counselors.
2. Identify effective individual and group counseling skills.
3. Identify therapeutic factors in individual and group counseling.
4. Identify types of groups and considerations in group facilitation.

• • •

It could almost go without saying that the world is becoming more complex each day, bringing new challenges for professional counselors, who need more skills and knowledge than ever before. Regardless of whether you are working with individuals or groups, it is imperative to consider clients within the context of the larger system composed of family, friends, community, school, work, religious organizations, and the like (Cook, 2012). Okun (2002) also emphasized the influence of race, ethnicity, class, sexual orientation, gender, and culture, stressing that counseling must always begin with an understanding of the client's cultural background and values. Suffice it to say that counseling does not occur in a vacuum, and the savvy counselor needs to understand how these factors impact assessment as well as treatment.

Because you are reading this book, you have made an initial commitment to becoming a professional counselor. In this chapter, you will learn about the fundamentals of individual and group helping relationships, which will give you a foundation for the important work you will do as a counseling professional.

Individual Counseling

One of the questions on the initial application for a graduate program in school and mental health counseling that I (Ann Vernon) coordinated required applicants to explain why they were interested in pursuing a counseling degree. After years of reading these applications, I could quite accurately predict that at least 75% would say something to the effect that their friends had always come to them for advice, so they figured this would be a good profession for them. Oops! Wrong response. In fact, an 8-year-old in my private practice was more on target when she said, "Dr. Vernon, sometimes it's frustrating that you won't tell me what to do, but I think it's because you really want me to figure it out for myself." And how right she was, because counseling typically is not about giving advice, contrary to popular opinion. Rather, "counseling is a professional relationship that empowers diverse individuals, families, and groups to accomplish mental health, wellness, education, and career goals" (American Counseling Association [ACA], as cited in Erford, 2014, p. 2). Implicit in this definition is that counseling is a collaborative relationship between counselor and client with the goal of promoting change and improving quality of life.

The Counseling Process

There has been a longstanding debate in the profession as to whether counseling is an art or a science. In reality, it is most likely a bit of both. Theory drives the way in which counselors implement the counseling process, but counselors must be intuitive, creative, culturally aware, and responsive to their clients if they are to be effective. In counseling, there is no "one size fits all," which is what makes this profession so challenging, intriguing, and rewarding. No two clients are alike, and as a professional counselor, you must remain cognizant of the fact that even clients who have very similar problems will have different perspectives and feelings. This obviously affects the way in which counselors approach treatment, which must be tailored to each client.

I (Ann) am reminded of a story I used to share with graduate students that is a powerful testament to the importance of listening to what the client is saying and feeling as opposed to jumping to conclusions, interpreting, or making assumptions. It also underscores the importance of being culturally competent. This story is about an

African American female, young and pregnant, who went to an older male Caucasian counselor. The client began to tell the counselor how she was feeling about being in her predicament, to which he replied, "I understand exactly how you feel." The client glared at him and said, "You don't have a clue how I feel. You aren't young, female, African American, or pregnant. So don't pretend to know what I'm feeling." The moral of the story is that although you need to do your best to step into your clients' shoes, they have the inside track on what they are thinking and feeling. Obviously you will not have experienced everything your clients have or necessarily come from the same background or culture, but as a professional counselor you will have to take your clues from the client, asking the right questions and using your skills to figure out the essence of the problem. Do not assume, interpret, or judge—just work the process with empathy and understanding, connecting with the client to develop an effective helping relationship that will facilitate the counseling process. Reflect on Sidebar 3.1 to begin to explore the process of empathy and understanding.

What Is Effective Helping?

This really is a rather complex question, but we hope that the answers provide you with some guidelines that will help you navigate your journey to becoming a professional counselor. First, let us look at what professional counseling is *not*. As previously mentioned, it is generally not about giving advice, because advice does not empower the client and can backfire on the counselor if the client takes the advice and the result makes the problem worse. However, there are times when giving advice might be appropriate. For example, if a person is in an abusive relationship, giving advice about steps to take for self-protection is appropriate.

Moreover, professional counseling is not about imposing one's values on the client. This is often very challenging, because values are influenced by personal experiences, culture, family systems, and so forth. However, as a professional counselor, you must be very aware of your own values and not jeopardize the counseling process by assuming that your clients share them. I (Ann) experienced this

Sidebar 3.1   Thought Questions

Do you think you can be an effective counselor if you have not had the same experiences as your clients?

Do you think you will be able to step into their shoes?

What challenges might this present for you?

• • •

67

when I sought counseling for the first time to deal with my apprehensions about becoming pregnant. After some initial discussion, the counselor said that I needed to understand that, to be a good mother, I would have to stop working. I was aghast, because I was a professional counselor and had no intention of quitting the job I loved. Furthermore, my husband and I intended to be dual career parents. I considered his response sexist and biased and definitely not what I had expected to experience in counseling. Needless to say, I was out the door long before the session ended and never went back.

Effective helping is also not about fixing clients or doing all the work for them. This is a trap that beginning counselors often fall into because they are inspired to help others and they want their clients to feel better. There is a thin line between sympathy and empathy: The sympathetic counselor often wants to fix the problem to take away the client's pain, whereas the empathetic counselor feels for the client but works with him or her to resolve the issues, with appropriate guidance.

So just what *is* effective helping? According to Sheperis and Ellis (2014), "Effective helping involves being present and attentive to clients through a variety of clinical approaches and techniques" (p. 170). As these authors noted, helping clients "combines the art of understanding and 'being with' another person with the research basis of what works" (p. 171). The counselor must understand and be attentive to important client cultural considerations, which is more important than a client–counselor cultural match, according to Sheperis and Ellis.

Effective helping also involves a high degree of self-awareness and a willingness to work on your own issues. Ridley, Mollen, and Kelly (2011) underscored the importance of this by stating that self-awareness and self-reflection are critical to a quality therapeutic relationship. In fact, who you are as a person will have an impact on your effectiveness as a counselor, because your values, beliefs, and background will undoubtedly have some degree of influence on your clients, no matter how hard you try to be neutral. Consequently, it is very important that you work through unfinished business so that you do not inadvertently harm your clients by working out these issues through them (Hutchinson, 2007). A lack of awareness of your own issues or unfinished business can also cloud your judgment as a counselor and result in an inaccurate hypothesis about the problem, which was the case with one of my (Ann's) supervisees. Because of her abusive past, she filtered many of her clients' issues through that lens, which often proved to be very detrimental to the client and to the counselor–client relationship.

Duan, Rose, and Kraatz (2002) posited that self-awareness facilitates the development of empathy for others, which is such a critical aspect of the counseling process, and Hutchinson (2007) stressed the importance of self-understanding as an ethical and professional obligation. According to Hutchinson, if your life as a counselor is in chaos, you cannot pay full attention to your clients. It may also be necessary to examine your own motives for becoming a professional helper: Do you *need* to be needed? It certainly is gratifying to be able to help others, but you must be cautious that you do not foster dependency. Although it may make you feel important, it is not healthy for the counselor–client relationship. Furthermore, if you depend on your clients needing you because it boosts your sense of self-worth, you have some work to do. As Corey and Corey (2016) noted, "If you aren't on the road to resolving your own pressing problems, it is unlikely that you will be effective in helping others find solutions to their problems" (p. 5).

According to Seligman (2004), effective helping is epitomized by a collaborative relationship in which counselor and client are working together to accomplish mutually agreed-on goals. The counselor provides a safe environment to encourage client sharing, which results in mutual respect and affirmation. Effective helping also revolves around personal characteristics and self-care of the counselor, the ability to develop a strong therapeutic alliance, and specific counseling skills. These topics are addressed subsequently. Reflect more on your personal motivation for entering the profession by referring to Sidebar 3.2.

Personal Characteristics and Self-Care

Numerous scholars have written about desirable personal characteristics of the ideal professional counselor (Corey & Corey, 2016; Erford, 2014; Hutchinson, 2007; Moss & Glowiak, 2013). As you read these, keep in mind that there is no such thing as a perfect person or a perfect counselor. However, as you begin your professional journey, you can be conscious of trying to develop the qualities you are presently lacking. Hutchinson (2007) identified "acceptance of others, self-confidence, emotional stability, empathy, flexibility, genuineness, open-mindedness, and sensitivity as important characteristics" (p. 29). Moss and Glowiak (2013) compiled a list from various sources and cited the following as desirable: "intelligent and knowledgeable,

Sidebar 3.2   Thought Questions

Think about your motivation for entering this profession. Is part of it based on your need to be needed?

Do you agree with the professionals who stress the importance of working on your own personal issues?

To what degree are you willing to do this?

• • •

energetic, caring, trustworthy, resourceful, a good listener, realistic, dependable, hopeful, respectful of individual differences, optimistic, self-aware, creative and insightful, nonjudgmental, ethical, friendly, comfortable with intimacy, able to clearly express oneself, hard working, and has a sense of humor" (p. 7). Moss and Glowiak also stressed that effective counselors are compassionate, are open to a wide range of experiences, and can get involved in their clients' problems and issues but remain somewhat detached at the same time.

Being able to remain somewhat detached is often difficult, especially for inexperienced counselors who are eager to begin their professional career and help others. Although it is rewarding to help clients work through their struggles, it can also be exhausting to listen to clients talk about their grim life circumstances and maintain some distance. Because you may be dealing with complicated issues, it is very easy to expend a great deal of time and energy taking care of others instead of yourself. As Simpson and Falkner (2013) stressed, a lack of self-care has serious implications for counselors, because it may lead to burnout and professional impairment or have a negative impact on the quality of care provided to clients. The fact is, counselors are human too and may be experiencing their own difficult circumstances as they attempt to work with clients. It is important to keep in mind that "mental and physical health are essential to maintaining competence as much or more than knowledge and skills" (Lawson, Venart, Hazler, & Kottler, 2007, p. 7).

The Therapeutic Alliance

A great deal has been written about the importance of the therapeutic alliance, with numerous studies affirming that, regardless of theory, the most important predictor of counseling outcomes is the quality of the therapeutic relationship (Meyers, 2014; Moss & Glowiak, 2013; Norcross, 2001). According to Kottler (as cited in Meyers, 2014), "Without the foundation of a constructive relationship, anything else that we do isn't going to work very well or last very long" (p. 34). At the same time, Kottler noted that, although it is a crucial component of the counseling process, clients usually need more than just a positive therapeutic alliance.

Carl Rogers, a pioneer in the counseling field, made significant contributions regarding key elements of the therapeutic alliance. In his seminal work *Client-Centered Therapy*, Rogers (1951) stated that "when the counselor is favorably perceived, it is as someone with warmth and interest for the client, someone with understanding" (p. 69). Rogers described core conditions that are necessary for developing a positive therapeutic alliance, including congruence and genuineness. Rogers, as well as Albert Ellis (2001), another influential pioneer, also stressed the importance of unconditional positive regard, which implies that the counselor accepts the client without evaluation or judgment. Another essential element of a beneficial relationship is empathy, which is the ability to put yourself in the shoes of your client and see things from his or her perspective (Sheperis & Ellis, 2014). When counselors are empathic, clients feel understood and are more willing to deal with difficult issues in an environment that feels safe.

Implicit in establishing and maintaining a positive therapeutic relationship is a sense of trust between the counselor and client as well as respect. Kottler and Shepherd (2008) emphasized that the counselor conveys respect by accepting the client as a worthy person who is capable of solving his or her problems. The counselor establishes trust by being warm and genuine, maintaining confidentiality, and behaving in an ethical manner.

A word of caution regarding the therapeutic alliance: Although it is important to be warm, empathic, genuine, and respectful, it is also important to remember that you are the counselor, not the client's friend. At times, you will need to confront clients for them to grow, and this can be done in a respectful manner that clients do not see as threatening if there is a safe, trusting alliance. As the counselor, you have the skills and expertise to facilitate their process, but you need to remain cognizant of the difference between being a helper and being a friend. In addition, you need to be careful about self-disclosure, which can be either powerful and appropriate or problematic. If the relationship is positive, the client will want to know more about you, but it is important to consider whether the self-disclosure will help clients increase their own disclosure and whether it will generate a more facilitative atmosphere (Moss & Glowiak, 2013).

Resistance Versus Reluctance

Over the years, there has been considerable discussion about how to deal with resistant clients. Personally I (Ann) have always had difficulty with this term because, in my opinion, it implies a tug of war between the counselor and client and is not a helpful term. According to Hagedorn, calling clients resistant "kind of takes counselors off the hook. It takes away our responsibility for finding a way to connect" (as cited in Meyers, 2016, p. 26).

Hagedorn (as cited in Meyers, 2016) posited that resistance is related to how the counselor approaches change. Specifically, when the counselor tries to impose change, assuming that clients are ready and willing when in fact they are not, clients push back, because change can be threatening. He maintained that counselors often rush into "making things right" (p. 26) by asking clients what they have tried or why they do not try something different. This approach may create defensiveness and, in turn, sabotage the counseling process. Instead, I (Ann) like to reframe resistance as reluctance, putting myself in clients' shoes and realizing how difficult it might be for them just to admit that there is a problem they need help with, let alone engage in a change process that may be threatening. In the long run, it is more important to empathize with the client, stop blaming him or her for the impasse, be patient, and gradually move forward (see Sidebar 3.3).

Basic Counseling Skills

Regardless of theory, certain fundamental skills can facilitate personal and social development. Ivey and Ivey (2018) and Egan (2010) identified attending skills and basic listening skills as essential.

Attending Skills

Attending behaviors include good eye contact, which conveys to clients that you are interested in them and their issues. It is important, however, to occasionally break eye contact and to be aware of cultural differences, because in some cultures clients resist making eye contact when they discuss serious issues.

Attentive body language is also an important variable. Egan (2010) developed the SOLER acronym: *Squarely* face the client, maintain an *open* body posture, *lean* forward, make *eye* contact, and be *relaxed*. These postures may seem awkward at first and may need to be adjusted depending on the response from the client. Tone of voice also matters: Clients will be more responsive if your tone is warm and caring as opposed to abrasive and brusque. When clients are too loquacious and it is difficult to follow their train of thought because they are providing too much detail that may be irrelevant, counselors need to use selective attention, tuning into what seems most pertinent to the issue at hand. There are times when silence can be very powerful, even

---

Sidebar 3.3   Implication for Practice

If you learn from a parent that his or her child or adolescent is reluctant or resistant about being in counseling, consider writing a letter of introduction about yourself and sending it prior to the first session. In this letter, you could simply explain that you are a counselor who helps kids their age solve problems, that you understand that he or she might not like to come to counseling, but that it could be helpful to give it a try. You could talk a bit about how you are looking forward to getting to know him or her and share something about yourself, such as the type of pet you might have, a favorite food, something you love to do in your spare time, or so forth. In my own personal experience, I (Ann) have found this to be very helpful.

• • •

though new counselors may feel uncomfortable or anxious and keep asking questions, which may not be the most appropriate response. Silence can actually help clients hear their own voice and gives the counselor more time to respond effectively (Moss & Glowiak, 2013).

Basic Listening Skills

Although attending skills contribute importantly to the counseling relationship, attending alone is insufficient to bring about change, a primary goal of the counseling process. Ivey and Ivey (2018) and Egan (2010), as well as others, can be credited with identifying the following basic listening skills that are fundamental to the counseling process.

First, it is critical to be an active listener, hearing the client accurately and trying to understand the problem from the client's point of view. Being a careful observer of clients' nonverbal behaviors, appearance, subtle body movements, eye contact, and so forth can also be helpful. Listen carefully to see whether you detect a discrepancy between what clients say and what they do. For example, a client may say that she is happy in her marriage but may break eye contact and shift uncomfortably as she talks about her partner. It is important to note this but not jump to conclusions until you have more information.

Second, the counseling interview is facilitated when the counselor uses encouragers, paraphrasing, reflection of feelings and meaning, and summarization skills. Encouragers are nonverbal head nods, smiles, and facial expressions that convey interest as well as verbal "um hums" and "uh-huhs." Encouragers are powerful, especially when the counselor uses a short key word or short phrase used by the client (Moss & Glowiak, 2013).

Paraphrasing is an especially effective skill. Paraphrasing is not just parroting what they client has said; rather, it is "feeding back to the client the essence of what has been spoken" (Cooper, 2014, p. 203). In essence, the counselor is like a mirror, rephrasing and conveying empathic understanding that helps the client clarify and explore the issues. When paraphrasing, it is important to check with the client: "Am I hearing you correctly?" Clients will also nod or say something like "exactly" when you are on target. Accurate paraphrasing strengthens the therapeutic bond.

Another essential skill is reflection of feelings and meaning. Reflecting feelings helps clients become more aware of their emotions, helps clients develop greater self-awareness, and facilitates self-disclosure (Cooper, 2014). Reflecting feelings also enhances the development of accurate empathy. When reflecting feelings, it is important not to mimic clients' exact words but rather say something such as, "It sounds like you feel angry . . . am I hearing that right?" Reflecting meaning helps clients go deeper and work through their thoughts and feelings. Simply asking, "What did that mean to you?" can be very powerful in helping clients develop greater self-understanding.

Summarizing is another important basic listening skill. Summarization helps the counselor tie together clients' thoughts and feelings to promote client self-understanding. Cooper (2014) noted that summarization is effective when clients are rambling or confused or when they are discussing unrelated ideas. Summarizing can be used at the beginning of the session to review what the client worked on in the previous session as well as at the end of the session to clarify what was addressed in the session. See Sidebar 3.4 for other basic counseling skills.

As you may have gathered, the counseling process involves many different variables and is easier said than done. So far in this chapter, you have learned about the counseling process and what constitutes effective helping. You have also read about key personal characteristics for professional counselors, the therapeutic alliance, the importance of self-awareness and self-care, and basic counseling skills. Although these concepts were discussed within the context of individual counseling, these same general principles also apply to group counseling. The remainder of this chapter addresses group counseling fundamentals, including therapeutic factors and group dynamics, group leadership skills that go beyond the basics needed in individual counseling, and types of groups and group settings.

Group Counseling

Training counselors to facilitate groups is essential because groups are therapeutically powerful. Working as a leader of a women's group, I (Darcie Davis-Gage) was able to witness this power and the transformation of members as they experienced the group process. The women were able to build strong connections and learn that they were not alone on their journeys. This sense of universality and cohesiveness encouraged the women to share their stories and practice healthy socializing behaviors. The women also benefited from valuable feedback that affected them and helped them gain insight into their own problems.

Sidebar 3.4   Implication for Practice

When you have finished a session, it might be helpful to ask the client how he or she felt about the session, what was learned, and what behaviors might change as a result of the session. Consider giving a short homework assignment related to the content of the session, something the client can try throughout the week to reinforce the counseling goals. Examples of homework assignments could include keeping a journal to get in touch with feelings, practicing assertive communication skills, or listening carefully before interrupting others.

• • •

The Council for Accreditation of Counseling and Related Educational Programs (2016) recognizes the importance of group work, as it is one of the eight core components of its accreditation standards. The Association for Specialists in Group Work (ASGW) also acknowledges the significance of group work in counseling. The *Professional Standards for the Training of Group Workers* (ASGW, 2000) define *group work* as "a broad professional practice involving the application of knowledge and skill in group facilitation to assist an interdependent collection of people to reach their mutual goals which may be intrapersonal, interpersonal, or work-related" (p. 2).

People participate in groups in their everyday lives, so adapting this format into counseling treatment makes sense. According to Erford, Vernon, and Davis-Gage (2016), using a group format has numerous advantages. Groups allow members to feel a sense of safety and belonging, are a place to practice interpersonal skills, and provide a cost-effective way of serving many people. In addition, group members are able to receive feedback from peers and have access to a greater number of resources given the various viewpoints of leaders and members. Burlingame, Fuhriman, and Mosier (2003) completed a meta-analysis of group counseling studies over a 20-year period and found that group members experienced significant improvement compared to their waitlisted counterparts. Reflect more on your experience in groups by referring to Sidebar 3.5.

Therapeutic Factors and Group Dynamics

As a counselor-in-training, you must understand group dynamics and therapeutic factors to be an effective group leader. Yalom and Leszcz (2005) identified 11 factors that operate within a group to make it therapeutic: universality, group cohesiveness, instillation of hope, imparting of information, altruism, corrective recapitulation of the family of origin, socializing techniques, imitative behavior, interpersonal learning, catharsis, and existential factors. When leaders adhere to these factors, groups flourish and members are more likely to increase their self-awareness and accomplish their goals (Ward, 2014; see Sidebar 3.6).

Along with therapeutic factors, as a future group leader, you must be aware of other group dynamics. In particular, you must understand

Sidebar 3.5   Thought Questions

What types of groups have you participated in throughout your life?

Have you experienced some of the benefits described in this chapter?

• • •

Sidebar 3.6   Implication for Practice

As a counselor, you are facilitating a group of women dealing with postpartum depression. Which of Yalom's therapeutic factors would be most helpful at the beginning of the group? How might you incorporate these factors into the transition stage of the group? Which factors would be most helpful as you work toward termination?

• • •

the stages of group development. There are many models of group development, and all identify either a four- or a five-stage process (Jacobs, Schimmel, Masson, & Harvill, 2016; Trotzer, 2007; Ward, 1982). Tuckman and Jensen's (1977) model is the most recognized and identifies a five-stage model of forming, storming, norming, performing, and adjourning. During the forming stage, the leader develops a rationale for the group, recruits members, and conducts the first few sessions. Leaders also process feelings of apprehension, establish ground rules, set goals, and promote positive interaction among members so that members can learn more about one another. During the storming stage, the group usually first works through resistance and reluctance. As members start to differentiate themselves from one another, conflict may occur during this stage. If the group is able to work effectively through this conflict, it enters the norming stage. Members then experience a sense of cohesion and togetherness. Next, the group enters the performing stage, in which members work on the personal goals that brought them to the group and receive feedback through interactions with others. The final stage, adjourning, includes reviewing and summarizing the group experience, assessing growth and change and how to apply it to everyday life, and expressing farewells. Understanding group development will help you, as a future group leader, facilitate more effective and efficient groups.

Group Leadership

As an aspiring counselor, you are learning microskills such as active listening, paraphrasing, reflection of feelings, and summarization that can be applied not only in individual counseling sessions but also in groups (Ivey, Ivey, & Zalaquett, 2014). To be an effective group counselor, you must also learn additional skills, such as linking, confronting, and managing the focus of the group. When linking, you facilitate connections between members by highlighting similar experiences or emotions shared in the group. You can make the connections stronger by encouraging members to speak directly to one another. As a leader, you must also be comfortable using confrontation skills such as protecting and blocking, which are not typically used in individual counseling but are important in groups. For instance, as members share, you may need to block unproductive activities or protect members from feedback if it becomes hostile, unnecessary, or unproductive (Gladding, 2016). Jacobs and colleagues (2016) emphasized the importance of managing the focus of the group to explore topics at a deeper level and learning to shift the focus if the group becomes stagnant. Group facilitators also need to be skilled at providing feedback, modeling, and helping members gain insight and attribute meaning to their experience (Milsom, 2016).

In addition to mastering basic group counseling skills, group leaders must also interact using various levels of communication. Connors and Caple (2005) referred to this as *group systems theory*. In individual counseling, the client and counselor engage in one-on-one communication. Although the counselor may direct the client to engage in role play or other activities, the primary mode of communication is between the counselor and the client. Groups are different and present many more opportunities for interaction between leaders and members. According to group systems theory, effective group leaders facilitate three types of communication: intrapersonal communication, interpersonal communication, and group-as-a-whole communication. Intrapersonal communication is helpful at the beginning of the group, when the leader is drawing out personal insights of the members and starting the process of disclosure. As the group members start to build their comfort level, leaders may initiate more interpersonal interaction by linking or using dyad discussions. These interactions encourage feedback exchange and relationship building between members. Finally, group-as-a-whole communication is helpful when addressing themes among members or when conflict occurs. Using all three levels of communication is crucial for the group to be productive and effective.

Champe, Atieno, Rubel, and Rubel (2013) suggested teaching emotional regulation skills to beginning group leaders, as they sometimes struggle with the intensity of groups. As a group leader, you must learn to become emotionally aware and then apply emotional regulation skills to yourself while leading the group. In so doing, you will use a variety of skills such as distraction, redirection, and alternative thinking to manage your emotions. Specifically, distraction is an avoidance technique used by leaders to decrease emotions internally by thinking of something else or externally by doing something else. You may also use cognitive change strategies to alter your thoughts about a situation, which ultimately will impact the associated emotions. In addition, you can use reappraisal to adjust the meaning attached to a situation, which will help decrease emotions. Finally, as a group leader, you may use response modulation strategies such as movement or deep breathing to affect your physiological, experiential, or behavioral responses to emotions. Champe et al. found that once they master these skills, leaders are more confident in their leadership abilities and believe that they can handle the intensity of groups more effectively. These effective leadership and emotional management skills can then be applied in a variety of group types and settings.

Types of Groups and Settings

Groups are facilitated in a variety of settings, such as schools, hospitals, college counseling centers, mental health centers, and substance abuse treatment centers. According to ASGW (2000), there are typically four different types of groups: task, psychoeducational, counseling, and psychotherapy. Although counselors may also lead support or self-help groups, the four types of groups identified here are the most common.

Task groups, which vary in size, are found in the community, the workplace, religious organizations, schools, and the like. The purpose of a task group is to accomplish a goal; when the goal is accomplished, the group typically disbands. Task groups vary greatly in size depending on the task. They generally do not focus on changing individuals but are often influenced by group dynamics. When leaders are aware and knowledgeable about group dynamics, task groups are more efficient and effective. Leaders may increase the effectiveness of task groups by encouraging introductions at the beginning of the group, clarifying the purpose of the group, and normalizing the conflict that sometimes occurs in normal group development (Erford, 2016).

Psychoeducational groups stress growth through knowledge. They are structured therapeutic groups with the main goal of preventing maladaptive behaviors, increasing coping skills, and teaching new life skills. The focus is on prevention and growth as well as remediation (Aasheim & Niemann, 2006; Conyne, 1996). This type of group is more issue specific and tends to be more leader led. As opposed to counseling groups, the focus is not on deep self-disclosure. Psychoeducational groups typically have six to 12 members but can have as many as 20 to 40 members in some settings. Larger psychoeducational groups may function more like lectures and should be broken into smaller groups for discussion, according to Gladding (2016). Typically, these groups last eight to 10 sessions but can include from four to 20 or more sessions, depending on how long it takes to address the objectives (Gladding, 2016). Counselors usually facilitate all types of psychoeducational groups on a multitude of topics appropriate to the age of the group members. For example, topics for school-age students might include sexual abuse prevention, study skills, or dealing with bullying. Adult members might benefit from groups on stress management, communication and assertion skills, or parenting techniques.

Counseling groups are typically theory driven and tend to be preventive, growth oriented, and remedial in nature (Gladding, 2016). Similar to psychoeducational groups, some information is imparted in these groups, but the emphasis is more on group dynamics, interpersonal relationships, and processing these interactions. The major advantage of counseling groups is the interpersonal interaction and feedback received from the other members. Counseling groups typically run six to 16 sessions and consist of six to 12 members, depending on the age of participants. Examples of group topics for adults might include grief and loss, managing anger and depression, relationship issues, or intimate partner violence. Groups for children or adolescents might address parental divorce, managing troublesome emotions, getting along with friends and family, and dating. In these groups, members have the opportunity to learn new skills and receive feedback from others who are not part of their normal support network.

Psychotherapy groups are also facilitated by highly trained counselors and address serious personal and interpersonal problems. Participants are usually experiencing severe or chronic maladjustment. These groups typically take place in inpatient or outpatient mental health facilities with three to 10 or 12 members. Often, psychotherapy groups are heterogeneous regarding the presenting problem and run for several weeks or months. The diverse nature of the problems addressed can be beneficial to group members as they learn from one another through disclosure, interaction, and applying these skills outside of group (Jacobs et al., 2016). Reflect more on your level of comfort facilitating various types of groups by referring to Sidebar 3.7.

Group Formation: Recruiting, Screening, and Selecting Members

Pregroup planning is very critical, because without careful planning, a group may not be successful. Jacobs et al. (2016) identified 15 therapeutic factors that should be considered when forming a group: clarity of purpose, relevance of the purpose for members, size of the group, length of sessions, frequency of meetings, adequacy of the setting, time of day, leader's attitude, closed or open format, voluntary or involuntary membership, members' level of trust, members' level of commitment, members' attitude toward the leader, leader's readiness to deal with groups, and coleadership harmony.

Sidebar 3.7   Thought Questions

Have you participated in any task, psychoeducational, counseling, or psychotherapy groups? If so, what was your experience?
Which types of groups do you think you would feel most comfortable facilitating, and why?

• • •

When planning a group, it is important to first establish and communicate the purpose of the group, which must be relevant to the members' development. As a group leader, you also must decide on the length and frequency of meetings. Most adult groups range from 60 to 90 minutes once a week, but groups for children and adolescents are shorter in duration, typically 30 to 45 minutes. The time of day chosen is typically driven by the topic; the targeted population; and in schools, for example, the teachers or administrators. The location should be convenient and accessible to group members. Another important consideration is choosing between an open or a closed format. In a closed group, members can only join at the beginning, whereas in an open group, they can join whenever they so choose. One advantage of a closed group is that the group is generally more cohesive and members typically develop deeper relationships as trust builds. However, open groups are more flexible, and members can receive new insights as others join the group. Once the leader establishes the structure of the group, he or she must start to recruit members (Jacobs et al., 2016).

As a future group leader, you must identify who will most likely benefit from participation in the group. As discussed previously, group size is driven by the type of group, with psychoeducational groups being larger and counseling and psychotherapy groups smaller. Some settings, such as schools and residential treatment centers, allow easier access to group members, as most of them are at the facility for many hours of the day, and counselors can reach out to teachers, residential treatment staff, and others to recruit members. Other settings, such as outpatient mental health clinics and college counseling centers, may have to make a more concerted effort to recruit members. Flyers, e-mails, and word of mouth are typical methods use to recruit group members (Bryan, Steen, & Day-Vines, 2016).

Although screening is not always possible in all settings, it really is important, because not everyone is appropriate for a group. If it is feasible to screen members, the leader should meet with potential members to determine their appropriateness as it relates to the purpose of the group, ascertain their expectations and reasons for participating, and assess their interpersonal communication skills and their ability to relate to others. Negative or overbearing members can ruin a group, so it is also important to balance group membership so that one or two members do not dominate or intimidate others and negatively affect the group dynamics.

Ethical Considerations

All counselors must adhere to ethical standards, but these standards are somewhat more complex when counselors are facilitating groups. ASGW developed its Best Practice Guidelines (Thomas & Pender,

2008) to clarify the application of the *ACA Code of Ethics* (ACA, 2014) to group work. This resource is particularly helpful for group leaders as they face ethical challenges in their work. Because of the sheer number of clients involved in group work, ethical considerations are compounded. Confidentiality and competency can be specifically challenging in group work (see Sidebar 3.8).

Maintaining confidentiality is essential in both individual and group counseling. In individual counseling, confidentiality is rather straightforward. In group counseling, it becomes more complicated and is an important factor to consider even when planning the group. Confidentiality must be carefully explained during group screening, in the first session, and throughout the subsequent sessions. Although leaders are bound to keep information confidential as they would when working with individual clients, members are not necessarily bound by the same standards. Group leaders must make it clear to members that the group is only as confidential as they choose to make it. Members may agree to keep information private, but leaders cannot guarantee the same level of confidentiality as in individual counseling (Rapin, 2014).

When leaders are properly trained in various aspects of group work and engage in adequate preparation and screening procedures, many ethical difficulties can be avoided. The ASGW practice guidelines encourage leaders to follow professional standards and workplace requirements, practice within their scope of training, provide a professional disclosure statement to members, secure informed consent from members, and use an ethical decision-making model when difficult ethical situations arise (Thomas & Pender, 2008).

Cultural Considerations

Whether you are counseling individuals or working in groups, cultural competency is a requirement. According to the Multicultural and Social Justice Counseling Competencies (Ratts, Singh, Nassar-McMillan, Butler, & McCullough, 2016), counselors must be aware of their own beliefs, biases, and privileges; be knowledgeable about a variety of cultures;

Sidebar 3.8   Implication for Practice

You are leading a friendship group for middle school girls. How would you explain confidentiality to the members of the group? A teacher approaches you with questions about who is attending this group and what is being discussed during group sessions. How would you respond to the teacher? Use the *ACA Code of Ethics* (ACA, 2014) to support your response.

• • •

engage in social justice advocacy; and demonstrate counseling skills that can be adapted for use with people from a variety of backgrounds.

ASGW has developed the Multicultural and Social Justice Competence Principles for Group Workers (ASGW, 2012) to guide in the training of group leaders. These guidelines suggest that group leaders be competent in choosing interventions and methods to facilitate change based on their understanding of members' worldviews. D'Andrea (2014) added that understanding cultural identity development is crucial in the process of facilitating effective groups. One must not only understand one's own identity developmental process but be able to recognize the developmental stages of group members and adapt accordingly. Singh and Salazar (2014) encouraged group leaders to be aware of the impact of privilege and oppression in groups:

> As leaders help members increase their ability to understand their individual and shared experiences of privilege and oppression and begin framing these experiences as systemic problems, members feel more empowered to change and become advocates for themselves and perhaps become agents of change for others. (p. 288)

Conyne (1998) suggested that group counselors consider and question their own assumptions about group process, such as expectations of verbal participation, emotional expressions, and other group norms. By becoming aware of their own expectations and cultural influences, group leaders can increase their cultural sensitivity.

Chapter Summary

In this chapter, we have addressed basic skills necessary for facilitating individual and group helping relationships and stressed the importance of adhering to ethical and cultural considerations when working with clients both individually and in groups. It should be apparent after reading this chapter that the foundation of an effective helping relationship is essentially the same for both individual and group approaches, although additional skills and knowledge of group dynamics are needed to facilitate groups. In addition, clients benefit in different ways from individual counseling (in which the total focus is on the client and his or her issues) and group counseling (in which clients have an opportunity to interact with and to give and receive feedback and support from other group members as well as from the group leader or leaders).

Both individual and group counseling can have a significant impact on clients' lives, and the professional counselor plays a major role in helping clients learn to help themselves. The information presented in this chapter is the first steppingstone in helping you to develop your counseling skills.

Learning Activities

1. Suppose you are a very religious person who does not believe in abortion. How would you deal with a young woman who was raped in college and now finds herself pregnant and wanting an abortion? Would it be possible for you to work with this young woman without imposing your values? If not, what would you do? Would your position change based on the *ACA Code of Ethics* (ACA, 2014)?
2. Suppose you had grown up in a very dysfunctional family and now have a client with similar issues. How would you work effectively with a client like this without your own issues getting in the way? Identify two things you could do to help keep your boundaries clear.
3. Conflict and resistance are a normal part of the group process. Think about how you handle conflict in your personal life. How effectively do you deal with it? How will this affect your work as a group leader?
4. Coleadership is common in many settings. What are some of your strengths and limitations as a coleader? What characteristics would you like to have in a coleader? How would you assess your effectiveness as a coleadership team?

Review Questions

1. After reading this chapter, what do you consider to be the most important characteristics for counselors working individually or in groups to develop?
2. Based on what you have read, what is your biggest concern about working with groups?
3. What is the most important piece of information that you took away from this chapter regarding ethical and cultural considerations?
4. What three things did you learn from reading this chapter that you did not already know?

Further Resources

Websites

Albert Ellis Institute
   http://albertellis.org/
American Counseling Association Competencies
   https://www.counseling.org/knowledge-center/competencies
Articles from *Counseling Today* related to group counseling
   https://ct.counseling.org/?s=group

Association for Specialists in Group Work
www.asgw.org/
Carl Rogers
www.goodtherapy.org/famous-psychologists/carl-rogers.html)
Irvin D. Yalom and Therapeutic Factors
www.yalom.com/
Psychotherapy
https://psychcentral.com/psychotherapy/

Books

Erford, B. T. (2016). *Group work in schools* (2nd ed.). New York, NY: Routledge.
Gladding, S. T. (2009). *Becoming a counselor: The light, the bright, and the serious* (2nd ed.). Alexandria, VA: American Counseling Association.
Perry, W. (2008). *Basic counseling techniques: A beginning therapist's toolkit* (2nd ed.). Bloomington, IN: Author's House.
Tyson, L. E., Perusse, R., & Whitledge, J. (2004). *Critical incidents in group counseling.* Alexandria, VA: American Counseling Association.

References

Aasheim, L. L., & Niemann, S. H. (2006). Guidance/psychoeducational groups. In D. Capuzzi, D. R. Gross, & M. D. Stauffer (Eds.), *Introduction to group work* (4th ed., pp. 269–293). Denver, CO: Love.
American Counseling Association. (2014). *ACA code of ethics.* Alexandria, VA: Author.
Association for Specialists in Group Work. (2000). *Professional standards for the training of group workers.* Retrieved from https://static1. squarespace.com/static/55cea634e4b083e448c3dd50/t/55d3f615e 4b0d900e228c831/1439954453323/ASGW_training_standards.pdf
Association for Specialists in Group Work. (2012). *Multicultural and social justice competence principles for group workers.* Retrieved from https:// static1.squarespace.com/static/55cea634e4b083e448c3dd50/t/55 d3f911e4b0ac4433ebd4cd/1439955217809/ASGW_MC_SJ_Prini- ciples_Final_ASGW.pdf
Bryan, J., Steen, S., & Day-Vines, N. L. (2016). Psychoeducational groups in the schools. In B. T. Erford (Ed.), *Group work in schools* (2nd ed., pp. 244–263). New York, NY: Routledge.
Burlingame, G. M., Fuhriman, A., & Mosier, J. (2003). The differential effectiveness of group psychotherapy: A meta-analytic perspective. *Group Dynamics: Theory, Research and Practice, 7,* 3–12.
Champe, J., Atieno, J. E., Rubel, O., & Rubel, D. (2013). Emotion regulation: Processes, strategies, and applications to group work training and supervision. *Journal for Specialists in Group Work, 38,* 349–368.

Connors, J. V., & Caple, R. B. (2005). A review of group systems theory. *Journal for Specialists in Group Work, 30,* 93–110.

Conyne, R. K. (1996). The Association for Specialists in Group Work training standards: Some considerations and suggestions for training. *Journal for Specialists in Group Work, 21,* 155–162.

Conyne, R. K. (1998). What to look for in groups: Helping trainees become more sensitive to multicultural issues. *Journal for Specialists in Group Work, 23,* 22–32.

Cook, E. P. (2012). *Understanding people in context: The ecological perspective in counseling.* Alexandria, VA: American Counseling Association.

Cooper, J. B. (2014). Counseling microskills. In B. Erford (Ed.), *Orientation to the counseling profession: Advocacy, ethics, and essential professional foundations* (2nd ed., pp. 194–214). Upper Saddle River, NJ: Pearson.

Corey, M. S., & Corey, G. (2016). *Becoming a helper* (7th ed.). Pacific Grove, CA: Cengage Learning.

Council for Accreditation of Counseling and Related Educational Programs. (2016). *2016 CACREP standards.* Retrieved from www. cacrep.org/for-programs/2016-cacrep-standards/

D'Andrea, M. (2014). Understanding racial/cultural identity development theories to promote effective multicultural group counseling. In J. L. Delucia-Waack, C. R. Kalodner, & M. T. Riva (Eds.), *Handbook of group counseling and psychotherapy* (2nd ed., pp. 196–208). Thousand Oaks, CA: Sage.

Duan, C., Rose, T., & Kraatz, R. (2002). Empathy. In G. Tryon (Ed.), *Counseling based on process research: Applying what we know* (pp. 197–231). Boston, MA: Allyn & Bacon.

Egan, G. (2010). *The skilled helper: A problem-management and opportunity-development approach to helping* (9th ed.). Pacific Grove, CA: Brooks/Cole.

Ellis, A. (2001). *Overcoming destructive beliefs, feelings, and behaviors.* Amherst, NY: Prometheus Books.

Erford, B. T. (Ed.). (2014). *Orientation to the counseling profession: Advocacy, ethics, and essential professional foundations* (2nd ed.). Upper Saddle River, NJ: Pearson.

Erford, B. T. (2016). Leading task groups in the schools. In B. T. Erford (Ed.), *Group work in schools* (2nd ed., pp. 223–243). New York, NY: Routledge.

Erford, B. T., Vernon, A., & Davis-Gage, D. (2016). The value of group work: Functional group models and historical perspectives. In B. T. Erford (Ed.), *Group work in schools* (2nd ed., pp. 3–27). New York, NY: Routledge.

Gladding, S. (2016). *Group work: A counseling specialty* (7th ed.). Englewood Cliffs, NJ: Merrill.

Hutchinson, D. (2007). *The essential counselor: Process, skills, and techniques.* Boston, MA: Lahaska Press.

Ivey, A. E., & Ivey, M. B. (2018). *Intentional interviewing and counseling: Facilitating client development in a multicultural society* (9th ed.). Belmont, CA: Cengage Learning.

Ivey, A. E., Ivey, M. B., & Zalaquett, C. (2014). *Intentional interviewing and counseling: Facilitating client development in a multicultural society* (8th ed.). Belmont, CA: Brooks/Cole.

Jacobs, E. E., Schimmel, C., Masson, R. L., & Harvill, R. L. (2016). *Group counseling: Strategies and skills* (8th ed.). Belmont, CA: Brooks/Cole.

Kottler, J. A., & Shepherd, D. S. (2008). *Introduction to counseling: Voices from the field* (6th ed.). Pacific Grove, CA: Brooks/Cole.

Lawson, G., Venart, E., Hazler, R. J., & Kottler, J. A. (2007). Toward a culture of counselor wellness. *Journal of Humanistic Counseling, Education and Development, 46,* 5–19.

Meyers, L. (2014). Connecting with clients. *Counseling Today, 56*(9), 32–39.

Meyers, L. (2016). Scaling client walls. *Counseling Today, 58*(7), 25–33.

Milsom, A. (2016). Leading groups in schools. In B. T. Erford (Ed.), *Group work in schools* (2nd ed., pp. 71–90). New York, NY: Routledge.

Moss, R., & Glowiak, M. V. (2013). Therapeutic alliance and the helping relationship. In D. Capuzzi & D. Gross (Eds.), *Introduction to the counseling profession* (6th ed., pp. 3–29). New York, NY: Routledge.

Norcross, J. C. (2001). Purposes, procedures, and products of the task force on empirically supported therapy relationships. *Psychotherapy, 38,* 345–356.

Okun, B. E. (2002). *Effective helping: Interviewing and counseling techniques* (6th ed.). Pacific Grove, CA: Brooks/Cole.

Rapin, L. S. (2014). Guidelines of ethical and legal practice in counseling and psychotherapy groups. In J. L. Delucia-Waack, C. R. Kalodner, & M. T. Riva (Eds.), *Handbook of group counseling and psychotherapy* (2nd ed., pp. 71–83). Thousand Oaks, CA: Sage.

Ratts, M. J., Singh, A. A., Nassar-McMillan, S. C., Butler, S. K., & McCullough, J. R. (2016). Multicultural and social justice counseling competencies: Guidelines for the counseling profession. *Journal of Multicultural Counseling and Development, 44,* 28–48.

Ridley, C. R., Mollen, D., & Kelly, S. M. (2011). Beyond microskills: Toward a model of counseling competence. *The Counseling Psychologist, 39,* 825–864.

Rogers, C. R. (1951). *Client-centered therapy.* Boston, MA: Houghton Mifflin.

Seligman, L. (2004). *Technical and conceptual skills for mental health counselors.* Upper Saddle River, NJ: Pearson.

Sheperis, D., & Ellis, C. M. (2014). The counseling process. In B. Erford (Ed.), *Orientation to the counseling profession: Advocacy, ethics, and essential professional foundations* (2nd ed., pp. 160–193). Upper Saddle River, NJ: Pearson.

Simpson, L. R., & Falkner, J. (2013). Self-care and self-growth: A professional responsibility. In D. Capuzzi & D. Gross (Eds.), *Introduction to the counseling profession* (6th ed., pp. 123–150). New York, NY: Routledge.

Singh, A. A., & Salazar, C. F. (2014). Using groups to facilitate social justice change. In J. L. Delucia-Waack, C. R. Kalodner, & M. T. Riva (Eds.), *Handbook of group counseling and psychotherapy* (2nd ed., pp. 288–300). Thousand Oaks, CA: Sage.

Thomas, R. V., & Pender, D. A. (2008). Association for Specialists in Group Work: Best Practice Guidelines 2007 revisions. *Journal for Specialists in Group Work, 33*, 111–117.

Trotzer, J. P. (2007). *The counselor and the group: Integrating theory, training, and practice* (4th ed.). Philadelphia, PA: Brunner-Routledge.

Tuckman, B. W., & Jensen, M. A. C. (1977). Stages of small group development revisited. *Group and Organizational Studies, 2,* 419–427.

Ward, D. E. (1982). The model for more effective use of theory in group work. *Journal for Specialists in Group Work, 7,* 224–230.

Ward, D. E. (2014). Effective processing in groups. In J. L. Delucia-Waack, C. R. Kalodner, & M. T. Riva (Eds.), *Handbook of group counseling and psychotherapy* (2nd ed., pp. 84–94). Thousand Oaks, CA: Sage.

Yalom, I. D., & Leszcz, M. (2005). *The theory and practice of group psychotherapy* (5th ed.). New York, NY: Basic Books.

Chapter 4

Research and Assessment in Counseling

Richard S. Balkin

Learning Objectives

1. Identify the role of research in counseling practice.
2. Differentiate the purposes of quantitative and qualitative inquiry.
3. Define the role of generalizability and design strategies in quantitative research.
4. Define the role of transfer and trustworthiness in qualitative research.
5. Explain the role of assessment in counseling practice.
6. Evaluate the integration of assessment in research.

• • •

I remember taking my first statistics class. We were learning about the properties of the normal curve and being introduced to the concepts of probability and distribution. It was at that moment that I thought, "Yeah . . . I want to be a counselor!" Okay, not really. That is not quite how it happened for me, and more than likely that is not how it happened for you either. Most graduate students in counseling do not approach the areas of research and assessment thinking that this is what drives the field. You likely chose counseling as a profession

89

because there is something inherent about you and your desire to help people. However, the tools we use in the helping and healing relationships we develop with clients are grounded in the areas of research and assessment.

Now you might be thinking, "That sounds great, but am I really going to be using this stuff?" The answer is a resounding *yes*. At the very least, professional counseling requires that you be an intelligent consumer of research, and this idea is grounded in our ethics code: "Counselors have a responsibility to the public to engage in counseling practices that are based on rigorous research methodologies" (American Counseling Association, 2014, p. 8). This mandate is not simply about practice as a professional counselor but also about protecting the public. Counselors can lose their license when they use practices that are not grounded in research. Being a frequent reader of research and understanding new methods is extremely important. Ultimately, you may need to justify your practice, and being familiar with research in the counseling profession provides a necessary framework for how we help others. Sidebar 4.1 provides an example of how research can apply to practice.

To further expound on the relevance of research in counseling, let's try to define research. Believe it or not, the federal government, through the Office for Human Research Protections (2009), has actually defined *research* as "a systematic investigation, including research development, testing and evaluation, designed to develop and contribute to generalizable knowledge" (p. 4). To truly understand this definition, we need to discuss what is meant by "contribute to generalizable knowledge" and how counseling research might deviate from this definition.

Sidebar 4.1   Reflection

As a counselor working with adolescents in psychiatric hospitalization, early in my career I was assigned a client diagnosed with anorexia. As part of her treatment, the nurses recorded her weight every day. A discussion ensued among staff as to whether the client should be weighed facing the scale so she could see her weight or facing away from the scale so she could not see her weight. The conflict became quite vigorous, but no one ever said, "Let's see what is in the research!" Research is not merely an academic exercise; its primary purpose is to improve practice and the care of our clients. Good research in the counseling profession has implications for the profession. The ultimate goal of a research article is to bridge the research project to the practice of counseling.

• • •

Generalizability refers to the extent to which findings can be applied across populations (Dimitrov, 2013). For example, among adults who are struggling with issues of forgiveness and conflict, the extent to which an offender has demonstrated remorse and changed behavior influences the decision of the victim to forgive and/or reconcile with the offender (Balkin, Perepiczka, Sowell, Cumi, & Gnilka, 2016). Generalizability, therefore, is the extent to which this finding can be applied to adults who are working through issues of forgiveness and conflict in counseling. However, not all counseling research is generalizable. A program evaluation being conducted at a mental health center is specific to the context and services of the mental health center, and the findings may not necessarily apply to other mental health centers. Furthermore, not all research is focused on generalizability. I discuss this more later, but suffice it to say that research need only *contribute* to generalizable knowledge.

What Type of Research Do Counselors Do?

The type of research conducted is guided not by a chosen study design but rather by the design that best answers the research question or addresses the research hypotheses posed by the researcher. To be clear on this, a researcher does not choose a particular design and then decide what is to be investigated. Rather, researchers set out with a premise of what they want to investigate. The nature of this investigation is usually identified through research questions or hypotheses. For example, Balkin, Perepiczka, Whitely, and Kimbrough (2009) studied the relationship between gender, sexual activity, sexual values, and emotional awareness. To investigate these relationships the research was guided by the following research questions: "(a) To what extent do sexual values differ based on gender and sexual activity level? (b) To what extent does emotional awareness relate to sexual activity? and (c) To what extent does emotional awareness relate to sexual values?" (p. 22). Sometimes, researchers prefer that hypotheses guide the reader in understanding the nature of a study. To demonstrate the effectiveness of a community-based program geared toward helping court-referred youth, Lancaster, Balkin, Garcia, and Valarezo (2011) hypothesized the following: "We hypothesized that youth who complete the program at a university-operated community center would have a lower rate of recidivism than would a matched sample of youth who participated in community probationary programs" (p. 489).

Generally speaking, researchers will use either research questions, hypotheses, or purpose statements to inform the reader about the goals of a study. Then the methods are provided to inform the reader how the questions were answered or how the research hypotheses were confirmed or disconfirmed. At other times, a researcher may simply identify the purpose of a study, particularly when the study is exploratory or addresses the development of a theory. For example, Gibson, Dollarhide, and Moss (2010) addressed professional identity development for new counselors: "This study was designed to provide a theory of professional identity development from entry into the program through the completion of internship, as described by the trainees" (p. 23). In this statement, the authors indicated that they would utilize a method that explains how counselor trainees develop a professional identity in their training.

Once the purpose of a study is delineated and either research questions or hypotheses are posed, the researcher identifies the appropriate method to conduct the study. Generally, counseling research can be categorized into three families of research: quantitative, qualitative, and mixed methods.

Quantitative Research

Quantitative methods are centered on the numerical measurement of variables relevant to the counseling profession. Some variables in counseling research, such as grade point average or income, can be directly observed. However, many variables of interest in counseling, such as self-esteem, mood states, or wellness, are *constructs*—phenomena that cannot be directly observed. I discuss the measurement of constructs later in this chapter, but the important point here is that quantitative research relies on statistical processes to answer research questions, explore hypotheses, or investigate the purpose of the study. The types of statistical processes used can become quite complex, but research in counseling is highly dependent on the use of statistics, which can demonstrate some objectivity on the part of the researcher but can also be fraught with error. Quantitative research most commonly consists of experimental research, correlational research, and meta-analyses.

Experimental Research

Experimental research is concerned with demonstrating the effectiveness of an approach or intervention or identifying differences between groups or among groups (Balkin & Kleist, 2017). As mentioned earlier, statistics are used to determine whether an effect or difference is occurring outside the realm of chance. In other words, are differences occurring simply due to chance, or are differences occurring due to a meaningful effect? To make this determination, researchers utilize what is known as *random assignment,* which refers to individuals in a study being randomly assigned to a *treatment group* (a group that receives an intervention) or a *control group* (a group that does not receive an intervention). The idea is that when individuals are randomly assigned to a group, the groups will be equivalent. In other words, random assignment ensures that both treatment and control groups will measure similarly across variables of interest. Does it work? Actually, it does! The reason it works is that when groups are large enough, the random assignment of individuals randomly disperses variables that could influence the study equally across the groups. The problem is that random assignment is not always possible. Counselors are often interested in differences based on demographic factors, such as sex and ethnicity, which are not variables that can be randomly assigned. In cases like this, researchers must establish group equivalence prior to conducting statistical tests to see whether an intervention was effective. When random assignment is used in a study, the study is referred to as a *true experimental* study. When random assignment is not used to compare two groups, the term *quasi-experimental* is used to describe the study. When the basis of comparison does not use random assignment or a comparison group, such as giving a group a pretest and then following up with a posttest with the same group, the design is known as *preexperimental.* You are not likely to see preexperimental studies published in academic journals. Without a comparison group there is no way to show that the changes in a preexperimental design, were due to an intervention or simply naturally occurring changes over time. Experimental research can be further categorized into between-groups designs and within-groups designs (Balkin & Kleist, 2017).

Between-groups designs refer to studies that compare groups. Sometimes, the groups are based on demographic variables, such as sex or ethnicity; other studies focus on true experimental designs in which a treatment group is compared to a control group. The purpose of these studies is to demonstrate that groups are statistically significantly different based on some factor of comparison (e.g., sex, ethnicity, treatment intervention).

Within-groups designs refer to studies that evaluate change over time or across repeated measures for participants. In other words, measurements of participants across a particular phenomenon occur at two different time periods. Tests of statistical significance help identify whether changes over time due to an intervention occurred. In classic within-groups designs, pretest or baseline scores serve as the control or point of comparison. Then an intervention takes place, and another measure is collected. If there is a significant effect between the pretest or baseline and the posttest scores, we can determine that the intervention was effective in changing the outcome between the pretest/baseline and posttest scores.

Correlational Research

Not all quantitative research falls into the realm of experimental design. As a matter of fact, most quantitative research published in counseling journals is correlational—that is, the research sets out to explain relationships between or among variables. For example, there is a significant relationship between the likelihood that a victim will forgive and reconcile with an offender and that the offender will demonstrate remorse and/or a change in behavior (Balkin et al., 2016). Such a relationship is demonstrated by measuring and evaluating victims' perceptions of forgiveness and the level of remorse/change in the offender. Correlational research is a wonderful tool for demonstrating relationships between or among variables of interest in the counseling profession, but such research is not evidence of causality. In this example, we cannot suggest that an offender's remorse or change in behavior causes the victim to forgive or reconcile; rather, we only know that there is a relationship between the offender demonstrating remorse or changing behavior and the victim being willing to offer forgiveness and reconcile the relationship with the offender.

Meta-Analyses

A body of research is composited when various authors and researchers contribute to a particular topic of interest. Do a search on a topic like trauma-focused counseling, and you will find a number of studies on the topic. When researchers want to summarize research and extend those summaries to empirically supported treatments—interventions with a record of effectiveness—then meta-analyses are conducted. Meta-analyses use quantitative processes to evaluate empirically supported articles and identify the extent to which techniques or interventions are effective (Lenz, 2017). Meta-analyses are extremely important to identifying best practices in the counseling profession, as such studies synthesize the existing research on a given topic and provide meaningful data about the efficacy of a treatment, intervention, or approach.

A Word About Statistical Significance

So far, we have focused on quantitative research and the idea of identifying statistically significant effects, relationships, or differences. A mistake that is often made about social science research is interpreting statistical significance as equating to meaningfulness. Quite plainly, statistical significance is a statement about the probability of an event occurring—such as the probability that group differences exist or that a relationship exists between or among variables (Balkin & Kleist, 2017). However, simply because an event occurs outside the realm of chance, that does not make it meaningful. For example, you might have made your bed this morning because your mother-in-law is coming over and you want her to see a clean house. Hence, this was an event that occurred outside the realm of chance, but it probably will not change your mother-in-law's opinion of you.

To demonstrate meaningfulness, counseling researchers use and interpret effect size—the magnitude of a relationship. Effect size informs the reader of the extent to which a statistically significant result has impact. Terms such as *small, medium* or *moderate,* and *large effects* are generally used to identify the meaningfulness of findings. Even if you are not familiar with measures of effect size, such as Cohen's *d,*

η^2, φ, r, or R^2, you can still look at the narrative explanation of the results, as a good research article will provide an interpretation of the effect. The important piece here is that, as a consumer of research, do not simply identify a statistically significant result as important. Look deeper at the magnitude of the effect to see whether this is really something you should pay attention to.

Qualitative Research

As mentioned previously, not all research is quantitative and generalizable. Much of the research conducted in counseling is qualitative research, which focuses on narrative data (i.e., interviews, observations, document collection). The goal of qualitative inquiry is to explain phenomena in depth that is *transferable*—where the reader ascertains that the findings are coherent, insightful, and useful (Lincoln & Guba, 1985). You might think that a reliance on and interpretation of narrative data such as interviews and observations would result in a research design that is highly subjective and lacking rigor. However, this is simply not the case. Qualitative research is essential for developing theory; quantitative research is essential for testing such theories. Findings from qualitative research are not generalizable. However, qualitative research eventually can lead to generalizable knowledge. To maintain objectivity in qualitative inquiry, researchers demonstrate various aspects of trustworthiness—the process of establishing the credibility of the analysis and results of the narrative data (Patton, 2015). A discussion of six aspects of trustworthiness follows.

Prolonged engagement refers to time on task in the field. In qualitative research, all data are filtered through the researcher. In this regard, the researcher is the instrument of data collection: The researcher interviews participants, makes observations, and analyzes the data. These tasks require that the researcher provide information that relates to time and intensity in the field of study. Let's take a look again at the aforementioned article by Gibson et al. (2010) on the professional identity development of new counselors. The 43 participants in the study each participated in one or two focus groups consisting of four to eight participants each so that each participant would have an opportunity to contribute. Considering the number of participants (qualitative research uses much smaller sample sizes than quantitative research) and the number of focus groups conducted, evidence of time spent in the field is established.

Persistent engagement refers to how the researcher manages discrepant data. As the researcher evaluates the interviews, observations, and documents (e.g., surveys, demographic information), he or she may find that not all data collected fit into the themes that the researcher identified. Researchers need to be transparent about how discrepant data were addressed.

Triangulation refers to the comparison of various data using a variety of sources, theories, and/or methods. For example, researchers may wish to compare data collected from different types of participants or from various focus groups. Perhaps survey data were collected in addition to interviews, and these can be compared. Again, when the researcher develops themes from the data, triangulation shows consistency with various data sources and/or methods.

Peer debriefing is a process by which the researcher engages with other experts or researchers and shares the data. This provides an opportunity to confirm the findings and address subjectivity and researcher bias. When another researcher evaluates the data, the results may be further confirmed.

Member checks occur when the researcher goes back to the participants who were interviewed, shares the findings, and establishes that what was said and the manner in which the data were interpreted are correct. Participants often have the opportunity to elaborate on the present findings, confirm the findings, or correct any misconceptions.

Finally, an *audit trail* is the raw data, consisting of surveys, interview transcripts, observation logs, and documents collected. Researchers need to be able to share the data and show them within reason should the results of the study be questioned. Often in a research study, quotes from respondents will be shared to establish how the data confirm the identified themes.

This description is merely a cursory presentation of qualitative inquiry. There are various themes and coding strategies that require much more elaboration. Furthermore, neither quantitative research nor qualitative research need stand alone; researchers may utilize mixed methods—a combined approach that involves both quantitative and qualitative inquiry. Mixed-methods research is obviously multifaceted, and the researcher needs to consider the sequence in which data were collected and analyzed. Should the quantitative findings inform the qualitative investigation or vice versa? Neither sequence is incorrect, but consideration of this is pertinent to such studies.

Linking Research to Assessment

Whether a researcher is focused on quantitative or qualitative inquiry, the process of gathering data is not only central to the research process but also inherent to the practice of counseling as well as life in general. Think about it. Perhaps at one time in your life you went to a bar and attempted to make eye contact with a particular individual. Assuming you made that eye contact, you evaluated the data. Did you get a come-hither look? Did you get an eye roll? Did you get a smile and a shy glance looking downward? Or did you get a flat-out rejection, like "I'm totally way out of your league"? The information you received from this process and your evaluation of that information is, in fact, an assessment. *Assessment* involves the "collection of information in order to identify, analyze, evaluate and address problems, issues, and circumstances" (Balkin & Juhnke, 2014, p. 1) within the context of counseling, such as client care or research. From this definition, you should note two primary functions of assessment:

1. Assessment relates to measurement; measurement is integral to research.
2. Assessment is a process, but not a final outcome, of counseling practice.

The Role of Assessment in Counseling

As an integral part of counseling practice, counselors use assessment for diagnosis, accountability, counseling outcomes, interventions, and research. Assessment can be both a formal or an informal process. In the case of informal assessment, counselors may evaluate a client's motivation, the working alliance, or a client's reaction to a confrontation during a session. Hence, assessment may occur within the context of the counseling relationship. In formal assessment, counselors may use a variety of tools and strategies, such as formal standardized interviews, a mental status exam, or established measures (e.g., symptom inventories, personality measures). Assessment covers the spectrum of client care, from crisis stabilization (such as a suicide assessment) to reporting abuse/neglect, to evaluating social history, to establishing criteria for a diagnosis, to evaluating symptom reduction and readiness to discontinue counseling services. Because of both the informal and formal processes, assessment is both a counseling skill and a vital resource within the context of counseling. For example, you will be expected to work with clients who are experiencing a variety of crises, such as situations of suicide and abuse, and you will need to evaluate their safety and stabilization. In addition, you may need to rely on formal assessment instruments to confirm diagnostic impressions and evaluate client progress. Counselors rely on both informal and formal functions of assessment, but assessment is often conceptualized as the more formal process, which includes the selection, administration, scoring, and utilization of assessment instruments essential to both client care and research. Let's turn our attention to the formal processes of assessment and the types of measures utilized.

How We Measure

Assessment in general, and especially formal assessment processes, focuses on measuring what we refer to in counseling as *constructs*—phenomena that cannot be directly observed. For example, some measures, such as height and weight, are very objective and observable. But areas of interest in counseling research are rarely directly observable. These include concepts such as achievement (e.g., competency testing in schools), aptitude (e.g., GRE, ACT, SAT), mood (e.g., Beck Depression Inventory–II, Hamilton Anxiety Rating Scale), personality (e.g., NEO Personality Inventory–3), career interests (e.g., Career Interest Profiler), working alliance (Working Alliance Inventory), symptom severity (e.g., Symptom Checklist–90–Revised), and so forth. Thus, we have to figure out ways to measure constructs that we deem important in counseling research but that can be difficult to assess. We can agree, for example, that depression exists, but can we agree that someone has mild, moderate, or severe symptoms? Consider a more complex construct, such as multicultural competence. How do we evaluate whether counselors are competent with respect to awareness, knowledge, and skills? Even when items are created to measure a construct, a degree of subjectivity is present. For example, consider the commonly used Likert-type scale, a scale from 1 to 5 that might indicate 1 = *strongly disagree,* 2 = *disagree,* 3 = *neither agree nor disagree,* 4 = *agree,* and 5 = *strongly agree.* When using such a scale, researchers often add the scores of the items and perform mathematical operations to obtain statistics that inform them about a group on the construct of interest. For example, Davis, Balkin, and Juhnke (2014) used a Likert-type scale like the one described here to evaluate life balance among adults in the development of the Juhnke–Balkin Life Balance Inventory (JBLI). But what is *life balance?*

As stated earlier, measuring constructs can be complex. Constructs such as life balance, wellness, and multicultural competence are multifaceted, and various experts and researchers in the field may define a construct differently. Therefore, each construct is dependent on an *operational definition*—a guiding description of a construct (Balkin & Juhnke, 2014). From the operational definition, items may be created to develop a measure. To develop the JBLI, Davis et al. (2014) used the following operational definition of *life balance:*

> Matuska and Christiansen (2008) defined life balance as "a satisfying pattern of daily activity that is healthful, meaningful, and sustainable to an individual within the context of his or her current life circumstances" (Matuska & Christiansen, 2008, p. 11). The JBLI was created to assess client life balance and determine areas of client imbalance, concern, and dissatisfaction. (p. 181)

Based on the operational definition of life balance, researchers would carefully select items to represent accurately the underlying construct. Reflect on the application of assessing life balance when working with a client (see Sidebar 4.2).

In addition to operationally defining a construct and developing items, counselors need to consider the type of measure to be used. Counselors

Sidebar 4.2   Implication for Practice

The Juhnke–Balkin Life Balance Inventory (JBLI; Davis et al., 2014) measures 10 domains related to life balance that the developers described in detail in a research article that presented the measure and provided validation data for it. After reading their article, you could administer the JBLI to a client and have a strong conceptualization of both deficits and protective factors affecting the client. This assessment tool could be used to address client concerns (such as stress, anxiety, or dysfunctional relationships) or identify positive aspects in the client's life (such as health or a positive outlook). In this way, assessment can move beyond mere diagnosis or labels; assessment instruments like the JBLI can be used to enhance the counseling process.

• • •

use assessment instruments or *measures* that fall into two categories: criterion referenced and norm referenced (Balkin & Juhnke, 2014). Scores on a *criterion-referenced* test are compared to a set standard or specification (i.e., criteria). An exam created by a classroom instructor or a driver's license exam are examples, because scores are compared to a pre-established criterion—how many you get right determines whether you have sufficient knowledge or mastery of the construct being measured. Scores on a *norm-referenced* test are compared to those of a normative sample; in other words, scores are based on other people's performance. For example, how do we determine whether someone has an extroverted personality or exhibits moderate to severe depression? When measures are developed, data are collected based on a population of interest, such as children, adolescents, or adults. Then scores of individuals can be compared to those of the normative group. If the normative group is representative of the population of interest, we can make evaluations based on how an individual scored on a measure compared to the normative group. When counselors evaluate clients using a norm-referenced instrument, such as indicating that someone is extroverted, depressed, angry, healthy, and so forth, that individual is being compared to a normative group—an indication of how individuals are expected to score on a particular construct of interest. Thus, the scores on criterion-referenced measures tell us something very different from what the scores on a norm-referenced measure do. Scores on a criterion-referenced measure explain what someone knows or understands about a particular construct; scores on a norm-referenced measure tell us how someone performed compared to a normative group. Most measures used in counseling are norm referenced (Balkin & Juhnke, 2014).

Psychometric Properties of Assessment

Obviously, there is some subjectivity to the way in which measures are developed, with the identification of an operational definition and reliance on scales that reflect how others respond as a way of establishing what might be considered average or normal. Even though scales, such as the Likert-type scale, may be used to score and quantify responses, such scales cannot be deemed totally objective. Let's say I ask readers to rate their agreement with this particular item using a Likert-type scale: "I enjoy this book chapter." Most would probably say *strongly agree*, but maybe some would say *agree*, and a few others might unwisely give a lower rating. The problem here is that, even though a scale is being used to rate responses, there is still a subjective quality—would everyone agree on what differentiates *agree* from *strongly agree?* Some people may be more difficult to please and give a lower rating, whereas others might be more inclined to give higher scores. What constitutes *agree* for one individual might be *strongly agree* for another individual. Reflect on Sidebar 4.3 to further assess this issue.

To demonstrate that items are scored accurately and consistently, researchers focus on *reliability*—the accuracy and consistency of scores on a measure. Reliability is a function of scores, not scale. In other words, a scale is never reliable. Rather, the scores on the scale indicate reliability. The accuracy and consistency of scores for a group are evidenced by statistics and specifically correlational procedures, which are used to demonstrate relationships among items and variables (Balkin & Juhnke, 2014). Discussing the computational strategies of reliability statistics is outside the scope of this chapter, but what is important to understand is that researchers need to show that responses to items on a measure are consistent. Take the JBLI I discussed earlier: According to the measure, individuals who exhibit higher levels of life balance will show higher scores on scales of the JBLI (e.g., Positive Orientation, Global Health, Sex/Intimacy), and individuals with lower levels of life balance will show lower scores on the same scales. Hence, such scores show evidence of consistency across populations. The most common measure of reliability is Cronbach's alpha (also known as *coefficient alpha*). Cronbach's alpha ranges from 0 to 1, with higher scores being closer to 1. Values around .70

Sidebar 4.3 Thought Questions

Would everyone agree on what differentiates *agree* from *strongly agree?*

How could the discrepancy between each person's perspective distort the results?

• • •

or higher are generally indicative of adequate evidence of *internal consistency*—consistency of the scores within a measure.

Another dimension to demonstrating the adequacy of a measure is *validity*—evidence that demonstrates the interpretation and use of scores on a measure (American Educational Research Association [AERA], American Psychological Association, & National Council on Measurement in Education, 2014). Simply because scores on a measure are accurate and consistent does not mean that the measure is being used appropriately. Although *reliability* refers to the accuracy and consistency of scores from a group of participants, reliability does not address how scores are used. The purpose for which scores are used is validity! For this reason, five basic types of validity evidence are essential to using scores on measures for counseling and research. Please note that not all of this evidence may be present in the validation of a measure, and the absence of such evidence should be highly scrutinized. In other words, if a lack of evidence or insufficient evidence is noted, the measure may not be very good.

Evidence based on test content refers to the "themes, wording, and format of the items, tasks or questions" (AERA et al., 2014, p. 14). Researchers generally demonstrate this type of evidence by demonstrating that the operational definition of the construct being measured is based on a thorough review of the literature and that the items derived for measuring the construct were based on expert reviews of the items and their relationship to the operational definition. For example, the construct of life balance, as measured on the JBLI (Davis et al., 2014), was tied to the literature from Matuska and Christiansen (2008). When creating the items, the authors used the following process:

> The items on the JBLI were developed by the authors in an attempt to assess the various domains of life balance. The authors of the JBLI consulted with eight experts during the item development phase. All the expert reviewers held doctoral-level degrees and were identified as having extensive clinical experience and having engaged in scholarly activities within the field of professional counseling. The reviewers were asked to rate the relevance (i.e., highly relevant to domain [4], relevant to this domain [3], neither relevant nor irrelevant to domain [2], irrelevant to domain [1], or highly irrelevant to domain [0]) of each of the 7 question stems within the 12 domains included in the JBLI. (Davis et al., 2014, p. 183)

Hence, the reader can look at the development of the JBLI and understand that the items were grounded in theory and evaluated for appropriateness.

Evidence based on response processes provides information about the cognitive processes used to respond to items (AERA et al., 2014). For example, the JBLI uses a Likert-type scale. Items are written as declarative statements, and respondents identify their level of agreement with each item. This is a common format used in counseling research to measure a construct of interest.

Evidence of internal structure refers to the statistical analyses used to demonstrate empirical evidence that the items measure the construct of interest (AERA et al., 2014). When items are moderately or strongly correlated and related in content, we can ascertain that they likely measure the same phenomenon.

Evidence of relationship to other variables is demonstrated by correlating scores on one measure to scores on another measure (AERA et al., 2014). The expectation is that, if two measures evaluate the same construct (e.g., the SAT and ACT both measure aptitude), then scores on the measures will be highly related. Sometimes, researchers attempt to demonstrate that the construct evaluated by one measure is similar to another, known as *convergent evidence;* at other times, researchers attempt to show how one measure is unique from another, resulting in weaker correlations and referred to as *divergent evidence.*

Evidence based on consequences of testing provides an indication of how scores should be interpreted and used (AERA et al., 2014). This is a difficult type of evidence to demonstrate but is important in protecting clients' welfare. The misuse of measures or the misinterpretation of scores can have detrimental consequences for clients. Hence, how measures are administered, scored, interpreted, and used should be clearly delineated in the development of a measure.

Chapter Summary

Regardless of specialization, counselors will practice assessment and integrate research into their work with clients, students, and the community. Clinical mental health counselors may use mood and diagnostic inventories to assist in client conceptualization or identify a reduction in client symptoms. Career counselors often use a variety of assessment tools to evaluate career interests, values, and abilities among the populations they serve. School counselors are responsible for understanding the functions of aptitude and achievement testing, along with a host of assessment measures that may be used in other settings, such as those mentioned here. Assessment is the foundation of demonstrating accountability and effectiveness (Balkin & Juhnke, 2014).

Within the area of program management, such as coordinating guidance curricula in a school, or consulting with external agencies, assessment is integral to needs assessment and program evaluation. Counselors may use informal processes (e.g., interviews) or formal processes (e.g., validated measures) to identify needs or evaluate existing programs or services. Such processes are essential in identifying best practices and serve to lend support to empirically supported treatments.

Counselors have the responsibility to be knowledgeable about assessment processes, to be intelligent consumers of research, and to stay current and practice ethically. When reviewing research and assessment processes, counselors should evaluate the extent to which they are grounded in the literature, thoroughly explained, and applicable to practice. What follows is a basic primer that reemphasizes the key points in this chapter.

A thorough review of the literature is essential to ascertaining the relevance of a research study or appropriateness of a measure. From the literature review, counselors should be able to obtain sufficient background on a given topic or construct and identify the importance of the development of the study. An explanation of how the study took place and what participants were involved is important to assessing whether the findings are generalizable and useful. From the Methods section of a study you should be able to identify the demographic characteristics of the participants (e.g., sex, age, ethnicity) and how participants were selected. These details provide an understanding of the extent to which the findings are generalizable to specific populations and therefore may or may not have cross-cultural implications. For example, a measure that was normed using predominantly high-income, White adolescents may not have much relevance to low-income, minority youth. Furthermore, the use of measures should be delineated with evidence of the reliability of the scores and the validity of the measure. The extent to which a measure is useful to special populations should be addressed. In qualitative inquiry, some explanation of what makes the researcher(s) qualified to undertake the study is essential.

Unfortunately, analyses, especially statistical analyses, can become quite complex and often difficult to understand—even with a terminal degree! You may not understand the complexity of an analysis, but the interpretation of the findings should be fairly straightforward. Look for key terms such as *statistical significance* and *small, moderate,* or *large effect.* Such terms help the reader place the findings in their proper context. With qualitative inquiry, make sure that the themes identified have adequate support from the narrative data collected. This is often demonstrated in the form of quotes.

Every research study requires a discussion, in which the results are put into perspective. Informed counselors make sure that the findings are appropriate to the discussion. Researchers should be cautious not to go beyond what the data provide. Furthermore, implications for counseling need to be explicated. How research should be integrated into practice or the appropriate use of assessment measures should be clearly delineated.

Research and assessment may be quite technical, but they provide the basis of the counseling profession. Understanding research and engaging in assessment practices are key to executing effective interventions and developing yourself as an expert in the counseling profession. Although research methodology may be highly nuanced, the practice of assessment within the context of counseling, and even in your daily life, is much more common. Within your counseling program, you will have courses that further develop these important skill sets.

Learning Activities

1. The American Counseling Association and most of its affiliated divisions publish journals. Select five counseling journals associated with the American Counseling Association or its affiliate divisions and provide an overview of the scope of articles published in each one. You will find a list of many counseling journals at https://www.counseling.org/publications/counseling-journals.
2. Using the Academic Search, PsycINFO, or *Mental Measurement Yearbook* databases or the test reviews from the Association for Assessment and Research in Counseling, provide a review of an assessment measure you might use in your counseling practice. Be sure to evaluate each of the five types of evidence of validity.
3. Find a quantitative article published in a counseling journal on a topic of your interest. Provide a summary of the research purpose/questions/hypotheses, the type of design (e.g., between groups, within groups, correlational), and the findings.
4. Find a qualitative article published in a counseling journal on a topic of your interest. Provide a summary of the research purpose/questions/hypotheses, evidence of trustworthiness, and a summary of the findings.
5. Interview a counselor in your specialization (e.g., clinical mental health; school; career; addictions; marriage, couple, and family counseling; clinical rehabilitation counseling; college counseling and student affairs). What type of assessment processes and measures does he or she use? How do you believe you may incorporate them or others into your future practice?

Review Questions

1. Differentiate between the major goals of quantitative and qualitative research.
2. How do counselors demonstrate adherence to using strategies based on "rigorous research methodologies" (American Counseling Association, 2014, p. 8)?
3. How is the process of assessment different in quantitative research, qualitative research, and counseling practice?
4. What is meant by *informal* and *formal assessment*? Provide examples of each.
5. What are some examples of assessment practices used in various specializations in counseling?

Further Resources

Articles

Balkin, R. S., & Sheperis, D. S. (2009). *A primer in evaluating quantitative research for counseling professionals* (ACAPCD-26). Retrieved from www.counseling.org/Resources/Library/ACA%20 Digests/ACAPCD-26.pdf

Falco, L. D., & McCarthy, C. J. (2013). Writing for publication: A guide for counseling practice articles. *Journal of Counseling & Development, 91,* 343–348. doi:10.1002/j.1556-6676.2013.00103.x

Goodwin, L. D., & Leech, N. L. (2003). The meaning of validity in the new standards for educational and psychological testing: Implications for measurement courses. *Measurement and Evaluation in Counseling and Development, 36,* 181–191.

Hays, D. G., & Wood, C. (2011). Infusing qualitative traditions in counseling research designs. *Journal of Counseling & Development, 89,* 288–295. doi:10.1002/j.1556-6678.2011.tb00091.x

Hunt, B. (2011). Publishing qualitative research in counseling journals. *Journal of Counseling & Development, 89,* 296–300. doi:10.1002/j.1556-6678.2011.tb00092.x

Trusty, J. (2011). Quantitative articles: Developing studies for publication in counseling journals. *Journal of Counseling & Development, 89,* 261–267. doi:10.1002/j.1556-6678.2011.tb00087.x

Watts, R. E. (2011). Developing a conceptual article for publication in counseling journals. *Journal of Counseling & Development, 89,* 308–312. doi:10.1002/j.1556-6678.2011.tb00094.x

Websites

American Counseling Association Practice Briefs
  https://www.counseling.org/knowledge-center/practice-briefs
Publication Guidelines for American Counseling Association Journals
  https://www.counseling.org/publications/counseling-journals
Test Reviews
  http://aarc-counseling.org/test-reviews

References

American Counseling Association. (2014). *ACA code of ethics.* Alexandria, VA: Author.

American Educational Research Association, American Psychological Association, and National Council on Measurement in Education. (2014). *Standards for educational and psychological testing.* Washington, DC: American Educational Research Association.

Balkin, R. S., & Juhnke, G. A. (2014). *Theory and practice of assessment in counseling.* Columbus, OH: Pearson.

Balkin, R. S., & Kleist, D. M. (2017). *Counseling research: A prac-titioner-scholar approach.* Alexandria, VA: American Counseling Association.

Balkin, R. S., Perepiczka, M., Sowell, S. M., Cumi, K., & Gnilka, P. G. (2016). The forgiveness reconciliation model: An empirically supported process for humanistic counseling. *Journal of Humanistic Counseling, 55,* 55–65.

Balkin, R. S., Perepiczka, M., Whitely, R., & Kimbrough, S. (2009). The relationship of values and emotional awareness to sexual activity in young adulthood. *ADULTSPAN Journal, 8,* 17–28.

Davis, R. J., Balkin, R. S., & Juhnke, G. A. (2014). Validation of the Juhnke-Balkin Life Balance Inventory. *Measurement and Evaluation in Counseling and Development, 47,* 181–198. doi:10.1177/0748175614531796

Dimitrov, D. M. (2013). *Quantitative research in education: Inter-mediate and advanced methods.* Oceanside, NY: Whittier.

Gibson, D. M., Dollarhide, C. T., & Moss, J. M. (2010). Professional identity development: A grounded theory of transformational tasks of new counselors. *Counselor Education and Supervision, 50,* 21–38.

Lancaster, C., Balkin, R. S., Garcia, R., & Valarezo, A. (2011). An evidence-based approach to reducing recidivism in court-referred youth. *Journal of Counseling & Development, 89,* 488–492.

Lenz, A. S. (2017). Synthesizing research results using meta-analysis. In R. S. Balkin & D. M. Kleist, *Counseling research: A practitioner-scholar approach* (pp. 161–186). Alexandria, VA: American Counseling Association.

Lincoln, Y. S., & Guba, E. G. (1985). *Naturalistic inquiry.* Newbury Park, CA: Sage.

Matuska, K., & Christiansen, C. (2008). A proposed model of lifestyle balance. *Journal of Occupational Science, 15,* 9–19.

Office for Human Research Protections. (2009). *U.S. Department of Health and Human Services, Code of Federal Regulations, Title 45 Public welfare, Part 46, Protection of human subjects.* Washington, DC: Author.

Patton, M. Q. (2015). *Qualitative research and evaluation methods.* Thousand Oaks, CA: Sage.

Section II

Counseling
Specialties

Chapter 5

Addictions Counseling

Virginia A. Kelly

Learning Objectives

1. List the etiological models of addictions described in the chapter.
2. Gain an understanding of the history and development of addictions counseling.
3. Identify the various impacts of addiction on significant others in the addict's life.
4. Understand a variety of contextual dimensions relevant to addictions counseling, including the various settings and roles of addictions counselors, co-occurring disorders, regulatory processes and substance abuse policies that impact addictions counseling, the professional organizations relevant to the practice of addictions counseling, and culturally relevant practices.
5. Gain knowledge in the assessment of addiction and addictive disorders.
6. Identify the treatment practices covered in the chapter.

• • •

Regardless of their setting or specific job, every professional counselor will encounter the issue of addiction. The universality of addiction is well established (National Council on Alcoholism and Drug Dependence, n.d.) and crosses all known boundaries. In addition, current notions of addiction include both alcohol and substance abuse and process addictions, increasing the likelihood that counselors will have contact with clients struggling with an addictive disorder.

It is estimated that 1 in every 12 adults struggles with alcohol abuse or dependence and that an estimated 20 million Americans (approximately 8% of the population) used an illegal drug in the past 30 days (National Council on Alcoholism and Drug Dependence, n.d.). The data concerning the prevalence of process addictions are not as well established, and researchers have noted this gap in the literature (Wilson & Johnson, 2013). However, the study of process addictions has gained traction (Smith, 2015). Specifically, researchers have identified 21 behaviors associated with the potential for addiction (Process Addictions, n.d.). Although more research in this area is necessary, available research addresses addiction as an underlying process regardless of whether the addiction is to a substance or a behavior (Seyyed et al., 2012). Thus, for the purposes of this chapter, process addictions and addictions to alcohol and drugs are treated as a single process.

Theories and Etiology of Addictions and Addictive Behaviors

There are a number of explanatory models of addiction and addictive behavior. Among the unidimensional models are moral models, the medical model, and the psychodynamic model. In addition, more current multidimensional models have been proposed that explain addiction from multiple perspectives. The most common of these is the biopsychosocial model (Tombs, 2013).

Moral Models

Moral models of addiction seek to explain addictive behavior as a moral failing and have been historically applied to drinking and alcoholism. In particular, the dry moral model proposes that addiction is simply and only due to poor moral choices on the part of the substance abuser. The wet moral model, in contrast, acknowledges that drinking is a normal part of society and may not always be considered an amoral behavior. However, this model suggests that implicit rules govern drinking behavior. Although most adults follow these rules, the individual with a substance use disorder does not and instead chooses to drink in a manner that opposes the normal social order. Most current-day practitioners do not use moral models as a way of explaining or understanding a substance use disorder. However, some professionals retain the belief that addiction can be explained by poor decision making. Specifically, some behavioral models explain the cause of addiction as rooted in behavior and thus under the control of the individual struggling with the addictive disorder (Heyman, 2013).

The Medical Model

The medical model of addictions explains addiction as a fatal, progressive disease. According to this model, the addict possesses a body chemistry or predisposition that promotes addiction. This model describes addiction as a disease that requires medical attention (Brooks & McHenry, 2015). The medical model is widely endorsed, and a medical explanation for addiction has become increasingly credible and mainstream. In fact, it has been argued that the neurobiological changes that occur for the addict prove that addiction cannot be characterized as a choice for these individuals (Leyton, 2013). This is perhaps the most widely expanding body of research currently available pertaining to the science of addictive disorders. Specifically, the ever-evolving understanding of what happens in the brain of the addict is adding to our understanding of addiction as a medical issue.

For example, addictive disorders have been conceptualized as a cycle of decreased functioning of brain reward systems (Koob & Le Moal, 2008). The neurobiological changes in the brain circuitry of an addict create a response whereby the individual either (a) is unable to stimulate a sense of reward from continued use of the same amount of a substance or engagement in the same behavior or (b) fails to experience the anti-reward responses typical of most individuals (e.g., fear of being arrested). It is hypothesized that the rewarding effects of addictive substances explain why humans use them and laboratory animals self-administer them (Volkow, Wang, Fowler, & Tomasi, 2012). Although the neurobiological processes that underlie vulnerability to addiction are still poorly understood, imaging studies provide evidence that variations in several neurotransmitters and brain circuitry, including circuits involved in reward and motivation, contribute to an explanation of addiction vulnerability (Ersche et al., 2012).

The Psychodynamic Model

Psychoanalysts explain addiction in much the same way as they describe other psychological disorders. From a psychoanalytic perspective, addiction is viewed as a symptom of underlying neurosis. The psychoanalytic view presumes that the addictive behavior has its roots in early experiences and relationships and that the behavior itself is a means of expressing unconscious, unresolved conflict (Brooks & McHenry, 2015).

Although most current-day practitioners will not treat addiction using a purely psychodynamic model, a focus on environmental factors, including those from early childhood, usually contributes to the overall treatment plan. In fact, at several well-known treatment facilities throughout the country, a psychodynamic approach is endorsed as a piece of an integrated model of treatment, and even in the medical community, support has been given for the application of a neuropsychoanalytic framework to understanding the complex nature of addictive disorders (Johnson, 2013).

The Biopsychosocial Model

The biopsychosocial model of addiction includes components of all of the aforementioned models (with the exception of the moral models). This model provides a comprehensive framework for exploring the interactions and intricacies of addictive disorders. The biopsychosocial model was first introduced by George Engel (1977) and has since been described and endorsed by other practitioners and researchers (Griffiths, 2005).

The biopsychosocial model of addiction attempts to capture the biological, psychological, and social components of addiction in one explanatory model. It recognizes the complexity of addiction and attempts to explain it as a multidimensional issue that can encompass all of these factors. For example, this model encourages practitioners to assess genetic predisposition, neurochemistry, and the fight-or-flight response from a biological perspective. In addition, psychological attributes such as learning, emotional regulation, stress management, and coping strategies are assessed. Finally, social variables are considered. Level of social support, family background, multicultural considerations, and interpersonal relationships are explored in the context of the substance use disorder. Essentially, in this model, practitioners are able to consider risk factors as well as protective factors in a holistic manner.

Although practitioners continue to debate the optimal explanatory model of addiction, the most robust and inclusive model is likely the biopsychosocial model. This model broadly accounts for the biological component of addiction, which is perhaps the most prominently researched area in terms of etiology at this point in time. In fact, the American Society of Addiction Medicine defines addiction with a heavy emphasis on the biological attributes of the condition. Its definition begins by claiming that addiction is a disease of the brain reward and motivation systems and goes on to discuss the role of genetics and brain circuitry. At the same time, the biopsychosocial model recognizes the psychological and social aspects of addiction and addresses these as well. In this way, the biopsychosocial model provides the broadest and most comprehensive means of conceptualizing a substance use disorder (see Sidebar 5.1).

Sidebar 5.1   Voice From the Field

Watch this short video of Hazelden Betty Ford's Vice President of Public Affairs and Community Relations, Bill Moyers, speak at the 51st Nobel Conference "Addiction: Exploring the Science and Experience of an Equal Opportunity Condition" in October 2015 (www.hazeldenbettyford.org/articles/advocacy-featured-videos).

• • •

The History and Development
of Addictions Counseling

Evidence suggests that humans have been using mind-altering substances since the beginning of time (Segal, 2014). However, national
awareness of drug addiction as a potential problem emerged slowly.
In the United States, the first drug identified as potentially harmful was opium. In response to an increase in the recreational use of
opium in San Francisco, the city passed the first law associated with
drugs when it banned opium dens in 1875. This law eventually led
to legislation, passed in 1906, requiring accurate labeling of patent
medicines containing opium. Subsequently, in 1914, the Harrison
Narcotic Act was passed, prohibiting the sale of large doses of opiates
or cocaine except by licensed physicians. Following this, the 18th
Amendment to the U.S. Constitution prohibiting the use of alcohol
was passed in 1919, remaining in effect until it was repealed in 1933
(Stevens & Smith, 2009).

After the end of Prohibition in the 1930s, drug education emerged
as a concept for the first time, and schools began to incorporate educational programs designed to intervene in adolescents' use of drugs
and alcohol. However, despite these efforts, drinking and drug use
increased. In the 1950s, the use of marijuana, amphetamines, and
tranquilizers increased dramatically (Brown, 1981).

The 1960s was a time of tremendous social upheaval, and a perception of increased use of drugs and alcohol was perpetuated. However,
despite this perception, a 1969 Gallup poll revealed that although
48% of American adults felt that drug use was a serious problem in
their communities, only 4% had tried marijuana. It was in the 1970s
that the use of marijuana increased dramatically. By 1973, 12% of
American adults reported using marijuana, and by 1977, this number
had doubled (Robison, 2002a).

By 1985, one third of American adults reported using marijuana,
and the use of cocaine was on the rise. It was at this time that President
Ronald Reagan signed the Anti-Drug Abuse Act of 1986, declaring the
nation's war on drugs, and First Lady Nancy Reagan began the Just
Say No campaign (Robison, 2002b). The 1986 bill imposed mandatory
minimum sentences for the possession of controlled substances in an
effort to deter the sale and use of newly introduced synthetic drugs,
including crack cocaine. As funding for this initiative became available,
programs began to emerge. Perhaps the most widely publicized and
utilized of these was the Drug Abuse Resistance Education (DARE)
program, introduced in schools across the country.

The 1990s was marked by the first reported decrease in drug use
since the 1960s. Although 34% of American adults still reported having used marijuana, a 1999 Gallup youth survey showed a decrease
in adolescents' trial use of all controlled substances. However, at the

same time, club drugs and methamphetamines began to emerge. Finally, in the later 1990s, an increase in the use of heroin was seen, as opiate-based prescription drugs hit the market for the treatment of pain (Robison, 2002b).

The United Nations Office on Drugs and Crime released a report in 2008 outlining the trends in drug use between the years 2000 and 2008. During that period, the United States saw a marked increase in the use of illicit drugs from 11% of the adult population in 2000 to 15% in 2008. Specifically, there was a moderate increase in the use of ecstasy and other synthetic drugs and a significant increase in the use of marijuana and hashish and in the use of pain relievers (United Nations Office on Drugs and Crime, 2008).

Since 2008, the use of heroin has increased, and the face of the heroin user has changed. Whereas the typical heroin addict in the 1960s was a young male with a mean age of 16.5, the heroin addict of today tends to be older, with a mean age of 22.9, and not necessarily male. In addition, heroin use has moved from predominantly urban areas to the suburbs. Finally, research suggests that the road to heroin use was historically initiated by the use of other increasingly impactful substances. However, 75% of current heroin users report that their use of heroin was initiated by the use of prescription pain medications (Cicero, Ellis, Surratt, & Kurtz, 2014). This trend has been highlighted in current news stories across the country, as the use of heroin continues to rise and spread to communities where it was rarely seen in past decades (Svrluga, 2014).

The Impact of Addiction on Significant Others

Addiction has been conceptualized as a family disease (Belles, Budde, Moesgen, & Klein, 2011). That is, the existence of an addiction in a family not only affects the addict but generally has an impact on the family in its entirety. Numerous consequences are linked to living with an individual with an addictive disorder. They generally fall into three categories: potential psychological effects, relational difficulties, and behavioral consequences.

Psychological Consequences of Living With an Addict

The potential psychological consequences of living with an addict include significant psychiatric disorders (Devine, 2013). For example, the link between parental addiction and depression has been consistently shown to be significant (Park & Schepp, 2014). In addition, individuals who live with an addict have been shown to be at risk for anxiety, borderline personality disorder, and covert narcissism (McDonald, 2013).

Family members of addicts also struggle with several predictable issues that, although not constituting diagnosable psychiatric disorders, nevertheless affect their level of overall psychological well-being. For example, this population of clients is vulnerable to feelings of learned helplessness, an internalized belief that they cannot change or affect what happens to them in their lives (Teodorescu & Erev, 2014). Dissociation, distancing, and disconnecting in the face of highly emotionally charged experiences (Blum, 2013) have also been shown to be higher among family members of addicts. Hypervigilance was also shown to be more common among individuals who have lived with an addict (Hussong et al., 2008). Finally, this population of clients has been shown to exhibit low levels of self-esteem (Park & Schepp, 2014).

Relational Consequences of Living With an Addict

In addition to possible psychological effects, individuals who live with an addicted family member are at an increased risk for experiencing a variety of consequences that affect relationships. Most profound is that family members of addicts have been shown to experience difficulty creating healthy bonds and may experience a lifelong inability to engage in relationships that are healthy and growth promoting (Kelley et al., 2010). Another issue typical of individuals who have lived with an addict is the inability to understand and create healthy boundaries in relationships (Kelly, 2016). Boundaries are considered essential to healthy relationships, as they serve the important function of helping to preserve the independence of both individuals and subsystems while maintaining interdependence with others (Marrett, Sprenkle, & Lewis, 1992). In addition, individuals who live with addicts are prone to low levels of healthy assertiveness (Mares, van der Vorst, Engels, & Lichtwarck-Aschoff, 2011). Finally, individuals who have lived with addicts have great difficulty creating and maintaining an authentic sense of self (Kelly, 2016). Essentially, the development of a stable and healthy self-image can be thwarted in a number of ways when development occurs in an environment in which the substance abuse of another individual has become a central and organizing feature.

Behavioral Consequences of Living With an Addict

Finally, individuals who live with addicts are at risk for a number of behavioral consequences. The ability to self-regulate the intensity of one's emotional response is a skill that is expected throughout adulthood. However, individuals who live with an addicted family member are at high risk for issues associated with a limited ability to self-regulate emotionally. In fact, young children of alcoholics display higher rates of externalizing behavior problems, and children of alcoholics in general have been shown to exhibit higher levels of acting-out behavior than children of nonalcoholics (Eiden, Edwards, & Leonard, 2007).

Another behavioral consequence related to substance use disorders is an increased likelihood of legal issues. According to DrugRehab. us (n.d.), a comprehensive resource for information on addictions, some legal issues commonly associated with addiction include driving under the influence, domestic violence, prescription fraud, theft, and prostitution. Consequences related to legal issues can range from a slap on the wrist to jail time, and often these consequences follow individuals throughout their lives, interfering with a variety of life activities (e.g., access to employment).

In addition, because of the unpredictable nature of addiction, the potential for child abuse and neglect is increased in families with a member struggling with a substance use disorder (Dandona, 2016). The same is true of sexual abuse (Edwards et al., 2017; Ulibarri, Ulloa, & Salazar, 2015).

Perhaps the most obvious potential consequence for those living with an addict is having an increased risk for developing an addictive disorder themselves. In fact, the prevalence of substance abuse is consistently higher among children of alcoholics than among children of nonalcoholics (Devine, 2013; Park & Schepp, 2014). In addition, parental substance abuse is one of the most frequently cited predictors for the development of a substance use disorder (Wilens, Yule, Martelon, Zulauf, & Faraone, 2014).

To conceptualize addiction as a family disease, consider the case of Naj, which highlights the impact that addiction has on an addict's significant others. Naj is a 38-year-old Indian male who has come for counseling for the first time in his life. Naj has been in the United States for 30 years and feels that he has grown accustomed to life here. He reports feeling generally happy but feels tremendous anxiety regarding relationships. He says that he is currently in a relationship that he is very hopeful about but fears that he is likely to "screw things up." Naj expresses this concern on the basis of a rocky relationship history.

As counseling continues, Naj begins to describe traumatic childhood experiences. He is the oldest of three children: He has a younger brother and a younger sister. Naj always felt pressure to subscribe to his parents' expectations, including those related to his cultural background. Naj agreed to enter into an arranged marriage against his instincts, and the marriage ended after less than 1 year. Although Naj has internalized this experience as a failing on his part, he has begun to question these beliefs. As Naj begins to discuss his childhood, he describes his early life as "scary" and wonders what impact these early experiences may have on his struggles with relationships.

As counseling continues, Naj begins to share more of the details of his childhood. He reports that his mother stayed at home, raising the children and maintaining the family home. His memories of his mother are of a timid, depressed woman who was very tired and overwhelmed much of the time. Naj's father worked sporadically, primarily in the field of construction. He describes his father as unpredictable and abusive. He is not sure whether he was an alcoholic, as this was not a term he knew or understood. However, he recalls that his father "drank a lot," stayed out a lot, and often stayed in bed well into the day. Naj says that when his father was awake and with the family, the atmosphere was tense; everyone was walking on eggshells. His father could be explosive, and predicting these episodes was impossible.

Naj's earliest memories include his mother frantically working to make sure that everything at home was "perfect." He recalls that in the event that she "failed" in this task, she was hit and verbally assaulted by his father. In addition, he reports several instances of being punished and "spanked" for such things as spilling a drink or failing to pick up a toy he had been playing with. Naj recalls school as a safe haven. However, he was extremely timid and always afraid that he would make a mistake that would be reported to his father.

Contextual Dimensions

In working with addicts, you will want to maintain an awareness of a variety of contextual factors and dimensions. Among these are the settings in which addictions counseling can occur and the role of the counselor in these settings, the prevalence of co-occurring psychological disorders associated with addiction, the regulatory processes that affect treatment, the professional organizations relevant to the practice of addictions counseling, and the importance of culturally relevant treatment.

Settings and Role

Although treatment centers exist that serve the needs of addicts exclusively, issues of substance abuse and addiction will be seen in virtually all mental health services settings. If you wind up working at a generic mental health counseling center, a school, a hospital, or a college counseling center, you will inevitably work with the issue of addiction. It is therefore essential that you possess a working knowledge of addiction. In addition, access to referral settings targeting the needs of addicted clients exclusively is critical. These can include residential treatment centers as well as outpatient programs.

Addictions counseling has traditionally occurred in programs specifically designed to meet the needs of this client population. Residential treatment is often recommended for addicts with a longstanding addictive disorder or for clients who have been unable to maintain sobriety after treatment at a lower level of care (National Institute on Drug Abuse [NIDA], 2016). However, issues of third-party payment and other practice and management considerations have made accessing residential treatment difficult for many clients. In these cases, clients are often referred to one of several outpatient options.

Residential Treatment

Residential treatment generally offers onsite 24-hour treatment and care for approximately 1 month to clients struggling with addiction. Most residential treatment centers include a detoxification (detox) component at the beginning of the treatment process. In the case that a client needs to detoxify from a substance, medical treatment is offered while that individual goes through this process. The detox portion of the treatment process generally lasts for 3 to 5 days. Once a client has completed the detox portion of the treatment program, he or she will begin to participate in the treatment portion of the residential program. Treatment varies but generally includes a significant amount of group work along with individual counseling. Many treatment centers simultaneously address co-occurring disorders that may exist for a large number of clients. The issue of co-occurring disorders is addressed more specifically later in this chapter.

Outpatient Treatment Programs

It is not uncommon for insurance companies to refuse to pay for residential treatment and instead insist that clients attempt outpatient treatment prior to the authorization of inpatient options. The most common outpatient treatment options available to clients struggling with addiction are intensive outpatient programs and partial hospitalization programs. Intensive outpatient programs are generally offered by large, comprehensive treatment centers that include a residential treatment option. Intensive outpatient treatment usually combines group and individual counseling to offer approximately 10 to 12 hours of services to clients per week.

Partial hospitalization programs offer a more intensive option than intensive outpatient programs. According to the Association for Ambulatory Behavioral Healthcare (n.d.), a *partial hospitalization program* is "a time-limited, ambulatory, active treatment program that offers therapeutically intensive, coordinated, and structured clinical services within a stable therapeutic milieu" ("1. What Is a Partial Hospitalization Program?"). Partial hospitalization programs typically offer services a minimum of 5 days per week and often include treatment on weekends.

In all of these settings, your role as a professional counselor is likely to include providing both group and individual counseling to clients. In addition, you may be involved in coordinating care, involving working with physicians, families, and other service providers. This may include coordinating meetings and establishing aftercare plans, which assist clients in transitioning to settings with progressively lower levels of care.

Co-Occurring Disorders

If you work with addicts, the issue of co-occurring disorders is likely to emerge (Mericle, Ta Park, Holder, & Arria, 2012). Specifically, this refers to the existence of other mental health issues or disorders that operate in conjunction with a client's addiction. The Substance Abuse and Mental Health Services Administration (SAMHSA; 2016a) estimates that 39.1% of addicts have a co-occurring disorder. In fact, many treatment providers consider the initial use of substances an attempt to self-medicate on the part of the addict, as clients will often disclose that their earliest use of mind-altering substances brought tremendous relief from long-term suffering.

Any disorder can potentially co-occur with addiction. The diagnosis and treatment of co-occurring disorders has been shown to be an integral part of treatment for addicts. In fact, the existence of depressive or anxiety symptoms among addicts has been linked to relapse, and it has been suggested that ongoing monitoring of symptomatology is a foundational component of follow-up care for addicts (Gil-Rivas, Prause, & Grelia, 2014).

Regulatory Processes and Substance Abuse Policies

A number of regulatory processes and policies have a direct impact on the treatment of addiction. As described in "The History and Development of Addictions Counseling," laws governing the sale and possession of controlled substances have evolved over time. Likewise, policies and regulations that affect the delivery of services to clients struggling with addiction continue to evolve. For example, the Affordable Care Act of 2010 (U.S. Department of Health and Human Services, n.d.) has made health insurance available to larger numbers of families and individuals. Although these benefits have not dramatically increased access to care for mental health disorders, having health insurance allows individuals to receive medical care that is affordable and offers a treatment avenue not historically available to all addicts. However, the future of access to health care is unknown, as it depends on the political climate. This fact highlights the importance of advocacy work among professional counselors. This includes engaging in activism, lobbying, and using our professional organizations as vehicles for the kinds of systemic change that will increase access to treatment. Currently, details pertaining to national-level access to care for mental health issues remain unclear, which makes this an important time in the history of our profession (Chen, 2017).

A fairly recent example of legal action affecting access to mental health care is the Mental Health Parity and Addiction Equity Act of 2008 (U.S. Department of Labor, Employee Benefits Security Administration, 2010). This act requires insurance companies to provide coverage for mental health disorders that is comparable to that provided for other medical conditions. Although this act affords mental health practitioners a vehicle for increasing the accessibility of mental health and substance abuse treatment, it has not been widely enacted. However, this legal provision provides a vehicle for advocacy as well as leverage that can be garnered now in the efforts to create legal mechanisms for ensuring access to treatment for substance use disorders. Although there are many reasons why the Mental Health Parity and Addiction Equity Act has not been fully enforced, professionals continue to discuss it as a primary issue in the field of addictions counseling. You might want to consider the questions in Sidebar 5.2.

Professional Organizations Relevant to the Practice of Addictions Counseling

A number of professional organizations and agencies are relevant to the practice of addictions counseling. Among them, SAMHSA represents the arm of the U.S. Department of Health and Human Services designated to reduce the impact of substance abuse and mental illness across the country. NIDA augments this work by advancing science on the causes and consequences of addiction and disseminating that knowledge. In addition to these government-affiliated agencies, numerous professional organizations exist to support professionals with expertise in the area of addictions counseling. The American Counseling Association has a division for professional counselors with this specific interest. The International Association of Addictions and Offender Counselors, founded in 1972, provides leadership in the advancement of the addictions counseling field.

Culturally Relevant Practices

We know that addiction crosses all known boundaries. Although this is true and important to recognize, it is equally important to consider the differences you will encounter in working with clients from diverse backgrounds. Counselors are trained to competently counsel individuals from a multicultural perspective, and this extends to working with addicts. Issues related to a client's cultural background must be integrated into conceptualization and treatment for any client strug-

---

Sidebar 5.2   Thought Questions

To what might you attribute the current lack of enactment of the Mental Health Parity and Addiction Equity Act of 2008, which requires insurance companies to provide coverage for mental health disorders that is comparable to that provided for medical conditions?

Is there a role for professional counselors in advocating for enforcement of this act? If so, what actions can we take?

• • •

gling with an addictive disorder. In fact, the counseling profession has made an explicit commitment to competently working with all clients regardless of socioeconomic status, ethnicity, race, or sexual orientation. This commitment has been supported through the development and endorsement of a set of multicultural competencies that guide our work with clients from all backgrounds (Ratts, Singh, Nassar-McMillan, Butler, & McCullough, 2016).

Socioeconomic Diversity

We are all aware of the significant range in socioeconomic circumstances in the United States, and this will most likely be reflected the population of clients we serve. In the case of work in the area of addictions, this vast socioeconomic spread affects treatment significantly. Right now, insurance companies are reluctant to pay for residential treatment. The trend is to provide hospitalization for a short period of time and refer clients for outpatient care. This may be in the form of a structured outpatient treatment program or a referral for individual counseling services. Often this is ineffective, and in the event that clients seem to require an intensive residential treatment setting, they may be left to their own financial devices. The premier residential treatment centers cost in excess of $30,000 for a 1-month stay (the typical amount of time suggested). This has created a serious dilemma around access to treatment that has yet to be resolved.

Race and Ethnicity

One of the significant issues related to race and ethnicity that has a profound impact on addictions treatment is stress. Specifically, differences exist in sources of stress and sources of resiliency among particular groups of clients. For example, compared with Caucasian individuals, African Americans experience a greater number of negative stressful events. In addition, the two groups are likely to differ in how they experience different types of stressors and in the types of coping strategies they use in response to these stressors (Gayman, Cislo, Goidel, & Ueno, 2014; Hoggard, Byrd, & Sellers, 2012). An additional and important source of stress for all non-Caucasian clients is racism, which has been shown to increase feelings of anger, hostility, alienation, and helplessness, all of which have been associated with negative health outcomes (Anderson, 2013), including addiction.

African American Clients. It has been suggested that core cultural values of African American clients be considered and assessed at the start of treatment for an addictive disorder. These include such things as communalism, religion/spirituality, expressiveness, respect for verbal communication skills, connection to ancestors and history, commitment to family, and intuition and experience versus empiricism (Resnicow, Soler, Braithwaite, Selassie, & Smith, 1999). Given these cultural attributes, several treatment implications arise. For example, the use of print in traditional substance abuse treatment (i.e., Alcoholics Anonymous [AA]) is highly regarded and does not generally include historical references or information that might be specific to particular cultural groups. However, the use of storytelling and a spiritual focus are also highly valued in the 12-step model and may provide a culturally relevant means of treatment.

Latina/o Clients. In several community-based studies investigating alcohol use among people of various ethnicities, Latinos were shown to be more likely to experience greater physical and social consequences compared with their male Caucasian peers (Rojas, Hallford, Brand, & Tivis, 2012). Therefore, identifying treatment modalities and techniques that are effective with the Latina/o population is essential. These might include attending to core cultural values that have been elaborated, such as *familismo* (the importance of family), *respeto* (respect for elders), *dignidad* (the value of self-worth), *caridad* (the value of rituals and ceremonies), fatalism, and *simpatía* (the importance of positive social interactions). It has been suggested that the novella format (i.e., the use of stories) be considered when exploring these themes, as the storytelling aspect of treatment may effect the greatest change for Latina/o clients (Lalonde, Rabinowitz, Shefsky, & Washienko, 1997).

Asian/Pacific Islander Clients. National surveys suggest that Asian Americans have a lower prevalence of alcohol use compared to other racial groups (SAMHSA, 2016b). However, more current research suggests that the incidence of reported problems related to alcohol and drug use among Asian Americans may not be reflective of the actual state of alcohol problems among this population (Cheng, Lee, & Iwamoto, 2012). In addition, Asian Americans report higher levels of depression compared with other ethnic groups, and, as I have discussed, depression and substance use and abuse are linked.

In terms of treatment, compelling evidence suggests that Asian American heavy drinkers experience a higher rate of negative consequences compared to heavy drinkers of other ethnicities (Park, Shibusawa, Yoon, & Son, 2010). Despite this, Asian Americans and Pacific Islanders are not as likely as other groups to access treatment. Cognitive, affective, value orientation, and physical barriers have been identified as factors contributing to the underutilization of mental health services by Asian Americans, despite the consequences these individuals may face as a result of their drug or alcohol use (Goebert & Nishimura, 2011).

Clients From Middle Eastern Cultures. The concept of *umma* in the Islam tradition discourages Arab individuals from seeking treatment for emotional or mental health issues (Dwairy, 2006). Although there is a primary focus and reliance on the family for support and direction in the Arab culture, even family therapy may not be welcomed, as this may be considered antithetical to cultural norms (McGoldrick, Giordano, & Garcia-Preto, 2005). The shame associated with participating in a behavior that is deemed theologically and culturally sinful may also keep Arab individuals, including Arab Americans, from seeking treatment. It is therefore assumed among treatment providers that substance use and abuse is underreported among this particular group. However, it has been suggested that if a Muslim Arab client were to reach out for assistance, the 12-step model might be well suited to his or her treatment needs. The reliance on a higher power may appeal to individuals who are already seeking spiritual guidance on a regular basis. In addition, the solidarity that exists in programs such as AA is consistent with Islamic law, as the construct of the *umma* refers directly to a collective consciousness around a common struggle (Abdel-Mawgoud, Fateem, & Al-Sharif, 1995).

Native American Clients. It is widely accepted that the Native American population has been disproportionately impacted by substance use and abuse (Legha, Raleigh-Cohn, Fickenscher, & Novins, 2014). Although the reasons for this are not completely understood, cultural conditions and differences are thought to have a tremendous impact on this phenomenon. Traditional treatment efforts have not been effective for this population of clients. In response to this, more tribe-centric treatment has been suggested. However, such barriers as funding and access to treatment have been cited as obstacles that have not yet been overcome (Eitle & Eitle, 2014).

Sexual Orientation

In every study comparing addiction between lesbian, gay, transgender, and queer adolescents and heterosexual adolescents, the former group has been shown to have higher rates of substance use (Cochran & Cauce, 2006). Researchers have offered several explanations for this phenomenon. One is that sexual minority teens may use drugs and alcohol as a tool to rationalize their same-sex feelings and behavior. Alternatively, it has been hypothesized that the additional stress related to being a sexual minority may contribute to elevated rates of addiction (Chaney & Brubaker, 2012).

Practice Dimensions

In addition to understanding and working with the contextual dimensions of counseling addicts, you will be responsible for managing practice dimensions. These include the assessment process and treatment for the addict.

Assessing Addiction and Addictive Disorders

The American Society of Addiction Medicine suggests that effective screening for addiction has the potential to forestall serious issues and provide an appropriate basis for treatment. NIDA (2014) supported this assertion and provided a listing of assessment tools that can be used to provide information pertinent to a sound assessment. In addition, the *Diagnostic and Statistical Manual of Mental Disorders, Fifth Edition* (*DSM–5;* American Psychiatric Association, 2013), provides criteria for a diagnosis of substance use disorder. According to the *DSM–5,* substance use disorders are patterns of symptoms resulting from the use of a substance that an individual continues to take despite the experience of negative consequences resulting directly from the substance use. The *DSM–5* allows clinicians (a) to specify how severe a substance use disorder is, depending on how many symptoms are identified; and (b) to identify clients as being in early remission, in sustained remission, on maintenance therapy, or in a controlled environment.

The only process addiction explicitly detailed in the *DSM–5* is gambling addiction. However, Internet gaming disorder is included in Section II of the *DSM–5.* Ultimately, further research is needed to explicitly list Internet gaming disorder, as well as other process disorders, as diagnosable according to the *DSM–5* (American Psychiatric Association, 2013).

Treating Addiction and Addictive Disorders

Cognitive Behavior Therapy

According to NIDA (2012), cognitive behavior therapy is endorsed as an evidence-based treatment option for working with individuals struggling with addiction. Cognitive behavior therapy is generally adapted for use with substance-abusing individuals as a means of assisting clients in the development of coping strategies. Specifically, clients are taught (a) to identify triggers and situations likely to induce cravings and (b) to develop strategies that can be used to manage these situations. Evidence suggests that the use of such strategies results in long-term benefits, as the skills that clients learn through cognitive behavior therapy remain beyond the completion of the therapy (Carroll et al., 2005; DeVito, Babuscio, Nich, Ball, & Carroll, 2014).

Group Counseling

Group counseling has been endorsed as a primary modality for working with addicts (Brooks & McHenry, 2015). In fact, it is used more frequently and with higher levels of success than individual counseling with this population of clients (MacGowan, 2006). This is the case in treatment programs that specifically target addicts as well as in the widely endorsed 12-step programs.

Motivational Interviewing (MI)

In addition to theoretical frameworks, several treatment models have been applied in working with addicts. Perhaps the most widely endorsed of these is MI. Originally described by Miller (1983), MI began as a means of working with problem drinkers. Subsequently, Miller and Rollnick (2013) detailed the development of a comprehensive treatment technique. MI is a technique centered on helping individuals identify and increase their level of motivation to change. The counseling involves a process whereby the counselor engages in a person-centered conversation with the client that is intended to strengthen that client's motivation and commitment to change.

MI is a collaborative process in which the counselor and the client participate as equal partners in assisting the client to change a behavior. A basic premise underlying MI is that change is difficult and requires a readiness that cannot be assumed. Clients may want changes to occur in their lives but may be at very different points regarding their genuine commitment to participate in the steps necessary to actualize the desired changes. Therefore, an initial focus in MI is to evaluate the client's readiness to change. The underlying assumption of this process is that individuals who are not ready will not change.

The Stages of Change. MI has adopted Prochaska, DiClemente, and Norcross's (2003) stages of change model as a means of assessing a client's readiness for change. This model describes five levels of readiness for change and assists the counselor and the client in understanding where the counseling process should begin. The identified stages are precontemplation, contemplation, determination, action, and maintenance. Accurately assessing where a client is along the change continuum is critical to the success of counseling.

An assumption associated with the change process is that individuals are virtually always ambivalent about change. Practitioners using MI view a lack of motivation as unresolved ambivalence. Intertwined with the notion of ambivalence is the construct of motivation. MI practitioners see motivation as a necessary element of change. It is assumed that talking through ambivalence and identifying its source leads to internalization of the motivation to change.

Strategies and Techniques. In addition to providing a framework for assessing a client's readiness for change, MI offers a number of strategies and techniques used to facilitate the working through of ambivalence and movement toward increased motivation (Sobell & Sobell, 2008). Many of these strategies are quite familiar to professional counselors, whereas other might be less well known. They include asking permission, change talk, exploring importance and confidence, open-ended questions, reflective listening, normalizing, decisional balancing, the Columbo approach, and statements supporting self-efficacy.

12-Step Programs of Recovery

In addition to treatment strategies that exist for clinicians, several self-help groups have become popular as supplemental supports for individuals struggling with an addictive disorder. Probably the most popular of these is AA (AA, n.d.-b). AA is a group based on the widely embraced 12-step recovery model for drug abusers and alcoholics.

The very early roots of AA can be traced to the Oxford Group, a religious group popular in the 19th century in which such actions as admitting wrongs, making amends, and using prayer and meditation were endorsed practices. In the early 1930s, Carl Jung referred an alcoholic he described as medically hopeless to the Oxford Group, as he felt that the only conceivable solution for his patient would be rooted in a spiritual experience. This man shared his experience with a friend of Bill W., who eventually shared the Oxford Group exercises with Bill W., who is commonly referred to as the founder of the current 12-step model of recovery (AA, n.d.-a). Originally, AA was structured to provide support for alcoholics who wanted to maintain sobriety. Over time, however, the 12-step model of recovery expanded to address the needs of those struggling with a variety of addictions (e.g., Narcotics Anonymous, Gamblers Anonymous, Overeaters Anonymous).

According to AA (n.d.-c),

> Alcoholics Anonymous is an international fellowship of men and women who have had a drinking problem. It is nonprofessional, self-supporting, multiracial, apolitical, and available almost everywhere. There are no age or education requirements. Membership is open to anyone who wants to do something about his or her drinking problem.

The program utilizes a text, *Alcoholics Anonymous,* originally published in 1939, to outline its principles and recovery steps. The model is based on a set of 12 steps that provide principles that, if practiced, are thought to interfere with an alcoholic's obsession to drink. In addition, AA has 12 traditions meant to protect the integrity of the program and its mission.

The 12-step model provides a structured framework for working on issues often associated with addiction. Individuals new to the program will often seek a sponsor—another addict who can help them work through the steps. Newcomers are welcome and are encouraged to attend meetings on a regular basis where they can share their experiences with other addicts. Working on the premise that being an addict promotes feelings, thoughts, and behaviors that limit an individual's functioning, AA seeks to provide a supportive environment and to promote healthier relationships and an increased sense of well-being (AA, n.d.-b).

Special Considerations in Addictions Counseling

The Increased Use of Opioids

The impact of the increased use and abuse of opioid-based substances on the field of addictions counseling cannot be overstated. The popular media has informed the public of the increase in addiction to opioid drugs and commonly refers to this issue as an *epidemic.* The attention given to this crisis has infiltrated mainstream consciousness in ways that discussion of drug use and abuse have not. This rise in awareness was perhaps best illustrated throughout the 2016 U.S. presidential election, with candidates from across the country vowing to make this issue a priority.

The current opioid crisis has been attributed to the huge increase in the distribution of prescriptions for such pain medications as OxyContin, Percocet, and Vicodin. It is estimated that more than 259 million opioid prescriptions were written in 2012, enough for every adult in the United States to have one bottle (National Safety Council, 2016). Although pharmaceutical companies have historically reported that these medications are not addictive, the rate of addiction to prescription pain medications has skyrocketed. This has led to an increase in the number of heroin addicts in general and among populations of individuals who have not historically been seen as at risk for heroin addiction. In 2013, 4 out of 5 heroin users reported that their addiction began with the misuse of prescription pain medication (Jones, 2013). Practitioners attribute this phenomenon to the fact that prescription pain medications are expensive, and pharmaceutical companies have altered the form of these medications so that they cannot be crushed into a powdered form that can be snorted. Thus, individuals addicted to opioids are gravitating to heroin, which is far less expensive and more readily available.

Although available statistics related to opioid addiction are fluid and change quickly, some of the current facts include the following:

- The number of overdose deaths involving opioids (including prescription opioids and heroin) has quadrupled since 1999 (Centers for Disease Control and Prevention, 2016).
- Of the 20.5 million Americans age 12 or older who had a substance use disorder in 2015, 2 million had a disorder involving prescription pain relievers, and 591,000 had a disorder involving heroin.
- Drug overdose is the leading cause of accidental death in the United States, with 52,404 lethal drug overdoses in 2015. Opioid addiction is driving this epidemic, with 20,101 overdose deaths related to prescription pain relievers and 12,990 overdose deaths related to heroin in 2015.
- A total of 91 Americans die every day from an opioid overdose (Centers for Disease Control and Prevention, 2016).
- Among respondents to a 2014 survey of people in treatment for opioid addiction, 94% reported choosing heroin as their drug of choice because prescription opioids were more expensive and more difficult to obtain (American Society of Addiction Medicine, 2016).

Access to Treatment

Access to treatment is a critical issue in the field of addictions counseling. Several barriers to treatment are cited in the literature, including lack

127

of funding, delays in getting clients into treatment, and no continuum of care (Pullen & Oser, 2014). This complex, multilayered issue inhibits progress in the field of addictions counseling (see Sidebar 5.3).

Strides in Neuroscience

Another special consideration in the field of addictions counseling is the increase in knowledge regarding the neuroscience of addiction. This relatively new science, which involves the use of brain scans to study the neurobiological component of the addiction process, is expanding our knowledge of addiction at a rapid pace. In an article published in the *New England Journal of Medicine*, Volkow, Koob, and McLellan (2016) provided a comprehensive analysis of the neurobiological advances in the field of addictions counseling. Through the lens of understanding addiction as a brain disease, this article breaks down the disease into three primary stages: binge and intoxication, withdrawal and negative affect, and preoccupation and anticipation. Among the findings these authors reported are the following:

- In all known addiction, the reward regions of the brain are activated, releasing dopamine.
- If the behavior associated with this release of dopamine is repeated, the stimuli that precede the behavior will elicit the same dopamine dump. In other words, activities that generally precede the addictive behavior, people associated with the addictive behavior, and so on will trigger cravings.
- Over time, ordinary, healthful rewards lose their power.
- For an addict, the reward and motivational systems become reoriented.

Sidebar 5.3   Voice From the Field

New Hampshire has one of the most significant opioid addiction problems in the United States. Another Way, a residential substance treatment program in Nashua, is always filled to capacity, with a typical 4-month waiting list. Although the program is comprehensive and utilizes medical and clinical techniques and strategies at the forefront of addictions counseling, it is unable to keep up with the need. Often, the work at such facilities is thwarted by the systems designed to help people access treatment. Primary among these are insurance companies. A substantial portion of resources dedicated to treatment goes toward working with insurance companies to provide clients with optimal time in inpatient treatment.

• • •

- Simply discontinuing the addictive behavior cannot reverse this reorientation in the brain's reward and motivational systems.

This line of inquiry offers hope for more accurately pinpointing the precise impact of addiction on the brain. As the science of addiction continues to advance, opportunities for treatment are likely to follow. As a professional counselor, you will want to continue to explore the area of neuroscience and its impact on our understanding of addiction.

The Increased Use of Synthetic Drugs

One of the most baffling current issues in the area of addictions counseling is the increased use of synthetic drugs. This issue affects both the law enforcement side and the treatment side of substance use and abuse. Manufacturers continue to develop new mind-altering substances at an alarming rate. Many of these substances are not illegal—at least until they are placed on the list of controlled substances. The issue for law enforcement is that by the time this occurs, several new legal synthetic drugs are likely to have hit the streets. These drugs are not known. Often, their chemical makeup is unknown, as is information pertaining to their addictive qualities. This has made treating individuals who use synthetic drugs an ongoing challenge for providers.

Chapter Summary

An understanding of addictions counseling is essential to your development as a professional counselor. Regardless of the setting in which you work, addiction is likely to be an issue that you will see. A basic understanding of the etiological models typically used to explain addiction, along with a sense of the historical context of this disorder, will allow you to conceptualize cases involving addiction in a manner that can facilitate treatment. In addition, it is essential that you know what services exist in your community and how to access them for addicted clients. With a firm understanding of the cultural implications of addiction and the laws and regulations related to addiction, you will be better prepared to assist clients in accessing the best treatment possible. Finally, a basic understanding of addiction assessment and treatment options will enable you to treat addicts effectively. Ultimately, clients struggling with addiction require specific treatment to live a life free of this disease, and professional counselors will often be in a position to facilitate that process.

Learning Activities

1. Attend a 12-step meeting and write a reflection paper on your experience. Share your reflections with a friend.

2. Interview an individual recovering from an addiction. For this activity, the following questions can be used as a guide:
   a. How did addiction affect your life?
   b. How did you achieve sobriety? What kinds of treatment did you access?
   c. How do you maintain your sobriety?
   d. What do you think is the most important thing a counselor-in-training should learn or understand about this disease?
3. Abstain from using something or doing something that you feel you may be addicted to (e.g., drinking coffee, eating chocolate, exercising) and keep a journal of you experience. Share your experience with a friend.
4. Watch *Rachel Getting Married* and analyze the characters in the movie who are directly affected by addiction in the family.

Review Questions

1. List three etiological models of addiction. Which model(s) make the most sense to you, and why?
2. What are the current trends in the field of addictions counseling?
3. Describe at least one potential psychological consequence, relational consequence, and behavioral consequence of living with an individual dealing with addiction.
4. What are the primary differences between SAMHSA and NIDA?
5. Describe at least one cultural consideration you might make in working with a Muslim Arab American client struggling with addiction.
6. What are the primary assumptions in using MI?

Further Resources

Print Materials

Brooks, F., & McHenry, B. (2015). *A contemporary approach to substance abuse and addiction counseling: A counselor's guide to application and understanding* (2nd ed.). Alexandria, VA: American Counseling Association.

Gladding, S. T. (2014). *Family therapy: History, theory and practice* (6th ed.). Upper Saddle River, NJ: Pearson.

Websites

National Institute on Drug Abuse
   https://www.drugabuse.gov
Official Blog of Dr. Gabor Maté
   https://drgabormate.com/blog/
Substance Abuse and Mental Health Services Administration
   www.samhsa.gov

References

Abdel-Mawgoud, M., Fateem, L., & Al-Sharif, A. I. (1995). Development of a comprehensive treatment program for chemical dependency at Al Amal Hospital, Dammam. *Journal of Substance Abuse Treatment, 12*(9), 369–376.

Alcoholics Anonymous. (n.d.-a). *Over 80 years of growth.* Retrieved from www.aa.org/pages/en_US/aa-timeline

Alcoholics Anonymous. (n.d.-b). *Welcome to Alcoholics Anonymous.* Retrieved from www.aa.org

Alcoholics Anonymous. (n.d.-c). *What is A.A.?* Retrieved from https://www.aa.org/pages/en_US/what-is-aa

American Psychiatric Association. (2013). *Diagnostic and statistical manual of mental disorders* (5th ed.). Washington, DC: Author.

American Society of Addiction Medicine. (2016). *Opioid addiction 2016 facts and figures.* Retrieved from www.asam.org/docs/default-source/advocacy/opioid-addiction-disease-facts-figures.pdf

Anderson, K. F. (2013). Diagnosing discrimination: Stress from perceived racism and the mental and physical health effects. *Sociological Inquiry, 83*(1), 55–81.

Association for Ambulatory Behavioral Healthcare. (n.d.). *An overview of the partial hospitalization modality.* Retrieved from https://www.aabh.org/partial-hospitalization-progra

Belles, S., Budde, A., Moesgen, D., & Klein, M. (2011). Parental problem drinking predicts implicit alcohol expectancy in adolescents and young adults. *Addictive Behaviors, 36*, 1091–1094.

Blum, H. (2013). Dissociation and its disorders. *Psychoanalytic Inquiry, 33*, 427–438.

Brooks, F., & McHenry, B. (2015). *A contemporary approach to substance abuse and addiction counseling: A counselor's guide to application and understanding* (2nd ed.). Alexandria, VA: American Counseling Association.

Brown, L. M. (1981). Substance abuse and America: Historical perspective on the federal response to a social phenomenon. *Journal of the National Medical Association, 73*, 497–506.

Carroll, K. M., Sholomskas, D., Syracuse, G., Ball, S. A., Nuro, K., & Fenton, L. R. (2005). We don't train in vain: A dissemination trial of three strategies of training clinicians in cognitive-behavioral therapy. *Journal of Consulting and Clinical Psychology, 73*(1), 106–115.

Centers for Disease Control and Prevention. (2016). *Drug overdose deaths in the United States continue to increase in 2015.* Retrieved from https://www.cdc.gov/drugoverdose/epidemic/

Chaney, M. P., & Brubaker, M. D. (2012). Addiction in LGBTQ communities: Influences, treatment, and prevention. *Journal of LGBT Issues in Counseling, 6*(4), 234–236.

Chen, M. (2017). *Trump's Obamacare repeal could lead to a mental-health crisis.* Retrieved from *The Nation* website: https://www.thenation.com/article/trumps-obamacare-repeal-could-lead-to-a-mental-health-crisis/

Cheng, A. W., Lee, C. S., & Iwamoto, D. K. (2012). Heavy drinking, poor mental health, and substance use among Asian Americans in the NLAAS: A gender-based comparison. *Asian-American Journal of Psychology, 3*(3), 160–167.

Cicero, T. J., Ellis, M. S., Surratt, H. L., & Kurtz, S. P. (2014). The changing face of heroin use in the United States: A retrospective analysis of the past 50 years. *JAMA Psychiatry, 71,* 821–826.

Cochran, B. N., & Cauce, A. M. (2006). Characteristics of lesbian, gay, bisexual, and transgender individuals entering substance abuse treatment. *Journal of Substance Abuse Treatment, 30*(2), 135–146.

Dandona, A. (2016). The impact of parental substance abuse on children. In M. Baker, J. Ford, B. Canfield, & T. Grabb (Eds.), *Identifying, treating and preventing childhood trauma in rural communities* (pp. 30–42). Hershey, PA: Information Science Reference Reference/IGI Global.

Devine, B. R. (2013). Students with parents involved in substance use or dependence. In E. Rosen & R. Hill (Eds.), *Supporting and educating traumatized students: A guide for school-based professionals* (pp. 119–128). New York, NY: Oxford University Press.

DeVito, E. E., Babuscio, T. A., Nich, C., Ball, S. A., & Carroll, K. M. (2014). Gender differences in clinical outcomes for cocaine dependence: Randomized clinical trials of behavioral therapy and disulfiram. *Drug and Alcohol Dependence, 145,* 156–167.

DrugRehab.us. (n.d.). *Legal consequences of addiction.* Retrieved from www.drugrehab.us/addiction/legal-problems/

Dwairy, M. A. (2006). *Counseling and psychotherapy with Arabs and Muslims: A culturally sensitive approach.* New York, NY: Teachers College Press.

Edwards, K. M., Murphy, S., Palmer, K. M., Haynes, E. E., Chapo, S., Ekdahl, B. A., & Buel, S. (2017). Co-occurrence of and recovery from substance abuse and lifespan victimization: A qualitative study of female residents in trauma-informed sober living homes. *Journal of Psychoactive Drugs, 49*(1), 74–82.

Eiden, R. D., Edwards, E. P., & Leonard, K. E. (2007). A conceptual model for the development of externalizing behavior problems among kindergarten children of alcoholic families: Role of parenting and children's self-regulation. *Developmental Psychology, 43,* 1187–1201.

Eitle, T. M., & Eitle, D. (2014). Race, coping strategies, and substance use behaviors: A preliminary analysis examining White and American Indian adolescents. *Substance Use and Misuse, 49*(3), 315–325.

Engel, G. L. (1977, April 8). The need for a new medical model: A challenge for biomedicine. *Science, 196,* 129–136.

Ersche, K. D., Jones, P. S., Williams, G. B., Turton, A. J., Robbins, T. W., & Bullmore, E. T. (2012, February 3). Abnormal brain structure implicated in stimulant drug addiction. *Science, 335,* 601–604.

Gayman, M. D., Cislo, A. M., Goidel, A. R., & Ueno, K. (2014). SES and race ethnic differences in the stress buffering effects of coping resources among young adults. *Ethnicity and Health, 19*(2), 198–216.

Gil-Rivas, V., Prause, J., & Grelia, C. E. (2014). Substance use after residential treatment among individuals with co-occurring disorders: The role of anxiety/depressive symptoms and trauma exposure. *Psychology of Addictive Behaviors, 23*(2), 303–314.

Goebert, D., & Nishimura, S. (2011). Comparison of substance abuse treatment utilization and preferences among Native Hawaiians, Asian Americans and Euro Americans. *Journal of Substance Use, 16*(2), 161–170.

Griffiths, M. (2005). A "components" model of addiction within a biopsychosocial framework. *Journal of Substance Use, 10*(4), 191–197.

Heyman, G. M. (2013). Addiction and choice: Theory and new data. *Frontiers in Psychiatry, 4,* Article ID 31.

Hoggard, L. S., Byrd, C. M., & Sellers, R. M. (2012). Comparison of African American college students' coping with racially and nonracial stressful events. *Cultural Diversity and Ethnic Minority Psychology, 18*(4), 329–339.

Hussong, A. M., Bauer, D. J., Huang, W., Chassin, L., Sher, K. J., & Zucker, R. A. (2008). Characterizing the life stressors of children of alcoholic parents. *Journal of Family Psychology, 22,* 819–832.

Johnson, B. (2013). Addiction and will. *Frontiers in Human Neuroscience, 7,* Article ID 545.

Jones, C. M. (2013). Heroin use and heroin use risk behaviors among non-medical users of prescription opioid pain relievers—United States, 2002-2004 and 2008-2010. *Drug and Alcohol Dependence, 132*(1–2), 95–100.

Kelley, M. L., Braitman, A., Henson, J. M., Schroeder, V., Ladage, J., & Gumienny, L. (2010). Relationships among depressive mood symptoms and parent and peer relations in collegiate children of alcoholics. *American Journal of Orthopsychiatry, 80*(2), 204–212.

Kelly, V. A. (2016). *Addiction in the family: What every counselor needs to know.* Alexandria, VA: American Counseling Association.

Koob, G. F., & Le Moal, M. (2008). Addiction and the brain antireward system. *Annual Reviews: Psychology, 59,* 29–53.

Lalonde, B., Rabinowitz, P., Shefsky, M. L., & Washienko, K. (1997). La esperanza del valle: Alcohol prevention novelas for Hispanic youth and their families. *Health Education & Behavior, 24,* 587–602.

Legha, R., Raleigh-Cohn, A., Fickenscher, A., & Novins, D. (2014). Challenges to providing substance abuse treatment services for American Indian and Alaska native communities: Perspectives of staff from 18 treatment centers. *BMC Psychiatry, 14,* 248–266. doi:10.1186/1471-244X-14-181

Leyton, M. (2013). Are addictions diseases or choices? *Journal of Psychiatry and Neuroscience, 38*(4), 219–221.

MacGowan, M. (2006). Measuring and increasing engagement in substance abuse treatment groups: Advancing evidence-based group work. *Journal of Groups in Addiction and Recovery, 1*(2), 53–67.

Mares, S. H. W., van der Vorst, H., Engels, R. C. M. E., & Lichtwarck-Aschoff, A. (2011). Parental alcohol use, alcohol-related problems, and alcohol-specific attitudes, alcohol-specific communication, and adolescent excessive alcohol use and alcohol-related problems: An indirect path model. *Addictive Behaviors, 36*(3), 209–216.

Marrett, K. M., Sprenkle, D. H., & Lewis, R. A. (1992). Family members' perceptions of Family boundaries and their relationship to family problems. *Family Therapy, 19*(3), 233–242.

McDonald, B. K. (2013). *Out of the mirror: A workbook of healing for adult children of covert narcissists.* Retrieved from www.alfredadler.edu/sites/default/files/McDonald%20MP%202013.pdf

McGoldrick, M., Giordano, J., & Garcia-Preto, N. (2005). *Ethnicity and family therapy* (3rd ed.). New York, NY: Guilford Press.

Mericle, A. A., Ta Park, V. M., Holder, P., & Arria, A. M. (2012). Prevalence, patterns, and correlates of co-occurring substance use and mental disorders in the United States: Variations by race/ethnicity. *Comprehensive Psychiatry, 53,* 657–665.

Miller, W. R. (1983). Motivational interviewing with problem drinkers. *Behavioural Psychotherapy, 11*(2), 147–172.

Miller, W. R., & Rollnick, S. (2013). *Motivational interviewing: Helping people change* (3rd ed.). New York, NY: Guilford Press.

National Council on Alcoholism and Drug Dependence. (n.d.). *NCADD: National council on alcoholism and drug dependence.* Retrieved from https://www.ncadd.org

National Institute on Drug Abuse. (2012). *Contingency management interventions/motivational incentives (alcohol, stimulants, opioids, marijuana, nicotine).* Retrieved from www.drugabuse.gov/publications/principles-drug-addiction-treatment-research-based-guide-third-edition/evidence-based-approaches-to-drug-addiction-treatment/behavioral-0

National Institute on Drug Abuse. (2014). *Chart of evidence-based screening tools for adults and adolescents.* Retrieved from https://www.drugabuse.gov/nidamed-medical-health-professionals/tool-resources-your-practice/additional-screening-resources

National Institute on Drug Abuse. (2016). *Treatment approaches for drug addiction.* Retrieved from https://www.drugabuse.gov/Publications/drugfacts/treatment-approaches-drug-addiction

National Safety Council. (2016). *Prescription nation 2016: Addressing America's drug epidemic.* Retrieved from www.nsc.org/RxDrugOverdoseDocuments/Prescription-Nation-2016-American-Drug-Epidemic.pdf

Park, S., & Schepp, K. G. (2014). A systematic review of research on children of alcoholics: Their inherent resilience and vulnerability. *Journal of Child and Family Studies, 24,* 1222–1231. doi:10.1007/s10826-014-9930-7

Park, S., Shibusawa, T., Yoon, S. M., & Son, H. (2010). Characteristics of Chinese and Korean Americans in alcohol treatment for alcohol use disorders: Examining heterogeneity among Asian American subgroups. *Journal of Ethnicity in Substance Abuse, 9*(2), 128–142.

Process Addictions. (n.d.). *Process addictions list.* Retrieved from www.processaddictions.com/process-addictions-list/

Prochaska, J. O., DiClemente, C. C., & Norcross, J. C. (2003). In search of how people change: Applications to addictive behaviors. In P. Salovey & A. J. Rothman (Eds.), *Social psychology of health* (pp. 63–77). New York, NY: Psychology Press.

Pullen, E., & Oser, C. (2014). Barriers to substance abuse treatment in rural and urban communities: A counselor perspective. *Substance Use and Misuse, 49,* 891–901.

Ratts, M. J., Singh, A. A., Nassar-McMillan, S., Butler, S. K., & Mc-Cullough, J. R. (2016). Multicultural and social justice counseling competencies: Guidelines for the counseling profession. *Journal of Multicultural Counseling and Development, 44,* 28–48. Retrieved from http://onlinelibrary.wiley.com/doi/10.1002/jmcd.12035/full

Resnicow, K., Soler, R. E., Braithwaite, R. L., Selassie, M. B., & Smith, M. (1999). Development of a racial and ethnic identity scale for African American adolescents: The Survey of Black Life. *Journal of Black Psychology, 25*(2), 171–188.

Robison, J. (2002a). *Decades of drug use: Data from the '60s and '70s.* Retrieved from www.gallup.com/poll/6331/decades-drug-use-data-from-60s-70s.aspx

Robison, J. (2002b). *Decades of drug use: The '80s and '90s.* Retrieved from www.gallup.com/poll/6352/decades-drug-use-80s-90s.aspx

Rojas, J. I., Hallford, G., Brand, M. W., & Tivis, L. J. (2012). Latino/as in substance abuse treatment: Substance use patterns, family history of addiction, and depression. *Journal of Ethnicity in Substance Abuse, 11*(1), 75–85.

Segal, B. (2014). *Perspectives on drug use in the United States.* Hoboken, NJ: Taylor & Francis.

Seyyed, S. A., Ferdosi, M., Jannatifard, F., Eslami, M., Alaghemandan, H., & Setare, M. (2012). Behavioral addiction versus substance addiction: Correspondence of psychiatric and psychological views. *International Journal of Preventive Medicine, 3*(4), 290–294.

Smith, R. L. (2015). *Treatment strategies for substance and process addictions.* Alexandria, VA: American Counseling Association.

Sobell, M. B., & Sobell, L. C. (2008). *Motivational interviewing strategies and techniques: Rationales and examples.* Retrieved from www.ncjfcj.org/sites/default/files/MI%20Strategies%20%26%20Techniques%20-%20Rationales%20and%20examples.pdf

Stevens, P., & Smith, R. (2009). *Substance abuse counseling: Theory and practice*. Upper Saddle River, NJ: Pearson.

Substance Abuse and Mental Health Services Administration. (2016a). *Co-occurring disorders*. Retrieved from www.samhsa.gov/disorders/co-occurring

Substance Abuse and Mental Health Services Administration. (2016b). *Racial and ethnic minority populations*. Retrieved from https://www.samhsa.gov/specific-populations/racial-ethnic-minority

Svrluga, S. (2014). *Fairfax mother of young heroin addict: "There were clues. But we had no clue."* Retrieved from www.washingtonpost.com/local/fairfax-mother-of-young-heroin-addict-there-were-clues-but-we-had-no-clue/2014/04/22/ab66b03c-b06b-11e3-9627-c65021d6d572_story.html

Teodorescu, K., & Erev, I. (2014). Learned helplessness and learned prevalence: Exploring the causal relationships among perceived controllability, reward prevalence, and exploration. *Psychological Science, 25,* 1861–1869.

Tombs, D. L. (2013). *Introduction to addictive behaviors* (4th ed.). New York, NY: Guilford Press.

Ulibarri, M. D., Ulloa, E. C., & Salazar, M. (2015). Associations between mental health, substance use, and sexual abuse experiences among Latinas. *Journal of Child Sexual Abuse, 24*(1), 35–54.

United Nations Office on Drugs and Crime. (2008). *2008 world drug report*. Retrieved from www.unodc.org/documents/wdr/WDR_2008/WDR_2008_eng_web.pdf

U.S. Department of Health and Human Services. (n.d.). *About the Affordable Care Act*. Retrieved from https://www.hhs.gov/healthcare/about-the-law/read-the-law/

U.S. Department of Labor, Employee Benefits Security Administration. (2010). *The Mental Health Parity and Addiction Equity Act of 2008 (MHPAEA)*. Retrieved from https://www.dol.gov/sites/default/files/ebsa/about-ebsa/our-activities/resource-center/fact-sheets/mhpaea.pdf

Volkow, N. D., Koob, G. F., & McLellan, A. T. (2016). Neurobiological advances from the brain disease model of addiction. *New England Journal of Medicine, 374,* 363–371.

Volkow, N. D., Wang, G., Fowler, J. S., & Tomasi, D. (2012). Addiction circuitry in the human brain. *Annual Reviews: Pharmacology and Toxicology, 52,* 321–336.

Wilens, T. E., Yule, A., Martelon, M., Zulauf, C., & Faraone, S. V. (2014). Parental history of substance use disorders (SUD) and SUD in offspring: A controlled family study of bipolar disorder. *American Journal on Addictions, 25,* 440–446.

Wilson, A. D., & Johnson, P. (2013). Counselors' understanding of process addiction: A blind spot in the counseling field. *The Professional Counselor, 3*(1), 16–22.

Chapter 6

Career Counseling

Mark Pope

Learning Objectives

1. Understand a variety of models and theories of career counseling and career development.
2. Understand the history, philosophy, and trends in career counseling.
3. Know the professional organizations relevant to the practice of career counseling.
4. Understand the role of multicultural issues in career counseling.
5. Understand the effects of racism, discrimination, power, privilege, and oppression in one's own life and career and those of the client.
6. Apply relevant research findings to inform the practice of career counseling.

• • •

First and foremost, career counseling is about helping, not just about career choice. To be sure, helping people make a career choice is an important focus for career counseling, but it is not the only one. From the little girl who daydreams of becoming an astronaut to the newly married couple who are having great difficulty dealing with their careers together as opposed to their careers when they were single, to the 75-year-old retired man who sits by the window of his apartment wondering what he should do today, to the single mother of four who has just lost her job, to the little boy who loves classical piano but whose parents are unable to pay for music lessons, to the teenage girl who just cannot figure out what she wants to do with the rest of her life, to the 20-something young man who is in the military and who has just realized that he is in the wrong gendered body, to the 50-year-old who drinks several cocktails every night because he is so stressed by his work and unable to sleep, to the family of four that is living on $16,000 a year and whose parents go hungry to ensure that their children have enough to eat, to the 60-year-old business executive who has just been fired by his board of directors. Career counseling is about helping people in each of these situations (and so many more) in their crises of doing and of being.

Career counseling as a profession is only 100 years or so old and is the predecessor of the entire field of professional counseling (Pope, 2000; Pope, Briddick, & Wilson, 2013). Career counseling has its roots in the social justice and Progressive movements of the late 1800s and early 1900s, as the United States moved from an agrarian society to an industrial one. Career counseling split off from the social work movement of that time and its predominant focus on case management as the core skill of that profession.

In this chapter, I trace the historic and philosophic traditions of the modern-day profession of career counseling, along with how it is practiced today. I look first at the definition of career counseling and then at the history, theories, and current practice trends in the career counseling profession.

The Definition of Career Counseling

To understand what career counseling is, we must first define key terms.

Career

Prior to the 1950s we used to think of *career* as simply a job or an occupation, with very narrow definitions of the work that human beings do. Ken Hoyt, a professor at the University of Iowa and Kansas State University who was director of the Office of Career Education for the U.S. Department of Education, wrote that *work* is "conscious effort, other than that [whose primary focus is] relaxation, aimed at producing [societally accepted] benefits for oneself [and/or] for oneself and others; [can be either paid or] unpaid activity" (Hoyt, 1976, p. 3). That was, however, only one piece of the career puzzle.

Then along came Donald Super, a professor at Columbia University, who had some other ideas about work and career. He stated that *career* is "the sequence and combination of roles that a person plays during the course of a lifetime" (Super, 1957, p. 27). So a career is not the work that you are doing right now ("I'm a janitor at Macy's"); it is the collection of work activities that you have done, are doing, and will do over the course of your lifetime. It is all of the various jobs or occupations that you have held, but even more than that, it is everything that you do, including what you do for fun (leisure), what you do to make money (job), and what you do when you retire ("to tire again"). The change in definition from a narrow perspective of career to one that is broad and inclusive became the sine qua non for our entire profession, even leading in 1985 to a change in the name of our primary professional association from the National Vocational Guidance Association (NVGA) to the National Career Development Association (NCDA; see Sidebar 6.1).

Counseling

The counseling part of the term *career counseling* also requires some attention, as it too has changed over time. Professional counseling has a distinct and evolving definition. The American Counseling Association (2004), the primary association in the United States representing professional counselors, defined *professional counseling* as "the application of mental health, psychological, or human development principles, through cognitive, affective, behavioral or systematic intervention strategies, that address wellness, personal growth, or career development, as well as pathology" ("The Practice of Professional Counseling," para. 1).

More recently, the American Counseling Association established a task force, called 20/20: A Vision for the Future of Counseling, to look at this definition. This led to the following definition, approved on October 28, 2010, by its Governing Council: "Professional counseling is a professional relationship that empowers diverse individuals, families, and groups to accomplish mental health, wellness, education, and career goals" (American Counseling Association, 2010, para. 2).

Note that *career* appears prominently in both definitions. This, along with very specific emphases on mental health, the use of psy-

---

Sidebar 6.1   Thought Question

In the newspapers or online, we see people talk about having had seven careers over their lifetimes. What they really mean are occupations, not careers. Donald Super defined career very broadly as everything we do over the course of our lives. From your first job mowing lawns to your retirement, you only have one career.

Why is it important to a student or client and to career counselors to understand career in such an all-encompassing way?

• • •

choeducational and developmental interventions (primary prevention as opposed to remedial), and the shunning of diagnosis as a primary tool, is what differentiates professional counseling from all other mental health fields. One role of career counseling in the larger field of professional counseling has been to keep professional counseling more focused on primary prevention rather than remediation, on mental health rather than mental illness, and on psychoeducational development rather than the diagnosing of disease. It has had a powerful role in shaping the path of professional counseling, counselor education, counseling psychology, and positive psychology in the mental health professions.

Career + Counseling

Career counseling then is a professional relationship that empowers diverse individuals, families, and groups to accomplish career goals in the context of the sequence and combination of roles that a person plays during the course of a lifetime. What career counselors do, therefore, is not simply assist others in their career decisions or career choice but also help others address career indecision, work performance, stress and adjustment, incongruence between the person and the work environment, social barriers and discrimination, dual career couples, and inadequate or unsatisfactory integration of life roles with other life roles (e.g., parent, citizen, leisurite). This is a huge task but so obviously important in human beings' lives. As can be seen, along with that big change in the definition of *career* in the 1950s, career counselors are now taking on substantially larger roles in their practice.

The History of Career Counseling

In the late 1800s and early 1900s in the United States, the profession of career counseling (and really counseling as a whole) was born. Several historians of career counseling have placed the date as 1913 (Aubrey, 1977; Brewer, 1942; Pope, 2000; Whiteley, 1984) and have attributed the founding to a small group of disaffected social workers who realized that case management, the traditional focus of that field, was simply not enough. People also needed a place to consider the barriers they faced and to gain knowledge about themselves so that they could learn to apply their internal, personal resources to the problems of everyday life.

Roots of the Profession of Counseling

The break from the profession of social work was personified historically by the work of Frank Parsons, who is credited as the founder of the field of professional counseling (Aubrey, 1977; Brewer, 1942; Davis, 1969; Pope & Sveinsdottir, 2005; Whiteley, 1984). Parsons and his colleagues at the Breadwinner's Institute of the Vocation Bureau of the Boston Civic Service House, a Jane Addams–styled settlement house that arose to help individuals who were migrating from rural areas to resettle in urban centers, found that they had to do more than just case management. They found that helping also meant helping people look at themselves through a process they called *vocational guidance*, which we now term *career counseling* (Brewer, 1942; see Sidebar 6.2).

Career counseling arose from the need to help people who were having financial, employment, and personal problems as a result of the transition from an agrarian society to an industrial one at the end of the 1800s and the beginning of the 1900s. Career counseling arose in response to, and as an immediate outcome of, this transition. Pope (2000) characterized this transition as follows:

> The societal upheaval giving birth to career counseling was characterized by the loss of jobs in the agricultural sector, increasing demands for workers in heavy industry, the loss of "permanent" jobs on the family farm to new emerging technologies such as tractors, the increasing urbanization of the [United States], and the concomitant calls for services to meet this internal migration pattern, all in order to retool for the new industrial economy. (p. 195)

Although societal transition and social insecurity can birth a new profession, it takes much more than such upheaval to sustain it over time. The other social factors that served to maintain this new field included the support of the progressive social reform movement, the rise of psychological testing as a scientific endeavor, and the emergence of laws that were supportive of vocational guidance and that received much societal support (Pope, 2000).

A critical factor in the establishment of career counseling was the early support for vocational guidance that came from the progressive

---

Sidebar 6.2 Thought Question

Sigmund Freud spoke of love and work as the hallmarks of a mature life. If you have a person whom you love and a job for which you have a passion, life is pretty good. There are, however, many jobs that people do for the money, not for the passion. Jobs like those in manufacturing, on assembly lines, are particularly monotonous.

What could workers do to meet their needs to feel passionate about their work when they are stuck on an assembly line everyday?

• • •

social reform movement (Pope, 2000). "The linkage between this movement and vocational guidance was largely built on the issue of the growing exploitation and misuse of human beings" (Aubrey, 1977, p. 290). Child labor laws provided much impetus for collaboration, as this crusade to prohibit the exploitation of children grew. Although some states, beginning with Pennsylvania, had established minimum age laws in the latter half of the 19th century, more than half a million children ages 10 to 13 years were still employed in the first decade of the 20th century (Bernert, 1958), and effective federal legislation did not come about until the passage of the 1938 Fair Labor Standards Act. Parsons was a prominent leader in the struggle to eliminate child labor.

Another important factor in the establishment of career counseling was the increasing use of psychological testing (Pope, 2000). Psychological tests became an important and necessary part of the first functional stage in career counseling; that is, self-assessment. Testing gave career counseling respectability in American society (Super & Crites, 1962; Whiteley, 1984). Without a scientific procedure to justify the first step of career counseling (i.e., self-assessment), it is unlikely that career counseling would have been so popularly accepted. In the late 1800s, Francis Galton, Wilhelm Wundt, James McKeen Cattell, and Alfred Binet each made important contributions to the newly emerging field of psychological testing and, by extension, to career counseling. In the 1920s, Edward Kellogg Strong, Jr., developed the Vocational Interest Blank (now the Strong Interest Inventory; Strong, 1927), the first career interest measure and the most successful of the many that have followed (see Sidebar 6.3).

Furthermore, laws that were supportive of vocational guidance were beginning to receive much social support (Pope, 2000). For example, the landmark Smith-Hughes Act of 1917 established secondary school vocational education training. This legislation was strengthened in succeeding years by the George-Reed Act (1929), George-Ellzey Act

Sidebar 6.3 Implication for Practice

Career assessment or psychological testing has an important role in career counseling, but it might take one of many forms. It might involve a semistructured interview such as the Career Style Interview. It might be objective assessment in the form of an interest inventory such as the Strong Interest Inventory. It might take the form of career daydreams, free association, a values card sort, a career genogram of the client's family, or one of many other forms. It depends on your theoretical orientation.

• • •

(1934), and George-Deen Act (1936). Each of these laws supported vocational education as an important part of public schools. Furthermore, in 1913, the U.S. Department of Labor was founded and the Bureau of Labor Statistics, which had been part of the Department of the Interior, was moved into the Department of Labor.

The Rise of Professional Institutions

Out of this transition also came the founding in 1913 of NVGA (now NCDA) in Grand Rapids, Michigan, at the Third National Conference on Vocational Guidance (Brewer, 1942; Pope, 2009). The founders of NVGA included Frank Leavitt (first president), Jesse B. Davis (second president and known as the first school counselor; Niles & Harris-Bowlsbey, 2017; Pope, 2009), Meyer Bloomfield (third president, Parsons's successor at the Vocation Bureau, and teacher of the first course in vocational guidance in 1911 at Harvard University), and John M. Brewer (fifth NVGA president and author of the definitive history of career guidance in the United States in 1942). They received much moral and financial support from Pauline Agassiz Shaw, a wealthy Boston philanthropist (Hershenson, 2006). NVGA/NCDA would go on in 1952 to be one of the four founding divisions of the American Personnel and Guidance Association, now the American Counseling Association, the preeminent association of professional counselors in the United States. NCDA is now recognized as one of the leading professional associations supporting the work of career counselors throughout the world.

Three Historic Periods

There have been three historic periods in the evolution of career interventions (Pope, 2015a). Career counseling has evolved over the past 100 years from the matching of an individual's traits with occupations of the vocational guidance period, with its focus on individual differences (Holland, 1997; Parsons, 1909; Strong, 1943), to the process-oriented approach to career decision making and career development over the life span of the career education period, with its focus on individual development (Super, 1953, 1954, 1957, 1990), to the individual construction of career through small stories of the life design period, with its focus on individual design (Hartung, 2010; Maree, 2007; Savickas, 2011; Savickas et al., 2009).

What has developed is a rich tapestry of career intervention. As the interventions of these three periods are conceptually additive, not mutually exclusive, each builds on and supplements the work of the preceding period (Savickas, 2010). Career counselors can thus choose an appropriate intervention from the total arsenal of career interventions that have arisen over these past 100 years based on the specific career problems of their specific client.

Theories of Career Counseling

As someone who is studying counseling, you might be asking, "Why is theory important?" The simple answer is that theory helps us make sense of our experiences. To be a successful practitioner, you must have a solid knowledge base in theory that provides you with a meaningful framework and context for working with clients. Theory gives you a better understanding of particular strategies, counseling approaches, and tools and helps you determine how to use them, when to use them, and why you use them. Finally, having the ability to use a number of theories and approaches better equips you to determine and meet the particular needs of each individual client. The bottom line is that research has shown that, as a practitioner, you will be more successful in working with your clients if you work from a theory (Pope, 2015b).

Although a thorough review of career counseling theories is not possible in this chapter, it is important to be aware of the key theories and theory categories that guide career counselors in their work. The philosophic traditions of career counseling have included a number of approaches or theories derived from important historic movements within the overall mental health professions—reflections of the major theories within all of professional counseling. These theories can be classified into larger categories as follows: differential, dynamic, reinforcement based, developmental, narrative, and contextual/cultural. Theories in each of these categories have made a critical contribution to career counseling practice.

Differential or Trait-Factor (or Person–Environment Fit) Theories

The basic approach in differential or trait-factor theories is to help the client identify key personality traits (values, interests, skills, etc.) and match them to job requirements. The idea is to help the person find the best fit in a congruent occupational environment. The trait-factor tradition arose from the work of Frank Parsons (1854–1908). His model of career counseling was largely without theoretical foundations and was grounded in "simple logic and common sense and relied predominantly on observational and data gathering skills" (Aubrey, 1977, p. 290). Parsons (1909) stated that:

> in the choice of a vocation there are three broad factors: (1) a clear understanding of yourself; . . . (2) a knowledge of the requirements and conditions for success . . . in different lines of work; (3) true reasoning on the relation of these two groups of facts. (p. 5)

His largely intuitive and experiential approach laid the foundation for career counseling.

The differential models or trait-factor approaches are represented here by John Holland's theory of vocational personalities and work environments. Holland (1997) focused on individual characteristics

144

and occupational tasks. Holland's theory expanded the concept of personality and posited the following:

1. Personalities fall into six broad categories: realistic, investigative, artistic, social, enterprising, and conventional (often referred to as *RIASEC*).
2. Because certain personalities are attracted to certain jobs, the work environments reflect these personalities and can be clustered into the same six themes (RIASEC).
3. Each individual is made up of all six themes rank ordered from "most like me" to "least like me."
4. Personalities can be matched with similar combinations of work environments using a problem-solving approach.
5. The closer the match between personality and job, the greater the satisfaction.

Holland took an easily understood matching approach to career planning, and this model has been extremely influential in career counseling. It has been used by popular assessment tools such as the Strong Interest Inventory, Self-Directed Search, and Vocational Preference Inventory to organize data. It has also resulted in practical resources like the *Dictionary of Holland Occupational Codes,* which applies Holland's codes to more than 15,000 occupations.

Dynamic or Parental Influence (or Psychodynamic) Theories

Dynamic career counseling takes a subjective perspective on career as a function of early parent–child relationships, childhood memories, family dynamics, and personal meaning. The dynamic approaches are represented here by Anne Roe's theory of career choice and development. Roe's initial interest in vocational psychology grew out of her work on clinical studies of artists and scientists. She received a grant to study the effect of alcohol on artists; used the Rorschach Inkblot Test, the Thematic Apperception Test, and life histories; and noticed a relationship between what and how artists painted and their personalities. She saw a need to go beyond the *Dictionary of Occupational Titles (DOT)* classification system (people, data, things) and the national census classification system. Roe wanted to incorporate interests and interpersonal relationships, tying these directly to Abraham Maslow's personality theory, based on unobservable personality needs as the primary determinants of choice. The primary tenets of her theory are as follows:

1. People select a certain occupation because it satisfies an important psychological need.
2. Genetic inheritance sets limits on the potential development of all characteristics, but the specificity of the genetic control and the extent and nature of the limitations are different for different characteristics.

3. The degrees and avenues of development of inherited characteristics are affected not only by experiences unique to the individual but also by all aspects of the general cultural background and the socioeconomic status of the family.

4. The pattern of development of interests, attitudes, and other personality variables with relatively little or nonspecific genetic control is primarily determined by individual experiences through which involuntary attention becomes channeled in particular directions.

5. The eventual pattern of psychic energies, in terms of attention directedness, is the major determinant of interests.

6. The intensity of these needs and of their satisfaction (especially as they remain unconscious) and their organization are the major determinants of the degree of motivation that reaches expression in accomplishment.

7. There are two basic orientations: toward persons and not toward persons. These are related to early childhood experiences and are then related to occupational choice.

8. Occupational choice is composed of the following factors: gender, the general state of the economy, family background, learning and education, special acquired skills, physical factors, chance, friends and peer group, marital situation, cognitive factors, temperament and personality, and interests and values. Each is weighted in different ways for each person, except there is no weight for gender. People have more control over some of the factors and less over others.

Reinforcement-Based or Social Learning or Cognitive (or Behavioral or Cognitive Behavior) Theories

Reinforcement-based career counseling focuses on what individuals believe or think about themselves and the world of work and considers how social learning, reinforcement patterns, and cognition shape trait development and mental representations of self and work. Reinforcement-based approaches came from behaviorism and cognitive behavior therapies in professional counseling and are represented here by John Krumboltz's social learning theory of career choice (Mitchell & Krumboltz, 1996). Krumboltz developed a theory of career decision making and development based on social learning. Career decisions are the product of an uncountable number of learning experiences made possible by encounters with the people, institutions, and events in a person's particular environment. In other words, people choose their careers based on what they have learned. Krumboltz proposed the following:

1. The four main factors that influence career choice are genetic influences, environmental conditions and events, learning experiences, and task approach skills (e.g., self-observation, goal setting, information seeking).

2. The consequences of these factors and, most particularly, learning experiences lead people to develop beliefs about the nature of careers and their role in life (self-observational generalizations). These beliefs, whether realistic or not, influence career choices and work-related behavior.
3. Learning experiences, especially observational learning stemming from significant role models (e.g., parents, teachers, heroes), have a powerful influence on career decisions, making some occupations more attractive than others.
4. Positive modeling, reward, and reinforcement will likely lead to the development of appropriate career planning skills and career behavior.

Krumboltz saw his theory as (a) a way of explaining the origin of career choice and (b) a guide to how career practitioners might tackle career-related problems (Mitchell & Krumboltz, 1996). The practitioner starts by understanding how clients came to their career-related views of themselves (i.e., their career beliefs) and the world and what is limiting or problematic about their beliefs.

Developmental Theories

Developmental career counseling incorporates both objective and subjective perspectives to examine how individuals can develop traits relative to the meaning and beliefs they give to themselves. The developmental approaches are represented here by the work of Donald Super. Super's life-span/life-space theory (Super, Savickas, & Super, 1996) is a very comprehensive developmental model that attempts to account for the various important influences on a person as he or she experiences different life roles and various life stages. Donald Super believed that humans are anything but static and that personal change is continuous. Some of Super's main tenets include the following:

1. Every individual has potential. The skills and talents that people develop through different life roles make them capable of performing a variety of tasks and numerous occupations.
2. In making a vocational choice, an individual is expressing his or her understanding of self—his or her self-concept. People seek career satisfaction through work roles in which they can express themselves and implement and develop their self-concept. Self-knowledge is key to career choice and job satisfaction.
3. Career development is lifelong and occurs throughout five major life stages: growth, exploration, establishment, maintenance, and disengagement. Each stage has a unique set of career development tasks and accounts for the changes and decisions that people make from career entry to retirement.

4. These five stages are not just chronological. People cycle through each of these stages when they go through career transitions.
5. People play different roles throughout their lives, including the role of worker. Job satisfaction increases when a person's self-concept includes a view of the working self as integrated with his or her other life roles.

Super's theory has greatly influenced how we look at career practices. Understanding the ages and related stages of career development assists practitioners in identifying where clients are in the career development continuum and suggesting appropriate career-related goals and activities. It also underscores the necessity of examining career development within the larger context of an individual's roles and lifestyle and how to achieve a life–work balance.

Narrative or Constructivist Theories

Narrative career counseling incorporates social construction and constructivist approaches to help individuals construct their career story so that they can change it. The narrative or constructivist model is a career development model by which human beings give meaning to their experience of temporality and personal actions. Narrative meaning functions to give form to the understanding of a purpose to a life and to join everyday actions and events into episodic units. It provides a framework for understanding the past events of one's life and for planning future actions. It is the primary process by which human existence is rendered meaningful. Narrative theory is more of a philosophical framework within which career counseling can be done. Two thinkers associated with this approach are Mark Savickas and Vance Peavy (see Niles & Harris-Bowlsbey, 2017). Constructivist career development is based on the concepts of constructivism, which include the following:

1. There are no fixed meanings or realities in the world; there are multiple meanings and multiple realities. Individuals create or construct their own meaning or reality of the world through the experiences they have.
2. People construct themselves and the world around them through the interpretations they make and the actions they take. These constructs or perceptions of events may be useful or may be misleading.
3. Individuals differ from one another in their construction of events. Two people may participate in the same or a similar event and have very different perceptions of the experience.
4. People are self-organizing and are meaning makers. Their lives are ever-evolving stories that are under constant revision. Individuals may choose to develop new constructs or write new stories in their lives.

5. Being an empowered or fulfilled person requires critical reflection on the assumptions that account for daily decisions and actions.

The constructivist career counseling approach is generally about life planning. The search for meaningful work is connected to constructivism's emphasis on deriving meaning from personal experience. To have meaningful careers, we need to reflect on our life experiences and the resulting constructs they may hold about life, work, or self. The career counselor and client work toward an awareness and openness of new constructs of one's life, work, or self that can provide the basis for meaning. Interventions include working directly with the client's life experience and using meaning-making processes such as narrative, metaphor, mapping, and critical reflection.

Contextual and Cultural Dimensions

In contextual/cultural approaches, the role of culture broadly defined is critical to the understanding of the individual and applies to all career counseling relationships. *Culture* was narrowly defined as race and ethnicity early in the development of this tradition within professional counseling (Pope, 1995d), but in career counseling, this tradition has always been more broadly inclusive in its definition and includes ethnographic variables (e.g., race, ethnicity, religion, history, and common ancestry), demographic variables (e.g., age, sex, sexual orientation, geographic location of residence), status variables (e.g., social, economic, and educational variables), and affiliation variables (both formal and informal variables).

This model is represented here by my approach to career counseling with underserved populations. Career counseling with underserved populations (Pope, 2009) came directly from the professional career counseling literature and was influenced by my early writings on sexual minority career development (Pope, 1992, 1995a, 1995b). It was later expanded to address the issues of ethnic and racial minorities (Pope, 1999; Pope et al., 2004; Pope, Cheng, & Leong, 1998) and now has been fully integrated into the model. Here are the 13 keys based on what we have learned about effective practice with ethnic, racial, and sexual/gender minorities:

1. *Take responsibility for your own biases and prejudices.* Bias can affect the interventions that are selected by career counselors as well as how such interventions are used.
2. *Know the process of cultural identity development and use it.* This is the one element that is consistently recommended in the research literature as a critical component of successful career counseling with culturally diverse adults.
3. *Know the special issues of specific cultures.* Career counselors must become knowledgeable and aware of the special issues of a culture to provide effective career counseling.

4. *Directly address issues of discrimination.* Openly addressing these issues and preparing clients to cope with the more overt manifestations of racism, sexism, heterosexism, ableism, ageism, and other forms of discrimination is an important and primary role of the career counselor.

5. *Remember that group career counseling has a strong appeal to many racial and ethnic minority clients.* Several characteristics of group-oriented or collectivist cultures—the primacy of group survival over individual survival, interdependency, and connectedness—make them especially suited to group career counseling.

6. *Pay particular attention to the role of the family.* The role of the family, defined as broad and extended, is exceptionally important in the provision of career counseling services to individuals from collectivist cultures.

7. *Pay attention to the special issues of dual career couples.* Dual career couples have been explored more in the sexual minority career development literature than in the ethnic and racial minority literature, where the focus has been more on the special role of the family in career decisions.

8. *Be aware of special issues when using career assessment inventories with individuals from various cultural communities.* Special procedures have been recommended for using formal assessment tools with diverse individuals.

9. *Help clients overcome internalized negative stereotypes or internalized oppression.* This is a critical role of the career counselor, as such stereotypes or internalized oppression can act as significant barriers to successful outcomes.

10. *Pay attention to coming-out issues with clients whose cultural membership is not obvious.* Whether to disclose their culture to others is a unique issue for clients whose cultural membership may not be obvious (gay/lesbian/bisexual/transgender, multiple race/ethnicity, political affiliation, religion, some [dis]abilities, and others). In the sexual minority counseling literature, this is termed *coming out* and is central for gay men and lesbian women who are seeking career counseling.

11. *To overcome societal stereotyping as a limitation on occupational choice, use occupational role modeling and networking interventions.* Occupational role modeling and networking interventions are very important for special populations that have historically been limited in their occupational choices.

12. *Maintain a supportive atmosphere in your office.* At the programmatic level, one simple and concrete way to inform others that you are supportive of the struggles of culturally diverse persons who are seeking career counseling is to create a supportive atmosphere in the office.

13. *Provide positive social advocacy for your culturally diverse clients.* Career counselors working with any special cultural group must be affirming of that group, going beyond the do-no-harm admonition to encompass positive advocacy for their clients and their rights.

As a result of more than 30 years of research, we now have some knowledge of how to proceed with career counseling with clients from a culture or cultures different from our own. Career counseling with underserved populations assists career services providers in developing a more nuanced approach that can help these individuals master their career issues and achieve successful career outcomes.

10 Ideas That Changed the Career Field

In 2013, on the occasion of its 100th anniversary, NCDA commissioned Mark Savickas to conduct a study to identify the 10 essential ideas in the evolution of career intervention. Savickas used the Delphi technique, a research design that allows the gathering of expert opinion, and a move toward consensus, without bringing a group of people together, guaranteeing anonymity so people do not have to defend their position.

The idea for this study originated from the most popular course at Kent State University for three decades: Seven Ideas That Changed Physics. For years, Savickas had wanted to identify the seven ideas that changed career counseling. Savickas began by listing 30 possible ideas. He spread the ideas across decades and across authors and attended to diversity— roughly three ideas per decade. To develop the list, Savickas "examined NCDA journals for the last 100 years to find the origins and trace the evolution of prominent concepts and activities" (Savickas, 2013, p. 1).

Then 12 people responded to his invitation to review the list and let him know which ideas they would revise, delete, and add to the list of 30 ideas. They were instructed to respond to the following question: "What are the 20 most essential ideas crucial in the development of career intervention since 1909? Identify big picture ideas for which counselors should have robust and flexible understanding" (Savickas, 2013, p. 2). They deleted some and added some to produce a list of 37. Then another group reduced that list to 20. Finally, 44 NCDA leaders individually ranked those ideas to produce the top 10 ideas, rank ordered here (Savickas, 2013):

1. *Career counseling:* The process of helping people to develop an integrated and adequate picture of themselves and of their role in the world of work, to test this concept against reality, and to convert it into a reality, with satisfaction to themselves and benefits to society (Super, 1951).
2. *Matching:* In the wise choice of a vocation, there are three broad factors: (a) a clear understanding of self, (b) a knowledge of occupations, and (c) true reasoning to make an occupational choice (Parsons, 1909).
3. *Career adaptability:* The postcorporate global economy requires that individuals develop the readiness and resources to cope with repeated vocational choices, occupational transitions, and work traumas (Savickas, 1997).

4. *Vocational guidance:* Vocational guidance is the process of assisting an individual in choosing an occupation, preparing for it, entering it, and progressing in it.

5. *Career education:* Career counselors must refocus American education and the actions of the broader community in ways that will help individuals acquire and utilize the knowledge, skills, and attitudes necessary for each to make work a meaningful, productive, and satisfying part of his or her way of living (Hoyt, 1976).

6. *Social justice:* Best practice requires that career counselors understand and appreciate cultural diversity and advocate for social justice (Pope, 1995a).

7. *Career construction:* People build careers by turning their preoccupations into occupations and thereby actively master what they passively suffer (Savickas, 2005).

8. *Congruence:* Probable success in entering an occupation depends on the correspondence between the requirements of the occupation and the qualifications the individual possesses for that particular occupation (Brewer, 1926).

9. *Happenstance:* The goal of career counseling is to help clients learn to take actions to achieve more satisfying career and personal lives—not to make a single career decision (Krumboltz, 2009).

10. *Career stages:* Careers develop over the life course through a predictable series of stages and tasks (Super, 1957).

Savickas (2013) then arranged the first 10 ideas into a statement to describe the career development field's core ideas:

> The field of career development privileges the idea of social justice as it helps people construct their work lives through the practices of vocational guidance, career education, and career counseling. Career development practitioners pursue the fundamental goal of helping individuals match themselves to congruent occupations as they traverse career stages, with each new era in life requiring that they adapt to new vocational development tasks, occupational transitions, and work traumas. Practitioners encourage their students and clients to remain open to possibilities created when new circumstances happen. (pp. 2–3)

Special Considerations in Career Counseling

> Individuals in the knowledge societies at the beginning of the 21st century must realize that career problems are only a piece of much broader concerns about how to live a life in a postmodern world shaped by a global economy and supported by information technology. (Savickas et al., 2009, p. 241)

As corporations evolve in the 21st century,

> the nexus of career moved from the organization to the individual (Hall, 1996). Rather than develop a career within a stable organization, the digital

revolution requires that individuals manage their own careers. This shift in responsibility from the organization to the individual posed the new question of how individuals may negotiate a lifetime of job changes. (Savickas, 2011, p. 5)

The world of work has changed drastically in the 21st century, and not necessarily for the better for the individual worker. In the 20th century, secure employment and stable organizations predominated and were part of the social compact between workers and employers (Duarte, 2009). As part of this compact, employment of that time and workers' expectations were based on a promise that if workers were loyal to the employer and performed well, they would have permanent employment to build their lives and secure their futures. At the beginning of the 21st century, with its emphasis on nimbleness, flexibility, temporary assignments, quick profits, and time-limited project-driven processes, that compact exploded, leaving workers of the period more insecure and anxious (Kalleberg, 2009; Kalleberg, Reskin, & Hudson, 2000; Savickas, 2011).

The project-focused model was previously the dominant model in certain occupations, such as construction, engineering, the arts, and entertainment (especially movie making, theater, music, and others), but the rise of large manufacturing and distribution companies as part of the more urbanized industrial era required large stable groups of workers to consistently perform their duties for these companies to exist, be successful, and make a profit (Duarte, 2009). With changes in technology, shortened boom-and-bust economic cycles, and increasing population densities of highly skilled and educated workers in metropolitan areas, this project-focused model has overtaken the more industrialized model and expanded its scope into many other organizations.

With such changes in organizations come changes in the structure of careers. Savickas (2011) noted this transition with data from several sources.

> For many workers, an assignment does not last even 2 years. More than half of the individuals born after 1980 left their first job within 5 months (Saratoga Institute, 2000). This was true not only emerging adults but also for those adults who in previous times had stabilized in jobs and families. Of the jobs started by workers between the ages of 33 and 38, 39% ended in less than a year and 70% ended in fewer than 5 years. One in four workers has been with his or her current employers for less than a year (Bureau of Labor Statistics, 2004). (2011, p. 9)

The result of these changes is insecure and anxious workers. Savickas (2011) provided a list of the terms used to identify such workers in the popular and professional literature: "temporary, contingent, casual, contract, freelance, part-time, external, atypical, adjunct, consultant, and self-employed" (p. 10). Benefits previously taken for granted as part of a job, including pensions, medical insurance, and others, may no longer be part of the compact. With the housing crash of the Great Recession (2008–2013), the dream of home ownership may be lost forever for many workers, and renting may be the better choice for persons with jobs of short duration and individual careers that require geographic mobility.

Another loss resulting from the new project-driven model involves the loyalty of workers, as employers who do not treat workers as long-term resources cannot expect their workers to just wait around for their next project or their next assignment. Workers have bills to pay and lives to lead. Individuals who must now take control of their own individual careers are no longer bound to an organization. Hall (1996) discussed protean careers, and M. B. Arthur (1994) wrote about boundaryless careers. Both reflect this new state of affairs for workers. As Savickas (2011) noted, "Rather than living a narrative conferred by a corporation, people must author their own stories as they navigate occupational transitions in the postmodern world" (p. 11).

Interventions: Practice Dimensions

The emerging career interventions of this period had their foundations in Super's (1954) career pattern work and Tiedeman's (1961) reflective career consciousness ideas, and "the individual design perspective finds [its] paramount embodiment in Savickas's (2002) career construction theory and practice and its recent advancement within a comprehensive model of individual life designing (Savickas et al., 2009)" (Hartung, 2010, p. 7).

Informal Qualitative Assessment
The individual life design perspective uses informal qualitative assessment methods, such as the Career-Story Interview (Savickas, 1998; M. L. Savickas, personal communication to P. J. Hartung, June 11, 2010; Savickas et al., 2009), which emphasizes subjective assessment of the individual's life story. "Practitioners apply career construction theory when they perform career counseling to (a) construct career through small stories, (b) deconstruct and reconstruct the small stories into a large story, and (c) coconstruct the next episode in the story" (Savickas, 2011, p. 5).

The central question that life design interventions address is this: How can I use school and work to make my life more meaningful and complete in a way that matters to society? Life design interventions use both informal and formal assessments to better evaluate and appreciate the rich tapestry of an individual's full life as told through his or her own story.

Occupational Information
The *DOT* was first published in 1938 by the U.S. Department of Labor and, as mentioned earlier, was a staple of the vocational guidance

period, with its nine-digit numeric codes for each of the thousands of occupations in the United States. These codes allowed for easy job matching. The *DOT* was updated on several occasions throughout its history, but it continued to have a distinctive industrial manufacturing focus, as would be expected for such a document from that period. It "emerged in an industrial economy and emphasized blue-collar jobs. Updated periodically, the DOT provided useful occupational information for many years. But its usefulness waned as the economy shifted toward information and services and away from heavy industry" (Mariani, 1999, p. 2).

The *DOT* was replaced in 1997 by a preliminary version of the Occupational Information Network (O*NET), a free online database sponsored by the U.S. Department of Labor and developed through a grant to the North Carolina Employment Security Commission. "O*NET allows everyone to access data on job characteristics and worker attributes. It includes information on the knowledge, skills, abilities, interests, preparation, contexts, and tasks associated with 1,122 O*NET occupations" (Mariani, 1999, p. 2), with Holland's RIASEC model as its organizing scheme.

The career exploration assessments that are available as part of O*NET include the O*NET Ability Profiler, O*NET Interest Profiler, O*NET Computerized Interest Profiler, O*NET Interest Profiler Short Form, O*NET Work Importance Locator, and O*NET Work Importance Profiler. These self-directed inventories are available for free on O*NET and provide valuable career information.

The Rise in Interest in Cultural Diversity and Social Justice

We are now witnessing a rise in interest in and research on the role of cultural diversity and social justice in career development and counseling, which is broadening the social groups to which career counseling is now becoming more effective and relevant. My colleagues and I led an insurgent movement within the profession that began to look at the effects of culture on the career counseling process, beginning with my work to establish and legitimize the study of career counseling with gays and lesbians (Pope, 1992, 1995a, 1995b, 1995c, 1996, 2008; Pope & Barret, 2002; Pope et al., 2004; Pope, Prince, & Mitchell, 2000; Pope, Singaravelu, Chang, Sullivan, & Murray, 2007); to expand the notions of career counseling with multiple diverse cultural groups in the United States (Pope, 2010; Pope & Pangelinan, 2010) and internationally (Leong & Pope, 2002a, 2002b; Pope, 2003, 2007, 2012; Pope, Musa, Singaravelu, Bringaze, & Russell, 2002; Pope & Russell, 2001; Pope et al., 2007; Puertas, Cinamon, Neault, Pope, & Rossier, 2012; Zhang, Hu, & Pope, 2002); to look at the social justice roots of career counseling (Pope, 2011; Pope et al., 2013; Pope & Sveinsdottir, 2005); and to integrate issues of culture into the processes of career intervention in the career education period (Hartung et al., 1998). This has led to the development of and focus on contextual/cultural theories, such as Arthur and Collins's multicultural career counseling (N. Arthur & Collins, 2011), my career counseling with underserved populations (Pope, 2011), and others. It has also elevated the understanding and effectiveness of career counseling interventions with a variety of people from a multitude of cultures (see Sidebar 6.4).

Chapter Summary

This chapter traced the historic and philosophic traditions of the modern-day profession of career counseling along with how it is practiced today. We looked at the definition of career counseling and then at the history, theories, and current practice trends in the career counseling profession.

Career counseling has a long historic tradition with professional counseling and is what makes that profession different from all other mental health professions. It is one of the most inherently positive types of counseling with consistently good client outcomes (Pope, 2003). It has evolved over the past 100 years from the matching of an individual's traits with occupations to a more process-oriented approach to career decision making and career development over the life span, and finally to the fostering of an individual's construction of career projects through narrative approaches. The positive outcomes that typically occur as a result of career counseling interventions are inspiring and empowering. Helping clients construct positive career goals and develop a sense of hope for the future is extremely reward-ing work and changes people's lives forever. Truly.

Sidebar 6.4   Implication for Practice

Cultural diversity and social justice are two ideas that permeate the career counseling profession. Social justice was a signifi-cant part of our profession from its beginning in the Boston social service houses of the late 1800s and the movement to abolish child labor practices. Cultural diversity is a relatively more recent phenomenon in the work of career counselors in the 1990s and on. We now know much more about what interventions are useful in career counseling with people from a variety of cultures, especially people from cultures different from our own, such as African Americans; lesbian, gay, bisexual, and transgender people; people with disabilities; older adults; and so many more.

• • •

Learning Activities

1. Elena is a 20-year-old Puerto Rican woman who has almost completed the second year of an associate's degree in business and is considering what she should do after finishing. She has really enjoyed both the information systems as well as the general business classes she has taken. She is currently having a hard time deciding whether she should continue on to get a bachelor's degree or whether she should just find a job and start working. Her academic advisor has told her that, with her 3.8 grade point average, it is likely that she would receive a scholarship from the local public university and that it is possible that she would even have all of her tuition expenses covered by a scholarship if she attends full time.

   Her father thinks an associate's degree is enough education to get a good job and is discouraging her from continuing her studies. Her mother agrees, but Elena knows that her mother is proud that she has done so well in school, especially because neither of her parents completed high school. She is the oldest child in the family and has had considerable responsibilities helping her mother with her three younger brothers and sisters. She has helped in her parents' small grocery store since she was young and enjoys talking to people who come to the store. Her uncle has a small real estate office and has offered to help her get started and assist her with getting a realtor license.

   What is Elena's main problem? Which career theories would be most helpful in helping Elena?

2. Namadi is a 33-year-old man who currently works as an accountant. He was born in Nigeria, but his family moved to the United States when he was a child, although his parents have since moved back to Lagos, the largest city in Nigeria, to take care of his grandparents. He has an older sister who lives in Los Angeles and two older brothers who live in Lagos. He has lived most of his life in the United States and feels like the United States is home, although he maintains close ties to Nigeria and goes back regularly to visit extended family. His family is Sunni Muslim and ethnically Yoruba, and one of his brothers is an imam at a local mosque in a suburb of Lagos.

   Namadi attended school and graduated from a local university and was active in a number of student organizations (International Business Club, Accounting Club, and African Student Association) and the campus newspaper. He had never worked before he graduated because his parents told him his education must always take priority.

   Namadi's first job was as a bookkeeper at a small graphic design business. He liked the job and the company, but his pay was too low. After 2 years, he found a different job at a large airplane manufacturing company. He was given the title of accountant at this new job, which was important to him.

He has been with this company for 8 years now, but recently he has been having difficulty with some of his coworkers and he has been passed over for promotion on four different occasions. Namadi is a hard worker and quite introverted. He has few friends at his workplace and prefers to be alone for breaks and lunch. He also is a strict Muslim, prays five times per day, and has requested Fridays off so that he can attend prayers at his local mosque. The company has agreed to this, but his supervisor was not happy with his request. Namadi has come to you for career counseling because he says he is not happy with his job and wants to find out what else he could do.

What is Namadi's main problem? Which career theories would be most helpful in helping Namadi?

3. Rose Ann, a recently separated 39-year-old Caucasian female, has sought career counseling in support of her need for self-sufficiency and personal growth. Rose Ann, a slender, professionally dressed woman, is presently employed as an administrative assistant. She attended college many years ago but did not receive a degree. Her immediate issues deal with her career planning in light of her pending divorce from her husband of 15 years. Of concern is the environment Rose Ann has been living in for the past 15 years. Her husband, described as controlling and not wanting to divorce, convinced Rose Ann not to work during their marriage and has isolated her from life outside their marriage.

What is Rose Ann's main problem? What are the barriers that Rose Ann faces?

4. Robert is a 39-year-old African American male who lives in San Francisco and has been married to a woman for 10 years. They have no children. He has worked for his family's construction business since he was in high school. While working in the construction industry, he went to college in the evenings and, after 7 years, completed a bachelor's degree in history, a field of study that he truly loves. It was also his parents' dream that he would go to college. When he completed his degree, he knew he did not want to stay in construction, and after much soul searching and many long talks with his wife, he decided that he would like to teach. He applied for and was hired for a teaching position at the high school level in San Francisco, where he taught for 5 years. He enjoyed his time teaching and working with students, as the subject matter he taught was quite interesting to him. He was not sure, however, that the low teacher salary would be something he could live with long term.

Unfortunately, during his time as a teacher, he was apprehended by federal drug officials for selling what he says was a "small amount" of marijuana to boost his low salary. He was found guilty and sentenced to 5 years in prison. He has almost completed his sentence and has come to see the career counselor as part of his prerelease program. He is very confused about his career options because of his drug conviction and time in prison. His wife has remained steadfast in her devotion to him and their relationship.

Robert starts by taking the Strong Interest Inventory and Myers–Briggs Type Indicator (MBTI), and his results indicate a RIASEC code of SAE (social, artistic, and enterprising) and an MBTI preference for ENFP (extroversion, intuition, feeling, and perceiving, with extroverted intuition as his dominant function).

What is Robert's main problem? How would you work with him?

Review Questions

1. What is the definition of career counseling?
2. What are the three historic periods in career intervention?
3. What are the six models of career counseling? Provide an example of each.
4. What are the 10 ideas that changed the career field?
5. What are the three intervention categories identified as special considerations in career counseling?

Further Resources

Brewer, J. M. (1942). *History of vocational guidance.* New York, NY: Harper.
Busacca, L. A., & Rehfuss, M. C. (Eds.). (2017). *Postmodern career counseling: A handbook of culture, context, and cases.* Alexandria, VA: American Counseling Association.
Maree, K. (Ed.). (2010). *Career counselling: Methods that work.* Cape Town, South Africa: Juta.
Ratts, M. J., Singh, A. A., Butler, S. K., Nassar-McMillan, S., & McCullough, J. R. (2016). *Multicultural and social justice counseling competencies: Practical applications in counseling.* Retrieved from the *Counseling Today* website: http://ct.counseling.org/2016/01/multicultural-and-social-justice-counseling-competencies-practical-applications-in-counseling/
Ratts, M. J., Singh, A. A., Nassar-McMillan, S., Butler, S. K., & McCullough, J. R. (2016). Multicultural and social justice counseling competencies: Guidelines for the counseling profession. *Journal of Multicultural Counseling and Development, 44,* 28–48. doi: 10.1002/jmcd.12035
Savickas, M. L. (2011). *Career counseling.* Washington, DC: American Psychological Association.
Strong, E. K. (1955). *Vocational interests eighteen years after college.* Minneapolis: University of Minnesota Press.

Thorndike, E. L. (1912). The permanence of interests and their relation to abilities. *Popular Science Monthly, 81,* 449–456.

References

American Counseling Association. (2004, July 26). *Definition of
professional counseling.* Retrieved from www.counseling.org/news/
updates/2004/07/26/definition-of-professional-counseling
American Counseling Association. (2010). *20/20: Consensus definition
of counseling.* Retrieved from www.counseling.org/knowledge-
center/20-20-a-vision-for-the-future-of-counseling/consensus-
definition-of-counseling
Arthur, M. B. (1994). The boundaryless career [Special issue]. *Journal
of Organizational Behavior, 15*(4).
Arthur, N., & Collins, S. (2011). Infusing culture in career counsel-
ing. *Journal of Employment Counseling, 47,* 147–149.
Aubrey, R. F. (1977). Historical development of guidance and
counseling and implications for the future. *Personnel & Guidance
Journal, 55,* 288–295.
Bernert, E. H. (1958). *America's children.* New York, NY: Wiley.
Brewer, J. M. (1926). *The vocational-guidance movement: Its problems
and possibilities.* New York, NY: MacMillan.
Brewer, J. M. (1942). *History of vocational guidance.* New York, NY: Harper.
Davis, H. V. (1969). *Frank Parsons: Prophet, innovator, counselor.*
Carbondale, IL: University of Southern Illinois Press.
Duarte, M. E. (2009). The psychology of life construction. *Journal
of Vocational Behavior, 75,* 259–266.
Hall, D. T. (1996). Protean careers of the 21st century. *Academy of
Management Executives, 10,* 8–16.
Hartung, P. J. (2010). Career assessment: Using scores and stories
in life designing. In K. Maree (Ed.), *Career counselling: Methods
that work* (pp. 1–10). Cape Town, South Africa: Juta.
Hartung, P. J., Vandiver, B. J., Leong, F. T. L., Pope, M., Niles, S.
G., & Farrow, B. (1998). Appraising cultural identity in career-
development assessment and counseling. *The Career Development
Quarterly, 46,* 276–293.
Hershenson, D. (2006). Frank Parsons's enablers: Pauline Agassiz
Shaw, Meyer Bloomfield, and Ralph Albertson. *The Career
Development Quarterly, 55,* 77–84.
Holland, J. L. (1997). *Making vocational choices: A theory of voca-
tional personalities and work environments* (3rd ed.). Odessa, FL:
Psychological Assessment Resources.
Hoyt, K. B. (1976, February 7). *Career education and work experience
education: Can we join together?* Speech given at the Western Associa-
tion of Cooperative and Work Experience Educators, Las Vegas, NV.
Retrieved from https://files.eric.ed.gov/fulltext/ED130043.pdf

Kalleberg, A. L. (2009). Precarious work, insecure workers: Employment relations in transition. *American Sociological Review, 74,* 1–22. doi:10.1177/000312240907400101

Kalleberg, A. L., Reskin, B F., & Hudson, K. (2000). Bad jobs in America: Standard and nonstandard employment relations and job quality in the United States. *American Sociological Review, 65,* 256–278.

Krumboltz, J. D. (2009). The happenstance learning theory. *Journal of Career Assessment, 17*(2), 135–154.

Leong, F. T. L., & Pope, M. (Eds.). (2002a). Challenges for career counseling in Asia [Special section]. *The Career Development Quarterly, 50,* 209–284.

Leong, F. T. L., & Pope, M. (2002b). Introduction to the special section on challenges for career counseling in Asia. *The Career Development Quarterly, 50,* 209–210.

Maree, J. G. (Ed.). (2007). *Shaping the story: A guide to facilitating narrative counselling.* Hatfield, South Africa: Van Schaik.

Mariani, M. (1999). Replace with a database: O*NET replaces the *Dictionary of Occupational Titles. Occupational Outlook Handbook, Spring,* 1–9.

Mitchell, L. K., & Krumboltz, J. D. (1996). Krumboltz's learning theory of career choice counseling. In D. Brown, L. Brooks, & Associates (Eds.), *Career choice and development* (3rd ed., pp. 233–276). San Francisco, CA: Jossey-Bass.

Niles, S. G., & Harris-Bowlsbey, J. E. (2017). *Career development interventions* (5th ed.). New York, NY: Pearson.

Parsons, F. (1909). *Choosing a vocation.* Boston, MA: Houghton Mifflin.

Pope, M. (1992). Bias in the interpretation of psychological tests. In S. Dworkin & F. Gutierrez (Eds.), *Counseling gay men and lesbians: Journey to the end of the rainbow* (pp. 277–291). Alexandria, VA: American Counseling Association.

Pope, M. (1995a). Career interventions for gay and lesbian clients: A synopsis of practice knowledge and research needs. *The Career Development Quarterly, 44,* 191–203.

Pope, M. (Ed.). (1995b). Gay/lesbian career development [Special section]. *The Career Development Quarterly, 44,* 146–203.

Pope, M. (1995c). Gay and lesbian career development: Introduction to the special section. *The Career Development Quarterly, 44,* 146–147.

Pope, M. (1995d). The "salad bowl" is big enough for us all: An argument for the inclusion of lesbians and gays in any definition of multiculturalism. *Journal of Counseling & Development, 73,* 301–304. doi:10.1002/j.1556-6676.1995.tb01752.x

Pope, M. (1996). Gay and lesbian career counseling: Special career counseling issues. *Journal of Gay and Lesbian Social Services, 4*(4), 91–105.

Pope, M. (1999). Applications of group career counseling techniques in Asian cultures. *Journal for Multicultural Counseling and Development, 27,* 18–30. doi:10.1002/j.2161-1912.1999. tb00209.x

Pope, M. (2000). A brief history of career counseling in the United States. *The Career Development Quarterly, 48,* 194–211.

Pope, M. (2003). Career counseling in the 21st century: Beyond cultural encapsulation. *The Career Development Quarterly, 51,* 54–60. doi:10.1002/j.2161-0045.2003.tb00627.x

Pope, M. (2007). Introduction to a new section: Global vision. *The Career Development Quarterly, 56,* 2–3.

Pope, M. (2008). Culturally appropriate counseling considerations with lesbian and gay clients. In P. B. Pedersen, J. G. Draguns, W. J. Lonner, & J. E. Trimble (Eds.), *Counseling across cultures* (6th ed., pp. 201–222). Thousand Oaks, CA: Sage.

Pope, M. (2009). Jesse Buttrick Davis (1871-1955): Pioneer of vocational guidance in the schools. *The Career Development Quarterly, 57,* 248–258.

Pope, M. (2010). Career counseling with diverse adults. In J. G. Ponterotto, J. M. Casas, L. A. Suzuki, & C. M. Alexander (Eds.), *Handbook of multicultural counseling* (3rd ed., pp. 731–744). Thousand Oaks, CA: Sage.

Pope, M. (2011). The career counseling with underserved populations model. *Journal of Employment Counseling, 48,* 153–156.

Pope, M. (2012). Embracing and harnessing diversity in the US workforce: What have we learned? *International Journal for Educational and Vocational Guidance, 12,* 17–30.

Pope, M. (2015a). Career intervention: From the industrial to the digital age. In P. J. Hartung, M. L. Savickas, & W. B. Walsh (Eds.), *APA handbook of career intervention* (pp. 3–19). Washington, DC: American Psychological Association.

Pope, M. (2015b). History and philosophy of the counseling profession. In V. F. Sangganjanavanich & C. A. Reynolds (Eds.), *Introduction to professional counseling* (pp. 25–46). Thousand Oaks, CA: Sage.

Pope, M., & Barret, B. (2002). Providing career counseling services to gay and lesbian clients. In S. G. Niles (Ed.), *Adult career development: Concepts, issues, and practices* (3rd ed., pp. 215–232). Tulsa, OK: National Career Development Association.

Pope, M., Barret, B., Szymanski, D. M., Chung, Y. B., McLean, R., Singaravelu, H., & Sanabria, S. (2004). Culturally appropriate career counseling with gay and lesbian clients. *The Career Development Quarterly, 53,* 158–177.

Pope, M., Briddick, W. C., & Wilson, F. (2013). The historical importance of social justice in the founding of the National Career Development Association. *The Career Development Quarterly, 61,* 368–373. doi:10.1002/j.2161-0045.2013.00063.x

Pope, M., Cheng, W. D., & Leong, F. T. L. (1998). The case of Chou: The inextricability of career to personal/social issues. *Journal of Career Development, 25,* 53–64. doi:10.1023/A:1022949929870

Pope, M., Musa, M., Singaravelu, H., Bringaze, T., & Russell, M. (2002). From colonialism to ultranationalism: History and development of career counseling in Malaysia. *The Career Development Quarterly, 50,* 264–276.

Pope, M., & Pangelinan, J. S. (2010). Using the ACA Advocacy Competencies in career counseling. In M. J. Ratts, R. L. Toporek, & J. A. Lewis (Eds.), *ACA Advocacy Competencies: A social justice framework for counselors* (pp. 209–224). Alexandria, VA: American Counseling Association.

Pope, M., Prince, J. P., & Mitchell, K. (2000). Responsible career counseling with lesbian and gay students. In D. A. Luzzo (Ed.), *Career counseling of college students: An empirical guide to strategies that work* (pp. 267–284). Washington, DC: American Psychological Association.

Pope, M., & Russell, M. (2001). A practitioner's view of career development policy in the United States. In B. Hiebert & L. Bezanson (Eds.), *Career development and public policy around the world* (pp. 1–13). Ottawa, Ontario, Canada: Canadian Career Development Foundation.

Pope, M., Singaravelu, H. D., Chang, A., Sullivan, C., & Murray, S. (2007). Counseling gay, lesbian, bisexual and questioning international students. In H. D. Singaravelu & M. Pope (Eds.). *A handbook for counseling international students in the United States* (pp. 57–86). Alexandria, VA: American Counseling Association.

Pope, M., & Sveinsdottir, M. (2005). Frank, we hardly knew ye: The very personal side of Frank Parsons. *Journal of Counseling & Development, 83,* 105–115.

Puertas, A., Cinamon, R. G., Neault, R., Pope, M., & Rossier, J. (2012). Career development for diverse and underserved populations. In J. Trusty (Ed.), *Bridging international perspectives of career development* (pp. 33–46). Broken Arrow, OK: National Career Development Association.

Savickas, M. L. (1997). Career adaptability: An integrative construct for life-span, life-space theory. *The Career Development Quarterly, 45*(3), 247–259.

Savickas, M. L. (1998). Career style assessment and counseling. In T. Sweeney (Ed.), *Adlerian counseling: A practitioner's approach* (4th ed., pp. 329–359). Philadelphia, PA: Accelerated Development.

Savickas, M. L. (2005). The theory and practice of career construction. In S. D. Brown & R. W. Lent (Eds.), *Career development and counseling: Putting theory and research to work* (pp. 42–70). New York, NY: Wiley.

Savickas, M. L. (2010). Foreword: Best practices in career intervention. In K. Maree (Ed.), *Career counselling: Methods that work* (pp. xi–xii). Cape Town, South Africa: Juta.

Savickas, M. L. (2011). *Career counseling.* Washington, DC: American Psychological Association.

Savickas, M. L. (2013). *Ten ideas that changed career development.* Broken Arrow, OK: National Career Development Association.

Savickas, M. L., Nota, L., Rossier, J., Dauwalder, J.-P., Duarte, M. E., Guichard, J., . . . van Vianen, A. E. M. (2009). Life designing: A paradigm for career construction in the 21st century. *Journal of Vocational Behavior, 75*(3), 239–250.

Strong, E. K. (1927). *Vocational interest blank.* Stanford, CA: Stanford University Press.

Strong, E. K. (1943). *Vocational interests of men and women.* Stanford, CA: Stanford University Press.

Super, D. E. (1951). Vocational adjustment: Implementing a self-concept. *Occupations, 30,* 88–92.

Super, D. E. (1953). A theory of vocational development. *American Psychologist, 8,* 185–190.

Super, D. E. (1954). Career patterns as a basis for vocational counseling. *Journal of Counseling Psychology, 1,* 2–20.

Super, D. E. (1957). *The psychology of careers: An introduction to vocational development.* New York, NY: Harper.

Super, D. E. (1990). A life-span, life-space approach to career development. In D. Brown, L. Brooks, & Associates (Eds.), *Career choice and development* (2nd ed., pp. 197–261). San Francisco, CA: Jossey-Bass.

Super, D. E., & Crites, J. O. (1962). *Appraising vocational fitness.* New York, NY: Harper & Row.

Super, D. E., Savickas, M. L., & Super, C. (1996). A life-span, life-space approach to careers. In D. Brown, L. Brooks, & Associates (Eds.), *Career choice and development* (3rd ed., pp. 121–178). San Francisco, CA: Jossey-Bass.

Tiedeman, D. V. (1961). Decisions and vocational development: A paradigm and implications. *Personnel & Guidance Journal, 40,* 15–20.

Whiteley, J. (1984). *Counseling psychology: A historical perspective.* Schenectady, NY: Character Research Press.

Zhang, W.-Y., Hu, X.-L, & Pope, M. (2002). The evolution of career guidance and counseling in the People's Republic of China. *The Career Development Quarterly, 50,* 226–236.

Chapter 7

Clinical Mental Health Counseling

Carla Adkison-Johnson

Learning Objectives

1. Understand how clinical mental health counseling is inextricably linked to better health and wellness.
2. Understand how the treatment of mental and emotional disorders has become multifaceted with the release of the *Diagnostic and Statistical Manual of Mental Disorders, Fifth Edition.*
3. Understand how integrated health care and collaborative care can be beneficial for clinical mental health counselors and clients.
4. Acquire the skills necessary to interact effectively with legal systems.
5. Understand why multicultural counseling in clinical mental health counseling is still an area of concern.

• • •

Clinical mental health counseling is one of the youngest programs in the counseling profession. This particular counseling specialization has a complex history and has been shaped and defined by counseling accreditation, licensure, and societal need (Bobby, 2013). However, it is a continuously evolving discipline that seeks to perfect its professional identity and influence public policy and client advocacy (Palmo, Weikel, & Borsas, 2011). Before a comprehensive discussion can take place regarding the roles, experiences, and trends in clinical mental counseling, it is important to reflect somewhat on its distinct past.

History

As a licensed professional clinical counselor who has been a counselor educator for more than 20 years, I have experienced the evolution of the clinical mental health counseling specialty as a counselor trainee, supervisor, and professor. In fact, it was when I entered my Council for Accreditation of Counseling and Related Educational Programs (CACREP)-accredited doctoral program in 1993 that I first heard of the internal split between community counseling and mental health counseling. Specifically, Bobby (2013), in her review of the evolution of specialties in CACREP standards, confirmed that the original draft of the 1988 CACREP Standards included only three sets of 48-credit-hour specialty standards: mental health counseling, school counseling, and student affairs. However, the American Mental Health Counselors Association (AMHCA) wanted a 60-credit-hour (minimum) mental health program (Pistole, 2001). Although there were arguments for and against the 60-hour requirement, the CACREP board agreed to offer a 60-credit-hour mental health counseling program along with a 48-credit-hour community counseling program (Bobby, 2013). Many writers (e.g., Cannon & Cooper, 2010; Gladding, 2003; Sweeney, 1992) who have documented the history of the counseling profession believe that this split between mental health and community counseling "affected the counseling profession's ability to view itself as one discipline" (Bobby, 2013, p. 36). It is taken almost 25 years for the two counselor preparation programs to reunite to form what we now identify as clinical mental health counseling.

Today, clinical mental health counseling is best exemplified by its focus on better health and wellness (Otis, 2011). That is, the diagnosis and treatment of mental and emotional conditions is necessary but not sufficient for optimal care. Our ultimate goal is to ensure that clients discover their best levels of overall mental health and well-being. The 2016 CACREP Standards (CACREP, 2016) have recently been implemented. The overall focus is on preparing clinical mental health counselors to address a wide variety of circumstances within a clinical setting.

The unique history, roles, and activities of clinical mental health counselors have been well documented in the counselor education literature. For example, Young and Cashwell (2017) and Field (2017) provided historical and comprehensive examinations of basic definitions, practices, and theoretical models identified with the clinical mental health counseling profession. This chapter speaks to the contextual and practice dimensions of this specialization with a focus on the roles and situations that counselors may face in future practice.

Contextual Dimensions of Clinical Mental Health Counseling

The passage of the Patient Protection and Affordable Care Act has made health care more available to everyone at an equitable price (Beronio, Po, Skopec, & Glied, 2013). The provision of additional coverage for mental health and addiction care has resulted in more people being eligible for mental health counseling (Beronio, Glied, & Frank, 2014; National Alliance on Mental Illness, 2013). As a result, the roles and settings of clinical mental health counselors have become more fluid. It is a popular notion that, for many patients, the doctor's office visit or routine checkup has become the entry point into the mental health system, especially for those patients who are economically disadvantaged (Kohn-Wood & Hooper, 2014). Consequently, both mental health counselors and primary care physicians are engaged in treating mental and emotional disorders with comorbid conditions (e.g., diabetes, high blood pressure).

Integrated Health Care and Collaborative Care

Integrated health care and *collaborative care* are terms often used to describe working relationships between mental health and primary care practitioners. *Integrated health care* is defined as the systematic coordination of general and behavioral health care (Alvarez, Marroquin, Sandoval, & Carlton, 2014). Collaborative care is one approach to integration in which the primary care provider and the mental health clinician work together to provide care and monitor a client's progress (Unutzer, Harbin, Schoenbaum, & Druss, 2013).

Collaborative care can be very beneficial for clients but is often a complex process. It occurs primarily in settings that serve individuals who are in need of a multitude of services (e.g., programming for children, clothes, food pantry) and do not have access to or are shut out of traditional counseling venues (e.g., private practice; Alvarez et al., 2014; Boyd-Franklin, Cleek, Wofsy, & Mundy, 2013; Kohn-Wood & Hooper, 2014). It is important to note that many clinicians in private practice and primary care physicians are reluctant to accept Medicaid as a form of payment or prefer not to deal with Medicaid clients at all. In fact, less than half of the physicians in 15 of the largest metropolitan cities accept Medicaid patients, which leaves this clientele, which is majority racially, culturally, and linguistically diverse, to obtain health care from federally qualified health centers (FQHCs; Alvarez et al., 2014; Merritt Hawkins, 2014). FQHCs

167

are federally funded nonprofit health centers or clinics that provide primary, preventive, dental, and mental health services regardless of the patient's ability to pay (HealthCare.gov, 2017).

The clinical mental health counseling literature has begun to address direct service delivery in collaboration with primary care professionals. For instance, the *Journal of Mental Health Counseling* dedicated a special issue to the benefits and process of clinical mental health counselors working in primary care settings. This issue highlighted the need to promote the transportability of counseling theories and culturally sensitive counseling practices associated with the counseling profession to primary care environments (Hooper, 2014).

As a counselor educator and clinical mental health counselor, I have experienced the complexity of engaging in the collaborative care process. An African American male counselor educator and professional counselor and I were recently asked to assist an agency with culturally responsive service delivery. Most of the clients struggled with mental health issues, such as adjustment disorder, posttraumatic stress disorder, or bipolar and anxiety disorders comorbid with high blood pressure, diabetes, and sleep apnea. Many of the clients at this agency did not have an ongoing primary care physician. Instead, they saw health care professionals at the local FQHC. We began to realize that to deliver optimal care to these clients, we needed to have an open line of communication with their primary care professional at the FQHC. Virtually all of the clients welcomed this proposed relationship. We assisted in helping clients recognize what their clinical symptoms were, when they became more pronounced, environments that aggravated these symptoms, and how they could articulate this information to their primary care physician. The physician often used this information to adjust medication levels so that patients could function normally with minimal side effects. When the physician willingly participated in the process, clients were pleased with their mental health care, and their relationships with their primary health care professionals improved (see Sidebar 7.1).

Treatment Planning and Clinical Mental Health Counseling

The treatment of mental and emotional disorders has become multifaceted with the release of the *Diagnostic and Statistical Manual of Mental Disorders, Fifth Edition*. For example, to address and monitor clinical symptoms related to a disorder, clinicians are encouraged to use new emerging assessment measures endorsed by the American Psychiatric Association to enhance the clinical decision-making process (American Psychiatric Association, 2014; see also King, 2015; Schmit & Balkin, 2014). These measures, along with the clinical interview, are purported to better identify symptoms or impairment and provide more precise information for evidence-based treatment

Sidebar 7.1 Thought Questions

According to the National Association of Community Health Centers (2010), the majority of states allow licensed professional counselors and licensed mental health counselors to be billable providers within the Medicaid system. Medicaid is a health insurance program that pays medical bills for eligible low-income individuals and families who cannot afford the cost of necessary medical services. States often pay these medical bills with federal and state tax dollars. Check with your state's Medicaid system to determine answers to the following questions:

1. What are the procedures to become a service provider once you become licensed to practice independently as a professional counselor?
2. Will you need to identify a subspecialty (e.g., substance abuse, counseling children and adolescents)?
3. Will you need post-master's supervision training?
4. How often will you need to participate in compliance and performance reviews?
5. How much payment will you receive per counseling session?
6. How many counseling sessions will be approved for each client?

• • •

planning. However, Schmit and Balkin (2014) advised that professional counselors proceed with caution when adopting these measures because of inconsistent validity evidence and a lack of alignment with diagnostic criteria.

Clinical mental health counselors are faced with addressing a multitude of issues with their clients while simultaneously reducing or alleviating client symptoms. According to Reichenberg and Seligman (2016), the overall goal of diagnosis and treatment planning is to make appropriate therapeutic decisions "that will help clients feel better about themselves and their lives, return to better functioning, and achieve their goals" (p. 2). To this end, treatment approaches often utilized in community mental health centers now embrace a more contextual, developmental perspective toward mental health treatment. Specifically, this framework is more humanistic in orientation, and the focus is on the client's strengths, dignity, and overall wellness. Although evidence-based therapeutic approaches such as cognitive and/or cognitive behavior therapies are also used to alleviate symptoms such as depression or anxiety, the use of these approaches alone is not sufficient to address human qualities such as self-determination and client agency, factors often associated with better health and overall well-being. Dr. Phillip D. Johnson, a counselor educator whose research has focused on the mental health and well-being of African Americans in general and African American men in particular, offers counselors a contextualized humanistic approach to clinical treatment. In a contextual humanistic perspective, the core principles of humanistic theory and the concrete realities of the African American experience are used to understand the psychological functioning of African Americans (Johnson, 2006, 2016). A concept embedded in this approach is the notion of somebodiness. Somebodiness is a multidimensional, culturally relevant idea that allows counselors to describe the actions of African Americans in general and African American men in particular in terms closer to their lived experience. African American men are considered to be human beings on a quest for a greater sense of worth, purpose, and community (Johnson, 2016). I asked Dr. Johnson how this distinct perspective would be useful for clinical mental health counselors addressing clinical symptoms with African American men. The following is his response:

It instructs counselors to first see African American men as human beings. Although this notion appears to be extremely simplistic, it is often not the case. African American men are time and again depicted in the media as unemployed, drug-addicted, animalistic predators who are armed and dangerous. These portrayals permeate the larger society, and counselors are not immune from adopting such dehumanizing views and attitudes.

If mental health practitioners hope to create an affirming therapeutic environment that supports African American men in their quest for a greater sense of somebodiness (worth, purpose, and community), they must be able to identify the internal and external barriers that block African American men from achieving their goals. To do so, they will need to listen and honor the stories and metaphors the men use to describe their aspirations and emotional pain. Often unmet needs in the area of self-worth, purpose, and community contribute to the anxiousness, frustration, anger, isolation, demoralization, and depression that many African American men experience.

The contextualized humanistic perspective helps mental health practitioners acknowledge the humanity of African American men by assuming that every African American man wants to experience himself as a person of infinite worth who is capable of making a meaningful contribution. It assumes that each man is on a quest for a greater sense of somebodiness within an anti-Black, White supremacist sociocultural context. No matter the outward appearance of a man, when this innermost desire is acknowledged and believed in patiently, counselors will help African American men achieve a greater sense of somebodiness. Thinking of African American men in this way can help counselors consider psychological functioning both apart from anti-Black racism and in response to it. As a result, mental health practitioners are better prepared to recognize and value the effective and constructive aspects of African American men's psychological functioning.

Treatment planning in clinical mental health counseling also includes an identification of addiction and substance abuse. As noted in the 2016 CACREP Standards (CACREP, 2016), clinical mental health counselors should be trained in understanding the etiology of addiction and co-occurring disorders and should recognize the potential for substance use disorders to mimic and/or co-occur with a variety of neurological, medical, and psychological disorders. Although recent studies of CACREP-accredited clinical mental health counseling programs have found that addiction content is being covered in required coursework (Iarussi, Perjessy, & Reed, 2012; T. K. Lee, 2014), little information is available on how this focus in clinical mental health counseling translates into actual practice in the field. To shed light on this issue, I asked Dr. Brian Russ, a White American doctoral-level professional counselor, for his thoughts on clinical mental health counseling and emerging issues in substance abuse treatment. Dr. Russ is an administrator at a rural community mental health center. He provides administrative and clinical oversight to the center's outpatient department, access center, medication clinic, and integrative behavioral health care team. He shared the following:

As the community support services director at a rural community mental health agency, an emerging issue I have seen is the rise of opioid substance dependence. The increase in those individuals that are addicted to prescription painkillers and heroin is upsetting. Even worse, we have seen an alarming amount of overdoses in the last year, and I imagine there are even more that we never hear about or that are not documented as an overdose due to the stigma attached to drug use.

The genesis of this problem lies in the increased pressure on medical doctors to manage pain over the past 15 years. This has led to overprescribing by physicians, allowing for patients to have access to large quantities of powerful opioid painkillers. What we are seeing now is prescribers being more conservative with their painkiller prescribing, which has led to a quick decrease in supply. Now those with opioid dependence are turning to the streets to get their drugs, and since painkillers are much more difficult to find and more expensive, people are turning to heroin. Heroin is much more dangerous, especially because of the potential for it to be laced with other drugs like fentanyl, a powerful synthetic opioid. This combination of factors has led to our current epidemic.

In order for clinical mental health counselors to be prepared to address this serious concern, they need to understand the issue and be adequately trained to work with clients with opioid dependence. First, counselors need to confront their own bias about those with opioid dependence. Opioid dependence is not about getting high; it is about avoiding getting sick. Opioid withdrawal is especially awful, and individuals continue to use simply to avoid detoxification. Second, counselors need to be able to recognize the signs and risk factors of opioid dependence. For example, a client who has access to painkillers following a medical procedure may be at increased risk, whereas frequent changes in prescribers may be a sign of opioid dependence. Third, counselors should be trained in addictions, with a special emphasis on those practices that have a strong evidence base, like motivational interviewing. Finally, counselors should be advocates in their communities to increase awareness and develop the necessary treatment options, like medication-assisted treatment programs. Medication-assisted treatment programs address opioid dependence by providing counseling and opioid maintenance medications like methadone and buprenorphine, but unfortunately they are still not readily available, especially in rural areas.

Practice Dimensions of Clinical Mental Health Counseling

A critical component of the practice dimension of clinical mental health counseling is practicum, internship, and postgraduate clinical experiences. For counselors-in-training, these experiences provide "for the application of theory and the development of counseling skills under supervision" (CACREP, 2016, "Section 3: Professional Practice," para. 1). However, clinical mental health counselors in private practice or agency settings must rely on continuing education opportunities such as attending state, regional, or national counseling conferences to update their skills and knowledge. Because counselor competence has a direct influence on the quality of mental health services received by clients, many efforts have been made by organizations such as AMHCA, the American Counseling Association (ACA), and CACREP to identify specific clinical mental health counseling skills in diagnosis and treatment planning. For example, skills training in psychopharmacology and the use of psychological assessments for treatment planning is now required for CACREP-accredited clinical mental health counseling programs; yet there is virtually no information on how licensed counselors who graduated prior to the implementation of the 2009 CACREP Standards (CACREP, 2009) acquire or maintain these important skills. This lack of normative data makes it difficult to determine what baseline competencies are necessary for clinical mental health counselors to establish proficiency in diagnostic testing and interpretation.

This is also the case for multicultural counseling skills training. For instance, the current CACREP standards (CACREP, 2016) indicate that programs should provide opportunities for students to counsel clients who represent the ethnic and demographic diversity of their community. However, even with this explicit CACREP requirement, it is likely that a large majority of professional counselors have never received hands-on multicultural counseling training and/or supervision (e.g., direct service delivery with clients of color or lesbian, gay, bisexual, and transgender populations). Maybe you have experienced embarrassment and/or frustration when attempting to provide responsive counseling to clients from underrepresented populations. This is a disturbing situation in counselor education, given the current racial tension in U.S. society as evidenced by continual news reports of unarmed African Americans being shot by the police; immigration reform backlash; and the undoing of legislation that supports lesbian, gay, bisexual, and transgender populations. Moreover, C. C. Lee's (2017) white paper prepared for the Association for Multicultural Counseling and Development underscored the fact that there continue to be serious challenges to the health and well-being of African Americans across the life span.

I thought it would be beneficial for you to hear the perspective of an African American professional clinical counselor who maintains a private practice that serves the needs of a diverse clientele. Dr. Shantel Thomas is president and chief executive officer of A Sound Mind Counseling Service, which serves the Greater Cincinnati, Ohio, area. Her private practice provides a full range of mental health services, including individual, group, and family counseling and addictions counseling. Her clinical staff, which is predominantly African American, consists of 13 clinicians (seven full-time and six part-time clinicians), the majority licensed and trained as professional clinical counselors. It is worth noting that Dr. Thomas's practice is on 26 insurance panels, including Blue Cross/Blue Shield, TRICARE, UnitedHealthcare, and Cigna. She also provides services to clients on Medicaid and Medicare. When asked to reflect on her experience building a practice that serves the needs of a diverse community, Dr. Thomas said the following:

> I started my private practice 16 years ago. I was the only clinician. My biggest obstacle was trying get helpful information from other professional counselors in the area. No one wanted to help me. I had to figure it out myself. I began calling insurance companies and I was eventually added to insurance panels. I slowly began to add more clinicians to my practice as my clientele grew. I wanted counselors who had a sincere interest in working with a diverse client population. I have hired White American clinical counselors in the past, but they eventually left due to feeling uncomfortable with working in a predominantly African American setting. It seems that they struggled with translating what they learned in counseling programs to working with actual people of color. Community engagement is very important to gain and maintain credibility. I offer city-wide forums and workshops on mental health awareness. Trauma, depression, and anxiety has been our main focus in response to recent police brutality and increasing suicide rates among our African American male youth. Counselors need to be trained to be responsive to the current needs of the community.

Interfacing With Legal and Child Welfare Systems

A by-product of working in mental health agencies or other public institutions is counseling clients who have been ordered by the court or Child Protective Services (CPS) to undergo individual, group, or family counseling. This is an important consideration given the power of the court and CPS to remove children from their home or to incarcerate individuals (Adkison-Johnson, Terpstra, Burgos, & Payne, 2016). Clinical mental health counselors can be influential in empowering their mandatory counseling clients to have intentional engagement with CPS and the court (Boyd-Franklin et al., 2013; Boyd-Franklin & Shenouda, 1990). Assisting clients with clearly articulating their needs and wants concerning their children to court officials can aid in establishing a trusting, therapeutic relationship. It is also important that counselors make a clear distinction between monitoring for the court or CPS and their own treatment role with the client and/or family (Boyd-Franklin & Shenouda, 1990). This is where client advocacy can be most effective. For example, counselors will often be called to report back to CPS or the court regarding their client's progress in therapy. It is important for counselors to be honest, reflective, and culturally knowledgeable in their expert opinion regarding their client's inner life as well as their observations in therapy.

Clinical mental health counselors are also called on to provide testimony as expert witnesses in the legal arena. An expert witness is an individual with comprehensive knowledge and experience in a specific field who is reasonably certain about the issues or questions concerning a case at hand (Brodsky, 2013; Faust & Ziskin, 1988). The expert testimony of clinicians can change the lives of adults and children. Based on the expert opinion of a clinician, a parent could lose custody of a child or an individual could be sent to or back to prison. The revised *AMHCA Code of Ethics* (AMHCA, 2015) includes specific standards on responding to subpoenas and offering expert testimony. These standards require mental health counselors to have appropriate knowledge and competence in performing court-related activities.

Over the past 10 years, I have provided expert testimony as a researcher and as a clinical mental health counselor. As a counselor educator/researcher, I have provided expert testimony in distinguishing for the court the difference between child discipline and child abuse. Most of these court cases involved African American mothers who used physical discipline as a child-rearing technique.

How a parent disciplines is one of the court's most important considerations in determining custody and/or placement. In most cases, the court looks to counselors to assist the court, caseworkers, and attorneys in that effort. In child custody cases, counselors may conduct parenting evaluations in which they assess the parenting abilities of the mother and father and advise all parties as to which parent does the better job (Adkison-Johnson et al., 2016).

As an expert witness, I had to present what I knew in terms of research and counseling expertise and define for the court who I was as a counseling professional (Brodsky, 2013). That is, I had to clearly articulate my role and training as a clinical mental health counselor and distinguish how counselor education is different from other helping professions. Most important, I also had to prove that my expertise could help the judge or jury reach a more valid conclusion than would be possible without my testimony (Faust & Ziskin, 1988). I believe that having a strong clinical mental health counseling identity (e.g., having master's and doctoral degrees in counselor education, being a licensed professional clinical counselor for more than 20 years) and an extensive publication record that focused on counselor training and child discipline reinforced my qualification to provide courtroom testimony. The following links will be helpful in making sure you are maintaining the highest level of ethical standards as you interface with the legal and child welfare systems:

ACA Code of Ethics
 www.counseling.org/docs/ethics/2014-aca-code-of-ethics.
 pdf?sfvrsn=4
AMHCA Code of Ethics
 www.amhca.org/HigherLogic/System/DownloadDocument
 File.ashx?DocumentFileKey=d4e10fcb-2f3c-c701-aa1d-
 5d0f53b8bc14&forceDialog=0
Multicultural and Social Justice Counseling Competencies
 https://www.counseling.org/docs/default-source/competencies/
 multicultural-and-social-justice-counseling-competencies.
 pdf?sfvrsn=20

Special Considerations in Clinical Mental Health: Emergent Issues

The primary focus of this chapter has been to reflect on various dimensions of clinical mental health counseling considering the implementation of the 2016 CACREP Standards (CACREP, 2016). It is important to note, however, that some current and emerging issues should be explored.

For example, now that all 50 states have professional licensure for counselors and the profession of mental health counseling is recognized by many insurance companies and managed care organizations, supervision competence has become an essential component of responsive service delivery. It is important to note, however, that most supervisors and even some counselor educators received their clinical training prior to the advent of the clinical mental health counseling specialization, and some may not have received specific coursework in the treatment of mental and emotional disorders. Although several states require continuing education for clinical supervisors, this may not be sufficient or the best way to monitor how supervisors are updating their skills (e.g., use of the *Diagnostic and Statistical Manual of Mental Disorders,*

Fifth Edition, and International Classification of Diseases–10, changes in managed care). One way to ensure that all supervisors are current with changes and trends in the mental health field is for state counseling boards to mandate annual or biannual training related to the prevention, diagnosis, and treatment of mental and emotional disorders. It is also noteworthy that the use of assessment instruments by clinical mental health counselors to evaluate mental and emotional conditions continues to be a litigious issue. For example, the American Psychological Association has been supporting legal interventions to restrict the use of tests, mainly at the C qualification level (tests that require a high level of expertise in test interpretation), to licensed psychologists (Naugle, 2009; Peterson, Lomas, Neukrug, & Bonner, 2014). However, Pearson Clinical Assessments (2016, "Qualification Level C") stated that Level C tests can be purchased by individuals with:

1. A doctorate degree in psychology, education, or closely related field with formal training in the ethical administration, scoring, and interpretation of clinical assessments related to the intended use of the assessment. OR
2. Licensure or certification to practice in your state in a field related to the purchase. OR
3. Certification by or full active membership in a professional organization . . . that requires training and experience in the relevant area of assessment.

Although the American Psychological Association may be seeking to restrict the use of psychological tests, ACA stands firm in its position that professional counselors have the right to administer projective tests, intelligence tests, and clinical diagnostic tests provided they have the appropriate training and experience (ACA, 2003; Peterson et al., 2014). The use of personality measures and other diagnostic assessments is fundamental to the role and duties of clinical mental health counselors. In fact, Naugle (2009) argued that "counselors who lose the right to assessment will lose the ability to diagnose, and they will have a valuable tool of treatment eliminated from their access" (p. 42). The Fair Access Coalition on Testing (FACT), led by Attorney David Bergman, has been instrumental in championing this important responsibility for professional counselors. FACT (whose office is located in the National Board for Certified Counselors headquarters) is a multidisciplinary, nonprofit coalition that advocates for consumer access to psychological and behavioral assessments performed by qualified health and education professionals. It also monitors state and national legislation and regulatory actions to ensure that counselors and other qualified professionals are permitted to administer and interpret psychological instruments. For instance, FACT was instrumental in blocking the Indiana State Board of Psychology from establishing and maintaining a restricted test list that would have prohibited mental health counselors from using several hundred psychological assessments (D. Bergman, personal communication, October 28, 2016; see also Naugle, 2009). In 2015, FACT also succeeded in convincing the Kentucky Board of Examiners in Psychology to withdraw restricting testing regulations.

As a counselor educator who is in a department with both counseling psychology and counselor education master's and doctoral programs, I recently had to consult with FACT concerning an assessment turf issue in our department. Specifically, the counseling psychology faculty attempted to prohibit the counselor education unit from teaching master's students how to administer (and interpret) Level C assessments. FACT responded immediately to my request for assistance and provided valuable information that helped our program maintain its ability to prepare master's students to administer and interpret advanced appraisal measures.

Clearly, clinical mental health counselors need to become more vigilant in their advocacy efforts. You can advocate for assessment use by working through your state counseling association to remove barriers and establish regulatory practices that promote clinical mental health counselors' use of diagnostic measures. ACA's Government Affairs Office (https://www.counseling.org/government-affairs/public-policy) can provide valuable information to support your legislative efforts.

Another emerging issue is the counseling profession's response to the numerous murders of African American men by police officers and the hateful rhetoric targeted at Latino and Middle Eastern immigrant families and children. With the United States becoming increasingly diverse, it is projected that racial tensions will only get worse. What type of techniques are clinical mental health counselors using to assist clients in addressing these oppressive and discriminatory life situations? Basic counseling skills of listening to and understanding a client's culture may be insufficient to alleviate the hurt, pain, and other clinical symptoms that can arise from having to endure daily attacks on one's humanity (Hardy & Laszloffy, 2005; Johnson, 2016). In fact, culturally competent clinical mental health counseling alone may not lead to responsive service delivery with racially oppressed client populations. AMHCA and ACA at the state regional and national levels must anticipate and clearly articulate to the public how the counseling profession will assist in dismantling institutional racism in society and in the mental health system in particular.

It is also important to mention that advocacy in clinical mental health counseling is inextricably linked to responsiveness to a client's basic needs. The CACREP standards mandate that clinical mental health counselors advocate for persons with mental health issues (CACREP, 2016). As counselors, we know firsthand the barriers and challenges that many of our clients face just when it comes to participating in the counseling process. Some of my own clients struggled with transportation to counseling sessions because they had no money for bus fare or the mental health agency was not on the bus line. Other clients, particularly families, would miss counseling appointments because they did not have access to appropriate child care. Responsive advocacy means attending to your client's true needs. This is the starting point from which we promote respect and human dignity for the people we serve.

Chapter Summary

How we think about the mental and emotional needs of our clients is how we respond to them. This chapter reviewed the roles, experiences, and trends in clinical mental health counseling. A brief history was given, as were contextual and practice dimensions that are unique to this specialization. A clinical mental health counselor will find that he or she has many of the necessary skills to meet the basic therapeutic needs of most clients but will need additional multicultural counseling and assessment preparation to be truly effective and competent.

Learning Activities

1. Visit an agency/organization in your community whose primary clients are racial minority, rural, and/or economically disadvantaged populations with the purpose of ascertaining information regarding diagnosis and treatment planning. In your contact with the treatment staff, explore the following: (a) What are some of the mental health issues often presented by these clients? (b) What assessment tools/measures are used to evaluate mental and emotional conditions? (c) What types of treatment plans or theoretical perspectives are used with clients with multiple issues? How is clinical work with racial minority clients different from that with White clients? (d) Are the mental health counselors specially trained in working with the mental health problems or challenges of racial minority and rural populations? How often is the clinical staff engaged in culturally responsive training? What aspects of culturally responsive training affect diagnosing, treatment planning, and the selection of evidence-based interventions? Finally, write a 5-page paper comparing the findings from your agency visit with current multicultural competencies endorsed by the Association for Multicultural Counseling and Development, the *ACA Code of Ethics* (ACA, 2014), and the *AMHCA Code of Ethics* (AMHCA, 2015).
2. Interview a licensed clinical mental health counselor who has court-mandated clients on his or her caseload. Explore the following questions: (a) What are some of the mental health issues often presented by these clients? (b) How often is the counselor called on to provide

information to the court regarding a client's progress in therapy? (c) How does the counselor prepare for courtroom testimony or develop client summaries/evaluations required by the court?

3. Juan and Inez Garcia sought counseling after their 15-year-old daughter Sonya went to visit a boy that she "liked" when she was told to come straight home from school. Both parents had become frustrated with their daughter's "attitude" problem over the past 6 months. Last week, Inez was investigated by CPS and required to see a counselor because Sonya told the school counselor that her mother had slapped her when she had told her mother, "I don't have to listen to you." Inez, who is African American, is a registered nurse and is being treated by her primary care physician for anxiety due to ongoing racism on her job. Juan, who is Mexican American, was recently downsized from his job as a middle-management banker. During the counseling session, Abbey, a White American female counselor, informed Juan and Inez that they should consider having their daughter live with her grandparents because Inez has a problem with anxiety and Juan does not appear to be able to control Inez's actions. The counselor also shared with the parents that, according to counseling research, African American and Latino parents abuse their children more than other parents, and therefore Juan and Inez would be at risk for harming Sonya again. Abbey submitted her views and conclusions to the assigned caseworker so that CPS could proceed with removing the child. She also recommended that Juan and Inez complete parenting and anger management classes. Abbey agreed to continue to work with Inez on her anxiety issues.

   a. Did the clinical mental health counselor handle this session in an appropriate manner?

   b. Prepare a response to this counseling situation that addresses the following: (a) an awareness of relevant ethical principles (e.g., autonomy, beneficence, nonmaleficence, justice, fidelity, veracity) involved in the case; (b) your knowledge and skill in the application of mental health counseling competencies that reflect an appreciation for the complexity of the case; (c) your professional role in the relationship between you and other human service providers; and (d) relevant strategies for collaboration and communication with other providers or agencies in addressing the client's concerns and/or situation.

4. Review the licensed professional clinical counseling/mental health counseling law in your state. What is the scope of practice for counselors concerning the use of Level C assessments? If there are restrictions for counselors, draft a letter in support of professional counselors using Level C assessments to evaluate the mental and emotional conditions of their clients. Submit this letter to your state counselor licensing board.

Review Questions

1. How did clinical mental counseling come into existence in the counselor education profession?
2. What is collaborative care? What role does the clinical mental health counselor have in this process/relationship?
3. Why is the use of evidence-based interventions not enough to promote optimal mental health in clients in general and in African American men in particular?
4. What is the cause for concern in rural communities regarding substance abuse?
5. What ethical concerns should clinical mental health counselors attend to when interfacing with legal and child welfare systems?
6. Explain a emergent issue in the clinical mental health counseling profession.

Further Resources

Articles

Ratts, M. J., Singh, A. A., Butler, S. K., Nassar-McMillan, S., & McCullough, J. R. (2016). *Multicultural and social justice counseling competencies: Practical applications in counseling.* Retrieved from http://ct.counseling.org/2016/01/multicultural-and-social-justice-counseling-competencies-practical-applications-in-counseling/

Ratts, M. J., Singh, A. A., Nassar-McMillan, S., Butler, S. K., & McCullough, J. R. (2016). Multicultural and social justice counseling competencies: Guidelines for the counseling profession. *Journal of Multicultural Counseling and Development, 44,* 28–48. Retrieved from http://onlinelibrary.wiley.com/doi/10.1002/jmcd.12035/full

Vogel, M. E., Malcore, S. A., Illes, R. A., & Kirkpatrick, H. A. (2014). Integrated primary care: Why you should care and how to get started. *Journal of Mental Health Counseling, 36,* 130–144.

Ward, E. (2005). Keeping it real: A grounded theory study of African American clients engaging in counseling at a community mental health agency. *Journal of Counseling Psychology, 52,* 471–481.

Websites

Fair Access Coalition on Testing (www.fairaccess.org)

Multicultural and Social Justice Counseling Competencies: Practical Applications in Counseling (http://ct.counseling.org/2016/01/multicultural-and-social-justice-counseling-competencies-practical-applications-in-counseling/)

Seeing Mental Illness as Real and Treatable (www.futureofpersonalhealth.com/advocacy/seeing-mental-illness-as-real-and-treatable)

References

Adkison-Johnson, C., Terpstra, J., Burgos, J., & Payne, D. (2016). African American child discipline: Differences between mothers and fathers. *Family Court Review, 54*(2), 203–220.

Alvarez, K., Marroquin, Y. A., Sandoval, L., & Carlton, C. I. (2014). Integrated health care best practices and culturally and linguistically competent care: Practitioner perspectives. *Journal of Mental Health Counseling, 36,* 99–114.

American Counseling Association. (2003). *Standards for qualifications of test users.* Alexandria, VA: Author.

American Counseling Association. (2014). *ACA code of ethics.* Alexandria, VA: Author.

American Mental Health Counselors Association. (2015). *AMHCA code of ethics.* Retrieved from www.amhca.org/HigherLogic/System/DownloadDocumentFile.ashx?DocumentFileKey=d4e10fcb-2f3c-c701-aa1d-5d0f53b8bc14&forceDialog=0

American Psychiatric Association. (2014). *Online assessment measures.* Retrieved from https://www.psychiatry.org/psychiatrists/practice/dsm/educational-resources/assessment-measures

Beronio, K., Glied, S., & Frank, R. (2014). How the Affordable Care Act and Mental Health Parity and Addiction Equity Act greatly expand coverage of behavioral health care. *Journal of Behavioral Health Services & Research, 41,* 410–428.

Beronio, K., Po, R., Skopec, L., & Glied, S. (2013, February 20). *Affordable Care Act expands mental health and substance use disorder benefits and federal parity protections for 62 million Americans.* Retrieved from https://aspe.hhs.gov/report/affordable-care-act-expands-mental-health-and-substance-use-disorder-benefits-and-federal-parity-protections-62-million-americans

Bobby, C. (2013). The evolution of specialties in the CACREP standards: CACREP's role in unifying the profession. *Journal of Counseling & Development, 91,* 35–43.

Boyd-Franklin, N., Cleek, E. N., Wofsy, M., & Mundy, B. (2013). *Therapy in the real world: Effective treatments for challenging problems.* New York, NY: Guilford Press.

Boyd-Franklin, N., & Shenouda, N. (1990). A multisystems approach to the treatment of a Black, inner-city family with a schizophrenic mother. *American Journal of Orthopsychiatry, 60*(2), 186–195.

Brodsky, S. (2013). *Testifying in court: Guidelines and maxims for the expert witness.* Washington, DC: American Psychological Association.

Cannon, E., & Cooper, J. (2010). Clinical mental health counseling: A national survey of counselor educators. *Journal of Mental Health Counseling, 32,* 236–246.

Council for Accreditation of Counseling and Related Educational Programs. (2009). *CACREP accreditation standards and procedures manual and application.* Alexandria, VA: Author.

Council for Accreditation of Counseling and Related Educational Programs. (2016). *2016 CACREP standards.* Retrieved from www.cacrep.org/for-programs/2016-cacrep-standards/

Faust, D., & Ziskin, J. (1988, July 1). The expert witness in psychology and psychiatry. *Science, 241,* 31–35.

Field, T. A. (2017). Clinical mental health counseling: A 40-year retrospective. *Journal of Mental Health Counseling, 39,* 1–11.

Gladding, S. (2003). *Community and agency counseling.* Upper Saddle River, NJ: Merrill Prentice Hall.

Hardy, K. V., & Laszloffy, T. A. (2005). *Teens who hurt: Clinical interventions to break the cycle of adolescent violence.* New York, NY: Guilford Press.

HealthCare.gov. (2017). *Federally qualified health center (FQHC).* Retrieved from https://www.healthcare.gov/glossary/federally-qualified-health-center-FQHC/

Hooper, L. (Ed.). (2014). Mental health services in primary care: Implications for clinical mental health counselors and other mental health provider [Special issue]. *Journal of Mental Health Counseling, 36.*

Iarussi, M. M., Perjessy, C. C., & Reed, S. W. (2012). Addition-specific CACREP standards in clinical mental health counseling programs: How are they met? *Journal of Addictions & Offender Counseling, 34,* 99–113.

Johnson, P. D. (2006). Counseling African American men: A contextualized humanistic perspective. *Counseling and Values, 50,* 187–196. doi:10.1002/j.2161-007X.2006.tb00055.x

Johnson, P. D. (2016). Somebodiness and its meaning to African American men. *Journal of Counseling & Development, 94,* 333–344.

King, J. H. (2015). *Clinical application of the* DSM-5 *in private counseling practice.* Retrieved from http://tpcjournal.nbcc.org/clinical-application-of-the-dsm-5-in-private-counseling-practice/

Kohn-Wood, L. P., & Hooper, L. M. (2014). Cultural competency, culturally tailored care, and the primary care setting: Possible solutions to reduce racial/ethnic disparities in mental health care. *Journal of Mental Health Counseling, 36,* 173–188.

Lee, C. C. (2017). *African Americans 2020: A wellness profile.* Alexandria, VA: Association for Multicultural Counseling and Development.

Lee, T. K. (2014). Addition education and training for counselors: A qualitative study of five experts. *Journal of Additions & Offender Counseling, 35,* 67–80.

Merritt Hawkins. (2014). *Physicians appointment wait times and Medicaid and Medicare acceptance rates.* Retrieved from www.merritthawkins.com/uploadedFiles/MerrittHawkings/Surveys/mha2014waitsurvPDF.pdf

National Alliance on Mental Illness. (2013, May). *Medicaid expansion and mental health care*. Retrieved from https://www.nami.org/getattachment/About-NAMI/Publications/Reports/2013MedicaidReport.pdf

National Association of Community Health Centers. (2010). *Health center reimbursement for behavioral health services in Medicaid*. Retrieved from www.nachc.org/wp-content/uploads/2015/11/MentalHealthSA_PPSReport-Final-Nov-2010.pdf

Naugle, K. A. (2009). Counseling and testing: What counselors need to know about state laws on assessment and testing. *Measurement and Evaluation in Counseling and Development, 42,* 31–45.

Otis, G. (2011). As clinical mental health counselors, where lies our future? *The Advocate, 34*(7), 3.

Palmo, A. J., Weikel, W. J., & Borsas, D. P. (2011). *Foundations of clinical mental health*. Springfield, IL: Charles C Thomas.

Pearson Clinical Assessments. (2016). *Qualifications policy*. Retrieved from www.pearsonclinical.com/psychology/qualifications.html

Peterson, C. H., Lomas, G. I., Neukrug, E. S., & Bonner, M. W. (2014). Assessment use by counselors in the United States: Implications for policy and practice. *Journal of Counseling & Development, 92,* 90–98.

Pistole, M. C. (2001). *Mental health counseling: Identity and distinctiveness*. Retrieved from https://www.counseling.org/resources/library/ERIC%20Digests/2001-09.pdf

Reichenberg, L., & Seligman, L. (2016). *Selecting effective treatments: A comprehensive, systemic guide to treating mental disorders*. New York, NY: Wiley.

Schmit, E. L., & Balkin, R. S. (2014). *Evaluating emerging measures in the* DSM-5 *for counseling practice*. Retrieved from http://tpc-journal.nbcc.org/evaluating-emerging-measures-in-the-dsm-5-for-counseling-practice/

Sweeney, T. J. (1992). CACREP: Precursors, promises, and prospects. *Journal of Counseling & Development, 70,* 667–672.

Unutzer, J., Harbin, H., Schoenbaum, M., & Druss, B. (2013). *The collaborative care model: An approach for integrating physical and mental health care in Medicaid health homes*. Retrieved from the Health Home Information Resource Center website: https://www.medicaid.gov/state-resource-center/medicaid-state-technical-assistance/health-homes-technical-assistance/downloads/hh-irc-collaborative-5-13.pdf

Young, J. S., & Cashwell, C. S. (2017). *Clinical mental health counseling: Elements of effective practice*. Thousand Oaks, CA: Sage.

Chapter 8

Rehabilitation Counseling

*Michael J. Leahy, Vilia M. Tarvydas, Annemarie Connor,
and Trenton Landon*

Learning Objectives

1. Explain the philosophy of rehabilitation counseling as it pertains to individuals with disabilities.
2. Explain empirically validated knowledge and skill requirements for professional practice.
3. Compare and contrast the practice of rehabilitation counseling with other counseling specialties.
4. Elaborate on both traditional and emergent practice settings specific to rehabilitation counseling.
5. Recognize professional associations affiliated with the practice of rehabilitation counseling.

• • •

Students considering a career in rehabilitation counseling, or any other counseling specialization, will be interested to know that although all counseling specialties rely on the practical application of counseling theories and techniques, the profession emerged from multiple specializations serving targeted populations (Hosie, 1995; Leahy,

Rak, & Zanskas, 2016; Myers, 1995; Sweeney, 1995). Rehabilitation counseling is one of these specialties and has even been termed a *super specialty.* "Rather than the profession of counseling evolving first, followed by a logical sequence of specialization of practice (as evident in the medical and legal professions), the specialty areas [of counseling] actually emerged first" (Leahy et al., 2016, p. 3), with one of those specific specializations being rehabilitation counseling. Jane Myers, a past president of the American Counseling Association and esteemed leader in the profession of counseling, characterized rehabilitation counseling as a specialization that:

> stands at the forefront in creating sustained positive change in the holistic wellbeing of persons with disabilities . . . the heart of the field lies in a desire to empower clients to be effective advocates and change agents for themselves, their families, their communities, and society. (Myers, 2012, pp. xv–xvi)

Currently, it is estimated that more than 120,000 rehabilitation counselors practice in the United States (U.S. Department of Labor, 2015), which makes the profession one of the most prevalent and longstanding counseling specializations. As specialists in providing counseling services for persons with disabilities, rehabilitation counselors promote adaptation, achievement, social justice, and improved quality of life for clients with an incredibly diverse range of developmental, congenital, and acquired disabilities, including psychiatric, neurological, muscular, cognitive, sensory, behavioral, systemic, orthopedic, and age-related conditions.

This chapter provides a historical perspective on the development and professionalization of rehabilitation counseling practice, discusses populations served through the rehabilitation process, describes some of the contemporary and emerging practice settings of the rehabilitation counselor, reviews the empirically validated knowledge and skill requirements used to regulate the professional practice of rehabilitation counseling, and introduces the professional associations that provide rehabilitation counselors with ongoing professional development and advocacy.

The History and Development of Rehabilitation Counseling

Among the specialty areas that emerged in direct response to human needs (Leahy et al., 2016), rehabilitation counseling has a long and storied history as one of the first specialty areas around which the larger field of counseling later coalesced. "Rehabilitation counselors play a central role in the extra-medical phase of the rehabilitation process, for individuals with both acquired and congenital disabilities" (Leahy, 2012, p. 193). However, like many other specialty areas at their inception, rehabilitation counseling had limited preservice education, lacked a defined code of ethics and regulatory oversight by accreditation and certification bodies, was limited in its scope of practice, and lacked empirical research in terms of the role and function of rehabilitation counselors as well as those practices that could be identified as evidence based (Capuzzi & Stauffer, 2016; Leahy et al., 2016).

Early Years of Services

Persons with disabilities were historically underserved, misunderstood, and often brushed to the fringes of society. Eugenics and inhumane practices, such as placing individuals with mental illness or intellectual disabilities in institutions, were commonplace (Wright, 1980). There were no established governmental organizations designed to serve persons with disabilities, and this led many to beg for daily sustenance or rely on alms. Charitable organizations and churches often took the lead in providing care for persons with disabilities. Some schools for disability-specific populations, such as the first school for deaf individuals (later, Gallaudet University), were organized and even had governmental funding. However, support for such programs waxed and waned with the political climate of the day. Service providers were typically volunteers and had little or no specialized training (Wright, 1980).

Beginning in 1908 with the first formal career counseling center in Boston, Frank Parsons began assisting young people in the consideration and selection of vocational paths and other career choices (Hartung & Blustein, 2002; Leahy et al., 2016). A contemporary of Parsons was Clifford Beers, who helped expose deplorable conditions in mental institutions of the day. Having been an inpatient, Beers was able to give a personal perspective on the inhumane treatment within institutional environments (Hartung & Blustein, 2002; Leahy et al., 2016). Parsons's early career development model along with Beers's advocacy for persons with disabilities helped to lay the foundation of career development and rights recognition for persons with disabilities.

Progress Toward Professionalization

Based on the recognition that difficulties arise with societal and work-related reintegration when an individual with a disability is neglected (Wright, 1980), and also stemming from the growing numbers of returning veterans from World War I, the passage of the 1918 Veterans Rehabilitation Act mandated vocational training for veterans injured in service to their country. This legislation was passed with the hope of helping veterans more fully reintegrate into community and work settings. The subsequent passage of the 1920 Civilian Rehabilitation Act (Smith-Fess Act of 1920, PL 67-236) extended this same vocational education training to civilian populations with physical disabilities. The passage of the Social Security Act of 1935 (PL 74-271), which established vocational rehabilitation as a permanent program, and the Vocational Rehabilitation Act Amendments of 1943 (PL 113) expanded service provision to previously excluded disability groups (e.g., those with mental illness or intellectual disabilities). This legislation paved the way for the formalization and professionalization of rehabilitation counseling practice.

Accreditation and Certification

As services for persons with disabilities began to expand to more diverse populations and states were being held accountable for the delivery of services, the lack of qualified providers came into acute focus. In the 1940s, the first three rehabilitation counseling education programs were established at New York University, The Ohio State University, and Wayne State University to address the need for adequately trained professionals. In addition, the U.S. government, through the Vocational Rehabilitation Act Amendments of 1954 (PL 82-565), sought to address concerns by appropriating funds to assist with the costs associated with master's-level university training in rehabilitation counseling and related rehabilitation disciplines (Leahy, 2012; Leahy et al., 2016). This funding continues to assist in the training and preparation of today's rehabilitation counselors.

As other universities created rehabilitation counseling education programs, the need for curriculum standardization grew and led to the organization of the Council on Rehabilitation Education (CORE) in 1972. Following the lead of the related fields of psychology and social work (Linkowski & Szymanski, 1993), CORE's primary focus was to review and accredit master's-level rehabilitation counseling training programs (Leahy & Tansey, 2008; Linkowski & Szymanski, 1993). This accreditation served to help employers, the public, and people with disabilities have access to highly trained professionals. As the oldest counseling accreditation body, CORE was officially recognized by the Council of Postsecondary Accreditation in 1975 (Leahy & Tansey, 2008; Linkowski & Szymanski, 1993).

The push for national certification of rehabilitation counselors was almost concurrent with the development of CORE. Growing out of concerns for the quality of practice and the need for practitioners to demonstrate competence in the field of rehabilitation counseling, the Commission on Rehabilitation Counselor Certification (CRCC) was established in 1974 (Leahy & Holt, 1993; Saunders, Barros-Bailey, Chapman, & Nunez, 2009; Wright, 1980). Today, CRCC is one of the oldest counseling certification bodies (Leahy et al., 2016; Saunders et al., 2009). The CRC designation, coupled with the completion of graduate degree training and state licensure, is the mark of a qualified provider of rehabilitation counseling services (Leahy, 2012); the CRC credential also gives persons with disabilities and other professionals the assurance that the individual practitioner has attained at least the minimum requirements set forth by CRCC and is operating according to and regulated by the discipline's code of ethics (Leahy & Holt, 1993).

Following standardization of the curriculum and the establishment of a nationally recognized certification process, the professionalization of rehabilitation counseling was further advanced in 1987, when a code of ethics was developed through close collaboration between professional associations and CRCC (Leahy & Szymanski, 1995; Tarvydas & Cottone, 2000). Although codes of ethics are meant to "define the responsibilities of the members to the profession, to client, to society, and to colleagues" (Rothman, 1987, p. 1), the *Code of Professional Ethics for Rehabilitation Counselors* is specifically intended to provide the public with assurance that rehabilitation counseling accepts its responsibility to provide knowledgeable, fair, and caring service to persons with disabilities (CRCC, 2010). To demonstrate this commitment and attend to constantly changing societal and technological advancements, the CRCC code of ethics has undergone periodic review (Tarvydas, Cottone, & Saunders, 2010), with the most recent code adopted in 2017.

Contemporary Practice

Regulation

Like all other counseling specialties, rehabilitation counseling is currently regulated by national certification standards and state licensure; served by professional organizations; and guided by a unique set of philosophies, principles, professional standards, and codes of ethics and conduct (Leahy et al., 2016; Tarvydas, Leahy, & Zanskas, 2009). Rehabilitation counseling led the field as the first counseling specialty to enact independent regulation of practitioner certification and graduate educational program accreditation (Leahy et al., 2016). Along with state licensure, the CRC credential indicates basic competence not only as a counselor but also as a rehabilitation counselor possessing specialized knowledge in both the medical and psychosocial aspects of disability (Leahy, 2012). Although some rehabilitation counselors practice in exempted settings without licensure, certification, or the regulation inherent to such credentials, the trend toward professionalization within U.S. contexts has greatly increased the need to obtain proper training and credentials before practicing as a rehabilitation counselor (Leahy, 2012).

Accreditation of preservice counselor education programs provides assurance to students, consumers, and state licensure boards that graduates possess entry-level competence as professional counselors. As the original accreditation body for rehabilitation counseling, CORE

compiled empirically derived standards of practice based on an iterative program of research that evaluated rehabilitation counseling roles
and functions every 5 years (Leahy, Chan, Sung, & Kim, 2013), thus
making rehabilitation counseling an early and leading contributor to
the evidence base of the counseling profession. A merger agreement
signed on July 20, 2015, took full effect in July 2017, dissolving
CORE and bringing it fully under the Council for Accreditation of
Counseling and Related Educational Programs (CACREP) family of
counseling specialty accreditation (see Sidebar 8.1).

Preservice Training

Master's-level training remains the entry level of practice for rehabilitation counselors, and nearly 100 universities in the United States
offer these types of graduate degree programs. Some rehabilitation
counselor education programs consist of 48 credit hours, but all are
transitioning to 60 credit hours under the new CACREP standards. In
July 2017, the CACREP board adopted a policy that programs accredited in the rehabilitation counseling specialization would be granted a
5-year period from the effective date of the CORE/CACREP merger
to meet the 60-hour degree requirement. With psychology as the science, counseling as the profession, and rehabilitation counseling as the
specialty area of practice (Leahy, 2012; Wright, 1980), rehabilitation
counselor training programs bring together faculty from counseling,
psychology, and related rehabilitation disciplines to provide students
with both the academic rigor and breadth of knowledge reflective of
contemporary, interdisciplinary service environments. As graduates of
preservice, master's-level training programs and qualified providers of
rehabilitation counseling services, licensed and certified practitioners
are required to maintain, expand, and deepen rehabilitation knowledge
and skills through professional development activities (Leahy, 2012).

Professional Associations

Professional development is offered primarily through professional
associations, which provide an organizational home for individuals
with similar professional identities, interests, backgrounds, and commitment to the further development and refinement of the discipline.
Professional identity remains a contemporary challenge to counseling
because of the atypical emergence of the counseling profession from

Sidebar 8.1   Reflection

What is the primary function of professional regulation?

• • •

multiple yet related specialty areas in conjunction with the diversity of practice settings and client populations served by counselors (Leahy et al., 2016; Remley, 1993; Sweeney, 2001; Tarvydas et al., 2009). Within the specialty of rehabilitation counseling, this struggle has played out in the emergence of multiple professional associations.

The American Rehabilitation Counseling Association was founded in 1958 as a professional division of the American Personnel and Guidance Association (now the American Counseling Association). The National Rehabilitation Counseling Association was also founded in 1958 as a professional division of the National Rehabilitation Association. The National Rehabilitation Counseling Association is now an independent association, and the National Rehabilitation Association has developed an additional division called the Rehabilitation Counselors and Educators Association. The International Association of Rehabilitation Professionals is a growing organization that focuses on the needs of practitioners in private practice from a global perspective. In addition, the National Council on Rehabilitation Education focuses on the discipline's research, training, and educational mission. The presence of multiple organizations, with similar missions and constituencies, has been the topic of much discussion and debate over the years (Leahy & Tarvydas, 2001; Leahy, Tarvydas, & Phillips, 2011). Hopefully, the discipline will soon take action on the need to create one national professional organization to represent rehabilitation counselors in the United States, marshal our strengths, clarify our identity to outside stakeholders and members of the public, and effectively utilize all of our resources to continue our leadership role in the counseling and disability fields.

Contextual Dimensions

Although rehabilitation counseling professional associations, practice settings, and client populations are diverse, rehabilitation counselor scholars and practitioners draw on a rich history of established and emerging models and training, targeting the need for adjustment and adaptation to disability within functional contexts.

Disability Populations

The need for counseling among persons with physical, cognitive, emotional, and psychiatric disabilities is growing partly because of increased incidence, awareness, integration, and advocacy for individuals with all types of disabilities (Smart & Smart, 2006). Although all counselors will work with individuals with disabilities, rehabilitation counselors possess specialized knowledge, training, and skills related to the medical, functional, environmental, and psychosocial aspects of disability, including sociopolitical–environmental factors that shape the disability experience (Jenkins, Patterson, & Szymanski, 1992; Leahy & Szymanski, 1995; Maki, 2012). Accordingly, rehabilitation counselors are primary providers of counseling services for individuals with not only physical disabilities but also mental health disabilities (Maki, 2012). Rehabilitation counselors serve a wide variety of individuals with developmental, congenital, and acquired disabilities, including psychiatric, neurological, muscular, cognitive, sensory, behavioral, systemic, orthopedic, and age-related conditions. Whether working with veterans experiencing physical, cognitive, and emotional trauma; individuals with severe psychiatric disabilities seeking engagement with their communities; or young adults with developmental disabilities as they transition from school to work, rehabilitation counselors use advanced mental health counseling skills and an individualized, ecological understanding of disability to help clients achieve functional outcomes, including employment, independent living, and education. Accordingly, rehabilitation counselor education and practice has been described as a hybridization of rehabilitation and mental health designed to holistically address the wide array of disability-related needs across practice settings (Maki, 2012).

Philosophy and Models

Although the broader concept of rehabilitation implies restoration, the rehabilitation counseling philosophy espouses client self-determination, the value and dignity of all people, and interdependence over prescriptivism (Maki, 2012). Having evolved from early traditions based on the medical model of disability, contemporary rehabilitation counseling is guided by the sociopolitical model of disability (Smart & Smart, 2006) and therefore seeks not to cure but to facilitate adjustment, adaptation, integration, participation, and improved quality of life for persons with disabilities. Using the power of collaborative therapeutic relationships as primary to client engagement (Connor & Leahy, 2016; Wampold, 2001), rehabilitation counselors draw from the theories of psychology to guide the delivery of mental health services while concurrently considering the effects of ecological constructs, including home, school, workplace, community, and culture. With this hybridized professional development, rehabilitation counselors are guided by a holistic framework that considers how the interplay of the counseling process, environmental resources, and barriers affects quality of life for persons with disabilities (Maki, 2012). With a solution focus, rehabilitation counselors evoke therapeutic change at the individual and environmental levels. For example, rehabilitation counselors may meet individually with clients in a traditional office setting but also provide consultation to employers on job accommodations or assistive technology (AT; Connor, Kuo, & Leahy, in press).

In addition to focusing on the person–environment fit (Kosciulek, 1993), rehabilitation counseling takes a longitudinal view of disability, intervening when other rehabilitation disciplines have done everything possible to cure, restore, or habilitate the individual.

Hershenson's (1996) model outlines fundamental differences between the rehabilitation counseling paradigm and other rehabilitation disciplines, such as medicine and psychology. Whereas physical medicine or psychiatry directs interventions toward preventing or limiting the effects of disease and disability, the rehabilitation counselor engages in tertiary prevention (i.e., preventing chronic conditions from causing further disability after restorative or habilitative progress has plateaued). Whereas primary prevention focuses mainly on the environment, and secondary prevention on the individual, tertiary prevention must equally consider the individual and the environment. From this tertiary prevention paradigm, rehabilitation counseling is further guided by conceptual models (Cottone & Emener, 1990; Maki & Tarvydas, 2012), with the ecological model perhaps representing the best example of a truly tertiary approach. Emerging from trait-factor theory (Parsons, 1967), the ecological model guides the practitioner to systematically evaluate person–environment fit and enlist client collaboration in developing a plan that empowers choice and maximizes fit and function.

Early scholars (Maki, McCracken, Pape, & Scofield, 1979) envisioned how a life-span, developmental orientation in conjunction with a trait-factor approach provides a theoretical framework for rehabilitation counseling (Maki, 2012). The contemporary ecological model of rehabilitation counseling (Maki, 2012) illustrates how each of the four functions of the rehabilitation counselor are used to facilitate correspondence between an individual's maximum and typical behaviors and the reinforcers and demands of the environment. As a counselor, the rehabilitation counselor assesses and explores the client's typical behaviors, including interests, temperament, values, and personality. Although the rehabilitation counselor may refer to psychologists or other rehabilitation professionals for assessments requiring specialized training, such as intelligence testing or functional capacity evaluations, most information pertinent to case conceptualization is gathered directly by the rehabilitation counselor through the use of interview, observation, and assessment instruments. As a case manager, the rehabilitation counselor facilitates restoration and optimization of behavior by referring the client for appropriate services, such as training, AT, or rehabilitation therapies with an emphasis on identifying and promoting maximum physical capacity, aptitude, and achievement. As an advocate, the rehabilitation counselor recommends environments that provide effective reinforcers and reasonable social demands. Finally, as a consultant, the rehabilitation counselor identifies limitations and residual capacities that shape client performance within the contexts of work, school, community, and independent living.

Although the ecological model of rehabilitation counseling focuses on assessing traits and factors, rehabilitation counselors also address psychosocial adaptation to disability. Thus, a comprehensive framework for rehabilitation counseling includes assessments and interventions to address client self-concept, self-efficacy, and response tendencies in relation to cultural standards and environmental contexts. With the belief that self-efficacy is a driver of meaning, persistence, purpose, and confidence in behavior, rehabilitation counselors seek to positively affect rehabilitation potential as clients navigate the array of state, community, and private services afforded them (Brodwin & Brodwin, 1992; Maki, 2012). Although functional independence and economic self-sufficiency are common rehabilitation outcomes, quality of life ultimately decides the success of any rehabilitation outcome (Maki, 2012; Roessler, 1990).

Contemporary rehabilitation frameworks, including the World Health Organization's International Classification of Functioning, Disability, and Health (ICF), provide constructs for considering disability-relevant factors, including body functions and structures, in conjunction with personal and environmental factors and with activities (World Health Organization, 2002). Rehabilitation researchers have capitalized on the biopsychosocial nature of the ICF, placing a focus on enablement and extending the model to include subjective and objective measures of quality of life as they relate to disability (Chan, Cardoso, & Chronister, 2009). Note that the ICF provides rehabilitation researchers with a common language and mechanism for identifying measures, exploring moderators that predict when or for whom a variable causes an outcome, and examining mediators that establish how or why one variable predicts another (Chan, Berven, & Thomas, 2004; Chan et al., 2009). Both the ecological model of rehabilitation counseling and the ICF have been, and will continue to be, instrumental in building the evidence base of rehabilitation counseling (see Sidebar 8.2).

Research-Based Foundations of Practice

Underlying the practice of any discipline or professional specialty area is the delineation of specific knowledge and skill competencies

---

Sidebar 8.2   Reflection

How might the different models discussed here affect the way society views disability?

Which model do you think has been most pervasive in your life and understanding of disability?

• • •

required for effective service delivery. *Job analysis, role and function, professional competency, critical incident,* and *knowledge-validation research* are all terms that describe a process whereby the professional practice of rehabilitation counseling has been systematically studied. This research identifies and describes important functions and tasks or knowledge and skills associated with the effective delivery of services to individuals with disabilities.

Over the past 50 years, through these various research methods, an extensive body of knowledge has been acquired that has empirically identified the specific competencies and job functions important to the practice of rehabilitation counseling. This longstanding emphasis on the development and ongoing refinement of a research-based foundation has served to define and validate the rehabilitation counseling scope of practice and also to distinguish it from other counseling specialties that are also seeking to define and validate their scopes of professional practice. These research efforts have also provided the discipline with evidence of construct validity of rehabilitation counseling knowledge and skill areas (Szymanski, Leahy, & Linkowski, 1993).

Although role and function approaches generally provide an empirically derived description of the functions and tasks associated with a role, the knowledge required to perform these functions is typically more indirectly assessed and inferred on the basis of the described functions and tasks. Roessler and Rubin (1992), in their review of major studies (Emener & Rubin, 1980; Leahy, Shapson, & Wright, 1987; Rubin et al., 1984), concluded that rehabilitation counselors must perform a diverse role requiring many skills if they are to effectively assist individuals with disabilities to improve the quality of their lives. They also concluded that the role of the rehabilitation counselor could be fundamentally described as encompassing the following functions or job task areas: (a) assessment, (b) affective counseling, (c) vocational (career) counseling, (d) case management, and (e) job placement.

Conversely, knowledge validation and professional competency approaches provide an empirically derived description of the knowledge and skills associated with a particular role, but the actual functions and tasks are more indirectly assessed and inferred on the basis of the knowledge and skills needed by an individual to practice. Research by Leahy and colleagues (2013) provided empirical support that the following 10 knowledge domains represent the core knowledge and skill requirements of rehabilitation counselors across practice settings: (a) assessment, appraisal, and vocational evaluation; (b) job development, job placement, and career and lifestyle development; (c) vocational consultation and services for employers; (d) case management, professional roles and practices, and utilization of community resources; (e) foundations of counseling, professional orientation and ethical practice, theories, social and cultural issues, and human growth and development; (f) group and family counseling; (g) mental health counseling; (h) medical, functional, and psychosocial aspects of disability; (i) disability management; and (j) research, program evaluation, and evidence-based practice. A complete listing of the knowledge domains and subdomains from this study is provided in Table 8.1.

The results of this study (Leahy et al., 2013) provide further empirical support for the description of the knowledge base underlying the practice of rehabilitation counseling and the content and construct validity of the knowledge domains identified in this replication and extension of the most recent study completed in 2009. Over the past 25 years, four large-scale national research initiatives (Leahy, Chan, & Saunders, 2003; Leahy et al., 2013; Leahy, Muenzen, Saunders, & Strauser, 2009; Leahy, Szymanski, & Linkowski, 1993) have identified and defined the specific competencies and job functions important to the practice of rehabilitation counseling and the achievement of positive outcomes with clients. The last three studies sampled the same population of interest and used parallel definitions of variables, research questions, and research instruments. Each successive replication and extension of this line of inquiry has added to the evidence-based foundation of practice (DePalma, 2002) in terms of underlying knowledge dimensions essential for effective rehabilitation counseling. These studies and prior research efforts (e.g., Berven, 1979; Emener & Rubin, 1980; Harrison & Lee, 1979; Jaques, 1959; Leahy et al., 1987; Muthard & Salomone, 1969; Rubin et al., 1984; Wright & Fraser, 1975) have provided the discipline with consistent empirically based evidence of an established and mature discipline that is able to respond appropriately to the evolutionary demands and pressures of a dynamic human service field (Leahy et al., 2013; Leahy, Muenzen, et al., 2009).

Knowledge Translation

In terms of research utilization and knowledge translation, these empirically derived descriptions of the rehabilitation counselor's role, function, and required knowledge and skill competencies have assisted the discipline in a number of important ways. First, they have helped in defining the professional identity of the rehabilitation counselor by empirically defining the uniqueness of the discipline and by providing evidence in support of the construct validity of its knowledge base. Second, the descriptions have been used extensively in the development of preservice educational curricula to provide graduate training in areas of knowledge and skill critical to the practice of rehabilitation counseling across major employment settings. Third, the longstanding emphasis on a research-based foundation for practice has greatly contributed to the rehabilitation counseling field's leadership role in the establishment and ongoing refinement of graduate educational

Table 8.1 Rehabilitation Counseling Knowledge Domains and Subdomains

Domain 1—Assessment, Appraisal, and Vocational Evaluation
  A. The tests and evaluation techniques available for assessing clients' needs
  B. Psychometric concepts related to measurement
  C. Interpretation of assessment results for rehabilitation planning purposes
  D. Computer-based job-matching systems
  E. Computer-based and online assessment tools

Domain 2—Job Development, Job Placement, and Career and Lifestyle Development
  A. Theories of career development and work adjustment
  B. Vocational implications of functional limitations associated with disabilities
  C. Methods and techniques used to conduct labor market surveys
  D. Transferable skills analysis
  E. Occupational and labor market information
  F. Job analysis
  G. Ergonomics, job accommodations, and assistive technology
  H. Job readiness including seeking and retention skills development
  I. Job placement and job development strategies
  J. Job modification and restructuring techniques
  K. Demand-side employment issues related to hiring, return to work, and retention
  L. Services available from one-stop career centers

Domain 3—Vocational Consultation and Services for Employers
  A. The workplace culture, environment, and business terminology
  B. Marketing strategies and techniques for rehabilitation services
  C. Employer development for job placement
  D. Consultation process with employers related to management of disability issues in the workplace
  E. Educating employers on disability-related issues

Domain 4—Case Management, Professional Roles and Practices, and Utilization of Community Resources
  A. Principles of caseload management
  B. Case management tools
  C. The case management process, including case finding, planning, service co-ordination, referral to and utilization of other disciplines, and client advocacy
  D. Case recording and documentation
  E. Professional roles, functions, and relationships with other human service providers
  F. Techniques for working effectively in teams and across disciplines
  G. Health promotion and wellness concepts and strategies for people with chronic illness and disability
  H. The services available for a variety of rehabilitation populations, including persons with multiple disabilities
  I. Techniques for working with individuals with limited English proficiency
  J. Negotiation, mediation, and conflict resolution strategies
  K. Advocacy processes needed to address institutional and social barriers that impede access, equity, and success for clients
  L. Human resource practices, diversity in the workplace, and workplace supports for people with disabilities
  M. Programs and services for specialty populations

(Continued)

Table 8.1 Rehabilitation Counseling Knowledge Domains and Subdomains *(Continued)*

Domain 4—Case Management, Professional Roles and Practices, and Utilization of Community Resources *(Continued)*

   N. Organizational structure of rehabilitation counseling practice settings
   O. Social security programs, benefits, work incentives, and disincentives
   P. Services available through client advocacy programs
   Q. Community resources and services for rehabilitation planning
   R. Supported employment strategies and services
   S. School to work transition for students with disabilities
   T. Financial resources for rehabilitation services
   U. Independent living services
   V. Health care benefits and delivery systems
   W. Laws and public policy affecting individuals with disabilities

Domain 5—Foundations of Counseling, Professional Orientation and Ethical Practice, Theories, Social and Cultural Issues, and Human Growth and Development

   A. Individual counseling theories
   B. Individual counseling practices and interventions
   C. Human growth and development
   D. Societal issues, trends, and developments
   E. Diversity and multicultural counseling issues
   F. Theories and techniques of clinical supervision
   G. Clinical problem-solving and critical-thinking skills
   H. Internet-based counseling tools and resources
   I. Risk management and professional ethical standards
   J. Ethical decision-making models and processes

Domain 6—Group and Family Counseling

   A. Family counseling theories
   B. Family counseling practices and interventions
   C. Group counseling theories
   D. Group counseling practices and interventions

Domain 7—Mental Health Counseling

   A. Behavior and personality theory
   B. Techniques for individuals with psychological disabilities
   C. Dual diagnosis and the workplace
   D. Human sexuality and disability issues
   E. Substance abuse and treatment
   F. Treatment planning for clinical problems
   G. *Diagnostic and Statistical Manual of Mental Disorders*

Domain 8—Medical, Functional, and Psychosocial Aspects of Disability

   A. Medical aspects and implications of various disabilities
   B. Medical terminology
   C. Rehabilitation terminology and concepts
   D. The psychosocial and cultural impact of disability on the individual
   E. The psychosocial and cultural impact of disability on the family
   F. Environmental and attitudinal barriers for individuals with disabilities
   G. The functional capacities of individuals with disabilities
   H. Implications of medications as they apply to individuals with disabilities
   I. Individual and family adjustment to disability

(Continued)

Table 8.1 Rehabilitation Counseling Knowledge Domains and Subdomains *(Continued)*

Domain 8—Medical, Functional, and Psychosocial Aspects of Disability *(Continued)*
  J. Appropriate medical intervention resources
  K. Work conditioning or work hardening resources and strategies
Domain 9—Disability Management
  A. Disability prevention and management strategies
  B. Managed care concepts
  C. Insurance programs
  D. Workers' compensation laws and practices
  E. Forensic rehabilitation
Domain 10—Research, Program Evaluation, and Evidence-Based Practice
  A. Historical and philosophical foundations of rehabilitation counseling
  B. Program evaluation procedures for assessing the effectiveness of rehabilitation services and outcomes
  C. Research databases for locating empirically validated interventions
  D. Rehabilitation research literature related to evidence-based practice
  E. Research methods and statistics
  F. Evidence-based practice and research utilization
  G. Evidence-based psychiatric rehabilitation practices
  H. Systematic review/meta-analysis

Note. From "Empirically Derived Test Specifications for the Certified Rehabilitation Counselor Examination," by M. J. Leahy, F. Chan, C. Sung, and M. Kim, 2013, *Rehabilitation Counseling Bulletin,* 56(4), pp. 212–213. Copyright 2012 by Hammill Institute on Disabilities. Reprinted with permission.

program accreditation through CORE and individual practitioner certification through CRCC. Finally, this body of knowledge has also been useful in identifying both common professional ground (shared competency areas) with the profession of counseling in general and the uniqueness of rehabilitation counseling among related rehabilitation disciplines (e.g., vocational evaluation, job placement) and other counseling specialties (e.g., career counseling, school counseling, mental health counseling). This process of further definition in the area of occupational competence is a normal sequence in the professionalization process for any occupation seeking public recognition.

Phases of Rehabilitation

As part of interdisciplinary rehabilitation or behavioral health teams, rehabilitation counselors follow the general sequence of service used by related professions, such as occupational therapy and psychology. The four phases are intake, assessment, service, and outcome. The process begins with intake, when eligibility is determined based on qualifying disability, level of impairment, and pertinent demographic factors established by the service agency or program. After eligibility or suitability for services is determined, the assessment phase begins. Initial evaluation procedures, which can include a records review, interviews, inventories, and consultation, are used to measure present levels of functioning, identify strengths and needs, and direct the initial rehabilitation plan. Although assessment is a vital early step in the process, it is also ongoing and iterative and is used to measure progress toward goals, determine the need for referral, and plan for termination of services. In settings that provide psychiatric or mental health services, assessment may also include an evaluation of mental status and clinical diagnostic interviewing (Maki, 2012).

As in any healthy counseling relationship, rehabilitation counselor and client work collaboratively to establish the bonds, goals, and tasks necessary to form a working alliance (Bordin, 1994). Based on intake data and in partnership with the client, the rehabilitation counselor identifies services and service providers to help move the client through the plan within a specified period of time. As mentioned previously, services provided directly by the rehabilitation counselor on behalf of the client include four overarching functions: (a) counseling and guidance, (b) case management or coordination of services, (c) consultation, and (d) advocacy (Maki, 2012). Whereas counseling and case management services target the individual client, consultation and advocacy operate at the larger systems level.

The last phase of the rehabilitation process is the outcome phase. In this phase, progress toward goals is assessed a final time and recommendations for placement, termination, follow-up, or extended services are made. The outcomes achieved are as diverse as the populations served and the service settings in which rehabilitation counselors work. Although specific outcomes can include employment, independent living, and improved mental health, the ultimate goal is improved quality of life for the individual with the disability.

Evidence-Based Practices

In recent years, there has been significant interest in and movement toward the concepts of evidence-based practice and knowledge translation efforts within health care, disability, and related practice settings. These initiatives have focused attention on the use of findings obtained through systematic research efforts to inform practice and clinical decision making for individual practitioners and to inform policy and continuous improvement strategies for organizations that serve people with disabilities (Leahy & Arokiasamy, 2010). Clearly, the emphasis in the future will be on the meaning of research findings to practitioners and consumers in improving services, interventions, and employment outcomes for persons with disabilities and on translating and disseminating evidence-based practices that come from research efforts to the level of the organization that will affect and inform practice and policy

(Leahy, Thielsen, Millington, Austin, & Fleming, 2009). The development of theory-driven or model-driven research to inform best practices in rehabilitation will undoubtedly be highly important as professionals in the field strive to improve the effectiveness of rehabilitation counseling services and outcomes, especially for subpopulations of consumers with the poorest rehabilitation outcomes (Chan et al., 2009).

Practice Dimensions

Work Settings

Rehabilitation counselors work in a variety of public and private practice settings. As interest in disability, mental health, and employment-related needs continue to grow, emerging practice settings offer an ever-increasing number of potential work settings for qualified rehabilitation counselors. CRCC (2016) provided a scope-of-practice statement that applies to all settings:

> Rehabilitation counseling is a systematic process which assists persons with physical, mental, developmental, cognitive, and emotional disabilities to achieve their personal, career, and independent living goals in the most integrated setting possible through the application of the counseling process. The counseling process involves communication, goal setting, and beneficial growth or change through self-advocacy, psychological, vocational, social, and behavioral interventions. The specific techniques and modalities utilized within this rehabilitation counseling process may include, but are not limited to:

- assessment and appraisal;
- diagnosis and treatment planning;
- career (vocational) counseling;
- individual and group counseling treatment interventions focused on facilitating adjustments to the medical and psychosocial impact of disability;
- case management, referral, and service coordination;
- program evaluation and research;
- interventions to remove environmental, employment, and attitudinal barriers;
- consultation services among multiple parties and regulatory systems;
- job analysis, job development, and placement services, including assistance with employment and job accommodations; and
- provision of consultation about and access to rehabilitation technology. ("Scope of Practice Statement")

State/Federal Settings
(Public Vocational Rehabilitation Program)
Funded by a combination of state and federal funds supported through congressional legislation, the public vocational rehabilitation program is the oldest and most traditional practice setting for rehabilitation

counselors. Currently, around 28% of all certified rehabilitation counselors work in the state/federal system (Saunders et al., 2009). Established as a formal practice for veterans (Soldiers Rehabilitation Act of 1918 [PL 65-178]) and later for civilians (1920 Civilian Rehabilitation Act [Smith-Fess Act of 1920, PL 67-236]), the state/federal vocational rehabilitation program was significantly expanded by the Rehabilitation Act of 1973 (PL 93-112) and its amendments. These agencies, at present, operate in each of the 50 states, the District of Columbia, and many of the territories of the United States (Fabian & MacDonald-Wilson, 2012), with the Rehabilitation Services Administration responsible for their oversight. Programs are based on eligibility, with eligibility determined by verification of a disability that impedes or presents a barrier to employment, the ability to benefit in terms of an employment outcome, and the need for vocational rehabilitation services to overcome significant work-related barriers (Fabian & MacDonald-Wilson, 2012; Workforce Investment Act of 1998, PL 05-220, Title IV). Consider the experience of this rehabilitation counselor in terms of state/federal vocational rehabilitation and higher education:

I obtained an MEd from an academic program that was both CACREP and CORE accredited where I was eligible to earn a certification as a rehabilitation counselor (CRC) as well as licensure as a professional counselor (LPC). I initially entered my master's program focusing on mental health counseling as my career goal, but after being exposed to the field of rehabilitation counseling, I knew I had found my professional calling. As a result, I decided to pursue my CRC and to work as a vocational rehabilitation counselor in my state's public vocational rehabilitation agency. In my role as a vocational rehabilitation counselor, I assisted adults, transition students, and youth with diverse circumstances to be successful with their employment goals. What I loved most about this position was developing collaborative relationships with consumers, their families, colleagues, community partners, service providers, and employers. It was deeply rewarding to have consumers allow me to enter their lives for assistance and guidance in navigating their challenges, adjusting to change, and celebrating their successes. Additionally, having the ability to be a social change agent for inclusiveness, accessibility, and opportunity was inherently rewarding.

I believe challenges are essentially opportunities for growth, and no matter what profession one pursues, there will be limitless growth opportunities. The aspect of my work as a vocational rehabilitation counselor where I had the most growth was finding balance in delivering high-quality services while also meeting the needs of quantitative outcomes. Additionally, there is still much opportunity for growth in employers acknowledging the benefits of hiring persons with a disability and understanding that providing accommodations to support accessible work environments promotes positive outcomes for both the employer and employee with a disability.

As a result of my life experiences, academic training, and professional pursuits, the importance of supporting and growing the field of rehabilitation counseling has become clear to me. It is for these reasons I have decided to pursue a PhD in rehabilitation counselor education. As an educator, I will be contributing to the field in terms of training future rehabilitation counselors, supporting the bridge between research and practice, and continuing to advocate for positive systems change. I never imagined I would be at this place in my life, and yet it seems as though I have been working towards this all along.

Veterans rehabilitation services are housed in the Veterans Benefits Administration within the federal Veterans Administration, and services are provided to enable veterans to obtain and maintain suitable employment (Fabian & MacDonald-Wilson, 2012). With ever-increasing involvement in global conflicts, service-related injuries, both physical and psychological in nature, have been on the rise. This has led to an increase in the number of veterans seeking, receiving, and benefiting from rehabilitation services on their return from service (Fabian & MacDonald-Wilson, 2012). One vocational rehabilitation counselor in the Veterans Administration describes his experience as follows:

As part of the Integrated Disability Evaluation System, the most rewarding aspect of being a Veterans Administration vocational rehabilitation counselor is assisting those who have served our country as they transition back to civilian life. In 2008, Congress passed an act to serve wounded soldiers who are no longer medically fit for duty; this act allows eligible veterans to have early access to vocational rehabilitation services before they are discharged from the military. Going through a medical board is often a confusing and scary time for those who have been serving in active duty, as the identity they have known is often no longer a reality. As an Integrated Disability Evaluation System vocational rehabilitation counselor, you are a critical component in aiding these veterans with their successful transition back to employment through referral services and the development of an appropriate rehabilitation plan. These rehabilitation plans often provide training so service members can obtain suitable employment in line with their service-connected impairments. The training I received from my master's program in rehabilitation/community counseling has prepared me to be able to cope, adapt, look for support, and remain positive so I can assist these service members as they deal with the complexities of their transition process, help them access resources that are available to them not only as soldiers but now as veterans as well, navigate their benefits, and explore their strengths and weaknesses in preparation for a successful future.

Private For-Profit Settings

Perhaps the fastest growing of the practice settings (Barros-Bailey, Benshoff, & Fischer, 2009), private for-profit settings operate on a fee-for-service model of service delivery (Brodwin, 2008). In addition to providing vocational counseling consultative services, rehabilitation counselors employed in these settings utilize their expertise in vocational planning, disability-related work limitations, and assessment. Examples of specific focuses include workers' compensation, forensic expert witness testimony for disability hearings, long-term disability, life care planning, disability consultation, and disability management (Brodwin, 2008). Insurance companies and employers themselves have begun hiring rehabilitation counselors as part of return-to-work and other disability-related initiatives. These long-term disability programs help to offset wages lost as a result of a physical or mental impairment causing work disruption for periods longer than 6 months (Fabian & MacDonald-Wilson, 2012). Private for-profit settings currently account for more than 30% of all work settings in which certified rehabilitation counselors practice (Saunders et al., 2009).

Private Not-for-Profit Settings
The state/federal system serves more than 1 million individuals each year, but this represents a very small portion of the more than 50 million Americans with disabilities (Fabian & MacDonald-Wilson, 2012). Community rehabilitation programs continue to play an ever-increasing role in the provision of counseling and direct services to persons with disabilities, particularly those with developmental disabilities and psychiatric disorders (Menz, Botterbusch, Hagen-Foley, & Johnson, 2003). Community rehabilitation programs seek to augment the services provided by state/federal agencies while also providing services to individuals who may require ongoing services not provided by the state/federal system (e.g., community-supported employment). More than 9,000 such agencies provide services to almost 10 million individuals, and these agencies coordinate service provision with a variety of community partners, including mental health agencies and hospitals, the Social Security Administration, the Department of Labor, probation and parole offices, and substance abuse programs (Fabian & MacDonald-Wilson, 2012; Menz et al., 2003). These practice settings are funded through a variety of state, federal, and private sources (Fabian & MacDonald-Wilson, 2012).

A few notable examples of practice settings in the private not-for-profit sector include university disability resource centers, centers for independent living (CILs), and community-based rehabilitation programs. More and more individuals with disabilities are seeking educational opportunities and training beyond high school. In 2011–2012, there was an estimated 2,563,000 undergraduate students, and 11.1% of them had a disability (Best Colleges, 2016). Disability resource centers exist on college campuses to provide counseling and advocacy and to help students with disabilities obtain necessary accommodations in classroom and campus settings (Best Colleges, 2016; Fabian & MacDonald-Wilson, 2012).

CILs are another type of nonprofit, community-based organization. CILs are primarily nonresidential centers that are controlled and run by persons with disabilities. CILs help to more fully integrate individuals with disabilities into society by providing peer counseling, information and referral, independent living skills training, and individual and/or group advocacy (Fabian & MacDonald-Wilson, 2012; Parkin & Nosek, 2001). CILs also provide assistance with AT, interpreter, and reader services as well as the planning and coordination of individual and group activities. CILs focus on "expressing the disability community's insistence on the removal of environmental barriers and disincentives in public policy that have a disabling effect [on persons with disabilities]" (Rubin & Roessler, 2008, p. 495).

Psychiatric Rehabilitation

Psychiatric rehabilitation is an even more focused specialization within rehabilitation counseling that has the mission to help "persons with long-term psychiatric disabilities to increase their functioning, so that they are successful and satisfied in the environments of their choice with the least amount of professional intervention" (Anthony, Cohen, & Farkas, 1990, p. 2). William Anthony, driven to effect outcomes in employment, independent living, education, and community participation, was a pioneer in psychiatric rehabilitation. He developed the Boston model of psychiatric rehabilitation, which was based on a premise of recovery. Since that time, a variety of psychiatric rehabilitation models have emerged. The psychosocial rehabilitation interventions utilized in these programs are often provided with rehabilitation counseling and recovery models as core elements. For example, the assertive community treatment approach, like the Boston model, calls for the inclusion of vocational rehabilitation counseling as part of the multidisciplinary approach to recovery (Kukla & Bond, 2011).

Supported employment, integrated dual disorders treatment, family psychoeducation, illness management and recovery, and medication management also demonstrate some of the strongest outcomes among mental health interventions within the evidence-based practice literature (Kukla & Bond, 2011; Mueser, Torrey, Lynde, Singer, & Drake, 2003). Essentially, psychiatric rehabilitation seeks to address functional needs that cannot be fully addressed through medication alone (Bond, Campbell, & DeLuca, 2005) while promoting the empowerment and integration of persons with mental illness. Consider the experience of the following vocational rehabilitation counselor who works with clients with serious mental health illness:

I work for a state rehabilitation agency as a vocational rehabilitation counselor with a specialty caseload focusing on serving individuals with mental diagnoses. Our agency has an interagency agreement with the health and welfare office for the purpose of better serving clients who are diagnosed with serious mental illness. A team approach is utilized to ensure that clients served by this agreement will benefit and successfully integrate into their communities from a psychological, psychosocial, and employment perspective. My office is housed within the Department of Health and Welfare's Human Development Center, and I am a part of several teams: the assertive community treatment team, crisis team, and mental health court. As a part of these teams, I work with clients to help them achieve an employment outcome. I have found it to be very helpful to work closely with the staff at the Human Development Center, as each team member provides valuable information as to the mental health status of clients we are jointly working with and how their current functioning may affect their ability to move forward with pursuing an employment outcome.

Working with clients with personality disorders can be very challenging, as this disorder will many times affect their ability to take responsibility for their actions, and they will tend to take a victim stance and blame others if things do not turn out as they want them to. It can be emotionally draining to work with clients who have significant mental health issues. Vocational rehabilitation is a process, and there are times when clients have unrealistic expectations of the program and expect it to be a quick fix.

The most rewarding part of working as a vocational rehabilitation counselor for me is watching clients grow in self-confidence as they gain skills in training programs and ultimately secure employment that is a good match with their skills and abilities. Being a part of assisting clients to gain self-confidence, employment, and stability in their lives is what makes this job worthwhile.

The Centers for Disease Control and Prevention (2016) estimated that, compared with all other types of illness, mental illness is the leading cause of disability in developed countries. Furthermore, approximately 25% of all U.S. adults have a mental illness, and almost 50% will experience mental illness at some point in their lifetime. With a focus on long-term community supports, contemporary psychiatric rehabilitation services incorporate strategies to address neurocognitive concerns (Corrigan, Mueser, Bond, Drake, & Solomon, 2012), interpersonal and coping skills (Rose, 1993), social support (Corrigan et al., 2012), informed consent and empowerment (Kosciulek, 2014), and vocational engagement (Falvo, 1999). As the well-established body of rehabilitation research has grown, specific psychiatric rehabilitation practices have been substantiated as evidence based, including supported employment, integrated dual disorders treatment, family psychoeducation, illness management and recovery, and assertive community treatment (Chan et al., 2009).

Rehabilitation counseling has a rich and longstanding tradition in psychiatric rehabilitation even though the earliest focus of rehabilitation counseling was physical disabilities. As early as 1943, federal legislation known as the *Barden-LaFollette Act* (Vocational Rehabilitation Act Amendments of 1943, PL 113) expanded state vocational rehabilitation services to persons with cognitive impairment and mental illness. Another significant philosophical shift occurred in the 1970s after states began deinstitutionalizing individuals with severe and persistent mental illness. However, 3- to 5-year rehospitalization rates as high as 75% highlighted the need for long-term community supports

(Anthony, Cohen, & Cohen, 1983). The Community Mental Health Centers Act was passed in 1963, and subsequent legislation in 1979 mandated the provision of rehabilitation services within community mental health. As the focus of intervention has shifted away from hospitals, federal and state allocations for community-based mental health services have continued to grow (Chan et al., 2009).

Even in those agencies in which primary service delivery is not centered on mental health or psychiatric issues, there is a high rate of co-occurring psychiatric disabilities among all other disability types. In 2008, the U.S. Census Bureau estimated that more than one third of consumers seeking rehabilitation services may also have a psychiatric diagnosis that affects cognitive functioning (Brault, 2009). At present, within the vocational rehabilitation context, rehabilitation counselors regularly serve clients with co-occurring mental health problems (Chan et al., 2009); moreover, the number of clients with a mental illness actually exceeds the number with a physical disability in some state vocational rehabilitation agencies (Chan, Berven, & Thomas, 2015). Clearly, rehabilitation counselors can, do, and will continue to serve a large percentage of individuals with mental illness in a variety of state and private service settings. The connection between clinical mental health counseling and rehabilitation counseling practice has been longstanding in psychiatric rehabilitation, as well as in the general field, despite historically competing credentialing models within the area (Tarvydas & Leahy, 1993).

Special Considerations in Rehabilitation Counseling

As rehabilitation evolves, so too do the needs of individuals with disabilities. Accordingly, rehabilitation counselors are playing a growing role in serving students as they transition from school to work, higher education and training, and independent living. In addition, rehabilitation counseling is now included under the CACREP family of counseling specialties and will be instrumental in bringing a historic and ongoing commitment to the empirical development and maintenance of practical and educational standards and increased disability-relevant knowledge, skills, and attitudes to counseling standards across specialty areas.

Transition Youth

As outlined by the 1990 Individuals with Disabilities Education Act, transition counseling is a dynamic process in which students with disabilities engage with rehabilitation counselors to solidify career and vocational options through a variety of activities (Riesen, Schultz, Morgan, & Kupferman, 2014). The number of students with disabilities seeking assistance with transition-related counseling has grown and will continue to grow (Plotner, Trach, & Strauser, 2012). To meet this need, rehabilitation counselors will increasingly need to engage in collaborative efforts with school administrators, counselors, transition coordinators, special education instructors, and family members to maximize the educational and eventual employment outcomes for students with disabilities (Plotner, Trach, Oertle, & Fleming, 2014).

AT

The Assistive Technology Act of 2004 (PL 108-364) describes *AT* as "any item, piece of equipment, or product system, whether acquired commercially, modified, or customized, that is used to increase, maintain, or improve functional capabilities of individuals with disabilities" (§3.4). Rehabilitation philosophy and the ecological model of rehabilitation counseling align naturally with an examination of how technology has the potential to increase participation in all aspects of life for individuals with disabilities. AT is considered an essential tool of rehabilitation professionals (Scherer & Sax, 2004), and rehabilitation counseling is the only counseling specialty with entry-level training in AT and training program accreditation standards for AT (CACREP, 2016). Furthermore, as case managers, consultants, advocates, and members of interdisciplinary rehabilitation service teams, rehabilitation counselors are in a unique position to address psychosocial adjustment to AT and thereby decrease problems of AT abandonment and maximize person–technology fit (Kuo, 2013; Phillips & Zhao, 1993; Riemer-Reiss & Wacker, 2000; Scherer, 2002). As technology continues to advance, rehabilitation counselor preservice training will need to continually adapt and advance preparation in this growing practice area (see Sidebar 8.3). A rehabilitator counselor who uses AT on the job shared the following:

> A significant portion of my job involves observing and assessing clients' performance on the job and developing AT solutions so that my clients can experience greater productivity and comfort at work. These AT solutions can be purchased off the shelf or can also be customized. The biggest challenge is not to find or make appropriate devices that can improve quality of life but to ensure that the device is a good match with the person. Promoting psychological satisfaction is the most difficult yet rewarding challenge of my job. The training I received from my master's rehabilitation counseling program has prepared me to effectively and ethically communicate with my clients

Sidebar 8.3   Reflection

In what ways do you use assistive technology (AT) for work, school, or communication?

• • •

regarding their needs and desires. This ability to establish productive working relationships with clients has made me a successful AT service provider. The rapid evolution of technology will continue to be a challenge for service providers who want to keep themselves informed about what AT options are available to their clients. While the devices I suggest will evolve, my training in counseling techniques ensures that I consistently prioritize individual needs and psychosocial adjustment in the AT process.

A New Chapter in CACREP Accreditation

Just prior to the earlier CORE/CACREP affiliation agreement, CACREP added the newly created specific area of clinical rehabilitation counseling as an accreditation program area. This was an attempt to extend CACREP accreditation to permit recognition of preparation in the clinical mental health areas of rehabilitation counseling. As educational standards were further refined through the subsequent merger, a traditional rehabilitation counseling program area within CACREP was provided so that the great majority of CORE-accredited rehabilitation counseling programs with this traditional focus could be accommodated with accreditation. Since the merger went into effect on July 1, 2017, CACREP has provided two counseling specializations to accredit rehabilitation counselor preparation programs: rehabilitation counseling, to prepare graduates for traditional vocational rehabilitation practice; and clinical rehabilitation counseling, to prepare graduates for clinical rehabilitation counseling practice and state licensure. The future evolution and reconciliation of these two accreditation areas within the larger field of rehabilitation counseling, and how they will influence the evolution of the overall specialty of rehabilitation counseling, remains to be determined. At a fundamental level, rehabilitation counselors will continue to need detailed but broad preservice training in counseling theories and techniques as well as the medical, psychosocial, and political aspects of disability to be prepared as master's-level generalists who specialize in serving people with disabilities according to the practice settings in which they serve. As part of the merger agreement, CACREP will infuse disability knowledge and awareness across all counseling specialties, and rehabilitation counselor educators will be instrumental in disseminating new and existing evidence on the unique needs of clients with both acquired and congenital physical, cognitive, emotional, and psychiatric disabilities across the life span (see Sidebar 8.4).

Sidebar 8.4 Reflection

Consider some ways in which counselors across specialty areas can infuse disability awareness into their practice settings.

• • •

Chapter Summary

Although rehabilitation counseling has been in existence for nearly a century, we have witnessed significant growth and development in this specialty area of practice over the past few decades. The occupation, as a professional discipline and specialty area of counseling, has had a rich history of professionalization spanning more than 60 years. Today, there are more rehabilitation counselors practicing in a variety of employment settings than at any time in our professional history, and the future market for these types of trained professionals looks excellent. Beyond the bright employment outlook, rehabilitation counselors reap the social and emotional rewards of knowing that their specialized disability knowledge and counseling expertise promote improved quality of life by assisting persons with disabilities to transition from dependence to interdependence, from disablement to empowerment, and from isolation to integration. As a growing specialty area and longstanding leader in promoting the holistic well-being of individuals with all types of disabilities, rehabilitation counseling will continue to advance social justice, advocacy, and empowerment for persons with disabilities within the contexts of school, work, independent living, and community.

Learning Activities

1. Tina is a 17-year-old high school junior with juvenile rheumatoid arthritis. She resides with her parents and 14-year-old brother. You have been working with Tina for the past year since the school district's transition coordinator referred her to you for school-to-work transition services. Currently, Tina is in special education classes for math, but all other courses are general education courses. She does have accommodations in place and can visit the resource rooms in the special education department as needed. Like many teenagers, Tina is active on social media and has sent you friend requests via Facebook and Instagram because, according to her, this is the best way for you to know what she is "up to." She even suggests that you can always instant message her through Facebook to schedule appointments. She has told you that she enjoys working with you and feels she can trust you. When you talk with her teachers, they describe Tina as a popular student with many friends, though recently she has appeared withdrawn and timid in class. You know that Tina has always felt close to her family, especially her mother. She is an excellent student and active in cheerleading, and you have been helping her pursue part-time work experience with a long-term goal of being admitted to college.

   Tina's mother recently called and expressed concern about her daughter's recent 10-pound weight loss. Tina counts calories and exercises each morning and evening. Tina's mother reports that, despite her weight loss and small–average size, Tina frequently describes herself as "fat" and weighs herself several times a day.

Tina's mom tells her that she looks too thin, but Tina still believes she needs to lose more weight. When confronted, Tina is quickly offended and reacts defensively. When Tina's father encourages her to eat more, she argues with him during dinner. Tina's brother teams up with Dad, sometimes calling Tina names. On several occasions, Tina has left the table and locked herself in her bedroom. Tina's parents are unsure whether she is showing some ordinary teenage rebellion or whether she is developing an eating disorder. Until now, Tina has never given them any problems.

a. What are three observations regarding the client?
b. Who are the stakeholders involved in this case study?
c. What are some potential ethical dilemmas within the case study?
d. What are three additional questions you might ask the client to clarify concerns you now have?

2. You have been asked to work with Brenda, an African American client with an acquired physical disability. Brenda has been employed at the same location for the past 10 years but recently suffered a work-related injury. She lost three fingers on her dominant hand, injured her knee, and now uses a cane for ambulation. As her work was primarily physical in nature, Brenda is no longer able to return to her previous position, but the company has found a front office position that is suitable for her. Brenda was recently cleared to return to work and was referred to your office for assistance with return-to-work services. During intake, Brenda reveals that a coworker has said hurtful things about her at work and during the Thursday night bowling league. Often, this is manifested in the form of inappropriate jokes in which Brenda is depicted as lazy and undeserving, particularly in regard to the promotion. In essence, Brenda's coworker implies that the only reason Brenda got the promotion is because of her disability. Based on her interaction with this particular coworker and the fact that other coworkers laugh at the jokes and have not stood up for her, Brenda believes that all coworkers, and even her supervisor, are racists. Brenda acknowledges that some coworkers are consistently nice and do not make similar statements; however, she is mistrustful of them. Brenda now believes that work is no longer an option for her because she believes she will repeatedly face discrimination in the workplace. Brenda's supervisor has expressed genuine concern, as he has noticed that Brenda seems withdrawn and is experiencing decreased work

performance. He has asked you to provide weekly updates on your work with Brenda.

 a. What are three observations regarding the client?
 b. Who are the stakeholders involved in this case study?
 c. What are some potential ethical dilemmas within the case study?
 d. What are three additional questions you might ask the client to clarify concerns you now have?

Review Questions

1. What is the rehabilitation philosophy, and how does it affect the delivery of counseling services to individuals with disabilities?
2. Explain the empirically validated knowledge and skill requirements for professional practice.
3. Name three or four empirically validated knowledge or skill requirements and discuss how these standards affect service delivery and outcomes.
4. Identify one or two evidence-based vocational rehabilitation practices and discuss why the field must continue to develop and validate existing and new evidence-based practices in counseling.
5. How does rehabilitation counseling align with other counseling specialties?
6. Why has rehabilitation counseling been referred to as a *super specialty*?
7. Discuss rehabilitation counseling's early influence on psychiatric rehabilitation.
8. Identify one co-occurring disorder and explain how rehabilitation counselors take a unique approach to treatment planning and intervention with this population.
9. Name two traditional and one emergent practice setting specific to rehabilitation counseling.
10. Discuss the credentialing of rehabilitation counselors, including certification and licensure.

Extension Activities for Discussion and Synthesis

1. You are a rehabilitation counselor working in an agency staffed primarily by social workers and vocational evaluators. Clients of the agency refer to all staff as *case workers* and may not understand the subtle differences in role and scope of practice among you and your colleagues. As the agency is focused on connecting clients with competitive employment, you and your colleagues typically develop similar goals and plans in collaboration with clients. As a certified rehabilitation counselor, what value do you add to service delivery in this agency? Where or how does your

role and scope of practice differ from that of your colleagues? Where or how might your role and scope of practice overlap with that of your colleagues? How do you communicate your unique philosophy and approach to clients, colleagues, and supervisors? How can you capitalize on the strengths of the team to provide the best service to your clients?

2. You are a certified rehabilitation counselor working as a transition coordinator for a regional educational service agency. The superintendent of schools is looking to reduce the district's costs. She calls you to her office to ask why the district needs a transition coordinator when each building is already staffed with a school counselor. She also wants to know why they need you as a liaison between school and community agencies when they could simply direct families and students to the local office of the state vocational rehabilitation agency after graduation. Construct a persuasive argument for the role of rehabilitation counselors in the postsecondary transition. Draw on counseling theory and empirical evidence to support your argument. Be sure to articulate how your preservice and continuing education affect your service delivery.

3. You are a certified rehabilitation counselor working in an outpatient clinic affiliated with a large physical medicine and rehabilitation hospital. You notice that many of your clients are issued assistive devices while on the inpatient unit, but few clients actually use their devices when they come for vocational evaluation and counseling services at your community reintegration clinic. Although you are not up to date on all the latest high-tech devices, you recognize the value of AT and see that AT might positively affect both evaluation and placement services for your clients. Given your limited technical expertise, how can you help to address your clients' AT needs? Discuss the roles of other rehabilitation professionals at both inpatient and outpatient sites with whom you can collaborate. Discuss how you can contribute to the AT process (evaluation, device selection, training, data collection, and ongoing support) within your scope of practice. Describe a scenario in which you would refer out for additional AT expertise.

Further Resources

American Rehabilitation Counseling Association
    www.arcaweb.org
Commission on Rehabilitation Counselor Certification
    https://www.crccertification.com
Counselor-License: A State-by-State Counselor Guide
    www.counselor-license.com

Employment Policy and Measurement–Rehabilitation and Research Training Center
    www.researchondisability.org/epm-rrtc/about
Job Accommodation Network
    https://askjan.org
Journal of Vocational Rehabilitation
    www.iospress.nl/journal/journal-of-vocational-rehabilitation/
National Council on Rehabilitation Education
    https://ncre.org
O*NET
    https://www.onetonline.org
Rehabilitation Counseling Bulletin
    http://journals.sagepub.com/home/rcb
Rehabilitation Research, Policy, and Education
    www.springerpub.com/journals/rehabilitation-research-policy-and-education.html

References

Anthony, W. A., Cohen, M. R., & Cohen, B. F. (1983). Philosophy, treatment process, and principles of the psychiatric rehabilitation approach. *New Directions for Mental Health Services, 1983*(17), 67–79. doi:10.1002/yd.23319831708

Anthony, W. A., Cohen, M. R., & Farkas, M. (1990). *Psychiatric rehabilitation.* Boston, MA: Boston University Center for Psychiatric Rehabilitation.

Assistive Technology Act of 2004, PL 108-364, 29 U.S.C. §§ 3001 *et seq.*

Barros-Bailey, M., Benshoff, J. J., & Fischer, J. (2009). Rehabilitation counseling in the year 2011: Perceptions of certified rehabilitation counselors. *Rehabilitation Counseling Bulletin, 52,* 107–113.

Best Colleges. (2016). *Overview of college resources for students with disabilities.* Retrieved from www.bestcolleges.com/resources/disabled-students/

Berven, N. L. (1979). The role and function of the rehabilitation counselor revisited. *Rehabilitation Counseling Bulletin, 22,* 84–88.

Bond, G. R., Campbell, K., & DeLuca, N. (2005). Psychiatric disabilities. In H. H. Zaretsky, E. F. Richter, III, & M. G. Eisenberg (Eds.), *Medical aspects of disability: A handbook for the rehabilitation professional* (3rd ed., pp. 509–541). New York, NY: Springer.

Bordin, E. (1994). Theory and research on the therapeutic working alliance: New directions. In A. Horvath & L. Greenberg (Eds.), *The working alliance: Theory, research and practice* (pp. 13–37). New York, NY: Wiley.

Brault, M. W. (2009, September 22). *Review of changes to the measurement of disability in the 2008 American Community Survey.* Retrieved from https://www.census.gov/people/disability/files/2008ACS_disability.pdf

Brodwin, M. G. (2008). Rehabilitation in private-for-profit sector: Opportunities and challenges. In S. E. Rubin & R. T. Roessler, *Foundations of the vocational rehabilitation process* (6th ed., pp. 503–523). Austin, TX: PRO-ED.

Brodwin, M., & Brodwin, S. (1992). Rehabilitation: A case study approach. In M. Brodwin, F. Tellex, & S. Brodwin (Eds.), *Medical, psychological and vocational aspects of disability* (pp. 1–19). Athens, GA: Elliott & Fitzpatrick.

Capuzzi, D., & Stauffer, M. D. (2016). *Foundations of addictions counseling* (3rd ed.). Boston, MA: Pearson Education.

Centers for Disease Control and Prevention. (2016). *CDC report: Mental illness surveillance among adults in the United States.* Retrieved from www.cdc.gov/mentalhealthsurveillance/fact_sheet.html

Chan, F., Berven, N. L., & Thomas, K. R. (Eds.). (2004). *Counseling theories and techniques for rehabilitation health professionals.* New York, NY: Springer.

Chan, F., Berven, N. L., & Thomas, K. R. (2015). *Counseling theories and techniques for rehabilitation and mental health professionals.* New York, NY: Springer.

Chan, F., Cardoso, E. D. S., & Chronister, J. A. (2009). *Understanding psychosocial adjustment to chronic illness and disability: A handbook for evidence-based practitioners in rehabilitation* (1st ed.). New York, NY: Springer.

Commission on Rehabilitation Counselor Certification. (2010). *Code of ethics.* Retrieved from https://www.crccertification.com/code-of-ethics-3

Commission on Rehabilitation Counselor Certification. (2016). *Rehabilitation counseling scope of practice.* Retrieved from https://www.crccertification.com/scope-of-practice

Connor, A., Kuo, H. J., & Leahy, M. J. (in press). Assistive technology in pre-service rehabilitation counselor education: A new approach to team collaboration. *Rehabilitation Research, Policy, and Education.*

Connor, A., & Leahy, M. J. (2016). Teaching the working alliance: Bridging the gap between counseling microskills and establishing meaningful and productive relationships. *Rehabilitation Research, Policy, and Education, 30*(4), 371–388.

Corrigan, P. W., Mueser, K. T., Bond, G. R., Drake, R. E., & Solomon, P. (2012). *Principles and practice of psychiatric rehabilitation: An empirical approach.* New York, NY: Guilford Press.

Cottone, R., & Emener, W. (1990). The psychomedical paradigm of vocational rehabilitation and its alternatives. *Rehabilitation Counseling Bulletin, 39,* 119–129.

Council for Accreditation of Counseling and Related Educational Programs. (2016). *2016 CACREP standards.* Retrieved from www.cacrep.org/for-programs/2016-cacrep-standards/

DePalma, J. A. (2002). Proposing an evidence-based policy process. *Nursing Administration Quarterly, 26*(4), 55–61.

215

Emener, W. G., & Rubin, S. E. (1980). Rehabilitation counselor roles and functions and sources of role strain. *Journal of Applied Rehabilitation Counseling, 11,* 57–69.

Fabian, E. S., & MacDonald-Wilson, K. L. (2012). Professional practice in rehabilitation service delivery systems and related system resources. In R. M. Parker & J. B. Patterson (Eds.), *Rehabilitation counseling: Basics and beyond* (5th ed., pp. 55–84). Austin, TX: PRO-ED.

Falvo, D. R. (1999). *Medical and psychosocial aspects of chronic illness and disability* (2nd ed.). Gaithersburg, MD: Aspen.

Harrison, D. K., & Lee, C. C. (1979). Rehabilitation counselor competencies. *Journal of Applied Rehabilitation Counseling, 10,* 135–141.

Hartung, P., & Blustein, D. (2002). Reason, intuition, and social justice. Elaborating on Parsons's career decision-making model. *Journal of Counseling & Development, 80,* 41–47.

Hershenson, D. (1996). A theoretical model for rehabilitation counseling. *Rehabilitation Counseling Bulletin, 33,* 268–278.

Hosie, T. (1995). Counseling specialties: A case of basic preparation rather than advanced specialization. *Journal of Counseling & Development, 74,* 177–180.

Jaques, M. E. (1959). *Rehabilitation counseling: Scope and services.* Boston, MA: Houghton Mifflin.

Jenkins, W., Patterson, J. B., & Szymanski, E. M. (1992). Philosophical, historic, and legislative aspects of the rehabilitation counseling profession. In R. M. Parker & E. M. Szymanski (Eds.), *Rehabilitation counseling: Basics and beyond* (2nd ed., pp. 1–41). Austin, TX: PRO-ED.

Kosciulek, J. (1993). Advances in trait-and-factor theory: A person × environment fit approach to rehabilitation counseling. *Journal of Applied Rehabilitation Counseling, 24*(2), 11–14.

Kosciulek, J. F. (2014). Facilitating the career development of individuals with disabilities through empowering career counseling. In N. C. Gysbers, M. J. Heppner, & J. A. Johsnton (Eds.), *Career counseling: Holism, Diversity, and Strengths* (pp. 129–139). Alexandria, VA: American Counseling Association.

Kukla, M., & Bond, G. R. (2011). Psychiatric disabilities. In S. R. Flannagan, H. Zaretsky, & A. Moroz (Eds.)., *Medical aspects of disability: A handbook for the rehabilitation professional* (4th ed., pp. 441–466). New York, NY: Springer.

Kuo, H. J. (2013). *Rehabilitation counselors' perceptions of importance and competence of assistive technology* (Unpublished doctoral dissertation). Michigan State University, East Lansing.

Leahy, M. J. (2012). Qualified providers of rehabilitation counseling services. In D. R. Maki & V. M. Tarvydas (Eds.), *The professional practice of rehabilitation counseling* (pp. 193–211). New York, NY: Springer.

Leahy, M. J., & Arokiasamy, C. V. (2010). Prologue: Evidence-based practice research and knowledge translation in rehabilitation counseling. *Rehabilitation Education, 24*(3–4), 173–175.

Leahy, M. J., Chan, F., & Saunders, J. L. (2003). Job functions and knowledge requirements of certified rehabilitation counselors in the 21st century. *Rehabilitation Counseling Bulletin, 46,* 66–81.

Leahy, M. J., Chan, F., Sung, C., & Kim, M. (2013). Empirically derived test specifications for the certified rehabilitation counselor examination. *Rehabilitation Counseling Bulletin, 56,* 199–214.

Leahy, M. J., & Holt, E. (1993). Certification in rehabilitation counseling: History and process. *Journal of Applied Rehabilitation Counseling, 24*(4), 5–9.

Leahy, M. J., Muenzen, P., Saunders, J. L., & Strauser, D. (2009). Essential knowledge domains underlying effective rehabilitation counseling practice. *Rehabilitation Counseling Bulletin, 52,* 95–106.

Leahy, M. J., Rak, E., & Zanskas, S. A. (2016). A brief history of counseling and specialty areas of practice. In I. Marini & M. A. Stebnicki (Eds.), *The professional counselor's desk reference* (2nd ed., pp. 3–8). New York, NY: Springer.

Leahy, M. J., Shapson, P. R., & Wright, G. N. (1987). Rehabilitation practitioner competencies by role and setting. *Rehabilitation Counseling Bulletin, 31,* 119–131.

Leahy, M. J., & Szymanski, E. M. (1995). Rehabilitation counseling: Evolution and current status. *Journal of Counseling & Development, 74,* 163–166.

Leahy, M. J., Szymanski, E., & Linkowski, D. C. (1993). Knowledge importance in rehabilitation counseling. *Rehabilitation Counseling Bulletin, 37,* 130–145.

Leahy, M. J., & Tansey, T. N. (2008). The impact of CORE standards across the rehabilitation educational continuum. *Rehabilitation Education, 22*(3&4), 217–226.

Leahy, M. J., & Tarvydas, V. M. (2001). Transforming our professional organizations: A first step toward unification of the rehabilitation counseling profession. *Journal of Applied Rehabilitation Counseling, 32,* 3–8.

Leahy, M. J., Tarvydas, V. M., & Phillips, B. N. (2011). Rehabilitation counseling's phoenix project: Re-visiting the call for the unification of the professional associations of rehabilitation counseling. *Rehabilitation Research, Policy, and Education, 25*(1/2), 5–14.

Leahy, M. J., Thielsen, V. A., Millington, M. J., Austin, B., & Fleming, A. (2009). Quality assurance and program evaluation: Terms, models, and applications. *Journal of Rehabilitation Administration, 33*(2), 69–82.

Linkowski, D. C., & Szymanski, E. M. (1993). Accreditation in rehabilitation counseling: Historical and current context and process. *Journal of Applied Rehabilitation Counseling, 24*(4), 10–15.

Maki, D. R. (2012). Concepts and paradigms in rehabilitation counseling. In D. R. Maki & V. M. Tarvydas (Eds.), *The professional practice of rehabilitation counseling* (pp. 83–107). New York, NY: Springer.

Maki, D. R., McCracken, N., Pape, D. A., & Scofield, M. E. (1979). A systems approach to vocational assessment. *Journal of Rehabilitation, 45*(1), 48–51.

Menz, F. E., Botterbusch, K., Hagen-Foley, D., & Johnson, P. T. (2003). *Achieving quality outcomes through community-based rehabilitation programs: The results are in.* Unpublished manuscript, University of Wisconsin–Stout, Stout Vocational Rehabilitation Institute, Research and Training Center.

Mueser, K. T., Torrey, W. C., Lynde, D., Singer, P., & Drake, R. E. (2003). Implementing evidence-based practices for people with severe mental illness. *Behavior Modification, 27,* 387–411.

Muthard, J. E., & Salomone, P. (1969). The roles and functions of the rehabilitation counselor. *Rehabilitation Counseling Bulletin, 13,* 81–168.

Myers, J. (1995). Specialties in counseling: Rich heritage or force for fragmentation? *Journal of Counseling & Development, 74,* 115–116.

Myers, J. E. (2012). Foreword. In D. R. Maki & V. M. Tarvydas (Eds.), *The professional practice of rehabilitation counseling* (pp. xv–xvii). New York, NY: Springer.

Parkin, E. K., & Nosek, M. A. (2001). Collectivism versus independence: Perceptions of independent living and independent living services by Hispanic Americans and Asian Americans with disabilities. *Rehabilitation Education, 15,* 375–394.

Parsons, F. (1967). *Choosing a vocation* [reprint of the 1909 ed.] New York, NY: Agathon Press.

Phillips, B., & Zhao, H. (1993). Predictors of assistive technology abandonment. *Assistive Technology, 5,* 36–45.

Plotner, A. J., Trach, J. S., Oertle, J. M., & Fleming, A. R. (2014). Differences in service delivery between transition VR counselors and general VR counselors. *Rehabilitation Counseling Bulletin, 57,* 109–116.

Plotner, A. J., Trach, J. S., & Strauser, D. R. (2012). Vocational rehabilitation counselors' identified transition competencies: Perceived importance, frequency, and preparedness. *Rehabilitation Counseling Bulletin, 55,* 135–143.

Rehabilitation Act of 1973, PL 93-112, 29 U.S.C. §§ 701 *et seq.*

Remley, T. P. (1993). A proposed alternative to the licensing of specialties in counseling. *Journal of Counseling & Development, 74,* 126–129.

Riemer-Reiss, M. L., & Wacker, R. R. (2000). Factors associated with assistive technology discontinuance among individuals with disabilities. *Journal of Rehabilitation, 66*(3), 44–50.

Riesen, T., Schultz, J., Morgan, R., & Kupferman, S. (2014). School-to-work barriers as identified by special educators, vocational rehabilitation counselors, and community rehabilitation professionals. *Journal of Rehabilitation, 80*(1), 33–44.

Roessler, R. (1990). A quality of life perspective on rehabilitation counseling. *Rehabilitation Counseling Bulletin, 34,* 82–90.

Roessler, R. T., & Rubin, S. E. (Eds.). (1992). Mission and role of the rehabilitation counselor. In *Case management and rehabilitation counseling* (2nd ed., pp. 1–16). Austin, TX: PRO-ED.

Rose, G. (1993). Mental disorder and the strategies of prevention. *Psychological Medicine, 23,* 553–555. doi:10.1017/S0033291700025320

Rothman, R. A. (1987). *Working: Sociological perspectives.* Englewood Cliffs, NJ: Prentice Hall.

Rubin, S. E., Matkin, R. E., Ashley, J., Beardsley, M. M., May, V. R., Onstott, K., ... Puckett, F. D. (1984). Roles and functions of certified rehabilitation counselors. *Rehabilitation Counseling Bulletin, 27,* 199–224.

Rubin, S. E., & Roessler, R. T. (2008). *Foundations of the vocational rehabilitation process* (6th ed.). Austin, TX: PRO-ED.

Saunders, J. L., Barros-Bailey, M., Chapman, C., & Nunez, P. (2009). Rehabilitation counselor certification: Moving forward. *Rehabilitation Counseling Bulletin, 52,* 77–84.

Scherer, M. J. (2002). *Assistive technology: Matching device and consumer for successful rehabilitation.* Washington, DC: American Psychological Association.

Scherer, M. J., & Sax, T. L. (2004). Technology. In T. F. Rigor & D. R. Maki (Eds.), *Handbook of rehabilitation counseling* (pp. 271–288). New York, NY: Springer.

Smart, J. F., & Smart, D. W. (2006). Models of disability: Implications for the counseling profession. *Journal of Counseling & Development, 84,* 29–40.

Smith-Fess Act of 1920, PL 67-236, 29 U.S.C. §§ 31 *et seq.*

Social Security Act of 1935, PL 74-271, 42 U.S.C. §§ 301 *et seq.*

Soldiers Rehabilitation Act of 1918, PL 65-178, U.S.C. §§ 501 *et seq.*

Sweeney, T. J. (1995). Accreditation, credentialing, professionalization: The role of specialties. *Journal of Counseling & Development, 74,* 117–125.

Sweeney, T. J. (2001). Counseling: Historical origins and philosophical roots. In D. Locke, J. Myers, & E. Herr (Eds.), *The handbook of counseling* (pp. 3–26). Thousand Oaks, CA: Sage.

Szymanski, E. M., Leahy, M. J., & Linkowski, D. C. (1993). Reported preparedness of certified counselors in rehabilitation counseling knowledge areas. *Rehabilitation Counseling Bulletin, 37,* 146–162.

Tarvydas, V. M., & Cottone, R. R. (2000). The code of ethics for professional rehabilitation counselors: What we have and what we need. *Rehabilitation Counseling Bulletin, 43,* 188–196.

Tarvydas, V., Cottone, R. R., & Saunders, J. S. (2010). A new ethics code as a tool for innovations in ethical practice. *Rehabilitation Counseling Bulletin, 53,* 195–196.

Tarvydas, V. M., & Leahy, M. J. (1993). Licensure in rehabilitation counseling: A critical incident in professionalization. *Rehabilitation Counseling Bulletin, 37,* 92–109.

Tarvydas, V., Leahy, M. J., & Zanskas, S. A. (2009). Reappraisal of rehabilitation movement toward licensure parity. *Rehabilitation Counseling Bulletin, 52,* 85–94.

U.S. Department of Labor. (2015). *Occupational Outlook Handbook: Rehabilitation counselors.* Retrieved from www.bls.gov/ooh/community-and-social-service/rehabilitation-counselors.htm

Vocational Rehabilitation Act Amendments of 1943, PL 113, Ch. 190, 57 Stat. 374, 29 U.S.C. §§ 3141 *et seq.*

Vocational Rehabilitation Act Amendments of 1954, PL 82-565, 36 U.S.C. §§ 101 *et seq.*

Wampold, B. E. (2001). *The great psychotherapy debate: Model, methods, and findings.* Mahwah, NJ: Erlbaum.

Workforce Investment Act of 1998, PL 105-220, 29 U.S.C. §§ 2801 *et seq.*

World Health Organization. (2002). *Towards a common language of functioning, disability, and health: ICF.* Geneva, Switzerland: Author.

Wright, G. N. (1980). *Total rehabilitation.* Boston, MA: Little, Brown.

Wright, G. N., & Fraser, R. T. (1975). *Task analysis for the evaluation, preparation, classification, and utilization of rehabilitation counselor track personnel* (Wisconsin Studies in Vocational Rehabilitation Monograph No. 22, Series 3). Madison, WI: University of Wisconsin.

Chapter 9

College Counseling
and Student Affairs

Perry C. Francis

Learning Objectives

1. Understand the difference between college counseling and student affairs.
2. Identify the ways in which college counselors and student affairs professionals work together for student success.
3. Be able to identify the current mental health issues of college students.
4. Understand the different ethical issues that affect college counseling and student affairs.

• • •

Counseling has been defined by the vast majority of the profession as "a professional relationship that empowers diverse individuals, families, and groups to accomplish mental health, wellness, educational, and career goals" (Kaplan, Tarvydas, & Gladding, 2014, p. 368). College counseling is the application of that definition by professional counselors on a college campus. This also includes those who use their education and skills in counseling in the various student affairs offices (e.g., career services, campus life, disabilities services, the wellness center; Remley &

Shaw, 2013). However, college counseling and student affairs are much more complex than the simple application of the counselor's knowledge and skills in a college setting. From the time Harvard University hired its first dean of students to administer advising, personal and vocational guidance, and discipline in 1870 to the development of one of the first college counseling centers to provide educational and vocational guidance to students at the University of Minnesota in 1932, college counseling and student affairs have been evolving to meet the needs of students and their educational institutions (Meadows, 2000; Rentz & Howard-Hamilton, 2011). College counseling has grown beyond personal and vocational guidance to now include counseling services (both long and short term), consultation with faculty and staff, the education and supervision of interns, career planning, crisis and emergency services, and much more (Brunner, Wallace, Reymann, Sellers, & McCabe, 2014; Francis, 2011; Hodges, Shelton, & Lyn, 2016). Student affairs has evolved from its early days of ensuring the moral and religious development of students to include a plethora of programs that complement the academic mission of the institution, support the personal and social development of students, and anticipate the continual changes in the needs of the student body (Rentz & Howard-Hamilton, 2011). The form and function of the services provided depend on the type of institution (e.g., community or technical college, 4-year college/university, large comprehensive research university), the campus environment and history of student services on campus, the budget, staff size, and the training of those involved (Francis & Horn, 2016).

This chapter introduces you to the specialties of student affairs and college counseling in the world of the counseling profession. I briefly review each area, its roles and functions within the college system, and how you as a professional counselor can fulfill those duties as part your larger identity as a counseling professional.

Counseling in Student Affairs

The role and function of student affairs has evolved in tandem with growth and change in the student body, the expectations of parents concerning the university's role as a caretaker of the student (e.g., *in loco parentis*), and the shifting role of the university in American society (Carpenter, 2011). As one counselor in student affairs reveals, counseling skills are a benefit in work with parents:

> So where does counseling fit into my job as orientation and family programs coordinator? On program days, I'm sure that you can imagine the listening and empathy skills I use as the families of 2,800 new students each year send their student off to college for the first time! I often find myself referring back to having learned to sense when there's a "question behind the question"; sometimes parents really *are* agitated over whether their students will be able

to find, for example, extralong twin sheets, but more often they are worried about how their student will find the resources necessary to navigate a new world, with new people and new places, all while testing the newfound independence that comes when students leave home for the first time.

Every single skill we learn in basic skills classes is invaluable, with a special shout-out to paraphrasing, summarizing, and the intentional use of silence. I create a space for my student staff members to use our weekly one-on-ones to hear their own voice so they can make meaning out of their own learning experiences. When they're all together I use group process skills and model for them how to be effective *and* supportive members of a team that will serve them wherever they go, in whatever they do.

There are so many great opportunities in student affairs to use the foundation that we build over the course of a counseling degree. Most of my student staff (and many of the families I serve), upon hearing that my background is counseling, have said something like, "Oh that makes sense." I take this to mean that my skills create an environment where they feel safe to ask questions or express uncertainty and that they trust that together we will do the work to empower them to set goals and then rise up to meet them.

The broad goal of a student affairs professional is to support the academic mission of the institution while promoting the social, intellectual, and emotional development of the whole student (Francis, 2011; Nuss, 2003). This is accomplished through offices such as campus life, career services, wellness centers, disabilities services, and leadership development. Your knowledge as a professional counselor in areas such as student development, wellness and prevention, therapeutic communication, the impact of stress on performance (e.g., personal and intellectual), relationships, and the development of mental illness gives you the skills and abilities to work within this profession (Remley & Shaw, 2013); yet to be successful in applying this knowledge, you must also have an understanding of what the American College Personnel Association (2008) identified as the student learning imperative:

- Hallmarks of a college educated person include: (a) complex cognitive skills such as reflection and critical thinking; (b) an ability to apply knowledge to practical problems encountered in one's vocation, family, or other areas of life; (c) an understanding and appreciation of human differences; (d) practical competence skills (e.g., decision making, conflict resolution); and (e) a coherent integrated sense of [identity], self-esteem, confidence, integrity, aesthetic sensibilities, and civic responsibility.
- The concepts of "learning," "personal development," and "student development" are inextricably intertwined and inseparable.
- Experiences in various in-class and out-of-class settings, both on and off the campus, contribute to learning and personal development. Indeed, almost any educationally purposeful experience may be a precursor to desired outcomes.

- Learning and personal development occur through transactions between students and their environments broadly defined to include other people (faculty, student affairs staff, peers), physical spaces, and cultural milieus.
- Knowledge and understanding are critical, not only to student success but also to institutional improvement.
- Student affairs professionals are educators who share responsibility with faculty, academic administrators, other staff, and students themselves for creating the conditions under which students are likely to expend time and energy in educationally-purposeful activities.

As you can see from this list, student affairs professionals share in the education of the students. Whereas the faculty educates students in both the general and major subject areas of the curriculum, student affairs professionals contribute to the social, emotional, intellectual, and career development of students through the unofficial curriculum that is part of the life of the campus. Examples of this can be found in the career exploration classes offered by the community college counseling center staff, the sexual assault prevention programming offered by the residential life staff at the beginning of each academic year, or the diversity training offered by the Office of Diversity and Community Involvement. In each case, the student affairs staff supports the development of students and contributes to their body of knowledge. The following extract highlights how one counselor has translated his education into his work in an Office of Disabilities Services:

One of the central goals of counseling is to help clients function as best as possible through the multiple challenges they face. That is also the goal in a disability services office at our college. We do not diagnose students, but we carefully analyze their disabilities and in collaboration with them create a plan to best serve and support them through college. These plans range from granting accommodations on tests and technology, to meeting weekly and working on improving certain essential skills, to goal setting. It parallels a lot of what is done in typical counseling sessions as we try to guide students in advocating for themselves and their wellness and help further evolve thoughts and behaviors that may be detrimental to their academic and personal success.

Our office deals with a wide range of diagnoses. When people hear *disability*, they often visualize a person in a wheelchair or with another noticeable limitation. While we do serve this population, the majority of the population we serve have what we call *invisible disabilities*. This includes depression, anxiety, dyslexia, dyscalculia, bipolar disorder, or other executive function disorders. My background in counseling has helped me understand how to view and work with these diagnoses, but in a more academic frame. I use accommodations and teach new behavior skill sets to help the students overcome obstacles.

My counseling education is used daily in my work as I conceptualize our students in a holistic manner. For many students, their disability has been a label and a way others identify them. Other students who were diagnosed later in life may have certain stigmas they struggle with. In either case, we know their disability is only part of who they are, and we work with them at the intersection of their lives and education in order to come up with the best services for their success.

College Counseling

As noted previously, college counseling is more than the application of counseling services to a specific population and environment. The size and type of the educational institution, funding, mission, staff size and training, and the configuration of student services will all affect the role of the counseling center on a college campus (Francis & Horn, 2016). The role of the counselor on campus is, therefore, dependent on the importance and mission of the counseling center in the life of the institution.

Community college counseling centers often provide the greatest variety of services by combining the counseling center (which provides short-term mental health counseling and crisis services, consultation with faculty, career services, and referrals to long-term counseling) with academic advising services (which provide students with help in choosing and registering for classes, determine students' need for developmental courses, and/or help with academic skills training; American College Counseling Association [ACCA], 2014; Kay & Schwartz, 2010; Sharkin, 2012). A survey of community colleges revealed that only 8% of 2-year colleges had psychiatric services available to their students on campus and 19% did not offer mental health services at all (ACCA, 2014). Of those campuses that did not offer any mental health services, 22% referred students to off-campus providers, 20% outsourced their mental health work, and 20% referred problematic behaviors potentially related to mental health concerns to behavioral intervention teams (BITs) or threat assessment teams (ACCA, 2014).

A large, well-funded university counseling center may offer few academic services, if any, but will offer more comprehensive mental health services, including psychiatric consultations for medications, long-term psychotherapy, internships, postdoctoral positions, and intensive supervision and training (Reetz, Krylowicz, & Mistler, 2014). When asked in 2014, college counseling directors at 4-year institutions revealed that 61% of their staff's time was taken up with direct counseling services and 22% was used for supervision/training, consultation, and outreach (Reetz et al., 2014).

Between the community college counseling center and the large university counseling center are a variety of types of counseling centers that provide different levels of services (Reetz et al., 2014; Vespia, 2007). The size of the counseling center and type of counseling services offered will affect the staffing configuration (i.e., counselors, psychologists, and/or social workers). Community colleges and smaller colleges generally employ more professional counselors, and midsize and larger counseling centers generally employ more psychologists or have a multidisciplinary staff that can specialize in specific populations or issues (e.g., substance abuse, eating disorders; Sharkin, 2012). The following extract from the counseling center director at a small, rural, high-achieving college highlights the reality of working in a smaller college setting:

> The only thing typical about a typical day at a college counseling center is that nothing is ever typical. The counseling center is often the place the college community turns to whenever anything bad happens. I have been flagged down by the director of human resources first thing in the morning as I am walking from my car to the office, coffee in hand, because a staff member tried to kill himself earlier that morning and he wants me to address the staff member's colleagues as soon as possible. I have received phone calls from the dean of students at 4:45 p.m. on a Friday to tell me that the swim coach was arrested for possessing child pornography and the swimming championships are this weekend and the dean wants to know how we should proceed. Working at a college counseling center is so much more than providing the day-to-day mental health care for students. Sometimes it feels like client sessions are a nice break from the other issues that we have been asked to address. And sometimes client sessions turn into the sole focus of the day. It is not uncommon for students to disclose during a counseling session that they are suicidal. They may even have a means and a plan but refuse to participate in an emergency psychiatric evaluation. So other client sessions scheduled for that day get canceled and we turn into case managers to develop a plan to ensure the student's safety. As the mental health needs of college students continue to increase, the demands on college counseling centers increase as well. This often causes a strain on resources but has also gone a long way to destigmatize mental health treatment and highlight the growing need for mental health resources. We are a field on the rise.

Students entering institutions of higher education are the most diverse we have ever seen (Watkins, Hunt, & Eisenberg, 2012). One in five students from the Millennial generation will come from a family in which at least one parent is an immigrant. One in 10 students will have at least one parent who is a not a U.S. citizen (Howe & Strauss, 2003). As part of your preparations to become a professional counselor working in a counseling center or a student affairs office, you will be exposed to and learn about many different cultures. These different cultural distinctions can be obvious (e.g., race) or invisible (e.g., religious or spiritual). In any case, it is incumbent on you as the counselor to be open to the many experiences that students and their families bring into the consultation room or the office of the dean of students. The first step in that process is to be aware of your own cultural history and heritage and how it affects how you view the world. Without that willingness to examine where you come from and how you see the world, any other education will be less than what it could be.

Developmental Theory and Student Affairs/College Counseling

Try and imagine the face of a traditional college student or simply remember what it was like for you to be a student on a college campus. Images of fresh-faced 18- to 24-year-old students studying, working, and playing on well-manicured lawns surrounding ivy-covered buildings come to mind for many people; yet you will find that the reality is far different. Depending on the institution, students vary in age, race/ethnicity, and gender and gender orientation, with the number of nontraditional students (25+ years of age) increasing at a slightly quicker pace than that of the number of traditional students (18–25 years of age) across the country. In addition, institutions of all types are seeing increases in the diversity of their student bodies (National Center for Education Statistics, 2015). Those professionals who work in student affairs and college counseling need a broad understanding of the developmental needs of each group. Having an understanding of the relevant developmental theories will help you to design and implement educational programming; social, emotional, and psychological interventions; and vocational and career planning and will help you support the overall mission of the institution to graduate students who are ready to enter (or re-enter) the world beyond the gates of the university. You will find an overview of human growth and development theories in Chapter 2.

Beyond the traditional developmental theories that encompass the human life span, additional theories address the specific issues of college students. Although it is beyond the scope of this chapter to give a detailed overview of each theory, a list of the relevant theories is offered in Table 9.1.

It would be difficult for anyone to have an in-depth knowledge of each one of these theories. However, having a working knowledge of each area of development will help you meet the unique needs of the diverse students who populate a college campus.

Professional Identity and Associations

Counseling is a profession (Francis & Dugger, 2014). It requires specific university-based education at the graduate level, requires expertise in specialized skills and knowledge beyond what would be found in the general population, and has a body of scholarly research that is disseminated through a professional association that helps to establish

Table 9.1   Relevant Student Development Theories
for Student Affairs and College Counselors

Theory Type	Theory
Identity development	Psychosocial development (Erickson, 1959)
	Ego identity status (Marcia, 1993)
	Seven vectors (Chickering & Reisser, 1993)
Intellectual and ethical development	Cognitive schemes (Perry, 1968)
	Women's ways of knowing (Belenky et al., 1986)
Moral development	Theory of moral development (Kohlberg, 1981)
	Theory of women's moral development (Gilligan, 1982)
Racial identity development	Racial and cultural identity development: five-stage model (Atkinson et al., 1993)
	Model of White identity development (Helms, 1995)
Sexual identity development	Model of sexual orientation formation (Cass, 1979)
	Model of gay and lesbian identity development (Fassinger, 1998)

a professional identity (Francis & Dugger, 2014). This professional identity is further divided into areas of specialization that themselves have their own particular identities and professional associations. This identity is developed by the shared values, ethics, and education that are organized by and disseminated through professional associations and their codes of ethics and provides a foundation for the development of future professional counselors (Gorman & Sandefur, 2011; Moss, Gibson, & Dollarhide, 2014; Reiner, Dobmeier, & Hernández, 2013). The identity of professional counselors is grounded in the shared philosophy of service focused on wellness; the prevention of mental illness; human growth and development; honoring the diversity of humanity; promoting social justice; and a shared belief in the worth, dignity, and potential of every human being (American Counseling Association [ACA], 2014; Reiner et al., 2013).

You will find that college counselors primarily identify with the counseling profession while having their own professional division (ACCA) within the main professional association (ACA; ACCA, 2016). Student affairs professionals have a more diffuse identity that is dependent on their area of specialization. Professionals within some of these specializations (e.g., academic affairs, assessment and evaluation, and campus safety) would not benefit from having an educational background in counseling. It would benefit you to explore the many professional organizations that represent counseling and student affairs as you begin to form your own professional identity (see "Further

Resources") and determine which one best fits your future career goals. Most professional associations have student memberships at a reduced cost and want to be a part of your development as a future professional in the field (see Sidebar 9.1).

Mental Health Issues on a College Campus: Contextual Dimensions

What you have read to this point in the chapter has provided you with a foundation for college counseling. Now, to help you gain a greater depth of knowledge, I provide you with the context for this specialty. As I noted previously, college counseling is more than just applying generic counseling knowledge and skills to a particular setting. It involves applying that knowledge to the special challenges, limitations, boundaries, and environment that are present on a campus of higher learning.

Attending college is an exciting time in anyone's life. It is filled with anticipation and anxiety as students try out new behaviors and try on new identities. Think about your own undergraduate days and the many different things you tried as you searched for your own identity and place in the world. For traditional undergraduate students (18–25 years of age) it is also a time when many mental illnesses begin to develop. If mental illness developed during students' high school years and was managed well with the help of parents, teachers, or counselors, students must now manage the illness on their own (Kessler et al., 2007).

The Increasing Complexity of Mental Health Issues on Campus

Although the utilization of counseling services has remained relatively stable at 10%–15% of the student population (Francis, 2015; Reetz et

Sidebar 9.1   Reflection Questions

Think back to your own time in college.
How diverse was the college you attended?
How did that shape your worldview?
Did any of your friends come from a different cultural background than you? If so, what did you learn from them? If not, how has that shaped your view of others?
What do you think is the difference between your college experience and the experience of students today?
How does this affect your approach to college counseling and student affairs?

• • •

al., 2014), the complexity of mental health issues has increased over the past decades (Benton & Benton, 2006; Brunner et al., 2014). The reasons for this increase in complexity are multifaceted and include the following:

- *Increased academic expectations:* Students who present at college counseling centers with depression and anxiety or seek help through support services (e.g., tutoring, writing labs) often cite academic problems as the cause of their issues (Flatt, 2013).
- *Increased financial burdens:* Student debt is at an all-time high, and concerns over defaulting and debt collection have increased levels of depression, anxiety, and worry (Morgenson, 2015; Watkins et al., 2012). The average student is also working more hours to earn the money necessary to pay an ever-increasing tuition (Narula, 2014).
- *Accessibility of higher education:* Going to college was once the privilege of the elite. Today, higher education has never been more accessible. In addition, the diversity of the student body has increased markedly. With this increased accessibility also comes an increase in the number of students with mental health concerns who once were unable to attend college (Watkins et al., 2012).
- *Increased use of psychotropic medication:* Students are being treated earlier for mental health issues (i.e., in high school) and arriving on the college campus with their pockets full of medications. Whereas once students would work with a therapist to discuss their feelings and work through their problems, according to Carter and Winseman (2003), they are now using the language of psychotropic medications and neurobiology and seeking services for medications instead of psychotherapy. In addition, students who might not have been able to attend college because of a persistent or chronic mental illness can now attend with the help of modern medications (Francis, 2015).

Anxiety and Depression

The two most common mental health issues that plague students are anxiety and depression (Beiter et al., 2015). Anxiety recently surpassed depression as the most common issue among students seeking services (Center for Collegiate Mental Health, 2015; Reetz et al., 2014). Beiter et al. (2015) attributed this high occurrence of anxiety to "academic performance, pressure to succeed, post-graduate plans, financial concerns, quality of sleep, relationships with friends, relationships with family, overall health, body image, and self-esteem" (p. 93). Ask yourself the following: How did you feel after you were accepted for graduate studies? After you celebrated your admission into your program, were there any feelings of self-doubt about your ability to do the required work? Were you at all concerned that you were on the correct path? Were you at all concerned with how you were going to pay for your education? These nagging questions can lead to anxiety and distract students from performing at best.

Although depression is now second to anxiety as the most common mental health concern among students, it continues to be a significant impediment to student success (Chung et al., 2011), affecting between 12% and 33% of students per year (American College Health Association, 2014; Lee, 2005). An annual American College Health Association (2014) survey of college health found that, in the past 30 days, students (n = 79,266) felt hopeless (7%), overwhelmed with all they had to do (16%), very lonely (11%), very sad (11%), so depressed it was difficult to function (5%), and overwhelming anxiety (9%). These same students were asked to identify factors that affected their individual academic performance, the effect of which may have resulted in a lower grade on an exam, project, or course; in an incomplete grade or withdrawal from a course; or in a substantial interruption in their research, thesis/ dissertation, or practicum. The top six of 32 unique factors identified were stress (30.3%), anxiety (21.8%), sleep difficulties (21%), cold/flu/ sore throat (15.1%), work (13.8%), and depression (13.5%).

Nonsuicidal Self-Injury

Students use various means to manage emotions and stress. One such way to manage anxiety and depression is through nonsuicidal self-injury (Whitlock et al., 2011). Whitlock and her colleagues (2011) surveyed a large group of college students (n = 14,372) and found that 15% had taken part in some form of nonsuicidal self-injury over the course of their lifetimes. This included behaviors such as carving words or symbols on their bodies; scratching, cutting, burning, or otherwise causing damage to the skin; and hitting an object or self. The purpose of such behavior is often to regulate troubling emotions, to engage in self-punishment, to engage in psychological or physiological stimulation, or to relieve overwhelming feelings and urges (Whitlock et al., 2011).

Alcohol Abuse

College students have been using and abusing alcohol and other substances for centuries. The impact of this abuse has exacted a tremendous toll on the personal, academic, and career futures of thousands of students (Johnston, O'Malley, Bachman, & Schulenberg, 2010). According to the National Institute on Alcohol Abuse and Alcoholism (2015), although alcohol use, abuse, and experimentation has often been seen as a rite of passage during college, the consequences of dangerous and underage drinking include the following:

- *Death:* More than 1,800 young adults die each year from alcohol-related accidents (injuries and automobile accidents).
- *Assault/violence:* As many as 686,000 students have been involved in violence or have been assaulted by another student who has been drinking.
- *Sexual assault:* Approximately 97,000 students have reported date rape or a sexual assault related to alcohol.
- *Academic problems:* About 25% of students report earning lower grades on papers and/or exams, missing classes and assignments, and falling behind in class as a consequence of alcohol use and abuse.
- *Alcohol use disorder:* As many of 20% of college students meet the criteria for alcohol use disorder.

Programs and strategies to reduce alcohol use on college campuses have met with mixed results and are often dependent on the environment or unique circumstances that is a part of each institution (e.g., its location, the presence of sports programs, the existence of fraternities and sororities; Licciardone, 2003a, 2003b; National Institute on Alcohol Abuse and Alcoholism, 2015). The National Institute on Alcohol Abuse and Alcoholism maintains a database and reviews of more than 60 educational and prevention programs and offers environmental strategies to compare and implement these programs on college campuses (CollegeAIM, 2016). Student affairs professionals develop or implement educational and prevention programming to curb the misuse of alcohol on college campuses. College counselors are often called on to provide programming as well as alcohol abuse assessments and counseling. Both student affairs professionals and college counselors are also involved in related activities that are often affected by alcohol abuse (e.g., sexual assault counseling, academic remediation).

What Does All of This Mean for Student Affairs and College Counseling Professionals?

Although all of this information may leave you with the impression that all college students are suffering from some sort of mental or emotional malady, the fact is the vast majority of students arrive on campus and successfully proceed to graduation with a minimum of problems. These same students also manage to navigate the developmental challenges and issues that are part of moving from adolescence to young adulthood, discovering within themselves resources and abilities that they never knew they had but their parents knew would develop. A review of 2014 data from the Higher Education Research Institute's Freshman Survey found that 50.7% of entering first-year students rated themselves above average or in the highest 10% for emotional health (Eagan et al., 2014). Although this is the lowest rating since the survey began in 1966, it still clearly demonstrates that the majority of students are doing well. What we can take from surveys like this is that the work of student affairs professionals and college mental health providers is very important in helping students move through this period of development and graduate college as productive citizens and healthy individuals. Reflect on how the following counseling center director at a midsize urban university helps students move through their college education and on to graduation:

> During graduate school, I completed my practicum in a college counseling center and absolutely loved it. I was lucky enough to get a full-time job in a college counseling center only 18 months after earning my master's degree in counseling. The director of that center provided me with board-approved supervision while I worked towards my license, which was a great bonus. And I really appreciated the work environment. College students are in this period of transition and identity development. They are also at an age where some significant mental illness can pop up for the first time. I've had clients come to the center describing symptoms indicative of a first manic episode or the onset of psychotic symptoms. So we see a diagnostic range from normal developmental issues all the way to severe and chronic mental illness. Within that range, there are some common themes of anxiety, depression, and relationship issues. There will also be urgent walk-ins and crisis situations requiring the counselor to assess harm to self or others and provide services to students coping with recent sexual assaults or domestic violence.
>
> Aside from doing a lot of individual therapy, we also provide periodic outreach programming to help students understand what the center offers while educating and working to destigmatize various mental health topics. The outreach will include tabling events in a main area of campus, hosting guest speakers on certain topics, conducting workshops to help students build coping skills, and even classroom presentations.

Working Together for Student Success: Practice Dimensions

You have been presented with the foundations and context of college counseling and student affairs. In this next section, I share with you how the practice of college counseling and student affairs is applied on the college campus, especially as these two related professions work together to help students overcome challenges, be successful learners, and prepare for a life beyond the classroom. In addition, you will read about how the practice of college counseling is guided by the ethics of our profession and the challenges the college environment places on those ethics.

Although college counselors and student affairs professionals may work in separate offices, they share the common goal of helping students succeed in an academic environment and ultimately preparing them to graduate to a life outside the institution. When students enter the institution, they are met by student affairs professionals, some of whom have a counselor orientation and education and work in various student success offices throughout campus. When students face social, emotional, and educational barriers, they can also find help in counseling center consultation rooms. At times, the work of these two related professions intersects on campus through shared services and programs. Two such examples are BITs and suicide prevention programs.

BITs

BITs were first created as threat assessment or crisis intervention teams following the shootings at Virginia Tech in 2007. Today, they are staffed by senior campus professionals, many of whom have student affairs, security, educational, and counseling backgrounds. Their task is to convene on a regular basis (usually weekly, depending on the type and size of the institution) to identify students who may be at risk for failure or are disruptive to campus life and to intervene with primary and tertiary services before a problem becomes serious (National Behavioral Intervention Team Association, 2015; Sharkin, 2012). The role of the student affairs professionals on a BIT is to identify and offer services that may be used to intervene with and help students proactively. The role of the counselor (often the counseling center director) is that of a consultant who offers a mental health perspective on what may be the cause of students' issues (Van Brunt, Reese, & Lewis, 2015). The counselor's ability to offer insights through the use of case studies, diagnostic impressions, and information about the tendencies of similar students is helpful, as the BIT crafts interventions for students (Van Brunt et al., 2015). At the same time, the role of the counselor is limited by the legal and ethical rules governing the practice of counseling. Specific information about students who may come before the BIT and who are clients of the counseling center cannot be released without the written consent of the student unless there are issues of serious and foreseeable harm to self and others (e.g., the potential for suicide, violence, or homicide; ACA, 2014; Eells & Rockland-Miller, 2011).

A college counselor may at times be asked to evaluate a student for a BIT to assess the level of dangerousness or potential for violence or suicidal ideation. Counselor education programs generally provide instruction on assessing and managing suicidal behaviors and crises (Council for Accreditation of Counseling and Related Educational Programs, 2016), but training in the assessment of violence or potential violence is not as extensive (Van Brunt, 2015). If counselors are asked to provide either service, it is incumbent on them to ensure that they are properly trained and/ or supervised and that the service is within their mission within the college counseling center.

Suicide Prevention and Education

The problem of student suicides on college campuses began to gain national attention with the death of Elizabeth Shin at the Massachusetts Institute of Technology in April 2000. Her death raised the subject of not only student suicides on college campuses but also how colleges were helping students with suicidal ideation and notification of the parents of students who had been hospitalized (Farrell, 2002; Sontag, 2002). Following the death of their son Jed to suicide on a college campus in 2000, Donna and Phil Satow created the Jed Foundation. It is now one of the premier organizations in the country providing programming, resources, and advocacy for suicide prevention, student wellness, and emotional health (Jed Foundation, 2016). Shin's death and a subsequent lawsuit against the Massachusetts Institute of Technology, as well as the creation of the Jed Foundation to foster prevention and treatment programming, helped bring the problem of student suicide to the attention of the nation. Finally, after the suicide of his son, Garrett Lee Smith, on the day before his 22nd birthday in 2003, U.S. Senator Gordon H. Smith of Oregon proposed legislation that would eventually become law (the Garrett Lee Smith Memorial Act) funding prevention and education grants for college campuses and Native American Indian reservations (Smith, 2007).

Despite their best efforts, college campuses continue to be challenged by student suicide and suicidal ideation. The level of suicidal ideation increased among college students from 24% in 2010–2011 to 31% in 2013–2014 (Center for Collegiate Mental Health, 2015). Although the prevalence of suicide is less among college students (6.5–7.5 per 100,000) than among individuals of the same age not enrolled in college (11 per 100,000), suicide continues to be the second leading cause of death among college students after vehicular and other accidents (Turner, Leno, & Keller, 2013). The death of a student by suicide in a residence hall can have a devastating effect on the other students in the dorm, second only to the impact it will have on the family of that student (Keyes, 2013).

College counselors and student affairs professionals work together on educational programming, prevention efforts, and gatekeeping training for faculty and staff (Taub et al., 2013). The common elements in many of these prevention programs are Web-based applications to help in the management of stress and bystander training of students, faculty, and staff (Drum & Denmark, 2012; Haas et al., 2008). In addition, student affairs specialists and college counselors train resident hall staff to recognize the signs and symptoms of depression, anxiety, and suicidal ideation/behavior and learn to intervene with appropriate referrals and reports to help ensure that students are obtaining the help they need to be safe and successful (Taub et al., 2013). It is important for you to become familiar with the many

235

suicide prevention programs that are offered at colleges and universities and to advocate for their use (see "Further Resources").

Ethics, College Counseling, and Student Affairs

Counseling is guided by a code of ethics that represents the values of the profession and its expectations for its members (ACA, 2014; Francis & Dugger, 2014). Although the *ACA Code of Ethics* (ACA, 2014) may be enforced only among its members, many state licensing boards that govern the practice of counseling either use the *ACA Code of Ethics* as part of their administrative rules, use the *ACA Code of Ethics* when reviewing the work of counselors whose behavior or practice is in question, or have the *ACA Code of Ethics* as part of state laws governing the practice of counseling (ACA, 2016; Wheeler & Bertram, 2015). Certain divisions within ACA have their own codes of ethics that reflect the special contexts or environments in which those professionals practice (e.g., American Mental Health Counselors Association, 2015; American School Counselor Association, 2011). The division within ACA that represents the profession of college counseling is ACCA. It has no specific code of ethics and endorses the *ACA Code of Ethics* (ACCA, 2012). In addition, the profession of college counseling is populated by other mental health professionals (e.g., psychologists and social workers) who align with their own professional associations and codes of ethics.

Counseling professionals who work in student affairs (e.g., academic advising, disabilities services, campus life) have several different professional organizations, each with its own code of ethics, statements of ethical principles, and statements of core values. It is incumbent on the professional to review appropriate documents and understand the impact such codes, statements, and values have on his or her practice. See Table 9.2 for a list of different codes or statements of values for counseling and student affairs.

Table 9.2 Selected Professional Codes of Ethics or Statements of Values for Counseling or Student Affairs

Professional Association	Document
Counseling	
American Counseling Association (ACA)	*ACA Code of Ethics* (ACA, 2014)
Counseling-related student affairs	
American College Personnel Association (ACPA)	*Statement of Ethical Principles and Standards* (ACPA, 2006)
National Academic Advising Association (NACADA)	*Statement of Core Values of Academic Advising* (NACADA, 2005)
National Association of Academic Advisors for Athletics (NAAAA)	*Code of Ethics* (NAAAA, 2016)
Association on Higher Education and Disability (AHEAD)	*AHEAD Code of Ethics* (AHEAD, 1996)

Common Ethical Issues in College Counseling and Student Affairs

Common issues arise when one is providing counseling services or student affairs services that are unique to the context of higher education. In addition, federal and state laws (e.g., the Family Educational Rights and Privacy Act, Title IX, the Violence Against Women Act, the Clery Act) affect both sets of professionals differently.

Confidentiality

All mental health professionals adhere to the practice of confidentiality for clients and their personal information. Without confidentiality, clients would not be able to trust that their most intimate concerns and issues would be kept between them and the counselor and would not be able to form the therapeutic alliance necessary to make change and progress toward health and healing. Although the environment of the college counseling center has the same limitations on confidentiality as any other counseling environment (i.e., the duty to warn in the case of suicide or violence), many members of the campus community do not understand the need for confidentiality. It becomes the counselor's job to continually educate the administration concerning when one can and cannot release information without students' expressed written permission.

These issues arise most frequently when others in the campus community are required to report specific incidents such as sexual harassment or assault that are defined under the federal law known as *Title IX* (Prince-Sanders, Lawson, Levitt, & Moorhead, 2013). Counselors are specifically exempt from reporting what is revealed to them in a counseling session (Francis & Raleigh, 2015; U.S. Department of Education, 2008). This causes concern among many administrators, who wrongly believe that counselors and their staff (i.e., secretaries, receptionists, etc.) are required to report and are putting the campus at risk. In other cases, student affairs administrators with no counseling background either (a) request confirmation that students they have referred to a counselor are following through with the referral or (b) seek access to the counselor's appointment book. In one such case of which I am aware, the dean of students at a small private college sought to have the counselor's appointment book put on the scheduling calendar for the department so he could review which students whom he had referred to the center were seeking services.

As you can see, it is necessary for college counseling professionals to become familiar with not only state laws that govern counseling but federal laws that mandate reporting or outline the management of student records. The Family Educational Rights and Privacy Act is one such law that affects how students' educational records are maintained on a college campus and allows the release of such records without students' permission in specific circumstances (U.S. Department of

Education, 2008). It specifically exempts medical and mental health records that meet three criteria:

1. The student is 18+ years of age or is attending postsecondary education.
2. The record is made or maintained by a physician or mental health professional or paraprofessional acting in a professional capacity.
3. The record is made, maintained, or used only in connection with treatment to the student and is not available to anyone (including the student), except by those providing the treatment or other medical (mental health) providers of the student's choice.

Any time a student's mental health file is used for any purpose beyond these three criteria, it becomes an educational record and is governed by the Family Educational Rights and Privacy Act. When that release is made, anyone with an educational need to know (e.g., faculty or an administrator) can review a student's educational record (U.S. Department of Education, 2008). It is therefore incumbent on the counselor to ensure that the counseling record is maintained properly to prevent any unintended release.

Scope of Practice and Competence

Counselors who are working in a student affairs capacity (i.e., in academic advising, campus life, etc.) need to have a clear understanding of their role and job description. Even though you may be a fully licensed counselor, unless provisions are made for counseling services as part of your job function, your work is not governed by the laws and ethics of counseling. When your job does allow for counseling services, such as in a counseling and academic advising office at a community college, the student must be clearly informed when the session has moved from being an advising session to being a counseling session and must give his or her permission through a clear informed consent process (see Section A.2. in the *ACA Code of Ethics* [ACA, 2014]). A college counselor's job can include many tasks, and understanding the scope of each task can help in placing it within the scope of practice for the position. Consider the experience of this counseling and advising center staff member at a midsize suburban community college:

> While it is cliché to say that there is no "typical day" being a counselor at a community college, there are some consistent and reoccurring working patterns that happen. To summarize a "typical day" may look something like this:
>
> 8 a.m.—Review your daily schedule and see if there are any meetings for which you need to prepare.
>
> 8:15 a.m.—Review and answer as many e-mails as you can before your first appointment arrives.
>
> 9 a.m. to noon—You see several academic advising appointments. Most of these appointments have questions regarding their program of study, trying to map out what classes to take next, and exploring what college they may matriculate to.

Noon to 1 p.m.—You have a standing personal counseling appointment with a student who has been struggling with adjustment issues related to her college experience. After this appointment you write up your case note and review more e-mails that have come in.

1:30 to 2:30 p.m.—You break for lunch; this is typically done at the school's fitness center. You return from your "lunch" and answer e-mails from students and various committee members throughout the college.

3 p.m.—Your career client has completed the Strong Interest Inventory, and you help interpret the results. You provide career searching resources such as the *Occupational Outlook Handbook*'s website to the student.

4 p.m.—You meet with several other team members to review and prepare for an upcoming workshop that your office is holding. The topic focuses on how to transfer to another college or university.

5 p.m.—You make sure your counseling file cabinet is locked, then you turn off the light and leave for the day!

Okay, so that is an ideal day with just some of the activities that you may be doing as a community college counselor. The reality is that you may be pulled in different directions throughout the day due to the increasing need for personal counseling services. It is fairly common for faculty or staff to refer or walk students over to the counseling office due to concerns for a student's welfare or safety. Other times throughout the day you may be consulting with another counselor about a concerning personal counseling case. Other days you may be doing presentations for the school's BIT. If you enjoy engaging with people and helping them reach their goals, then college counseling is a great fit!

Special Considerations in College Counseling and Student Affairs

Like any profession, college counseling and student affairs faces new challenges and issues as the college population changes, the learning environment evolves, and institutions adjust to meet these demands. Student affairs has gone through massive changes since the early days when the goal was to act in place of parents (*in loco parentis*) and now includes myriad different offices to meet the demands of the student population. College counseling centers continue to provide short- and long-term counseling, but issues have moved beyond home sickness and relationship issues to include crisis and trauma work and the treatment of complex mental health issues. Here, I discuss some of the current changes and challenges in the profession.

Sexual Violence

Over the past several years, more attention has been focused on the problem of sexual violence on college campuses. Research on the issue identifies it as a "pervasive problem on university and college campuses" (Fedina, Holmes, & Backes, 2016, p. 1). The White House and Congress have highlighted sexual assault as a problem that needs to be addressed to ensure the safety of students and their ability to acquire an education in a safe environment (Fedina et al., 2016). The implications for college counseling and student affairs are many and include the following:

- Traumatization of the victim/survivor and an increased need for counseling services in an already overtaxed system (Hodges et al., 2016)
- The creation, funding, and staffing of a Title IX office to investigate sexual violence cases on campus (Francis & Raleigh, 2015)
- Increased training, funding, and staff time on outreach and programming to prevent sexual violence on campus (Hodges et al., 2016)

Integrative Approaches

The increased complexity of issues and diagnoses of students coming to counseling centers has prompted many centers to take a more integrated approach to prevention and treatment. Although counseling has always had a foundation in development and wellness/prevention, counseling center staff are now increasingly incorporating biological, social, and cultural factors into treatment (Hodges et al., 2016). It has become clear that there is a need for increased understanding of the neurobiological foundations of some mental health issues as well as a strong background in many of the cognitive behavioral approaches to treatment. When this is combined with the wellness model of identifying client strengths and developmental stages, a holistic approach is created that addresses the multiple needs that students present in session.

Provision of Services

A perennial issue in student affairs and college counseling is levels of staffing in the face of increasing demands for services at both the community college and university levels. As many as 19% of community colleges do not offer any formal mental health services, and only 8% have some kind of psychiatric services available (Francis & Horn, 2016); yet 58% of 4-year institutions offer some kind of psychiatric services (Francis & Horn, 2016). Given the increasingly complex mental health issues students face; the fact that 10% to 15% of the college population utilizes counseling, disabilities, and advising services; and the greater access to higher education among individuals today, a strong argument can be made for increased staffing and funding of student affairs and counseling services (Francis & Horn, 2016).

Anxiety and Depression

The two most common issues for which students seek treatment on college campuses are depression and anxiety (Center for Collegiate Mental Health, 2015; Reetz et al., 2014), with depression historically being the most prevalent issue. Anxiety has now overtaken depression as the most common issue. Some have attributed this change to the need to succeed, financial concerns, relationships with others (peers, professors, etc.), and academic performance (Beiter et al., 2015). Depression continues to affect students' lives, with an estimated 12% to 33% of students reporting problems (American College Health Association, 2014). The consequences of untreated or undertreated anxiety and depression include many threats to student success, such as poor academic performance, difficulty concentrating, and relationship problems (Baez, 2005).

Chapter Summary

A degree in counseling offers the flexibility to work in higher education in a number of positions beyond just those found in the counseling center. From academic advising and disabilities services to campus life and wellness, counselors with the proper education and pre- and postgraduate training can find themselves helping to prepare students of all types to succeed not only while they are in college but also beyond the walls of the classroom and in the world. A degree in counseling also offers the opportunity to work in a college counseling center where you can provide a much-needed service to a student who struggles with relationship issues, developmental concerns, developing mental health issues, or chronic mental illness so that the student can persist and successfully traverse the educational requirements needed to become a graduate and a functioning citizen in society. It also offers you the opportunity to provide preventive services so that students can learn to stop problems from developing.

Working on a college campus either as a professional counselor or in the office of student affairs provides you with a mix of opportunities that will keep you interested, challenged, and motivated. The variety of students continues to change each year as more and more people, young and not so young, take up the challenge of pursuing higher education and improving their lives. The reward that is offered is the knowledge that you have had a hand in helping to shape the future.

Learning Activities

1. You are a counselor in a midsize urban regional university. Your center director has given you the task of planning and implementing a screening day for depression and anxiety. This is the first time your center and university have implemented a screening day. You have been given a modest budget to purchase brochures and supplies to advertise the event. Working with a team of your fellow students, plan a screening day for your university. Search the Web and identify screening days resources available to you. How would you advertise the screening day to the student body? Which student affairs offices would you involve in your screening day?

2. Many universities have BITs that seek to intervene with struggling students before their problems become overwhelming and negatively impact their academic and personal futures or those of others. You are preparing to become a member of your university's BIT. Explore and list all of the student support services at your institution and how they might be deployed to help a struggling student. Then explore the student support services of a community college and see whether or how they differ. What do you think is the reason for the difference?

3. Ethics are a reflection of the common values and expectations of a profession (Francis & Dugger, 2014). Look up the *ACA Code of Ethics* (ACA, 2014) and one other code in Table 9.2. related to student affairs. Compare and contrast the codes, looking for where they complement each other and where they diverge. What are the areas of agreement? What are the areas of divergence? How might a student affairs professional approach an issue such as confidentiality differently from a college counselor?

4. How do the professional associations of college counseling and student affairs differ? Explore different professional association websites and find their mission statements or professional identity definitions. How do they differ? What do they have in common? As you explore these websites, take a look at the many different jobs and careers that are highlighted on the sites and imagine yourself in several of those jobs. What skills do you think you would need to do the jobs well, and how could you leverage your education to prepare yourself to be successful in one of those jobs?

Review Questions

1. How would you describe the differences and similarities between a college counselor and a student affairs professional?

2. What are the different tasks for a college counselor in a community college and a 4-year university?

3. What are the major factors contributing to the increasing complexity of mental health issues among the college student population?

4. How do the roles of a college counselor and a student affairs professional differ on a BIT?

5. How are the ethics of counseling applied to and challenged on a college campus?

Further Resources

Websites

American College Health Association
www.acha.org

Association for University and College Counseling Center Directors
www.aucccd.org/public
Center for Collegiate Mental Health
ccmh.psu.edu/
Higher Education Research Institute and Cooperative Institutional
Research Program
www.heri.ucla.edu/

Professional Associations

American College Counseling Association
www.collegecounseling.org
American College Personnel Association
www.myacpa.org
American Counseling Association
www.counseling.org
Higher Education Case Managers Association
www.hecma.org
National Academic Advising Association
www.nacada.ksu.edu
Student Affairs Administrators in Higher Education
www.naspa.org

Common Suicide Prevention Programs

Kognito, At-Risk for Students
https://kognito.com/products/at-risk-for-college-students
LivingWorks Education, Applied Suicide Intervention Skills Training
https://www.livingworks.net/programs/asist/
QPR Institute, Gatekeeper Training for Suicide Prevention
https://www.qprinstitute.com/
Reconnecting Youth Inc., Coping and Support Training
www.reconnectingyouth.com/programs/cast/

References

American College Counseling Association. (2012). *ACCA by-laws.* Retrieved from www.collegecounseling.org/ACCA-By-Laws
American College Counseling Association. (2014). *Community college survey.* Alexandria, VA: Author.
American College Counseling Association. (2016). *Mission statement.* Retrieved from www.collegecounseling.org/mission-statement
American College Health Association. (2014). *American College Health Association-National College Health Assessment II: Reference group executive summary spring 2014.* Hanover, MD: Author.
American College Personnel Association. (2006). *Statement of ethical principles and standards.* Washington, DC: Author.

American College Personnel Association. (2008). *The student learning imperative: Implications for student affairs.* Retrieved from www. myacpa.org/student-learning-imperative-implications-student-affairs

American Counseling Association. (2014). *ACA code of ethics.* Alexandria, VA: Author.

American Counseling Association. (2016). *Licensure requirements for professional counselors: A state-by-state report.* Retrieved from http:// web.oru.edu/current_students/class_pages/grtheo/mmankins/ CounselingLicensure/ORU%20Counseling%20Licensure%20 Requirements%20Website%20Update%202-16-16/state%20licensure%20requirements%202016%20edition.pdf

American Mental Health Counselors Association. (2015, October). *AMHCA code of ethics.* Retrieved from http://connections. amhca.org/HigherLogic/System/DownloadDocumentFile. ashx?DocumentFileKey=d4e10fcb-2f3c-c701-aa1d-5d0f53b8bc14

American School Counselor Association. (2011). *Ethical standards for school counselors.* Alexandria, VA: Author.

Association on Higher Education and Disability. (1996). *Resources.* Retrieved from www.ahead.org/learn/resources

Atkinson, D. R., Morten, G., & Sue, D. W. (1993). *Counseling American minorities: A cross-cultural perspective* (4th ed.). Madison, WI: Brown & Benchmark.

Baez, T. (2005). Evidence-based practice for anxiety disorders in college mental health. In S. E. Cooper (Ed.), *Evidence-based psychotherapy practice in college mental health* (pp. 33–48). New York, NY: Haworth Press.

Beiter, R., Nash, R., McCrady, M., Rhoades, D., Linscomb, M., Clarahan, M., & Sammut, S. (2015). The prevalence and correlates of depression, anxiety, and stress in a sample of college students. *Journal of Affective Disorders, 173,* 90–96. doi:10.1016/j. jad.2014.10.054

Belenky, M. F., Clinchy, B. M., Goldberger, N. R., & Tarule, J. M. (1986). *Women's ways of knowing.* New York, NY: Basic Books.

Benton, S. A., & Benton, S. L. (Eds.). (2006). Responding to the college student mental health problem. In *College student mental health: Effective services and strategies across campus* (pp. 233–244). Washington, DC: National Association of Student Personnel Administrators.

Brunner, J. L., Wallace, D. L., Reymann, L. S., Sellers, J.-J., & McCabe, A. G. (2014). College counseling today: Contemporary students and how counseling centers meet their needs. *Journal of College Student Psychotherapy, 28*(4), 257–324. doi:10.1080/875 68225.2014.948770

Carpenter, S. (2011). The philosophical heritage of student affairs. In N. Zhang & Associates (Eds.), *Rentz's student affairs practice in higher education* (4th ed., pp. 3–29). Springfield, IL: Charles C Thomas.

Carter, G. C., & Winseman, J. S. (2003). Increasing number of students arrive on college campuses on psychiatric medications: Are they mentally ill? *Journal of College Student Psychotherapy, 18*(1), 3–10.

Cass, V. C. (1979). Homosexual identity formation: A theoretical model. *Journal of Homosexuality, 4*(3), 219–235. doi:10.1300/J082v04n03_01

Center for Collegiate Mental Health. (2015, January). *2014 annual report* (Publication No. STA 15-30). University Park, PA: Author.

Chickering, A. W., & Reisser, L. (1993). *Education and identity* (2nd ed.). San Francisco, CA: Jossey-Bass.

Chung, H., Klein, M. C., Silverman, D., Corson-Rikert, J., Davidson, E., Ellis, P., & Kasnakian, C. (2011). A pilot for improving depression care on college campuses: Results of the College Breakthrough Series-Depression (CBS-D) Project. *Journal of American College Health, 59,* 628–639. doi:10.1080/07448481.2010.528097

CollegeAIM. (2016). *CollegeAIM: Alcohol intervention matrix.* Retrieved from www.collegedrinkingprevention.gov/collegeaim/

Council for Accreditation of Counseling and Related Educational Programs. (2016). *2016 CACREP standards.* Retrieved from www.cacrep.org/for-programs/2016-cacrep-standards/

Drum, D. J., & Denmark, A. B. (2012). Campus suicide prevention: Bridging paradigms and forging partnerships. *Harvard Review of Psychiatry, 20*(4), 209–221. doi:10.3109/10673229.2012.712841

Eagan, K., Stolzenberg, E. B., Ramirez, J. J., Aragon, M. C., Suchard, M. R., & Hurtado, S. (2014). *The American freshman: National norms fall 2014.* Los Angeles, CA: University of California at Los Angeles, Higher Education Research Institute.

Eells, G. T., & Rockland-Miller, H. S. (2011). Assessing and responding to disturbed and disturbing students: Understanding the role of administrative teams in institutions of higher education. *Journal of College Student Psychotherapy, 25*(1), 8–23. doi:10.1080/87568225.2011.532470

Erickson, E. H. (1959). Identity and the life cycle. *Psychological Issues, 1,* 1–171.

Farrell, E. F. (2002, May 24). A suicide and its aftermath. *The Chronicle of Higher Education, 48,* A37–A39.

Fassinger, R. E. (1998). Lesbian, gay, and bisexual identity and student development theory. In R. L. Sanlo (Ed.), *Working with lesbian, gay, bisexual, and transgender college students: A handbook for faculty and administrators* (pp. 13–22). Westport, CT: Greenwood Press.

Fedina, L., Holmes, L. H., & Backes, B. L. (2016). Campus sexual assault: A systematic review of prevalence research from 2000 to 2015. *Trauma, Violence, & Abuse.* Advance online publication. doi:10.1177/1524838016631129

Flatt, A. K. (2013). A suffering generation: Six factors contributing to the mental health crisis in North American higher education. *College Quarterly, 16*(1). Retrieved from http://collegequarterly.ca/2013-vol16-num01-winter/flatt.html

1

Francis, P. C. (2011). Student affairs and counseling in college setting. In S. C. Nassar-McMillan & S. G. Niles (Eds.), *Developing your identity as a professional counselor: Standards, settings and specialties* (pp. 232–262). Belmont, CA: Brooks/Cole.

Francis, P. C. (2015, March). *10 years of the Gallagher College Counseling Center Survey: A look at the past, present, and future.* Paper presented at the annual conference of the American Counseling Association, Orlando, FL.

Francis, P. C., & Dugger, S. M. (2014). Professionalism, ethics, and value-based conflicts in counseling: An introduction to the special section. *Journal of Counseling & Development, 92,* 131–134. doi:10.1002/j.1556-6676.2014.00138.x

Francis, P. C., & Horn, A. S. (2016). *Counseling services and student success.* Retrieved from www.mhec.org/sites/mhec.org/files/201602counseling_services.pdf

Francis, P. C., & Raleigh, M. J. (2015, October). *Ethics, Title IX, and the Clery Act.* Paper presented at the annual conference of the American College Counseling Association, Louisville, KY.

Gilligan, C. (1982). *In a different voice: Psychological theory and women's development.* Cambridge, MA: Harvard University Press.

Gorman, E. H., & Sandefur, R. L. (2011). "Golden age," quiescence, and revival: How the sociology of professions became the study of knowledge-based work. *Work and Occupations, 38*(3), 275–302. doi:10.1177/0730888411417565

Haas, A. P., Koestner, B., Rosenberg, J., Moore, D., Garlow, S. J., Sedway, J., … Nemeroff, C. B. (2008). An interactive Web-based method of outreach to college students at risk for suicide. *Journal of American College Health, 57*(1), 15–22. doi:10.3200/JACH.57.1.15-22

Helms, J. E. (1995). An update of Helm's White and people of color racial identity models. In J. G. Ponterotto, J. M. Casas, L. A. Suzuki, & C. M. Alexander (Eds.), *Handbook of multicultural counseling* (pp. 181–198). Thousand Oaks, CA: Sage.

Hodges, S., Shelton, K., & Lyn, M. (2016). *The college and university counseling manual: Integrating essential services across the campus.* New York, NY: Springer.

Howe, N., & Strauss, W. (2003). *Millennials go to college.* Washington, DC: American Association of Collegiate Registrars and Admissions Officers.

Jed Foundation. (2016). *About us.* Retrieved from https://www.jedfoundation.org/who-we-are/

Johnston, L. D., O'Malley, P. M., Bachman, J. G., & Schulenberg, J. E. (2010). *Monitoring the future: National survey results on drug use, 1975–2009: Vol. 2. College students and adults ages 19–50* (NIH Publication No. 10-7585). Bethesda, MD: National Institute on Drug Abuse.

Kaplan, D. M., Tarvydas, V. M., & Gladding, S. T. (2014). 20/20: A vision for the future of counseling: The new consensus definition of counseling. *Journal of Counseling & Development, 92,* 366–372. doi:10.1002/j.1556-6676.2014.00164.x

Kay, J., & Schwartz, V. (Eds.). (2010). *Mental health care in the college community.* Hoboken, NJ: Wiley-Blackwell.

Kessler, R. C., Amminger, G. P., Aguilar-Gaxiola, S., Alonso, J., Lee, S., & Üstün, T. B. (2007). Age of onset of mental disorders: A review of recent literature. *Current Opinion in Psychiatry, 20*(4), 359–364. doi:10.1097/YCO.0b013e32816ebc8c

Keyes, L. (2013). Suicide and its prevention on college campuses. *Alabama Counseling Journal, 38*(2), 3–8.

Kohlberg, L. (1981). *The philosophy of moral development: Moral stages and the idea of justice.* New York, NY: Harper & Row.

Lee, C. L. (2005). Evidenced-based treatment of depression in the college population. In S. E. Cooper (Ed.), *Evidence-based psychotherapy practice in college mental health* (pp. 23–32). New York, NY: Haworth Press.

Licciardone, J. C. (2003a). Outcomes of a federally funded program for alcohol and other drug prevention in higher education. *American Journal of Drug and Alcohol Abuse, 29,* 803–827. doi:10.1081/ADA-120026262

Licciardone, J. C. (2003b). Perceptions of drinking and related findings from the Nationwide Campuses Study. *Journal of American College Health, 51*(6), 238–246. doi:10.1080/07448480309596356

Marcia, J. E. (1993). The ego identity status approach to ego identity. In J. E. Marcia, A. S. Waterman, D. R. Matteson, S. L. Archer, & J. L. Orlofsky (Eds.), *Ego identity: A handbook for psychosocial research* (pp. 1–21). New York, NY: Springer-Verlag.

Meadows, M. E. (2000). The evolution of college counseling. In D. C. Davis & K. M. Humphrey (Eds.), *College counseling: Issues and strategies for a new millennium* (pp. 15–40). Alexandria, VA: American Counseling Association.

Morgenson, G. (2015, October 11). *A student loan system stacked against the borrower.* Retrieved from https://www.nytimes.com/2015/10/11/business/a-student-loan-system-stacked-against-the-borrower.html?mcubz=1

Moss, J. M., Gibson, D. M., & Dollarhide, C. T. (2014). Professional identity development: A grounded theory of transformational tasks of counselors. *Journal of Counseling & Development, 92,* 3–12. doi:10.1002/j.1556-6676.2014.00124.x

Narula, S. K. (2014, April 1). *The myth of working your way through college.* Retrieved from https://www.theatlantic.com/education/archive/2014/04/the-myth-of-working-your-way-through-college/359735/

National Academic Advising Association. (2005). *NACADA statement of core values of academic advising*. Retrieved from www.nacada.ksu.edu/Resources/Clearinghouse/View-Articles/Core-values-of-academic-advising.aspx#sthash.oNKUVk2Y.dpuf

National Association of Academic Advisors for Athletics. (2016). [Code of ethics]. Retrieved from http://grfx.cstv.com/photos/schools/nacda/sports/nfoura/auto_pdf/2011-12/misc_non_event/codeofethics.pdf

National Behavioral Intervention Team Association. (2015). *Behavioral intervention teams*. Retrieved from https://nabita.org/behavioral-intervention-teams/

National Center for Education Statistics. (2015). *Digest of Education Statistics: 2013: Chapter 3: Postsecondary education* (NCES 2015-011). Retrieved from http://nces.ed.gov/programs/digest/d13/ch_3.asp

National Institute on Alcohol Abuse and Alcoholism. (2015). *College drinking*. Washington, DC: Author.

Nuss, E. M. (2003). The development of student affairs. In S. R. Komives, D. B. Woodard, Jr., & Associates (Eds.), *Student services: A handbook for the profession* (3rd ed., pp. 65–88). San Francisco, CA: Jossey-Bass.

Perry, W. G., Jr. (1968). *Forms of intellectual and ethical development in the college years: A scheme*. New York, NY: Holt, Rinehart & Winston.

Prince-Sanders, J., Lawson, G., Levitt, D. H., & Moorhead, H. J. H. (2013). Title IX and reporting. In D. H. Levitt & H. J. H. Moorhead (Eds.), *Values and ethics in counseling: Real-life ethical decision making* (pp. 96–102). New York, NY: Routledge.

Reetz, D. R., Krylowicz, B., & Mistler, B. (2014). *The Association for University and College Counseling Center Directors annual survey*. Retrieved from www.aucccd.org/assets/documents/2014%20aucccd%20monograph%20-%20public%20pdf.pdf

Reiner, S. M., Dobmeier, R. A., & Hernández, T. J. (2013). Perceived impact of professional counselor identity: An exploratory study. *Journal of Counseling & Development, 91,* 174–183. doi:10.1002/j.1556-6676.2013.00084.x

Remley, T. P., Jr., & Shaw, B. M. (2013). College counseling and student affairs. In D. Capuzzi & D. R. Gross (Eds.), *Introduction to the counseling profession* (6th ed., pp. 471–494). New York, NY: Routledge.

Rentz, A. L., & Howard-Hamilton, M. (2011). Student affairs: An historical perspective. In N. Zhang & Associates (Eds.), *Rentz's student affairs practice in higher education* (4th ed., pp. 30–62). Springfield, IL: Charles C Thomas.

Sharkin, B. S. (2012). *Being a college counselor on today's campus: Roles, contributions, and special challenges*. New York, NY: Routledge.

Smith, G. H. (2007). *Remembering Garrett: One family's battle with a child's depression.* New York, NY: Basic Books.

Sontag, D. (2002, April 28). Who was responsible for Elizabeth Shin? *The New York Times Magazine,* p. 57, Section 56.

Taub, D. J., Servaty-Seib, H. L., Miles, N., Lee, J.-Y., Morris, C. A. W., Prieto-Welch, S. L., & Werden, D. (2013). The impact of gatekeeper training for suicide prevention on university resident assistants. *Journal of College Counseling, 16,* 64–78. doi:10.1002/j.2161-1882.2013.00027.x

Turner, J. C., Leno, E. V., & Keller, A. (2013). Causes of mortality among American college students: A pilot study. *Journal of College Student Psychotherapy, 27*(1), 31–42. doi:10.1080/8756822 5.2013.739022

U.S. Department of Education. (2008, November). *Joint guidance on the application of the Family Educational Rights and Privacy Act (FERPA) and the Health Insurance Portability and Accountability Act of 1996 (HIPAA) to student health records.* Washington, DC: Author.

Van Brunt, B. (2015). *Harm to others: The assessment and treatment of dangerousness.* Alexandria, VA: American Counseling Association.

Van Brunt, B., Reese, A., & Lewis, W. S. (2015). *The NaBITA 2015 whitepaper: Who's on the team? Mission, membership, and motivation.* Retrieved from https://nabita.org/wordpress/wp-content/uploads/2015/07/2015-NaBITA-Whitepaper.pdf

Vespia, K. M. (2007). A national survey of small college counseling centers: Successes, issues, and challenges. *Journal of College Student Psychotherapy, 22*(1), 17–40. doi:10.1300/J035v22n01_03

Watkins, D. C., Hunt, J. B., & Eisenberg, D. (2012). Increased demand for mental health services on college campuses: Perspectives from administrators. *Qualitative Social Work: Research and Practice, 11*(3), 319–337. doi:10.1177/1473325011401468

Wheeler, A. M. N., & Bertram, B. (2015). *The counselor and the law: A guide to legal and ethical practice* (7th ed.). Alexandria, VA: American Counseling Association.

Whitlock, J., Muehlenkamp, J., Purington, A., Eckenrode, J., Barreira, P., Baral Abrams, G., … Knox, K. (2011). Nonsuicidal self-injury in a college population: General trends and sex differences. *Journal of American College Health, 59,* 691–698. doi:10.1080/07448481.2010.529626

Chapter 10

Marriage, Couples, and Family Counseling

Richard E. Watts, Rick Bruhn, Mary Nichter, and Judith Nelson

Learning Objectives

1. Understand families from systemic and developmental perspectives.
2. Understand the history and development of couples and family counseling.
3. Understand characteristics of well-functioning families and common patterns of family problems and distress.
4. Understand various approaches to couples and family counseling.
5. Understand the training and credentialing of couples and family counselors.
6. Understand couples and family counseling as a career path.
7. Understand ethical issues unique to couples and family counseling.

• • •

Marriage, couples, and family counseling is a young profession. Although it is true that Alfred Adler and Rudolf Dreikurs originally proposed and demonstrated the importance of working with the family as a unit in the 1920s (Bitter, 2014; Carlson, Watts, & Maniacci, 2006; Sherman & Dinkmeyer, 1987), professional associations related to the profession did not begin to form until the 1940s and 1950s, and it was not until the last quarter of the 20th century that family counseling attained universal acceptance with the mental health profession (Bitter, 2014; Gladding, 2015; Goldenberg & Goldenberg, 2013). This is not really surprising because, historically, most counselors were trained to view clients as individuals, ignoring the role of the family and societal influences in the development and continuation of psychological problems. Over the past 40+ years, however, mental health professionals have increasingly recognized that counseling individuals without considering, and often including, the family unit frequently limits the success of counseling (see Sidebar 10.1).

Although marriage, couples, and family counseling is a young profession, our understanding of what constitutes a family has changed significantly since the beginning of the family counseling movement. Originally, the focus of family counseling was the nuclear or traditional intact family, and the typical family discussed in the initial literature was White, middle class, and heterosexual. Our understanding of family is now significantly different and includes single-parent families, blended (remarried) families, dual career families, adoptive families, foster families, child-free families, families with children with special needs, interracial or multiple-heritage families, gay or lesbian families, aging families, multigenerational families, grandparent-led families, military families, and families with chronic medical issues as well as nuclear families (Browning & Pasley, 2015; Gladding, 2015). You might be able to identify some others. It is clear that there is enormous diversity regarding couple and family systems.

In addition to the increased diversity in our understanding of couple and family relationships, the demands on today's couples and families are greater than ever before. Consequently, because of the increasing demands and accompanying levels of stress experienced by couples and families, mental health professionals need to be prepared to work with clients' counseling issues within a family systems context and with an appreciation of diverse client populations and family system formations.

The purpose of this chapter is to provide a brief introduction to the field of couples and family counseling in hopes of whetting

Sidebar 10.1   Personal Reflection on
                Family and Societal Influence

How have you seen family and societal influences affect the development and continuation of psychological problems?

• • •

your appetite for intense study and practice of counseling couples and families. We begin by addressing the history of the couples and family counseling movement. Next, we discuss the characteristics of the family from a systemic and developmental perspective. In the following section, we address characteristics of well-functioning families and family problems and distress. We then overview several widely recognized approaches to couples and family counseling. Next, we briefly address ethical issues that are largely unique to couples and family counseling. Then we present information on the careers, training, and credentialing of couples and family counselors. We conclude by addressing special topics and further considerations regarding couples and family counseling.

The History and Development of Family Counseling

According to Gladding (2015), three major trends in history that contributed to the development of family counseling were (a) the rise in the divorce rate after World War II, (b) the changing role of women in terms of social status and employment opportunities, and (c) increased life spans for both men and women in the United States. These social changes, along with the acceptance of counseling as a viable process for problem solving and decision making, created a need for increased training and research in working with families.

Major events in the early development of family counseling included the beginning of marriage and premarital counseling, the child guidance movement, the early use of group dynamics or processes in counseling, and research studies on the role of the family in the development of schizophrenia (Bitter, 2014; Goldenberg & Goldenberg, 2013). As early as the 1920s and 1930s, professionals in a variety of settings developed and used marriage interventions and premarital counseling programs; however, the focus was largely intrapsychic rather than interpersonal and remained so for several decades thereafter (Bitter, 2014; Goldenberg & Goldenberg, 2013). The child guidance movement, founded by Adler in Vienna in the early 1900s, strongly influenced practitioners working with families, and Dreikurs in the United States expanded the notion of intervening in child problems by working with the entire family. Also, early in the 1900s, Jacob Moreno developed psychodrama within the context of group therapy and helped participants work through interpersonal situations that produced distress and dysfunction. Beginning in the late 1930s and early 1940s, researchers and practitioners worked with schizophrenic patients in hospital settings, attempting to determine the relationship between family dynamics and schizophrenia. Pioneers like Nathan Ackerman, James Framo, and Murray Bowen integrated systemic ideas into their practices and developed new theoretical perspectives on mental illness (Framo, 1996).

253

The 1950s is generally considered the official beginning of family counseling and therapy. No one person, however, may be singled out as the first to adopt a systemic approach to working with families. At this time, several practitioners across the United States were meeting with families and viewing symptoms of identified patients as a function of family interactional patterns, and they began to learn about one another's work. In 1956, the Palo Alto Group—which included Gregory Bateson, Don Jackson, Jay Haley, and John Weakland—wrote its seminal paper on the double bind, which described a theory of the relationship between family communication patterns and schizophrenia (Bitter, 2014; Gladding, 2015; Goldenberg & Goldenberg, 2013).

Beels (2002) noted that the 1960s was a time of family centeredness and group welfare that contributed to the evolution of family therapy. During this decade, family counseling became a recognized topic at professional meetings, and the 1960s was a very productive period for persons working from a systems perspective. In 1962, Don Jackson and Nathan Ackerman founded the first family therapy journal, *Family Process*, and Virginia Satir published her book *Conjoint Family Therapy*. In the 1960s and early 1970s, the work of Jay Haley (strategic family therapy), Salvador Minuchin (structural family therapy), and Carl Whitaker (experiential family therapy) emerged in the literature (Bitter, 2014; Gladding, 2015; Goldenberg & Goldenberg, 2013).

The 1970s and 1980s continued the productivity established in the 1960s. During this time, significant expansion to the traditional systems perspective occurred. Leading these changes, which argued for a more circular understanding of family counseling, was the Milan group, led by Maria Selvini-Palazzoli, Harry Goolishan, and Harlene Anderson of the Houston Galveston Family Institute and Karl Tomm from the University of Calgary. Also during this time, Michael White and David Epston in Australia began developing their narrative therapy approach to helping families. According to Kaslow (2000), the feminist movement in the 1980s brought an emphasis on gender sensitivity and the role of gender in family dynamics to family counseling. Also in the 1980s, family counselors examined the role and impact of cultural and ethnic diversity on family functioning and family counseling (McGoldrick, Giordano, & Garcia-Preto, 2005).

Family counselors in the 1990s responded to managed care constraints with brief and solution-focused perspectives in their work with couples and families. Steve de Shazer, William O'Hanlon, and Michelle Weiner-Davis published numerous journal articles and books presenting their brief, solution-focused (or solution-oriented) methods, which emphasized solutions and possibilities rather problems (Bitter, 2014; Goldenberg & Goldenberg, 2013).

Contemporary issues in family counseling continue to center around the changing role and understanding of the family and family process in a multicultural and pluralistic society and changing perspectives regarding family counseling. You may see these changes in (a) the movement away from strict adherence to one particular theoretical perspective or school of thought toward integration; (b) the increasing interest in and appreciation of constructivist and constructionist ways of helping couples and families; (c) the changing patterns of couples and family counseling within the constraints of managed care, including the use of evidence-based interventions; (d) the ever-increasing attention paid to the role of gender and cultural issues, societal oppression, and spirituality and religious values in the lives of clients and client families; (e) the impact of technology on couples and families; and (f) changes in our understanding of the neurophysiology of the brain and its impact on couple and family relationships (Bitter, 2014; Fishbane, 2015; Gladding, 2015; Goldenberg & Goldenberg, 2013; Peluso, 2007; Siegel, 2012; see Sidebar 10.2).

The Family: Systemic and Developmental Perspectives

What is a family? All of us have basic emotional and physical needs. Although physical needs are fairly obvious, emotional ones are much less easily recognized. According to Foley (1989), emotional needs can be reduced to three dimensions: intimacy, power, and meaning. Humans have a need to belong, to be in close relationship with others. We have a need for self-expression, to be unique. Last, we have a need to find meaning and purpose in our lives. One might suggest that fulfilling these needs is possible without being involved in a family unit. Foley argued, however, that the possibility of meeting these needs apart from being in a family—in some form or fashion—is remote. Thus, one definition of a *family* is the social unit in which people by mutual consent attempt to fulfill their needs for intimacy, self-expression, and meaning and purposefulness.

Although Foley's (1989) definition is good as far as it goes, it does not adequately address (or even allude to) the many contextual factors that influence the family as a whole or the individual persons who make up the family system. A more encompassing definition of the family was offered by Goldenberg and Goldenberg (2013):

Sidebar 10.2 Class Discussion on the Definition of a Family

How do you define *family*?
What personal influences or information guide your definition?
What are some other ways that *family* might be defined?

• • •

A family is a natural social system that occurs in a diversity of forms today and represents a diversity of cultural heritages. Embedded in society at large, it is shaped by a multitude of factors, such as its place and time in history, race, ethnicity, social class membership, religious affiliation, and number of generations in this country. The way it functions—establishes rules, communicates, and negotiates differences between members—has numerous implications for the development and well-being of its members. Families display a recurring pattern of interactional sequences in which all members participate. (p. 23)

Perspectives on Family Functioning: Contextual Dimensions

Until the 1980s, the family research literature focused primarily on characteristics and symptoms of dysfunctional families. Addressing only negative aspects of family functioning provides a myopic perspective, however.

I would not dream of teaching someone to play tennis by only telling them how *not* to do it: "Now you do *not* hold a racket this way. You do *not* do a backstroke this way." A coach would not succeed if he (or she) only made remarks like, "This is wrong, don't stand like this, this is terrible," while never telling the person how to stand right and how to hold the tennis racket correctly. But to a large extent we have done this in the area of family life. For example, we've told people what families of delinquents or runaways are like, and we've said, "Now don't let your family be like that." We have not used the positive model approach. We have not said, "Here's what a strong family is like and your family can work on these positive qualities." (Stinnett, 1985, p. 37, emphasis in the original)

In this section, we address characteristics of well-functioning families and family dysfunction. Issues such as ethics, career path, and training and credentialing as they relate to marriage, couples and family counselors are discussed in detail later in the chapter (see Sidebar 10.3).

Characteristics of Well-Functioning Families

Beginning in the late 1970s, some family researchers began focusing on the characteristics of strong, well-functioning families. This

Sidebar 10.3 Reflecting on Well-Functioning Families

Before you read the section "Characteristics of Well-Functioning Families," make a list of what you think are key characteristics of well-functioning families.

How do the characteristics on your list contribute to productive family functioning?

• • •

research has continued over the recent decades (Beavers & Hampson, 1990, 2003; Curran, 1983; Epstein, Bishop, & Baldwin, 1982; Epstein, Ryan, Bishop, Miller, & Keitner, 2003; Gladding, 2015; Stinnett, Chesser, & DeFrain, 1979; Stinnett, DeFrain, King, Knaub, & Rowe, 1981; Walsh, 2003, 2009; Watts, Trusty, & Lim, 1996). The following characteristics of well-functioning families were the ones most often mentioned in the literature. Ancillary characteristics were often discussed in the literature as being part of or subsumed under these core characteristics.

Commitment
Commitment is understood from both the marital/partner dyad and parent perspective. In well-functioning families, members of the marital or partner couple are committed to each other. There is a high level of trust and security in the relationship. In addition, parent(s) are consciously committed to the development and well-being of the family. There is a high level of trust and security within the family as a whole.

Communication
Healthy communication may be the most important characteristic of all because the other characteristics are so heavily influenced by communication styles and patterns. In well-functioning couples and families, members strive to actively listen to and empathize with one another. They strive to be honest and genuine when attempting to communicate. Members feel permission to appropriately express their own thoughts and feelings. Furthermore, conflict and negotiation are considered a normal part of the family process. When faced with divergent opinions, members choose to respond in a respectful and constructive manner rather than a condemnatory and destructive one.

Clear Boundaries
Well-functioning families have firm but permeable boundaries for both the marital/partner relationship and parent–child relationships. The marital/partner couple is affectionate and intimate, consistently sets aside time apart from children for the dyadic relationship, and has other couples as friends. Parents meet intimacy and social needs through their relationships with adults rather than their children. In addition, families are part of a social network of families that provide enjoyment, support, and a sense of community for family members.

A Positive Family Atmosphere
In well-functioning couples and families, the family atmosphere is encouraging, affirming, and optimistic. The family environment allows members to freely express appreciation and love for one another. Family members seek to support one another and express their love in an unconditional manner by being caring, compassionate, respectful,

and accepting of individual differences. In addition, these families have a sense of humor, but not at the expense of one another. Members are able to see and appreciate the humor in everyday living and can readily laugh at themselves.

Connectedness

In well-functioning couples and families, members share a feeling of belongingness. They enjoy one another and purposefully spend time together in both planned and spontaneous activities; they make spending both quality and quantity time together a priority. Time is divided into time for the marital dyad, parent and child interactions, and the family as a whole. Furthermore, families seek to create and continue family traditions, and parents attempt to instill and pass on cultural and family heritage to their children.

Adaptability

Well-functioning couples and families have sufficient adaptability to constructively address and take responsibility for problem prevention and/or resolution. Consequently, individual and family developmental transitions are handled in a flexible manner. When families are faced with a crisis beyond their capacity to cope, however, they will readily admit problems and seek help outside the family.

Spirituality

Spirituality is understood here as family members have meaning and purpose to life that may or may not be evidenced by some form of organized, formal religious commitment. Spirituality in these families influences the moral development of members and the development of relationship-enhancing qualities such as love, patience, kindness, support, and altruism (see Sidebar 10.4).

When working with couples and families, it is important that you look at strengths and assets and not merely limitations and liabilities. The characteristics of well-functioning families can help you and families identify family strengths and can serve as points for dialogue to address areas for growth. You also need to understand these char-

---

Sidebar 10.4 Thought Questions: Using the Characteristics of Well-Functioning Families

How might you use the list of characteristics of well-functioning families in counseling couples and families?

What concerns do you have about using such a list in couples and family counseling?

How might you use the list and address your concerns?

• • •

acteristics as a process across a continuum. That is, families will never completely or perfectly manifest all of these characteristics. Perhaps most important, the characteristics must be understood contextually in terms of family stressors and in the context of a couple's or family's culture. Contextual influences such as job changes, unemployment, or other economic stressors, as well as the impact of substance abuse and domestic or interpersonal violence (often perpetrated against women and children), must be considered in assessing family functioning. In addition, it is crucial to understand the characteristics of well-functioning families in the cultural context of the client. Although these characteristics are commonly discussed in the literature (e.g., Gladding, 2015), couples and family counselors must be sensitive to how culturally diverse clients or client systems understand these characteristics and must work within clients' cultural framework. As noted by Goldenberg and Goldenberg (2013), it is crucial for couples and family counselors to thoroughly attend to a couple's or family's cultural background to avoid misunderstanding and pathologizing culturally diverse families "whose behavior is unfamiliar; taking care not to misdiagnose or mislabel family behavior in the process" (p. 65). A useful technique in this regard for couples and families, as well as counselors-in-training, is the cultural genogram developed by Hardy and Laszloffy (1995; see also Goldenberg & Goldenberg, 2013). This process helps participants "trace their kindship (race, social class, gender, religion, family migration history) networks over several generations" (Goldenberg & Goldenberg, 2013, p. 79). Participants examine their family cultural issues and identities over several generations. Important questions include the following:

> What were their family's migration patterns? Under what conditions did they enter the United States (immigration, political refugee, slavery, etc.)? Did race play a part? What is the family's dominant religion? How are gender roles defined within the family? What prejudices and stereotypes does their family have about itself and other groups? (p. 80)

In addition, clients (or students) are asked to explore which aspects of their cultural heritage they willingly embrace and which aspects they may tend to avoid. The cultural genogram can help couples and families significantly increase their self-understanding. It can help counselors-in-training increase their own cultural self-awareness prior to engaging in work with culturally diverse couples and families (Goldenberg & Goldenberg, 2013).

Common Patterns of Family Problems or Distress

Many patterns of family problems or distress are discussed in the literature. Because of space limitations, we discuss here three patterns of family problems commonly addressed in the literature: problems with boundaries, communication, and family structure.

Problems With Boundaries

Boundaries within a family are the means by which members perceive their function within the system and the subsystems contained therein. A crucial task of the marital/couple subsystem is the development of boundaries that allow for the satisfaction of the dyad's needs but protect the subsystem from the intrusion of in-laws, children, and others. Boundaries between other subsystems within the family system are equally necessary. There must be a clear hierarchy of power with parents leading the family in a unified manner. Parents must avoid interfering with sibling conflicts, adolescents must not expect or be expected to take on parental or spousal responsibilities, and extended family members (e.g., in-laws) must not be involved with the conflicts of a family subsystem (Gladding, 2015; Goldenberg & Goldenberg, 2013; Minuchin, 1974; Minuchin & Fishman, 1981; Nichols, 1988).

Problems With Communication

In surveying more than 500 family professionals, Curran (1983) discovered that healthy communication was the number one trait of healthy families. The importance of healthy communication to the healthy functioning of families is well documented in the research literature (e.g., Beavers & Hampson, 2003; Curran, 1983; Epstein et al., 2003; Gladding, 2015; Goldenberg & Goldenberg, 2013; Stinnett et al., 1979, 1981; Walsh, 2003, 2009; Watts et al., 1996).

Communication is more than one person speaking and another listening. All communications have two different levels or functions: report and command. The report (or content) level is the information conveyed by the words we use. The command (or metacommunication) level communicates how the report level is to be understood and provides a commentary on the nature of the relationship. The metacommunication level is the more powerful influence on human relationships, albeit the more difficult to notice and understand (Gladding, 2015; Goldenberg & Goldenberg, 2013; Watzlawick, Beavin, & Jackson, 1967).

Dysfunctional couples and families exhibit deficits in their ability to constructively express thoughts and feelings and actively listen to one another. Communication dysfunction occurs when communication is *incongruent*; that is, when the verbal (report or content) and nonverbal (command or metacommunication) levels of communication do not agree. Examples of nonverbal communication include body position or posture, breathing rhythm, facial expression, muscle constriction or relaxation, and vocal tone and intensity (Satir, 1983). In well-functioning families, there is agreement or *congruence* between the verbal and nonverbal aspects of communication.

Problems With Family Structure

A family's structure is the invisible set of functional demands that organize family relations. The structure represents the rules the family has developed for relational patterns between family members indicating how, when, with whom, and in what manner members relate. In other words, family rules are the processes by which the family operates and gets things done. Stated and unstated rules exist all families and may or may not be understood by all family members. Rules indicate beliefs and values. Rules are expressive of the belief system whereby the family operates and are based primarily on the beliefs and values of the parental subsystem. Each family has its own unique set of rules because each family has its own unique beliefs and values (Gladding, 2015; Goldenberg & Goldenberg, 2013; Minuchin, 1974; Satir, 1972).

Family rules also delineate family roles. The term *role* refers to the socially expected behavior for a person occupying a place in a particular family system. In all families, there are both formal and informal roles. Formal or traditional roles are assigned, and certain role-congruent behaviors are expected. Informal roles, conversely, are assigned to members so that a family's social and emotional needs may be met. Family members are typically unaware of the role assignment process but may be able to identify their role(s) if questioned about the family's rules and roles. Family roles are not necessarily dysfunctional, however, and the performance of roles is a significant indication of how a family is functioning. In well-functioning families, roles are flexible and easily interchanged, and family stressors are handled creatively. Roles in distressed families, however, are rigidly inflexible, and family stressors are handled by rigid, inflexible, and cyclical patterns of behavior (Gladding, 2015; Goldenberg & Goldenberg, 2013; Minuchin, 1974; Satir, 1972).

In assessing the rules and role enactment of a family system, counselors must pay careful attention to the ethnic and cultural norms of the culturally diverse families with whom they work. Knowledge of different values, customs, and traditions—and understanding of how these elements affect the family's understanding of rules and roles—is crucial for culturally sensitive counseling with diverse families (Goldenberg & Goldenberg, 2013; McGoldrick, Giordano, et al., 2005).

Some Contemporary Couple and Family Stressors

A number of contemporary couple and family stressors may generate distress, and these difficulties are typically amplified by the problem patterns just mentioned. Therefore, couples and family counselors should also assess for the following stressors: the impact of substance use and addictions; the impact of Internet activity on couple and family interactions; couple and family interpersonal violence; unemployment

261

and other socioeconomic issues and stressors; family members with mental health issues; physical issues due to injuries, accidents, and illnesses; and the impact of living with and/or caring for aging family members (Berenson, 1979; Browning & Pasley, 2015; Epstein, Werlinich, & LaTaillade, 2015; McCrady & Epstein, 2015; Peluso, 2007; Peluso, Watts, & Parsons, 2013; Ruddy & McDaniel, 2015; Whisman & Beach, 2015).

Approaches to Couples and Family Counseling: Practice Dimensions

Numerous models of family counseling are addressed in the literature. In addition, many traditional individual-focused approaches have developed couple and family applications (e.g., cognitive behavioral couples and family therapy; Watts, 2001). Discussing in detail the various approaches to couples and family counseling is beyond the scope of this brief chapter. Therefore, in this section, we briefly discuss several prominent theories and approaches that inform the work of counselors practicing within a couples and family counseling framework. These theories and approaches include Bowen family systems, structural, strategic, human validation process, experiential, narrative, solution-focused, Gottman couples, and emotion-focused couples therapies.

Bowen Family Systems Therapy

Bowen family systems therapy, developed by Murray Bowen in the 1950s, was among the first systemically based approaches for working with families (Gladding, 2015). This therapy, sometimes referred to as *transgenerational family therapy*, conceptualizes the family as an emotional unit, a network of interlocking relationships best understood when analyzed within a multigenerational framework (Bowen, 1978; Goldenberg & Goldenberg, 2013). Through a Bowenian lens, dysfunction in the family results when members of the marital dyad have poor differentiation of self and are emotionally stuck together with their families of origin. An individual's level of differentiation or fusion with his or her family of origin can best be observed when the individual experiences anxiety-producing family situations. A therapist using Bowen family systems therapy, a primary technique that serves as both an assessment and an intervention, would guide the family in constructing a multigenerational genogram with the purpose of helping family members understand multigenerational patterns and influences from their families of origin. A genogram is a graphic layout that provides a visual picture of a family tree (Goldenberg & Goldenberg, 2013; McGoldrick, Gerson, & Shellenberger, 2005). Becvar and Becvar (2006) suggested that the genogram provides a visual mapping that may help family members see patterns and relationships in a new light, creating a more objective assessment of their families of origin. Although Bowen family systems therapy is not a technique-focused approach to therapy, some other techniques of this theoretical approach include detriangulation (whereby the counselor helps clients to be both in contact with and emotionally separate from their families) and the therapist as coach (whereby the counselor serves as an active expert who asks factual questions, helps family members clarify their roles and relationships in the family, and helps family members in defusing emotions and avoiding blame).

Structural Family Therapy

Structural family therapy, one of the most influential theories of the 1970s, originated with the work of Salvador Minuchin at the Philadelphia Child Guidance Clinic. The foundational constructs of structural family therapy emphasize that an individual's symptoms are best understood as rooted in the context of family transactional patterns and that a change in family organization or structure must take place before the symptoms are relieved (Bitter, 2014; Goldenberg & Goldenberg, 2013). According to this approach, symptoms within the family arise when family structures are inflexible and appropriate structural adjustments are not made. As noted earlier, family members relate to one another according to certain structures that, according to Minuchin (1974), form an "invisible set of functional demands that organizes the ways in which family members interact" (p. 51). Symptoms within the family are believed to arise when family structures are inflexible, whether enmeshed or disengaged, and appropriate structural adjustments are not made. In addition, when boundaries, which are the unwritten rules that help define the roles and functions of family members, become rigid or confused within or between subsystems, family dysfunction occurs. The therapist working from a structural family therapy perspective must enact a directive leadership role in changing the structure or context in which a symptom is embedded. According to Goldenberg and Goldenberg (2013), the major focus of the structural therapist is to "actively and directly challenge the family's patterns of interaction, forcing the members to look beyond the symptoms of the identified patient in order to view all of their behavior within the context of family structures" (p. 224). To help the family accomplish this, the structural therapist would use the technique of reframing, or changing a perception by explaining a situation from a different and often more positive context (Gladding, 2015). Additional techniques include engaging clients in enactments (a procedure whereby family members role-play the family conflict rather than merely talking about it, thus giving the counselor an opportunity see the family dysfunction) and creating structural family maps (a procedure whereby the counselor draws a map indicating the family structure, including boundaries and subsystem relationships within the family). Structural maps also serve as blueprints for the counselor's plan to support structural shifts.

Strategic Family Therapy

Jay Haley, strongly influenced by the work of Gregory Bateson and Milton Erickson, is credited with the development of the strategic approach to family therapy, and Chloe Madanes helped to further develop it (Bitter, 2014; Carlson, 2002; Goldenberg & Goldenberg, 2013). Haley used the term *problem-solving therapy* to describe his approach to family therapy. He contended that current interactions of the family rather than historical events or family-of-origin issues create family problems. According to this approach, problems or symptoms are not successfully resolved within the family, because family members are locked in repetitive and nonproductive communication patterns (Nugent & Jones, 2005). Family problems can be solved under the direction of an innovative, active, and directive therapist who will challenge the power and unspoken rules that govern many of the behaviors of family members. Strategic therapists view themselves as experts in therapy and take responsibility for directly influencing the family with concrete actions and strategies that bring about change and resolution of the presenting problem. The therapist may use the strategies of reframing or relabeling (whereby problem behaviors are more positively interpreted), directives (whereby clients are given homework or outside assignments to encourage family members to behave differently), and paradoxical intervention or prescribing the symptom (whereby clients are encouraged to continue or increase the presenting problem; compliance demonstrates that they have at least some control over the problem, and noncompliance usually results in significant lessening or cessation of the problem).

The Human Validation Process Approach

Developed by Virginia Satir, the human validation process approach to family therapy views dysfunctional families as consisting of persons whose freedom to grow and develop has been blocked. Dysfunctional behavior results from the interplay of low self-esteem, incongruent communication, and dysfunctional rules and roles (Bitter, 2014; Satir, 1972, 1983). The approach has three overarching goals. First, family members will grow in their understanding of self and in their ability to communicate congruently. Second, family members will develop increased respect for the uniqueness of each member. Third, family members will view individual uniqueness as an opportunity for growth (Bitter, 2014). In the human validation process approach, the family therapist is a facilitator; a resource person; an observer; a detective;

and a teacher or model of congruent communication, warmth, and empathy. The therapist is highly active and personally involved in the system yet able to confront when necessary. The marital or couple dyad is typically seen first, and then conjoint family therapy is convened. The approach is humanistic and highly experiential, using techniques such as the family life fact chronology (a chronology of significant events in the life of the family—and the extended family—typically obtained at the beginning of counseling), family sculpting (whereby one or more family members during a counseling session physically places family members in positions that signify their role or position in the family), and family reconstruction (in this procedure, typically done in group settings, a family member enlists persons to role-play family members and enact significant family events; Bitter, 2014; Satir, 1972, 1983).

Experiential Family Therapy

Experiential family therapy, developed by Carl Whitaker, characterizes family dysfunction in terms of interactional rigidity and emotional deadness. The specific presenting problem is often related to pre-established roles for—and collusions between—family members. Symptoms often serve to maintain the status quo (Goldenberg & Goldenberg, 2013). The primary goal of experiential therapy is growth and creativity rather than mere symptom reduction, because individual growth and creative freedom will reduce the need for the symptom. According to this approach, growth occurs when family members are able to experience the present moment and communicate that experience with other family members. Experiential family therapists focus on being fully with the client family and using themselves to help family members fully express what they are experiencing. Typically working with a cotherapist, experiential family therapists are very active but usually not very directive, serving as a coach or surrogate grandparent. In this approach, which uses a conjoint family therapy framework, the therapeutic relationship or therapist as a person is the primary technique. Additional techniques include reframing (e.g., the therapist suggests that presenting problems are attempts at growth), modeling of fantasy alternatives (e.g., role-playing behavioral possibilities), therapeutic use of self (whereby therapists share fantasies, images, and personal metaphors from their lives), and use of as-if situations (whereby family members enact new roles and experience new perspectives; Gladding, 2015; Goldenberg & Goldenberg, 2013).

Narrative Therapy

Narrative therapy, developed by Michael White and David Epston, deviates from traditional systems thinking. According to this approach, a family is a microsystem embedded in a cultural macrosystem. Families have their own belief and value systems, but these are significantly influenced by beliefs and values of the larger cultural system. According to narrative therapy, dysfunction stems from oppressive forces external to families that generate family problems. Families fail to recognize their strengths and abilities and develop personal and family narratives that are centered on the problem and are failure oriented (White & Epston, 1990). The goal of narrative therapy is to help the family restory the problem-saturated narrative, thereby authoring a new and ongoing narrative of success and empowerment. Narrative therapists make extensive use of reflection-oriented questions to help the family (a) assess the problem, (b) externalize the problem (e.g., "How does anger try to control your interactions?"), (c) find strengths by discovering unique outcomes (times when the problem is not present or distressing; e.g., "Tell me about a time when anger tried to take control and you did not let it. What was different about his time?"), (d) discover preferred outcomes (e.g., "What will your relationship look like when you are consistently not letting anger take control?"), and (e) create a new story (whereby clients liberate themselves from their problem-saturated narrative and create a new story about themselves that re-envisions their past, present, and future). The therapist serves as editor, reader, and publisher of the family's new story (with the family's permission; Freedman & Combs, 1996; Gladding, 2015; Goldenberg & Goldenberg, 2013; Watts, 2003; West, Watts, Trepal, Wester, & Lewis, 2001).

Solution-Focused Brief Therapy (SFBT)

Originally developed by Steve de Shazer, SFBT also deviates from traditional systems thinking and shares with narrative therapy the notion that knowledge is chronologically and culturally embedded. According to this approach, clients and client families can change these realities by doing and viewing things differently (O'Hanlon & Weiner-Davis, 2003). Clients and client families present for counseling because they develop ongoing, recurring patterns of problem solving that do not work, and consequently, they become demoralized and discouraged. The fundamental goal of SFBT is to assist families in the process of restoring patterns of hope (Guterman, 2013; Littrell, 1998). The client–counselor relationship in SFBT is cooperative, collaborative, optimistic, and respectful. SFBT counselors seek to help clients change family members' behavior and attitudes from a problem or failure focus to a focus on solutions and success and to discover latent assets, resources, and strengths that may have been overlooked as family members focus primarily on problems and liabilities (Watts & Pietrzak, 2000). Similar to narrative therapists, SFBT counselors make extensive use of reflection-oriented questions as they work with clients and client families. Techniques commonly used in SFBT include the presession change question (e.g., "Between the time you made the appointment and right now, have you made any movement toward a solution to your problem?"), the miracle question (e.g., "If a miracle occurred tonight and you awoke tomorrow and the problem was gone, what would be different in your life that would indicate that the problem was solved?"), the first sign question (e.g., "What would be the first indication to you that the miracle had occurred? What can you start doing right now to begin making some of this miracle occur?"), exception-finding questions (e.g., "Are there times when the problem does not occur? How are things different at those times?"), scaling questions (e.g., "On a scale from 1 to 10, how committed are you to solving this problem? If I asked your wife, how would she answer?"), and cheerleading (e.g., "Wow, that's great. How were you able to do that?"; DeJong & Berg, 1998; Guterman, 2013; Littrell, 1998; O'Hanlon & Weiner-Davis, 2003; Watts, 2003; West et al., 2001).

Gottman Couples Therapy

In 1980, John Gottman and Robert Levenson began their research on couples communication and relationship analysis. Their research included seven longitudinal studies with a total of 677 couples, some of whom they followed for 15 years (Gottman & Gottman, 2014). Specifically, Gottman and Levenson were researching divorce predictions and marital stability through direct observations. They were surprised by the enormous stability of couples' interaction over time and by the data's ability to predict the longitudinal course of relationships (Gottman & Gottman, 2015).

Gottman, joined by his wife Julie Gottman, continued to study couples to observe distressed relationships and well-functioning heterosexual and same-sex relationships (Gottman & Gottman, 2015). Gottman claims that, based on observations along with physiological responses of the couple, self-report, and assessments, they can predict with 90% accuracy whether a couple will divorce (Gottman & Gottman, 2014).

Dysfunctionality and Functionality in Relationships

Gottman and Gottman (2014) described dysfunctionality in an ailing relationship and identified several predictors of divorce. Some of the predictors are as follows:

1. *More negativity than positivity:* When couples discuss conflict, the ratio of positive to negative interactions in dysfunctional relationships is 0.8:1 rather than 5:1, as it is among couples in stable relationships.
2. *Emotional disengagement and withdrawal:* There is an absence of negative and positive affect during conflict. Couples who engage in this dysfunctional pattern have a negative style in everyday interaction as well, and any attempt at emotional connection is met with withdrawal.

3. *The failure of repair attempts:* When one partner tries to end the conflict by offering a regret or resolve, the other partner rejects the attempt.
4. *A refusal to accept influence:* One partner is unwilling to respond favorably to the other partner's requests, suggestions, or ideas.
5. *Escalation of negative affect: The "Four Horsemen of the Apocalypse":* When a couple is in conflict, four behaviors—criticism, defensiveness, contempt, and stonewalling—are prevalent and are highly predictive of divorce.

Gottman and Gottman (2014) also identified predictors of relationship satisfaction, or what they identified as functionality in relationships. These include the following:

1. *Good relationships are matched in preferred conflict style.* There are three types of couples when it comes to conflict: avoiders, validators, and volatiles. Couples who are matched rather than mismatched in their preferred conflict style are more stable and happy if the ratio of positive to negative interactions during conflict is greater than or equal to 5:1.
2. *Good relationships are characterized by dialogue rather than gridlock with perpetual issues.* Gottman contended that only 31% of relationship conflict is solvable and that functional problem solving about resolvable issues has specific characteristics. Some of these characteristics are as follows:

   - Softened startup versus harsh startup is used when raising an issue. Ideally, the partner who raises the issue will begin with something positive.
   - Partners accept influence rather than escalate or bat back. De-escalation of negativity is functional.
   - Attempts at repair are successful.
   - More positive than negative affect is displayed, leading to physiological soothing.

3. *Individuals in good relationships make peace with the problem to some degree.* Making peace with the problem requires that the couple acknowledge and accept the problem. Couples need to view the problem like a chronic physical condition that they must adapt to but cannot expect to completely cure (Gottman & Gottman, 2014).

The Sound Relationship House

Gehart (2016) discussed two components that, according to Gottman, make marriages work: an overarching sense of positive affect and reducing negative affect when in conflict. Gehart stated that Gottman "has designed a marriage therapy to increase these two qualities in ailing marriages in a model called he terms *The Sound Marital House,* which has seven aspects" (p. 258, emphasis in the original). Gottman explained that the first three levels of the house—build love maps, share fondness and admiration, and turn toward instead of away—make up the necessary components of the couple's friendship. The fourth level is a positive perspective and is contingent on the friendship of the couple or the successful building of the first three levels. The fifth level of the house requires the couple to manage conflicts effectively. This means that the couple accepts the unsolvable and avoids gridlock by finding a way to talk about its perpetual problems. Make life dreams and aspirations come true is the sixth level of the house. When partners support each other in pursuing their dreams, a bond is formed, which helps couples unlock gridlock. The seventh level or the attic completes the house. At this level, couples work together to build their own culture and decide together their shared meaning of life together. To finish off the house, Gottman added two walls, one on either side of the house. The two walls are trust and commitment, and they serve to make the house sound by reinforcing and strengthening the structure.

Emotion-Focused Therapy (EFT)

EFT, developed in the early 1980s by Leslie Greenberg and Sue Johnson, is an evidence-based experiential approach based on 50 years of scientific research focused primarily on treating couples (Johnson, 2015). According to Johnson (2004), EFT is influenced by the work of three pioneers in the field of human development and therapy: Carl Rogers, Salvador Minuchin, and John Bowlby. These pioneers influenced the development of an approach to therapy based on an integration of experiential and systemic perspective (Reiter, 2014) along with attachment and bonding to help understand the nature of close relationships. Strongly influenced by Bowlby's attachment theory, Johnson (2004) asserted that most of the issues couples struggle with are related to the need for secure attachment relationships across the life span, not just in infancy and early childhood. EFT is the only model of couples intervention that uses a systematic empirically validated theory of adult attachment and bonding as the basis for understanding and alleviating relationship problems (International Centre for Excellence in Emotionally Focused Therapy, n.d.).

EFT practitioners focus on the emotional systems of couples, which involve both intrapersonal (within the individual) and interpersonal (between individuals) functioning, to understand how people interact, attach, and bond (Gehart, 2016; Reiter, 2014). By emphasizing both interpersonal and intrapersonal experiences, emotion-focused therapists target interactional cycles and change each person's intrapsychic experiences of the relationship, which maintains, and is maintained by, the cycle (Greenberg & Johnson, 1988).

EFT Interventions

The EFT practitioner borrows concepts and language from attachment theory and frames couples' and family members' experiences in terms of deprivation, isolation, and loss of secure connectedness (Nichols & Schwartz, 2004). With an emphasis on the experiences and unmet needs of the individual, therapy shifts from blaming and finding fault in one's partner or other family members to focusing on one's own desires and longings.

EFT practitioners focus on the present (Johnson, 2004) and follow a treatment design of three stages with nine steps. Gehart (2016) noted that the steps are not perfectly linear, and clients can be expected to cycle back and forth within the nine steps. She added that the steps are primarily designed to be instructive and help guide the therapy process and track progress and setbacks. Stage 1 consists of four steps and involves assessment and de-escalation of problematic interactional cycles. The goal of Stage 1 is for the therapist and couple to create an expanded view of the problem that validates each partner's reality and help the members of the couple begin to see that they are, in part, responsible for their problem and relationship disappointment. In Stage 2, the couple (or family) moves through Steps 5, 6, and 7 and must change interactional patterns and create new and corrective bonding and emotional experiences. The goal of this middle stage is that the blaming partner "soften" (Johnson, 2004, p. 116) and ask for his or her attachment needs to be met by his or her partner. Stage 3, with Steps 8 and 9 of the treatment model, involves consolidation of change and integration of the change into the couple's relational patterns. EFT practitioners help members of the couple (or family) learn to relate to one another differently and work through old unresolved issues using healthier, more respectful ways to communicate. The goal of Stage 3 is to consolidate new responses and cycles of interaction by reviewing the couple's (or family's) growth and successes and helping them create a meaningful narrative of their journey into and out of distress (Johnson, 2004). Throughout the nine steps, the therapist attempts to help each partner or family member identify and express his or her emotional experiences and confront the negative cycle of interactions that characterizes the relationship. Finally, the EFT therapist helps to reorganize patterns of interactions, replacing the negative hurtful cycle of interactions, with both partners or all family members becoming more responsive to one another so that bonding interactions can occur. Johnson (2015) stated, "This bond allows for open communication, flexible problem solving, and resilient coping with everyday issues" (p. 114).

Unique Ethical Issues in Couples and Family Counseling

Every professional mental health discipline and association has a code of ethics that addresses issues such as client welfare, confidentiality, counselor competence, and dual relationships. We would be remiss in failing to address, albeit briefly, some ethical issues that are typically not addressed in individual and group-oriented ethical guidelines.

As professional counselors, we need to be thoroughly familiar with the *ACA Code of Ethics* (American Counseling Association [ACA], 2014) and stay up to date with federal and state laws affecting the counseling relationship (Section A) and managing confidentiality and privacy (Section B). Couples and family counselors consider several systems issues when addressing legal and ethical issues in counseling. As Wilcoxon, Remley, Gladding, and Huber (2007) indicated, treating a couple or family expands the treatment context. Counselors are treating not only the individuals but also the couple's relationship or the whole family. Remaining neutral in counseling is more challenging for counselors treating a couple or family, as couples and family members often try to recruit the counselor to one or the other's side. It is important that counselors act in such a way as to remain neutral. Thus, if asked, "Whose side is the counselor on?" each client would realize that the counselor was on his or her side and also on everyone's side at the same time.

It is also useful to ask yourself: Who has the privilege to sign consent for treatment? How many participants must sign a release of protected health or mental health information? Prior to the start of treatment, couples and family counselors need to communicate to clients how confidentiality extends to all of the adults in the session and how all of the legal adults' signatures are required to release the whole record. Related to this question is another: If you see members of the couple or family individually or in smaller groups, will you need a separate file? If you do not keep separate files for individuals seen separately from conjoint couples or family sessions, are you ready to redact confidential information that includes the mention of someone who has not given permission to release information? This condition comes up when one client from the couple or family or a court of law requests a disclosure of information but another adult in the conjoint session(s) declines to give consent.

Counselor neutrality and the capacity to manage confidentiality can be affected by who attends a session. Complications arise when one member of a couple or family starts counseling and then asks for others to attend conjoint sessions. The reverse may also be true when a couple starts counseling and then just one member attends a session. In several approaches to couples counseling, counselors will initially see the couple conjointly, have individual sessions for assessment purposes, and then see the couple conjointly again (Gottman & Gottman, 2015; Johnson, 2015; see Sidebar 10.5).

A Career as a Marriage and Family Counselor/Therapist (MFC/T)

Although numerous graduate programs prepare MFC/Ts, there is still concern that there will not be enough mental health workers

> **Sidebar 10.5   Case Study: What Would You Do?**
>
> You are seeing a couple for conflict in their marriage. The day after your first session with the couple, one of the partners asks to meet with you privately to "clarify some information that was not presented correctly in yesterday's counseling session." How might you respond?
>
> • • •

to serve the nation's needs in the future. A report of the Annapolis Coalition on the Behavioral Health Workforce expressed concerns that there is "an anemic pipeline of new recruits to meet the complex behavioral needs" of the population (Hoge et al., 2007, p. 2). Many MFC/T graduates like to stay close to larger cities, where most mental health workers are concentrated, which leaves rural areas underserved (Center for Health Statistics, 2006; Hogg Foundation for Mental Health, 2007). Another issue is the aging of MFC/Ts. Northey (2004) reported more than 10 years ago that the average age of marriage and family therapists was 54.

Work Locations and Income for MFC/Ts

Employment sites for MFC/Ts include community mental health agencies, private practice, inpatient facilities and hospitals, social service agencies, churches, universities and research centers, courts and prisons, business and consulting companies, employee assistance programs, and health maintenance organizations (American Association for Marriage and Family Therapy [AAMFT], 2017). The 2016–2017 Bureau of Labor Statistics (2017b) website for the *Occupational Outlook Handbook* shows that, in May 2016, MFC/Ts had a median annual wage of $49,170 compared to $42,840 for mental health counselors. The median annual wage for marriage and family therapists working in state and local government, excluding education and hospitals, was $67,460. The median income for marriage and family therapists working in individual and family services was $44,560.

Job Outlook for MFC/Ts

The U.S. Bureau of Labor Statistics (2017a) predicts that the number of MFC/Ts in the United States will increase from 33,700 in 2014 to 38,700 in 2024, an increase of 15%. The growth for MFC/Ts is projected to be faster than the national average. The AAMFT (2016) website states that there are approximately 50,000 marriage and family therapists. It is important to note that AAMFT includes members in all 50 states, in U.S. territories, and in Canada (AAMFT, 2016). Consider this more personal perspective on the issue:

My name is Sara, and I am a master's-level licensed marriage and family therapist in private practice working in a small county seat city. I work full time with as many as 32 client hours scheduled each week, although with cancellations and schedule changes I typically see only 28–30 face-to-face hours each week. Additionally, I am licensed as both a professional counselor and a social worker.

I have over 35 years of professional experience, starting as a therapist in a long-term adolescent treatment program followed by several years as a community mental health worker in a major city. Three years into my career I added a part-time private practice. Following a move to the small city, I developed contacts within the community, focusing on marketing my practice to physicians, clergy, and social service agencies in the community. Today I carry the lease for a multioffice suite, subletting space to a psychologist (full time), and one part-time marriage and family therapist. I hire and train one part-time receptionist and one part-time billing clerk. I pay bills, clean toilets, call exterminators, buy computer equipment, and make sure the office has adequate office supplies. Since time management is crucial to profitability, I frequently use hours freed by cancellations to attend to record keeping, case follow-up, bill paying, supply purchases, and catching a bite to eat. There are other tasks to attend to between client sessions. Insurance companies must be called requesting additional sessions, 30-page packets must be filled in each year for recredentialing with each provider panel (I'm on over 20 panels). Client-permitted calls are made to school personnel, physicians, and other mental health care personnel for purposes of planning treatment, consultation, and exchanging records. Other spare moments are used to consult with my colleagues or to supervise the work of my employees. Since some insurance companies require electronic submission, I carefully select office software, select billing formats, and attend to Health Insurance Portability and Accountability Act requirements. In order to maintain my licenses, I obtain continuing education units at state, regional, and sometimes national conferences, although I am keenly aware that if I don't work, I don't get paid.

I highly value the freedom to set my own schedule and to manage my own practice. I typically start my week with a 10-hour day followed by three 8-hour days and a 6-hour day, starting and ending at different times during the day. I don't work weekends but work four evenings per week (my children are grown and my husband works several evenings per week). My self-imposed limit is 5 hours of clients in a row. Although I often see couples and families on a cash-only basis, my practice is primarily insurance work, seeing individuals of all ages. I sustain a strong referral base with physicians due to regularly spending 5–10 minutes consulting with the families of my insurance clients. I supplement talk therapy with sand tray and creative arts/activity therapy, trading off the cost of the additional office space needed for those modalities for the flexibility of moving to rooms specifically set up for those modalities, and the benefits each provide in working with children and adolescents especially.

Because time is such a premium, I take some notes during the session and then quickly complete the note before the next session starts. I use a laptop computer in my office to look up resources for clients during sessions; I've become good at Googling for client resources.

I prevent burnout by taking care of myself. I arrange my work week to allow personal time for exercise, good nutrition, and time with my family. My wellness focus includes attending to my spiritual needs, maintaining pets and plants, and enjoying recreational reading. And I leave my work at the office.

Training and Credentialing of Couples and Family Counselors/Therapists

Couples and family counselors have been sharing information and informally training potential colleagues since the late 1950s. Some of the early training was provided through workshops at national meetings of the American Association of Marriage Counselors and the American Orthopsychiatric Association, through workshops held at various agencies, and through research projects focusing on families across the country. Throughout the 1960s and into the 1970s, education in the field came through workshops, conferences, and staff training through organizations. This tradition continues and expands as current and potential MFC/Ts seek workshops, conferences, training programs, and graduate coursework.

Professional Associations for MFC/Ts

By the late 1970s, the American Association for Marriage and Family Counselors (AAMFC) set standards for student, associate, and clinical memberships. In 1978, AAMFC changed its name to the American Association for Marriage and Family Therapy (AAMFT). Other professional associations have influenced the direction of training of MFC/Ts (Gladding, 2015). A group of practitioners created the American Family Therapy Academy in 1977. In 1986, Division 43 (Society for Couple and Family Psychology) of the American Psychological Association was formed. ACA also has a division for MFCs. The International Association of Marriage and Family Counselors (IAMFC) was formed in 1986 and affiliated with the American Association for Counseling and Development (now ACA) in 1990 (Smith, Carlson, Stevens-Smith, & Dennison, 1995). Each association created standards for membership that, in turn, have been codified into specific graduate coursework and training programs (e.g., Council for Accreditation of Counseling and Related Educational Programs, 2016). The most influential organizations for couples and family counselors and therapists are IAMFC and AAMFT. You can find Internet links to these (and other) associations in the "Further Resources" section located at the end of this chapter. You will also find in-depth information regarding professional training standards for both IAMFC (see also Council for Accreditation of Counseling and Related Educational Programs, 2016) and AAMFT.

State Licensure

Both ACA and AAMFT have worked with state-level counseling and marriage and family therapy organizations to seek licensure in states for MFC/Ts. All 50 states and the District of Columbia have licensure for MFC/Ts. Each state has its own standards for academic preparation and postdegree supervised internships. The Association of Marital and Family Therapy Regulatory Boards website (www.amftrb.org) contains information regarding licensure in each state. In addition, the AAMFT website (www.aamft.org) offers a handy reference listing of contact information for each state in the United States and province in Canada. As states have achieved licensure of MFC/Ts, university programs have adjusted their curricula to prepare program graduates to meet the academic and clinical experience requirements for licensure in their respective states or provinces.

Special Topics and Further Considerations

As we noted earlier, couples and family counseling is a continually evolving field. Although addressing the many evolving topics in the field is beyond the scope of this brief chapter, we would like to address two key topics: the introduction of systems counseling in school settings and the use of online or distance modalities for couples and family counseling.

Systems Counseling in School Settings

Since the 1980s, family counselors have recognized the influence that society's larger systems have on family systems. Lusterman (1988) introduced the idea of adopting an ecosystemic approach to working with families presenting with a child who is having school problems. If you use this approach in family counseling, you must have knowledge of both the family system and the school system and how the interaction of these two systems may impede or enhance the child's progress. You will "map the ecosystem" (p. 1) to decide whom to include in the treatment plan and how to invite change in a way that does not blame either system for the problem but rather encourages both systems to work toward a solution that will benefit the child. In this role, you become a sort of systems consultant who facilitates a family–school collaboration leading to systemic change (Wynne, McDaniel, & Weber, 1986).

More recently, experts in the fields of both school counseling and family counseling have suggested that professional school counselors would benefit from training in family counseling and systems theory to better serve students in schools (Davis & Lambie, 2005; Holcomb-McCoy, 2004; Kraus, 1998). Since the inception of the vocational school counseling model of the 1950s, school counseling has been viewed from an individual perspective. The growing shift from an individual focus in counseling to a systems approach has affected schools as well as other counseling settings. Schools and families are the primary socializers of children; therefore, school counselors who have the training and ability to work within a systemic approach are able to assist their clients in attaining both educational and family goals.

Online Couples and Family Counseling

The use of the Internet to deliver counseling services to clients who are unable to be in face-to-face meetings with a counselor is becoming more commonplace and acceptable. ACA has established norms and guidelines for online counseling (ACA, 2014). Some of the Internet tools available for online counseling are e-mail consultation, text-based chat rooms, and videoconferencing (ACA, 2014; Jencius & Sager, 2001). Although the idea of being able to provide services to families who live in remote areas or are confined to their homes because of illness is appealing to family counselors, many issues relevant to Internet counseling need to be addressed (ACA, 2014; Pollock, 2006). If you are going to use online resources for family counseling, you must consider the following implications: (a) the inability to guarantee confidentiality in online counseling; (b) the problem of setting clear boundaries when the Internet is available 24 hours a day, every day; (c) the problem of counseling over the Internet across state lines and the inconsistency of licensure and regulations from state to state; (d) the refusal of many insurance companies to cover Internet counseling; and (e) the risks of not being able to clearly discern the facial expressions, body language, and other dispositions of your clients, which may lead to you overlooking serious pertinent information about clients. As increasingly more therapy-friendly modalities of online counseling become available, couples and family counselors will need to engage in rigorous research regarding the efficacy and ethical implications of this new field.

Chapter Summary

Family configurations have changed significantly in recent decades, and today's counselors work with diverse family structures and dynamics. Counselors working with couples and families face significant challenges and must be knowledgeable and well trained in the theory and practice of couples and family counseling and the professional issues involved with the discipline. This chapter was merely an overview of the couples and family counseling field. If you are interested in working with couples and families, you should actively pursue training and supervision in couples and family counseling both during and after your formal counseling education. In conclusion, we present a summary of the contents of this chapter:

1. Some basic characteristics of the family as a system include holism, communication, circular causality, coexisting subsystems, morphogenesis, and homeostasis.
2. Just as individuals must negotiate various developmental tasks throughout the human life cycle, so must families negotiate developmental tasks throughout various family life cycles.
3. Although Adler and Dreikurs began working with the family as a unit in the 1920s, it was not until much later in the 20th century that family counseling received universal acceptance within the mental health profession. Furthermore, the profession of couples and family counseling has evolved significantly over the past three decades, largely because of significant societal and economic changes.
4. Characteristics of well-functioning families most commonly mentioned in the literature include commitment, communication, clear boundaries, a positive family atmosphere, connectedness, adaptability, and spirituality. Three commonly discussed characteristics of family dysfunction are dysfunctional boundaries, dysfunctional communication, and dysfunctional family structure. It is crucial for counselors to be sensitive to culturally diverse clients' understandings of family functioning and how they may differ across cultures.
5. There are numerous approaches to family counseling, and many of the traditional individual-focused approaches have developed applications for use with couples and families. Seven of the most prominent approaches specific to family counseling are Bowen family systems therapy, structural family therapy, strategic family therapy, the human validation process approach, experiential family therapy, narrative therapy, and SFBT. In addition, two of the most influential couples therapy approaches are Gottman couples therapy and emotion-focused couples therapy.
6. Ethical issues unique to couples and family counseling include the manner in which problems are defined, the determination of who should attend counseling sessions, therapist use of power to facilitate systemic change, the use of paradoxical interventions, and the importance of considering numerous contextual issues when working with couples and families.
7. The two most influential associations for couples and family counselors and therapists are IAMFC and AAMFT. In addition, counselors can be credentialed via professional certification and state licensure.

Learning Activities

1. The chapter addresses the idea of the family as an interrelated system in which the system influences each part and each part influences the system as a whole. Besides families, what are some other examples of systems? Identify some systemic functional similarities between these other examples and families.
2. Reflect on the family environment(s) in which you grew up. What were the strengths? What problem areas do you recall? In what ways do you see the influence of your family environment(s) in your life today? How might your family environment(s) affect your work as a counselor? Discuss your answers with a classmate.
3. In a group setting, discuss with classmates the portrayal of couples and families in movies and television. Is the focus typically on well-functioning couples and families, or is the focus more on dysfunctional ones? Discuss how portrayals of couples and families in movies and television might positively and/or negatively influence couple and family functioning.
4. Now that you have read this chapter, what questions would you like to ask a counselor whose primary practice focus is working with couples and families? Interview a counselor who meets that description and include your questions in the interview.

Review Questions

1. Define and explain the family from a systemic and developmental perspective.
2. Discuss how couples and family counseling has developed as a profession.
3. Describe the differences between well-functioning families and poorly functioning ones.
4. Discuss similarities among the various approaches to family counseling. What differences do you see?
5. What aspects of training and credentialing are unique to couples and family counseling compared to the requirements for the National Certified Counselor credential or your state's professional counseling license?
6. What ethical issues unique to couples and family counseling appear to be the most problematic to you?

Further Resources

American Association for Marriage and Family Therapy
    www.aamft.org
American Family Therapy Academy
    www.afta.org

American Psychological Association, Division 43 (Society for
    Couple and Family Psychology)
        www.apadivisions.org/division-43/
Association of Marital and Family Therapy Regulatory Boards
    www.amftrb.org
Council for Accreditation of Counseling and Related Educational
    Programs
        www.cacrep.org
International Association of Marriage and Family Counselors
    www.iamfc.org
International Family Therapy Association
    www.ifta-familytherapy.org/

References

American Association for Marriage and Family Therapy. (2016).
    About marriage and family therapists. Retrieved from www.aamft.
    org/imis15/AAMFT/Content/About_AAMFT/Qualifications.
    aspx?hkey=2d5f6fac-24c6-40fd-b74f-5f3eaf214e55
American Association for Marriage and Family Therapy. (2017, Sep-
    tember). *Marriage and family therapists: The friendly mental health
    professionals.* Retrieved from www.aamft.org/iMIS15/AAMFT/
    Content/consumer_updates/marriage_and_family_therapists.aspx
American Counseling Association. (2014). *ACA code of ethics.* Retrieved
    from www.counseling.org/docs/default-source/ethics/2014-aca-
    code-of-ethics.pdf?sfvrsn=fde89426_5
Beavers, W. R., & Hampson, R. B. (1990). *Successful families.* New
    York, NY: Norton.
Beavers, W. R., & Hampson, R. B. (2003). Measuring family
    competence: The Beavers systems model. In F. Walsh (Ed.),
    Normal family processes (3rd ed., pp. 549–580). New York, NY:
    Guilford Press.
Becvar, D. S., & Becvar, R. (2006). *Family therapy: A systemic inte-
    gration* (6th ed.). Boston, MA: Allyn & Bacon.
Beels, C. (2002). Notes for a cultural history of family therapy.
    Family Process, 41, 67–82.
Berenson, D. (1979). The therapist's relationship with couples with
    an alcoholic member. In E. Kaufman & P. N. Kaufmann (Eds.),
    Family therapy of drug and alcohol abuse (pp. 233–242). New York,
    NY: Gardner.
Bitter, J. R. (2014). *Theory and practice of family therapy and counsel-
    ing* (2nd ed.). Belmont, CA: Brooks/Cole.
Bowen, M. (1978). *Family therapy in clinical practice.* New York,
    NY: Jason Aronson.
Browning, S., & Pasley, K. (Eds.). (2015). *Contemporary families:
    Translating research into practice.* New York, NY: Routledge.

Bureau of Labor Statistics. (2017a). *Occupational Outlook Handbook: Mental health counselors and marriage and family therapists: Job outlook.* Retrieved from https://www.bls.gov/ooh/community-and-social-service/mental-health-counselors-and-marriage-and-family-therapists.htm#tab-6

Bureau of Labor Statistics. (2017b). *Occupational Outlook Handbook: Mental health counselors and marriage and family therapists: Pay.* Retrieved from https://www.bls.gov/ooh/community-and-social-service/mental-health-counselors-and-marriage-and-family-therapists.htm#tab-5

Carlson, J. (2002). Strategic family therapy. In J. Carlson & D. Kjos (Eds.), *Theories and strategies of family therapy* (pp. 80–97). Boston, MA: Allyn & Bacon.

Carlson, J., Watts, R. E., & Maniacci, M. (2006). *Adlerian therapy: Theory and practice.* Washington, DC: American Psychological Association.

Center for Health Statistics, Health Professions Resource Center. (2006, February). *Highlights: The supply of mental health professionals in Texas—2005* (Publication No. 25-12347). Austin, TX: Author.

Council for Accreditation of Counseling and Related Educational Programs. (2015). *2016 CACREP standards.* Retrieved from www.cacrep.org/for-programs/2016-cacrep-standards/

Curran, D. (1983). *Traits of healthy family.* New York, NY: Winston.

Davis, K. M., & Lambie, G. W. (2005). Family engagement: A collaborative, systemic approach for middle school counselors. *Professional School Counseling, 9,* 144–151.

DeJong, P., & Berg, I. K. (1998). *Interviewing for solutions.* Pacific Grove, CA: Brooks/Cole.

Epstein, N. B., Bishop, D. S., & Baldwin, L. M. (1982). The McMaster model: A view of healthy family functioning. In F. Walsh (Ed.), *Normal family processes* (pp. 115–141). New York, NY: Guilford Press.

Epstein, N. B., Ryan, C. E., Bishop, D. S., Miller, I. W., & Keitner, G. I. (2003). The McMaster model: A view of healthy family functioning. In F. Walsh (Ed.), *Normal family processes* (3rd ed., pp. 581–607). New York, NY: Guilford Press.

Epstein, N., Werlinich, C., & LaTaillade, J. (2015). Couple therapy for partner aggression. In A. Gurman, J. Lebow, & D. Snyder (Eds.), *Clinical handbook of couple therapy* (5th ed., pp. 389–411). New York, NY: Guilford Press.

Fishbane, M. (2015). Couple therapy and interpersonal neurobiology. In A. Gurman, J. Lebow, & D. Snyder (Eds.), *Clinical handbook of couple therapy* (5th ed., pp. 681–701). New York, NY: Guilford Press.

Foley, V. D. (1989). Family therapy. In R. J. Corsini & D. Wedding (Eds.), *Current psychotherapies* (4th ed., pp. 455–500). Itasca, IL: Peacock.

Framo, J. (1996). A personal retrospective of the family therapy field: Then and now. *Journal of Marital and Family Therapy, 22,* 289–316.

Freedman, J., & Combs, G. (1996). *Narrative therapy: The social construction of preferred realities.* New York, NY: Norton.

Gehart, D. (2016). *Theory and treatment planning in family therapy: A competency-based approach.* Boston, MA: Cengage Learning.

Gladding, S. T. (2015). *Family therapy: History, theory, and practice* (6th ed.). Upper Saddle River, NJ: Prentice Hall.

Goldenberg, H., & Goldenberg, I. (2013). *Family therapy: An overview* (8th ed.). Belmont, CA: Brooks/Cole.

Gottman, J. M., & Gottman, J. S. (2014). *Level 1 clinical training. Gottman method couples therapy: Bridging the couple chasm.* Seattle, WA: Gottman Institute.

Gottman, J. M., & Gottman, J. S. (2015). Gottman couple therapy. In A. Gurman, J. Lebow, & D. Snyder (Eds.), *Clinical handbook of couple therapy* (5th ed., pp. 129–160). New York, NY: Guilford Press.

Greenberg, L. S., & Johnson, S. M. (1988). *Emotionally focused therapy for couples.* New York, NY: Guilford Press.

Guterman, J. T. (2013). *Mastering the art of solution-focused counseling* (2nd ed.). Alexandria, VA: American Counseling Association.

Hardy, K. V., & Laszloffy, T. A. (1995). The cultural genogram: Key to training culturally competent family therapists. *Journal of Marital and Family Therapy, 21,* 227–237.

Hoge, M., Morris, J., Daniels, A., Stuart, G., Huey, L., & Adams, N. (2007). *An action plan on behavioral health workforce development.* Cincinnati, OH: Annapolis Coalition on the Behavioral Health Workforce.

Hogg Foundation for Mental Health. (2007). *The mental health workforce in Texas: A snapshot of the issues.* Austin, TX: Author.

Holcomb-McCoy, C. (2004). Using the family autobiography in school counselor preparation: An introduction to a systemic perspective. *The Family Journal, 12,* 21–25.

International Centre for Excellence in Emotionally Focused Therapy. (n.d.). *What is EFT?* Retrieved from http://iceeft.com/index.php/about-us/what-is-eft

Jencius, M., & Sager, D. (2001). The practice of marriage and family counseling in cyberspace. *The Family Journal, 9,* 295–301.

Johnson, S. M. (2004). *The practice of emotionally focused marital therapy: Creating connections* (2nd ed.). New York, NY: Brunner/Mazel.

Johnson, S. M. (2015). Emotionally focused couple therapy. In A. Gurman, J. Lebow, & D. Snyder (Eds.), *Clinical handbook of couple therapy* (5th ed., pp. 97–128). New York, NY: Guilford Press.

Kaslow, F. (2000). Continued evolution of family therapy: The last twenty years. *Contemporary Family Therapy, 22,* 357–386.

Kraus, I. (1998). A fresh look at school counseling: A family-systems approach. *Professional School Counseling, 1,* 12–17.

Littrell, J. M. (1998). *Brief counseling in action.* New York, NY: Norton.

Lusterman, D. D. (1988). Family therapy and schools: An ecosystemic approach. *Family Therapy Today, 3,* 1–3.

McCrady, B., & Epstein, E. (2015). Couple therapy and alcohol problems. In A. Gurman, J. Lebow, & D. Snyder (Eds.), *Clinical handbook of couple therapy* (5th ed., pp. 555–584). New York, NY: Guilford Press.

McGoldrick, M., Gerson, R., & Shellenberger, S. (2005). *Genograms: Assessment and intervention* (3rd ed.). New York, NY: Norton.

McGoldrick, M., Giordano, J., & Garcia-Preto, N. (Eds.). (2005). *Ethnicity and family therapy* (3rd ed.). New York, NY: Guilford Press.

Minuchin, S. (1974). *Families and family therapy.* Cambridge, MA: Harvard University Press.

Minuchin, S., & Fishman, H. C. (1981). *Family therapy techniques.* Cambridge, MA: Harvard University Press.

Nichols, M. P. (1988). *The power of the family.* New York, NY: Fireside.

Nichols, M. P., & Schwartz, R. C. (2004). *Family therapy concepts and methods.* Boston, MA: Pearson.

Northey, W., Jr. (2004, November/December). Who are marriage and family therapists? *Family Therapy Magazine, 3,* 10–13.

Nugent, F. A., & Jones, K. D. (2005). *Introduction to the profession of counseling* (4th ed.). Upper Saddle River, NJ: Prentice Hall.

O'Hanlon, B., & Weiner-Davis, M. (2003). *In search of solutions* (rev. ed.). New York, NY: Norton.

Peluso, P. R. (Ed.). (2007). *Infidelity: A practitioner's guide to working with couples in crisis.* New York, NY: Routledge.

Peluso, P. R., Watts, R. E., & Parsons, M. (2013). *Changing aging, changing family therapy: Practicing with 21st century realities.* New York, NY: Routledge.

Pollock, S. L. (2006). Internet counseling and its feasibility for marriage and family counseling. *The Family Journal, 14,* 65–70.

Reiter, M. D. (2014). *Case conceptualization in family therapy.* Upper Saddle River, NJ: Pearson.

Ruddy, N., & McDaniel, S. (2015). Couple therapy and medical issues. In A. Gurman, J. Lebow, & D. Snyder (Eds.), *Clinical handbook of couple therapy* (5th ed., pp. 659–680). New York, NY: Guilford Press.

Satir, V. (1972). *Peoplemaking.* Palo Alto, CA: Science and Behavior Books.

Satir, V. (1983). *Conjoint family therapy* (3rd ed.). Palo Alto, CA: Science and Behavior Books.

Sherman, R., & Dinkmeyer, D. (1987). *Systems of family therapy: An Adlerian integration.* New York, NY: Brunner/Mazel.

Siegel, D. J. (2012). *The developing mind: How relationships and the brain interact to shape who we are.* New York, NY: Guilford Press.

Smith, R. L., Carlson, J., Stevens-Smith, P., & Dennison, M. (1995). Marriage and family counseling. *Journal of Counseling & Development, 74,* 154–157.

Stinnett, N. (1985). Six qualities that make families strong. In G. A. Rekers (Ed.), *Family building: Six qualities of a strong family* (pp. 35–50). Ventura, CA: Regal.

Stinnett, N., Chesser, B., & DeFrain, J. (Eds.). (1979). *Building family strengths.* Lincoln, NE: University of Nebraska Press.

Stinnett, N., DeFrain, J., King, K., Knaub, P., & Rowe, G. (Eds.). (1981). *Building family strengths 3: Roots of well-being.* Lincoln, NE: University of Nebraska Press.

Walsh, F. (Ed.). (2003). *Normal family processes* (3rd ed.). New York, NY: Guilford Press.

Walsh, F. (Ed.). (2009). *Spiritual resources in family therapy* (2nd ed.). New York, NY: Guilford Press.

Watts, R. E. (2001). Integrating cognitive and systemic perspectives: An interview with Frank M. Dattilo. *The Family Journal, 9,* 472–476.

Watts, R. E. (2003). Selecting family interventions. In D. Kaplan (Ed.), *Family counseling for all counselors* (pp. 121–160). Greensboro, NC: Educational Resources Information Center/Counseling and Personnel Services Clearinghouse.

Watts, R. E., & Pietrzak, D. (2000). Adlerian "encouragement" and the therapeutic process of solution-focused brief therapy. *Journal of Counseling & Development, 78,* 442–447.

Watts, R. E., Trusty, J., & Lim, M. G. (1996). Characteristics of healthy families as a model of social interest. *Canadian Journal of Adlerian Psychology, 26,* 1–12.

Watzlawick, P., Beavin, J. H., & Jackson, D. D. (1967). *Pragmatics of human communication.* New York, NY: Norton.

West, J. D., Watts, R. E., Trepal, H. C., Wester, K. L., & Lewis, T. F. (2001). Opening space for client reflection: A postmodern consideration. *The Family Journal, 9,* 431–437.

Whisman, M., & Beach, S. (2015). Couple therapy and depression. In A. Gurman, J. Lebow, & D. Snyder (Eds.), *Clinical handbook of couple therapy* (5th ed., pp. 585–605). New York, NY: Guilford Press.

White, M., & Epston, D. (1990). *Narrative means to therapeutic ends.* New York, NY: Norton.

Wilcoxon, S. A., Remley, T. P., Jr., Gladding, S. T., & Huber, C. H. (2007). *Ethical, legal, and professional issues in the practice of marriage and family therapy* (4th ed.). Upper Saddle River, NJ: Prentice Hall.

Wynne, L. C., McDaniel, S. H., & Weber, T. T. (1986). *Systems consultation: A new perspective for family therapy.* New York, NY: Guilford Press.

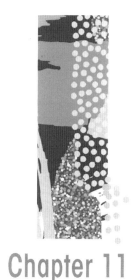

Chapter 11

School Counseling

Amy Milsom

Learning Objectives

1. Articulate the role of school counselors.
2. Describe components of a comprehensive, developmental school counseling program.
3. Discuss the importance of collaboration in school counseling.
4. List important knowledge areas and skills needed by school counselors.
5. Identify current priorities for school counselors.

• • •

The specialty area of school counseling is one of the oldest, having originated in the late 19th century and evolving greatly over the past century. In this chapter, I highlight how school counseling has changed over time, with a strong emphasis on current models and trends in the profession. I also review the various roles school counselors assume and the different factors that influence their work. You will learn about accountability and the importance of data in school counseling. You will also learn a little about some of the current issues that are at the forefront of school counseling and the roles that school counselors play in relation to them.

From Guidance Counselor to School Counselor

What is school counseling? To answer this question, you would need to consider the point in history at which you ask it. Societal trends and government influence are evident in the evolution of school counseling. To start, consider what you learned in Chapter 1 about the important roles that people like Frank Parsons and Jesse B. Davis played in the history of counseling as a profession. The emphasis on vocational guidance in the early 1900s resulted in the role of the school counselor being mainly that of career advisor. Teachers were asked to incorporate into their days classroom lessons on careers and character education in an effort to help students become aware of occupational options and develop behaviors that would be expected in the workplace. Defined as "advice or counseling, especially that provided for students choosing a course of study or preparing for a vocation," the term *guidance* was a very accurate descriptor of what school counselors provided at that time ("Guidance," n.d.).

Vocational guidance activities in schools became more formalized through the 1920s and 1930s through the use of assessments and a more directive approach, as you learned in Chapter 1. The increased focus on assessment through the psychometric movement as well as the availability of assessments used by the armed forces (the Army Alpha and Army Beta tests) led to school counselors using formal assessments to identify students' interests, abilities, and personality characteristics. Furthermore, using the directive counseling approach introduced by E. G. Williamson (1950), school counselors were able to use these kinds of assessments to analyze and synthesize information about their students before offering suggestions about potential future occupations.

A number of significant events in the history of school counseling that occurred during the 1950s and 1960s helped enhance the role of school counselors and increase their presence in schools. The National Defense Education Act of 1958 ultimately helped increase the number of counselors in schools as well as the number of counselor training programs. The Elementary and Secondary Education Act of 1965 (most recently reauthorized as the Every Student Succeeds Act) also included a provision for funding to support training for school counselors (which continues to this day). Furthermore, the American School Counselor Association (ASCA) was established in 1952. With input from ASCA leaders, Gilbert Wrenn was able to offer a new vision for school counseling. In his 1962 report, *The Counselor in a Changing World*, he offered a view of school counseling that included a focus on the development of students and the provision of individual and group counseling, in addition to an emphasis on vocational guidance. Shortly after the publication of this report, the federal government provided funding, through the National Defense Education Act, to support the training of elementary school counselors. The end result of all of these things was an increase in the number of school counselors employed across all building levels, an acknowledgment of the important contributions school counselors can make.

Despite increased funding for the training of school counselors, a lack of uniform or standardized requirements for training existed. Furthermore, school counselors were still being pulled from the teaching ranks, as most individuals who entered school counseling were required to have teaching experience. Coy (1999) discussed the focus on developing professional standards for training school counselors that emerged in the 1960s. Nearly 20 years later, in 1981, the Council for Accreditation of Counseling and Related Educational Programs (CACREP) was formed and published counseling accreditation standards that helped highlight the importance of counseling knowledge and skills for the role of school counselors. The CACREP standards offer a uniform set of standards agreed on by the profession, and currently more than half of the 466 school counselor preparation programs (ASCA, 2016b) in the United States are accredited; CACREP lists 258 accredited school counseling master's degree programs in its online directory (CACREP, 2016).

It is interesting that the 1970s and early 1980s brought good and not-so-good things to school counseling. Declining school enrollments led to many school counseling positions being cut. Baker (2001) attributed much of this to school counselors not being able to show how they made a difference in schools—when schools need to make cuts, they eliminate the staff positions they deem less important. The good was that out of this concern arose discussions of accountability in school counseling. I discuss accountability in more detail later in this chapter, as it is pivotal to the future of school counseling. The 1970s and 1980s were also characterized by an unclear professional identity. Fortunately, Gysbers and Henderson (2012) introduced the idea of a goal-driven, comprehensive kindergarten–Grade 12 developmental approach to school counseling that focused on prevention and the holistic development of students rather than on crisis approaches to service provision. This idea that school counselors should have in place a thoughtful, comprehensive program rather than just engage in a series of disconnected activities would serve as the basis for what school counseling looks like today.

It is also interesting that the turn of the century was a turning point for school counseling, with extensive efforts made to unify the profession and promote a clear identity (Lambie & Williamson, 2004). The publication of the *ASCA National Standards for School Counseling Programs* (Campbell & Dahir, 1997) was a first, important step, as that document offered guidance to help school counselors identify relevant academic, career, and personal/social areas to target when working with students. Around this time, ASCA (2003) also highlighted the more contemporary and comprehensive role school counselors assume by promoting use of the term *school counselor* as opposed to *guidance counselor*. Unfortunately, progress has been slow in relation to that shift in language, as even today many states still credential people as guidance counselors. Nevertheless, progress was made in a different way through the publication of *The ASCA National Model: A Framework for School Counseling Programs* (ASCA, 2003). This document derived from Gysbers's concept of a comprehensive, developmental program and was a major step toward advocating for a unified approach to school counseling.

The *ASCA National Model* (in its third edition as of 2012) emphasizes the role of school counselors in addressing students' academic, career, and socioemotional concerns; collaborating with others; using data to inform their work; and using leadership and advocacy skills to influence systemic change. It also highlights the importance of integrating the school counseling program with the academic mission of the school and ensuring that all students receive equitable access to services and programs. In that document, ASCA provides guidance regarding how to develop a strong foundation for a program, what components go into the management of the program, the kinds of activities school counselors ideally should engage in for the delivery of the program, and the ways in which school counselors can demonstrate accountability.

The publication *Mindsets and Behaviors for Student Success: K-12 College and Career Readiness Standards for Every Student* (ASCA, 2014) reflects the most recent effort ASCA has made to unify school counseling and help school counselors connect what they do to the school's academic mission. This document describes knowledge, skills, and attitudes students should be able to demonstrate as a result of participating in the school counseling program; therefore, school counselors are encouraged to use the standards in that document as a guide when developing program activities and interventions. The standards can also be aligned with state or district-wide initiatives, thus helping connect what school counselors do with broader agendas.

Contextual Dimensions in School Counseling

As you can see, the role of the school counselor has changed quite a bit over time. From an initial emphasis on assessment and advising for vocational development to a current focus that spans academic, career, and socioemotional concerns and integrates skills related to counseling, collaboration, and advocacy, school counselors wear many hats throughout the year. The amount of time and/or the extent to which you will engage in various roles and perform different activities as a school counselor will vary based on the context in which you work (ASCA, 2012). In particular, the building level at which you work, the district in which you work, the characteristics and needs of the students in your school, the existing counseling staff and program, and the expectations of and relationships with your principal (Clemens, Milsom, & Cashwell, 2009) all can influence what your day-to-day activities look like.

For example, an elementary school counselor might find herself spending a lot of time engaging in activities to help students have healthy and happy personal lives (e.g., teaching classroom lessons on topics such as healthy coping strategies and making friends), whereas a high school counselor likely would spend much of her time working with individuals on setting and achieving career and college goals. Or, in a school that serves a lot of students in the foster care system, a school counselor might find himself frequently engaging in consulting and advocacy activities with community agencies and families, whereas a school counselor working in a school in a high-violence area might find himself engaging in a lot of crisis intervention or grief counseling activities or working in collaboration with local law enforcement or other agencies.

The district in which you work can definitely set the tone for what school counseling looks like. Although every school district will vary in size and structure (from county-wide districts composed of 20+ high schools and their feeder schools to districts that are formed around one high school and its feeder schools), the school board and district-level administrators make decisions that affect the work of school counselors. The local district near me is a large one that employs a director of school counseling who oversees the work of nearly 200 school counselors, and that individual is able to inform school counseling practice throughout the district by working with administrators and the school board. In his role, he has been successful in getting the district to support not having school counselors serve as testing coordinators—their time is now freed up to engage in other activities. In a smaller district that does not have an advocate like that at the district level, school counselors might have a more difficult time defining or influencing their roles.

School districts also establish policies that affect school counselor caseloads, which ultimately affect school counselor roles. For example, it is not uncommon for a district to establish a minimum or maximum school counselor caseload and to hire school counselors based on desired ratios. ASCA (2016c) recommends a 250:1 student-to-counselor ratio, but most school counselors throughout the country are assigned to work with much larger numbers of students. In fact, ASCA (2016c) reported a national average of 491:1 during the 2013–2014 school year. Is it realistic for a high school counselor to provide adequate levels of individual counseling or advising to students when she has a caseload of 350 students? How much time would a middle school counselor have to monitor all of his students' grades and follow up with them on socioemotional concerns if he were responsible for 500 students? What about the elementary counselor who has a caseload of 675 and spends a third of her day in classrooms—how much time does she have to address individual student needs, consult with parents or caregivers, or help plan middle school transition programs? Caseload size often drives what kinds of activities are possible and leaves school counselors having to prioritize their roles and activities.

No matter what their caseload, ideally, school counselors should assess the needs in their school and make decisions about how to spend their time based on those needs. Nevertheless, your first year as a school counselor might be more a reflection of the school context than of what a needs assessment might indicate. This is because the roles you engage in as a school counselor are often greatly affected by your colleagues, in relation to whom you work with, what those individuals already do, and what those individuals expect of you. Coming in as a new counselor, you might anticipate that how you spend your time that first year will be influenced not only by what the previous counselor did but also by what any other counselors at that school are doing. If the school administration and faculty were happy with the previous counselor, they might expect you to do things just as he or she did, whereas if they were not happy, you might have more flexibility to approach the job differently. Similarly, if your new colleagues have a clearly defined counseling program, you might be expected to come in and do what they are doing or to just pick up any roles or activities assumed by the previous counselor. Consider the experience of Kristi Kendrick, a school counselor at Monaview Elementary:

> I started my first school counseling job in January at a very diverse Title I elementary school. Our population then was 97% free and reduced lunch, and our demographics were 60% Hispanic, 25% Caucasian, 13% African American, and 2% mixed or other. I was so excited to be at a Title I elementary school, and I was eager to jump in and create my own program. However, I found myself faced with a job description that was not aligned with the ASCA model and a principal and staff who were not familiar with the current role of a professional school counselor. Here I was trying my best to get to know the needs of my school and put together a comprehensive counseling program, and yet I was also serving as state testing coordinator for every standardized test and records clerk responsible for sending and receiving every record for our transient population of students. I felt like my time was not being spent in the best interest of my students, and I struggled with what my role was going to be in this school.
>
> I went to my principal with a calendar at the end of that first half year on which I had highlighted every week that I spent coordinating testing rather than working with students. I also took a graph of my percentage of time spent doing records and the number of referrals that were given to me. I was eager to keep track of these data because I was becoming discouraged that I had to spend my time doing administrative duties rather than working with

kids. Slowly but surely things began to change. I started an advisory council with teachers and administrative leaders in my building, and there was a shift in what everyone saw as the role of the school counselor. I'm happy to say that with amazing support and buy-in at the district level, I no longer serve as testing coordinator, and my principal has hired a full-time records clerk so that I can now more fully align my program with ASCA.

I spent the next year keeping close track of how I was spending my time. I paid attention to the number of student, parent, and teacher referrals I was receiving for individual counseling. Because of the needs of my population, I realized that I was spending the majority of my time dealing with responsive services to address either conflict resolution among my students or stressful and traumatic events that came up in my students' lives, such as having their parents deported, witnessing domestic violence, or sadly having gone through an abusive situation. Realizing that I needed to be available to address these needs as they came up, but also knowing how important classroom lessons are to reach all students, I set up a system where I visit each classroom on a monthly basis. I create my own curriculum based on needs assessments from teachers that I still collect at the end of each year and data from my students' self-referrals so that I can address the issues that kids typically ask for the most help with. I focus on a mix of conflict resolution skills and coping skills because those tend to be the needs of my kids.

I find small groups to be really helpful in seeing students that teachers have referred for behavior issues because I'll often have three to five kids in each grade level with a similar concern. I also use small groups for pulling together some of my high-flyers for a regular appointment to give them skills they can use and practice in between our meetings. I also spend a good bit of my time consulting with teachers and parents as concerns come up or changes happen in the classroom or at home.

I've learned that there is a certain give and take when looking at the different roles that a school counselor should assume in the best interest of time and the students. When my principal first told me that she needed me to take over our daily morning news show I was less than excited. As it turned out, I have been able to transform our news show to include character and career education every day that impacts each student schoolwide. I also love working with my news crew, which is a small group of fourth and fifth graders that I get to teach leadership skills and allow them to be school role models. Another one of the roles I take on at my school is the Section 504 coordinator. I feel that in this role I am able to look out for the best interest of my population of students with a disability in the general education setting. I spend time coordinating various schoolwide programs to recognize and support my students through our Positive Behavior Intervention and Support program as well as coordinating Terrific Kids and our mentor program. The job of a school counselor undoubtedly looks different depending on the school level, district support, and student and community needs. I've found that it takes time to figure out the most appropriate roles for the counselor to assume, but being really in tune with the needs of my kids helps me stay focused on the mission of my program, which is to deliver a comprehensive, developmental counseling program that provides every child with an opportunity to learn and practice skills and competencies that will empower them socially, emotionally, and academically while preparing them to be kind and contributing citizens of our community.

I would be remiss if I did not mention what is probably the most influential factor in school counselor roles: public education. Trends in, as well as legislation pertinent to, public education cannot help but influence what school counselors do, as funding often dictates how time must be prioritized. This influence is evident when you review the history of counseling and that of school counseling in particular. The roles school counselors assume are often directly related to legislation (Dollarhide & Lemberger, 2006). In fact, sometimes the career and assessment emphasis makes it difficult for school counselors to engage in counseling activities focused on students' socioemotional development (I address this concern later in the chapter). Furthermore, the manner in which school counselors conduct their roles is often influenced by legislation. For example, the Family Educational Rights and Privacy Act offers guidelines for record keeping, and the Individuals with Disabilities Education Act delineates possible roles for school counselors as providers of related services for students with disabilities. School counselors have a responsibility to be aware of the laws that drive public education in their state and to ensure that their practice is consistent with those laws. It is beyond the scope of this chapter to offer detailed information about all of these laws, especially because their implementation often varies from state to state and district to district. I do, however, want to shift to discussing what school counseling looks like in practice to better illustrate the influence of many of these contextual factors (see Sidebar 11.1).

Sidebar 11.1 Reflection: Your Kindergarten–Grade 12 School Experience

Think back to the kindergarten–Grade 12 schools you attended. In what types of communities were they located?

What were the demographic characteristics of the students and teachers?

How do you think these factors might have influenced school counselor roles?

Did you have a counselor in elementary, middle, and high school? If so, do you know how that counselor spent his or her time?

How does what you experienced compare with what you have read so far?

• • •

Practice Dimensions in School Counseling

So what does school counseling look like in practice, given that no two school counseling positions are exactly the same? Consider a general overview of what your year might look like as a school counselor who is attempting to implement a comprehensive, developmental program.

Foundation

Ideally, you would already have a program mission in place, and you would have identified annual goals that are aligned with both your program mission and any current district-wide initiatives (ASCA, 2012). If the school district wants to crack down on bullying, for example, it would make sense for one of your program goals to be connected to that bullying agenda. Also, prior to or at the start of the school year, you would have ideally worked with the other counselors in your building and in your district to map out a plan for implementing the standards identified in ASCA's (2014) *Mindsets and Behaviors for Student Success*. For example, you might choose to address a social skills standard via an elementary classroom lesson about making friends or through a high school lesson addressing job interview skills. You might spend some time in your counseling graduate program exploring what it looks like to work on these types of activities.

Management

ASCA (2012) suggests that the program goals you develop will inform the kinds of interventions and activities you integrate into your school counseling program, and the standards crosswalk you create will delineate the specific topics you will address via classroom lessons, small groups, and other schoolwide interventions. Data you collect on your program should inform your practice as well. ASCA highlights the importance of examining data specifically related to student achievement and behaviors and of disaggregating data (i.e., breaking it down so you can examine results for specific subgroups) in an effort to identify any differences among groups. For example, you might ask that a report be run from the school database to examine course enrollment patterns (e.g., how many students enroll in Advanced Placement courses or honors courses) or student suspensions. Then you would want to disaggregate those data to determine whether any differences exist by factors such as gender, race, or socioeconomic status, to name a few. The results you find would help you determine whether any targeted interventions should be offered to certain subgroups of students or whether any schoolwide programming needs to be considered. Interventions and activities that are derived from the data would then be integrated into your existing program.

293

With all of these interventions and activities in mind, you can create an annual calendar (ASCA, 2012) that will outline, month by month, any significant program activities. Beginning-of-the-year activities in your calendar might include things like introducing yourself to students and staff and reminding them of your role, conducting a needs assessment (more on that topic later), updating the program Web page, and developing program goals. Transition programming for students moving to and from building levels could be integrated into both the beginning (checking in on how it went) and end (planning for upcoming transition) of the year. The bulk of the academic year could be filled with things like career development activities (formal advising meetings, career days, etc.); college planning events (e.g., financial aid night, college fairs); dates for standardized testing; meeting dates for things like the program advisory board or school leadership teams; and academic-related activities such as course registration, study skills groups, and preset times for conducting individual advising meetings after reviewing report card data. At the end of the year, school counselors might find their calendars filled with activities that include reviewing program data, planning for the next year, and disseminating information about summer remedial and/or enrichment opportunities for students.

Delivery

ASCA (2012) recommends that 80% of a school counselor's time be spent in the delivery of the program. Activities in the delivery system include what are referred to as *direct* student services and *indirect* student services. The easiest way to remember the difference is that direct services are activities you implement in which you are working directly with students in some way—there must be interaction with students. Indirect services, in contrast, are activities you engage in on behalf of students and that benefit students in some indirect way.

Direct services are delivered through large-group activities or classroom lessons, through small-group or targeted interventions, or individually. They typically include things like individual counseling, academic advising, college and career planning (including relevant assessment), counseling and psychoeducational groups, classroom lessons, and crisis intervention activities. Given the size of their caseloads and the array of services they need to provide across academic, career, and socioemotional domains, school counselors are limited to the use of short-term counseling interventions (ASCA, 2015).

Making referrals to mental health providers or community agencies falls into the indirect services category, and school counselors might provide selected direct services to a student but also refer that student and/or family to other service providers who might be able to address specific needs (ASCA, 2015). For example, a school counselor would continue to engage in academic and career planning with a student but also recognize the need to refer her to a specialist who can treat her eating disorder (a diagnosis for which most school counselors would not be adequately trained to provide treatment). In these kinds of instances, school counselors should encourage caregivers to sign a release of information that would enable them and other mental health providers to coordinate their efforts to best help the student (ASCA, 2016a). It is important that school counselors check in with a student or family after making a referral to monitor the follow-through or inquire about progress.

Consulting and collaborating with others are the other two indirect services activities in which school counselors might frequently engage in an effort to help students (ASCA, 2011). Parents or caregivers, teachers, community agencies, colleges, and local businesses all might be involved in some way in collaborative efforts to help students through sharing information and resources and/or combined efforts. For example, a school counselor might initiate a team meeting to discuss concerns related to a middle school student who is struggling with organization and social skills. The team might develop an intervention that involves individual counseling and support from the school counselor, reinforcement of behaviors in class by the teacher, and monitoring and support from someone at home.

The delivery of your school counseling program will definitely reflect the context in which you work, in terms of both the frequency with which you engage in activities and the manner in which you approach them. For example, elementary school counselors typically teach more classroom lessons than do high school counselors, but middle and high school counselors spend more time engaging in academic advising and career and college planning activities than do elementary school counselors. Probably most different, however, is the manner in which you will prepare for and implement direct services activities.

Using the counseling, ecological, human development, and career development theories you will learn about throughout your program, you will work with students to address a variety of academic, career, and socioemotional concerns. The developmental level of the students with whom you are working and their unique needs will influence the way in which you implement those theories and what you will emphasize in your work. For example, although all students can benefit from opportunities to become aware of their own strengths and skills in relation to future careers, the way in which this information is explored and the depth with which it is explored will differ based on students' grade level and cognitive abilities (Akos, Cockman, & Strickland, 2007). Similarly, if you are working in a school that has a lot of students who speak English as a second language, or if a lot of students in the classroom you will be visiting have cognitive or learning disabilities, you will need to consider the ways in which you can differentiate your lessons to provide opportunities for all students to grasp and benefit from the information. Hopefully, you will have opportunities throughout your counseling program to learn more about how to tailor your interventions to the unique needs of the school you are in as well as to the individual students with whom you work (see Sidebar 11.2).

Accountability

An important aspect of being a school counselor is engaging in accountability (ASCA, 2012), and I share more about this a little later in the chapter. In terms of what accountability looks like in practice, think generally about how you might use data to identify needs and to evaluate the effectiveness of your work. I already talked briefly about examining school data and disaggregating those data. School counselors also might develop and implement needs assessment surveys, administering them to students or teachers or to parents or caregivers in an effort to identify areas of focus. Maybe they want to know what teachers are seeing as main concerns in their grade level, or maybe they want to know how many parents or caregivers would be interested in attending workshops throughout the year and on what topics. That kind of information can be gathered through needs assessments, and the results could be used to inform program activities.

Another important aspect of accountability is evaluation. Think back to the idea of generating school counseling program goals. Ideally, school counselors should at some point evaluate whether they have achieved those goals. In developing goals, they need to consider the ways in which they will measure, or evaluate, the outcomes. ASCA (2012) references three types of data: process, perception, and outcome. These terms, respectively, refer to the ideas of noting the

Sidebar 11.2 Reflection: School Counseling Delivery System

Think about the different kinds of activities that fall into the school counseling delivery system. Which ones most appeal to you, and why? Slightly different skill sets are required to effectively deliver individual counseling versus classroom instruction, for example, or to handle crisis situations or explain achievement test results. Where do you think your strengths lie currently? What skills do you believe you will need to develop to competently deliver the range of services expected of school counselors? How will you work on those skills?

• • •

number of people involved in an intervention and the frequency of that intervention, what people think they know or learned or can do as a result of an intervention, and actual outcomes (e.g., behaviors, knowledge) resulting from an intervention. ASCA indicates that these outcomes often are measured through school data such as grades, attendance, and course enrollment. It is through collecting these types of data that school counselors are able to demonstrate whether and how they have made a difference.

Key School Counseling Roles

Despite the contextual differences and the different types of roles school counselors assume, a common set of skills can be used by school counselors across the different components of counseling described earlier. You will learn more about these core roles as you progress through your graduate program, but let me provide a very brief overview here.

Counselor

At their core, school counselors must be excellent counselors, and the relationship they develop with students and others will be at the heart of their work. As you will learn in your counseling program, the effectiveness of most counseling interactions has more to do with the relationship between the counselor and client than with the type of interventions used (Lambert, 1992). People with whom you interact as a school counselor need to feel heard and understood—this holds true whether you are counseling a student, consulting with a teacher, or fielding a caregiver's concern. Core counseling skills will be essential to your job.

Collaborative Consultant

In a very simplistic way, *consultation* refers to interacting with others (e.g., parents, teachers) to solve problems. School counselors will often be sought out to help someone figure out what might be going on with a student and what kinds of interventions could be helpful. The collaborative aspect of being a consultant refers to school counselors partnering with others, appreciating that multiple perspectives on an issue and the shared knowledge of others might be most beneficial in fully understanding and conceptualizing the situation. School counselors can foster this collaborative consultation approach by inviting others to contribute ideas rather than simply offering their own advice or suggestions.

Leader

Most students do not enter school counseling programs thinking that they will be leaders in their schools, but it is important that you adopt the mindset of a leader. Mason and McMahon (2009) found that the most common ways in which school counselors exhibited leadership were in relation to fostering collaborative relationships, listening, being supportive, encouraging others, and modeling what they expected of others. Notice the similarity to counseling? School counselors can also assume leadership roles in more obvious ways, through speaking up and identifying concerns and offering suggestions, similar to the role they will assume as advocates.

Advocate

Although you are probably drawn to the idea of advocating on behalf of others, you might not be as excited to advocate for yourself or your program. School counselors must possess the skills to do all of these things, because sometimes advocating for yourself or for your program ultimately will lead to outcomes that benefit your students. Trusty and Brown (2005) discussed the importance of school counselors developing advocacy dispositions, knowledge, and skills to effectively assume the role of advocate.

Special Considerations in School Counseling

Although numerous topics could be highlighted here, I want to focus on a few key areas that are driving school counseling in the present day.

Accountability and Outcome Research

Since the 1970s, school counselors have been encouraged to collect data to demonstrate their effectiveness (Baker, 1977). I would not say that accountability is any more or less important today, but school counselors need to collect and use accountability data to advocate for their positions in schools. The 1970s serve as a good reminder of how easily school counseling positions can be cut when budgets get tight— it is up to you to ensure that your role is recognized and supported.

Numerous researchers have reported how unprepared school counselors feel to work with data and share the outcomes of their work (Milsom & McCormick, 2015; Young & Kaffenberger, 2015), but hopefully, you will have opportunities in your graduate program to gain skills in accountability. Opportunities to design needs assessments and then collect and summarize data or to collect pre- and posttest data to determine the effectiveness of a group counseling intervention can occur during your internship or other field-based courses. Fortunately, you do not need to be an expert statistician to focus on accountability. In addition to the formulas in Excel that enable you to summarize data via the calculation of means or percentages, many online surveys (e.g., Google Forms) offer options for summarizing individual item data. In addition, some school districts have sophisticated student record databases in which data can be sorted and compiled (often with the help of technology personnel). By showing how they spend their time, how many students they serve, and the impact of their interventions, school counselors can help to secure their positions. Consider the experience of Lorraine Holeman, Lauren Tingle, and Laura Tolbert, school counselors at Wade Hampton High School:

As high school counselors, we use data to assess the needs of our students and parents, track the progress of our students in various areas, and assess the outcome of programs and initiatives that we put into place to address our population's needs. Here is a sample of our daily processes and yearly initiatives.

To collect information on counselor time spent with drop-in students, parents, or other visitors, we keep an automated sign-in on a laptop at the front desk in our school counseling office. It shows the volume of students that we assist daily in addition to our various other counseling duties. Another way we track our use of time within ASCA's standards for use of time is through Google calendars. We color code our time spent based on the following categories: individual counseling, consultation, school support, and so on.

To survey student learning, we use an online mobile quiz called Kahoot to check for student understanding after classroom guidance lessons. We also use pre- and posttests to collect perception data to check for both student understanding and progress on the particular need the small-group counseling is addressing.

Naviance, a college and career database used for student postsecondary planning, is a new tool that our district has provided this year. Through Naviance, we collect meaningful data through student surveys. Every year, we meet with student and parents for an Individual Graduation Plan meeting. This year, we used an Individual Graduation Plan survey to identify career clusters of interest, goals, and postsecondary plans.

In August, we conduct an electronic needs assessment to identify academic, career, and personal/social counseling needs. Questions asked on these surveys might include postsecondary plans, goals, and needs for individual or group counseling. This year, our school's top three career clusters were (a) arts, audiovisual technology, and communications; (b) health science; and (c) science, technology, engineering, and mathematics. We packaged these data in an infographic created with Piktochart, a free online resource. These data support our course offerings and inspire conversations about future program development at our school. Teachers can put confident energy towards recruiting students at the middle school level because the data support these initiatives. The data are also now being used to validate to our administrative and district level decision makers our need for more health science course offerings and more health science teachers.

Stakeholders at our high school are also examining data on a regular basis. Quarterly, the leadership team collaborates to discuss at-risk student progress through the Data Action Team Meeting. The outcome data discovered in this meeting inform some of our school counseling interventions. For example, through a teacher survey and quarterly failure reports, our counselors found that there was a high association between students with multiple absences and failing grades. Teachers commented that this was the most significant problem in their classes and that they simply could not teach students that are not in school. We brainstormed ways to increase attendance for our failing students and examined data from the Early Warning Response System. Our analysis formed a target group of 42 students across grade levels. A common thread among these students was their lack of internal motivation to come to school. Abraham Maslow's hierarchy of needs also provided a framework for our attendance intervention, keeping in mind that students need to feel a sense of belonging before working on higher level thinking. We named the intervention *Generals Connect,* highlighting the importance of positive student–teacher relationships to encourage student success. Mentor responsibilities are pretty simple: Randomly meet with assigned students twice during the week to check in, encourage them to come to school, ask about their day, and give them a raffle ticket when they are present. The counselors hold a weekly raffle for small gift cards, and students are enjoying the chance to win prizes. So far, we have seen a huge improvement in attendance for our target group resulting in passing grades. Generals Connect is an example of effective programming made possible through targeted data collection and analysis.

In addition to assessing the outcomes of individual interventions, school counselors should be concerned about the extent to which their programs in general make a difference to students. In a summary of school counseling outcome research, Whiston and Quinby (2009) reported connections between school counseling interventions and positive student outcomes related to discipline, career knowledge, problem-solving skills, and academic achievement. Recent research has focused on the impact of fully implemented comprehensive, developmental programs, with numerous research studies having been conducted around the country through the Ronald H. Fredrickson Center for School Counseling Outcome Research and Evaluation. *Empirical Research Studies Supporting the Value of School Counseling* (ASCA, n.d.) includes a review of many of the research studies that have addressed the impact of comprehensive school counseling programs and of individual school counseling interventions. In general, however, more outcome research is needed in school counseling, particularly at the middle and high school levels (Whiston, Tai, Rahardja, & Eder, 2011).

School–Family–Community Partnerships

When families, schools, and communities assume a shared responsibility, students learn more (Epstein, 1987). In fact, benefits of partnerships include increased academic achievement, improved student attendance, improved student behavior, and correspondingly decreased disciplinary referrals, to name a few (Epstein & Van Voorhis, 2010). School counselors can play an important role in fostering this kind of shared responsibility in relation to student learning and success, and Epstein and Van Voorhis

(2010) offered examples of ways in which schools can envision the six types of involvement that were originally described by Epstein (1987).

The importance of partnering with families and communities becomes more evident when you consider the diversity of communities and families with which you might be involved. Barriers to school involvement (such as lack of transportation, language barriers, or negative or racist attitudes exhibited by school personnel) prevent many families from being involved in their child's schooling. Sometimes the school staff set a negative tone by the way in which they approach or interact with parents or caregivers or often because they do not initiate interactions or reach out to families. Sometimes, however, families feel insecure about being involved even when schools do attempt to interact positively with them. Imagine you are a parent who did not graduate from high school. How comfortable would you feel if called to attend a meeting with your child's teachers to discuss his failing grades and behavior problems? If you chose to attend the meeting and they asked for your feedback, would you feel comfortable speaking up or asking questions?

Not only must schools recognize the importance of parent or caregiver involvement, but they must also be creative in terms of how they attempt to engage families (Van Velsor & Orozco, 2007). In many instances, by reaching out to the communities in which families might already be engaged or to individuals in the community who might be trusted by families, school counselors can increase their understanding of the needs of those communities and families. They might learn about existing community resources or supports, or they might identify a community need and figure out a way to offer services or provide resources at the school. For example, school-based health centers (which might offer basic medical and mental health care services) can be valuable resources in low-income, rural communities where families have difficulty locating or accessing services. The point is that by demonstrating interest in families and making efforts to support them, schools might see increased family involvement.

Mental Health in Schools

The past few years have seen an increase in the number of research articles addressing issues related to school counseling and mental health issues in schools. In the introduction to his special issue of *Professional School Counseling* on that topic, Auger (2013) cited numerous statistics reflecting increases in diagnoses, especially anxiety disorders, among school-age students as well as the negative outcomes experienced by many of these students. Furthermore, other articles have addressed the negative socioemotional outcomes of students who have experienced bullying (in particular, students who identify as lesbian, gay, bisexual, transgender, or queer or students who have disabilities), school violence, or other crises. DeKruyf, Auger, and Trice-Black (2013) argued that school counselors have a responsibility to address the mental health needs of students in their schools. I have already suggested that school counselors are not in the business of providing long-term therapy, so what are the appropriate roles they can assume in relation to addressing the mental health needs of students? Given that so many students have mental health needs that go unaddressed, it is imperative that school counselors do what they can.

Identification is one thing school counselors can keep in mind when focusing on mental health (Thompson, Robertson, Curtis, & Frick, 2013). In addition to becoming aware of warning signs and characteristics of various mental health disorders (Is a psychopathology course required in your counseling program? If not, in what other class will you learn about mental health disorders in children and adolescents?), school counselors can use one of the many inexpensive, and sometimes free, assessments that are available to help screen for various diagnoses (and, hopefully, you will be exposed to some of these in your assessment course). When those assessments suggest the possibility of any diagnosable condition, school counselors can refer families to a school psychologist or other local mental health provider for a formal evaluation. It is important to remember that diagnosing students is beyond the scope of practice for a school counselor (ASCA, 2016a).

In addition to helping to identify mental health disorders, school counselors can provide short-term individual or group counseling and psychoeducational interventions and work collaboratively with families and teachers in their implementation (Thompson et al., 2013). By *short-term*, I am referring to interventions that might last four to six sessions as opposed to longer durations. For example, if a teacher notices that a number of students in her classroom seem to get pretty worried right before taking tests, even without a formal diagnosis of anxiety, a school counselor might pull those students in for a time-limited (e.g., four- to six-session) small-group intervention focusing on cognitive behavioral strategies for reducing those feelings. Strategies taught in the group can be introduced to parents or caregivers so that they can monitor and help reinforce them at home as well as to the teacher so that he or she can integrate them into pretesting routines in the classroom. By educating teachers and families about mental health conditions, school counselors not only can help them recognize potential warning signs but also can help them better understand how to support students struggling with these conditions.

I mentioned earlier in this chapter that school counselors sometimes need to refer students to other mental health providers who have expertise in specific areas. In instances when financial or other legitimate barriers prevent families from seeking additional help for students, school counselors should try to help families overcome those barriers (e.g., provide families with a list of counselors or agencies that offer sliding-scale services, connect them with social workers who might be able to identify community resources, advocate for a school-based mental health counselor). In instances when a caregiver refuses to seek help for a student with a potentially severe or life-threatening condition (e.g., schizophrenia), school counselors might need to make a referral to Child Protective Services on the basis of concerns of neglect.

College Readiness

In recent years, the number of students attending college has increased, with the greatest gains evident among minorities (Carnevale, Smith, & Strohl, 2010), but disparities become evident when you examine the percentage of students attending college by race—with higher percentages of Asian and White students enrolled compared to Black and Hispanic students. In addition, Brock (2010) suggested that although women outnumber men at 4-year colleges, both women and minorities are overrepresented at 2-year institutions. Much has been written about the unique needs of diverse individuals pursuing college, including students with disabilities, first-generation college students, racial minorities, students who speak English as a second language, or those who are undocumented, to name a few (with many students falling into more than one of those groups), and school counselors need to be familiar with those populations (see Holcomb-McCoy, 2010; Marsico & Getch, 2009; Milsom & Hartley, 2005).

Conley (2007) defined college readiness not only in relation to possessing academic and higher order thinking skills for academic success but also in terms of knowing what to expect and having a desire and commitment to develop the skills and knowledge to successfully navigate college. For many students, especially those who have no friends or family members who went to college, the greatest challenge is not knowing. They might have strong academic skills and be incredibly motivated, but without help gathering information about college in general, they may never achieve their goals. This is where school counselors can play the greatest role.

The Barack Obama Administration did great things to promote both the importance of college readiness and the role of school counselors in relation to helping students become college ready. First Lady Michelle Obama, speaking at the ASCA conference in 2014 about the Reach Higher initiative and again in her final remarks as First Lady, which coincided with the 2017 School Counselor of the Year ceremony, validated the efforts that school counselors can make to help encourage and support all students to pursue some type of education beyond high school. She also addressed the challenges that school counselors face in relation to high caseloads, limited graduate training related to college readiness, and limited support and resources in schools to facilitate helping students prepare for and pursue college.

Research suggests that school counselors matter when it comes to college: Students who had interactions with a school counselor were more likely to apply to college (Bryan, Moore-Thomas, Day-Vines, & Holcomb-McCoy, 2011). This does not mean that those students will attend or complete college, but getting students to apply to college is a starting point. Through a variety of interventions implemented across all building levels, school counselors can help ensure that all students have opportunities to learn about and be exposed to college. Although it is beyond the scope of this chapter to review the many ways in which school counselors can and should play a role in college readiness, I would leave you to think about the four key roles identified earlier in this chapter—counselor, collaborative consultant, leader, and advocate—and how, through these roles, school counselors can address college readiness.

Chapter Summary

In this chapter, I briefly reviewed some of the key events that have shaped school counseling over the years. I also examined the different roles that school counselors assume and the multiple factors that influence these roles. You were introduced to the basic components of a comprehensive, developmental school counseling program and learned a little about some of the current topics that are at the forefront of school counseling today. You will have many opportunities throughout your graduate program to continue to explore what school counseling looks like in practice, including how school counselors apply the skills and theories you will learn to their work with diverse students and families.

Learning Activities

1. Interview one or two school counselors and ask them how their role is viewed in their school, what their typical week looks like, what factors influence how they spend their time, and what challenges they regularly face in their jobs. Reflect on how what they shared compares to what you have learned in this chapter.
2. Search online for school counseling program calendars. What did you learn about the types of activities counselors engage in throughout the year? Compare calendars for different building levels.
3. Look up the laws in your state related to public education. In what way do they affect school counselor roles?
4. Thinking about the various roles that school counselors assume. Generate a list of adjectives that you believe reflect important school counselor characteristics. Compare your list to those generated by your peers and come to an agreement on what you believe to be the five most critical characteristics. Rate yourself on each, and develop plans to maintain or develop those characteristics.

5. Develop a school counseling program goal, and generate a plan for addressing and evaluating it.
6. With a group of peers, brainstorm ways in which college and career readiness activities could be integrated into a school counseling program across all building levels. Identify at least one school counseling intervention and one collaborative schoolwide intervention that could be integrated at each building level (elementary, middle, and high).

Review Questions

1. In what way has the role of school counselors changed over time? Compare school counseling in the early 1900s to school counseling today.
2. How have societal trends and governmental initiatives influenced school counseling?
3. What are the key components of a comprehensive, developmental school counseling program, and what kinds of activities fall under those components?
4. What are appropriate roles for school counselors in relation to addressing mental health concerns in schools?
5. In what ways is collaboration important in school counseling?

Further Resources

Websites

American Counseling Association School Counselor Connection
    https://www.counseling.org/knowledge-center/school-counselor-connection
American School Counselor Association
    www.schoolcounselor.org
EZAnalyze
    www.ezanalyze.com
Ronald H. Fredrickson Center for School Counseling Outcome Research and Evaluation
    www.umass.edu/schoolcounseling/
State Certification Requirements
    https://www.schoolcounselor.org/school-counselors-members/careers-roles/state-certification-requirements
What Works Clearinghouse
    http://ies.ed.gov/ncee/wwc/

Books

Kouzes, J., & Posner, B. (2008). *The student leadership challenge: Five practices for exemplary leaders.* San Francisco, CA: Jossey-Bass.

References

Akos, P., Cockman, C. R., & Strickland, C. A. (2007). Differentiating classroom guidance. *Professional School Counseling, 10,* 455–463.

American School Counselor Association. (2003). *The ASCA national model: A framework for school counseling programs.* Alexandria, VA: Author.

American School Counselor Association. (2011). *The professional school counselor and the identification, prevention and intervention of behaviors that are harmful and place students at-risk.* Retrieved from www.schoolcounselor.org/asca/media/asca/PositionStatements/PS_AtRisk.pdf

American School Counselor Association. (2012). *The ASCA national model: A framework for school counseling programs* (3rd ed.). Alexandria, VA: Author.

American School Counselor Association. (2014). *Mindsets and behaviors for student success: K-12 college and career readiness standards for every student.* Alexandria, VA: Author.

American School Counselor Association. (2015). *The school counselor and student mental health.* Retrieved from www.schoolcounselor.org/asca/media/asca/PositionStatements/PS_StudentMentalHealth.pdf

American School Counselor Association. (2016a). *ASCA ethical standards for school counselors.* Retrieved from https://www.schoolcounselor.org/asca/media/asca/Ethics/EthicalStandards2016.pdf

American School Counselor Association. (2016b). *School counseling degree programs.* Retrieved from www.schoolcounselor.org/school-counselors-members/careers-roles/school-counseling-degree-programs

American School Counselor Association. (2016c). *Student-to-school-counselor ratio 2013-2014.* Retrieved from www.schoolcounselor.org/asca/media/asca/home/Ratios13-14LowestToHighest.pdf

American School Counselor Association. (n.d.). *Empirical research studies supporting the value of school counseling.* Retrieved from https://www.schoolcounselor.org/asca/media/asca/Careers-Roles/Effectiveness.pdf

Auger, R. W. (2013). School counseling and children's mental health: Introduction to the special issue. *Professional School Counseling, 16,* 208–210.

Baker, S. (1977). An argument for constructive accountability. *Personnel and Guidance Journal, 56,* 53–55.

Baker, S. (2001). Reflections on forty years in the school counseling profession: Is the glass half full or half empty? *Professional School Counseling, 5,* 75–83.

Brock, T. (2010). Young adults and higher education: Barriers and breakthroughs to success. *Future of Children, 20,* 109–132.

Bryan, J., Moore-Thomas, C., Day-Vines, N. L., & Holcomb-McCoy, C. (2011). School counselors as social capital: The effects of high school college counseling on college application rates. *Journal of Counseling & Development, 89,* 190–199.

Campbell, C. A., & Dahir, C. A. (1997). *Sharing the vision: The national standards for school counseling programs.* Alexandria, VA: American School Counselor Association.

Carnevale, A. P., Smith, N., & Strohl, J. (2010). *Help wanted: Projections of jobs and education requirements through 2018.* Retrieved from http://cew.georgetown.edu/jobs2018/

Clemens, E. V., Milsom, A., & Cashwell, C. S. (2009). Using leader-member exchange theory to examine principal-school counselor relationships, school counselors' roles, job satisfaction, and turnover intentions. *Professional School Counseling, 13,* 75–85.

Conley, D. (2007). *Toward a more comprehensive conception of college readiness.* Retrieved from https://docs.gatesfoundation.org/documents/collegereadinesspaper.pdf

Council for Accreditation of Counseling and Related Educational Programs. (2016). *Directory.* Retrieved from www.cacrep.org/directory/?state=&dl%5B%5D=M&pt_id=27&pc_logic=any&keywords=&submitthis=

Coy, D. R. (1999). The role and training of the school counselor: Background and purpose. *NASSP Bulletin, 83,* 2–8.

DeKruyf, L., Auger, R. W., & Trice-Black, S. (2013). The role of school counselors in meeting students' mental health needs: Examining issues of professional identity. *Professional School Counseling, 16,* 271–282.

Dollarhide, C. T., & Lemberger, M. E. (2006). "No Child Left Behind": Implications for school counselors. *Professional School Counseling, 9,* 295–304.

Epstein, J. L. (1987). Toward a theory of family-school connections: Teacher practices and parent involvement. In K. Hurrelman, F. Kaufmann, & F. Losel (Eds.), *Social intervention: Potential and constraints* (pp. 121–136). New York, NY: DeGruyter.

Epstein, J. L., & Van Voorhis, F. L. (2010). School counselors' roles in developing partnerships with families and communities for student success. *Professional School Counseling, 14,* 1–14.

Guidance. (n.d.). Retrieved from www.dictionary.com/browse/guidance?s=t

Gysbers, N. C., & Henderson, P. (2012). *Developing & managing your school guidance & counseling program* (5th ed.). Alexandria, VA: American Counseling Association.

Holcomb-McCoy, C. (2010). Involving low-income parents and parents of color in college readiness activities: An exploratory study. *Professional School Counseling, 14,* 115–124.

Lambert, M. J. (1992). Implications of outcome research for psychotherapy integration. In J. C. Norcross & M. R. Goldfried (Eds.), *Handbook of psychotherapy integration* (pp. 94–129). New York, NY: Basic Books.

Lambie, G. W., & Williamson, L. L. (2004). The challenge to change from guidance counseling to professional school counseling: A historical proposition. *Professional School Counseling, 8,* 124–131.

Marsico, M., & Getch, Y. Q. (2009). Transitioning Hispanic seniors from high school to college. *Professional School Counseling, 12,* 458–462.

Mason, E. C. M., & McMahon, H. G. (2009). Leadership practices of school counselors. *Professional School Counseling, 13,* 107–115.

Milsom, A., & Hartley, M. T. (2005). Assisting students with disabilities transitioning to college: What school counselors should know. *Professional School Counseling, 8,* 436–441.

Milsom, A., & McCormick, K. (2015). Evaluating an accountability mentoring approach for school counselors. *Professional School Counseling, 19,* 27–35.

Thompson, E. H., Robertson, P., Curtis, R., & Frick, M. H. (2013). Students with anxiety: Implications for professional school counselors. *Professional School Counseling, 16,* 222–234.

Trusty, J., & Brown, D. (2005). Advocacy competencies for professional school counselors. *Professional School Counseling, 8,* 259–265.

Van Velsor, P., & Orozco, G. L. (2007). Involving low-income parents in the schools: Communitycentric strategies for school counselors. *Professional School Counseling, 11,* 17–24.

Whiston, S. C., & Quinby, R. F. (2009). Review of school counseling outcome research. *Psychology in the Schools, 46*(3), 267–272.

Whiston, S. C., Tai, W. L., Rahardja, D., & Eder, K. (2011). School counseling outcome: A meta-analytic examination of interventions. *Journal of Counseling & Development, 89,* 37–55.

Williamson, E. G. (1950). *Counseling adolescents.* New York, NY: McGraw-Hill.

Wrenn, G. C. (1962). *The counselor in a changing world.* Washington, DC: American Personnel and Guidance Association.

Young, A., & Kaffenberger, C. (2015). School counseling professional development: Assessing the use of data to inform school counseling services. *Professional School Counseling, 19,* 46–56.

Section III

Current Issues for
Personal and
Professional
Development

Chapter 12

Current Issues and Trends in the Counseling Profession

Thelma Duffey and Shane Haberstroh

Learning Objectives

1. Describe current counselor licensure portability plans.
2. Discuss challenges from other professional groups related to counselors' use of assessments and scope of practice.
3. Describe the role of supervisors, models of supervision, and credentialing of supervisors.
4. Describe the unique attributes and career options associated with being a private practitioner.
5. Compare and contrast the medical model with the wellness model as they relate to assessment and diagnosis.
6. Describe ethics, applicability, and approaches when using technology in counseling practice.

• • •

The passion and commitment of professional counselors, leaders, and advocates along with politics and social change continue to propel the growth and development of the counseling profession. Over the past several decades, counselors, educators, and organizations have promoted various perspectives related to the definition of counseling, the roles and training of professional counselors, and licensure standardization and portability needs (American Counseling Association [ACA], 2016; Chang, 2012; Kaplan, Tarvydas, & Gladding, 2014; Mascari & Webber, 2006, 2013). These dialogues continue to center on unifying the profession through common definitions, practice competencies, and training curricula to provide greater clarity to the public, future clients, and legislators (Bergman, 2013).

Through our leadership work with ACA, we have seen tremendous movement toward unity and clarity in recent years. I (Thelma Duffey) served as the 2015–2016 ACA president and chaired the proceedings of the ACA Governing Council. And I (Shane Haberstroh) served as the Association for Creativity in Counseling representative to the ACA Governing Council. As part of this work, the Governing Council discussed, debated, and passed decades-long deliberated motions related to accreditation, portability, and advocacy. It also passed a motion to relocate the ACA 2017 Conference & Expo from Tennessee because the state had recently passed a bill legalizing a counselor's right to refuse services because of personally held values (Meyers, 2016). This bill stood in opposition to the *ACA Code of Ethics* (ACA, 2014) and our value of nondiscrimination. Each of these issues aligned with two ACA presidential initiatives on (a) professional advocacy and (b) social action related to anti-bullying and interpersonal violence.

These decisions generated impassioned discussions within the ACA membership and leadership, and they created opportunities for collaboration, increased public awareness of the profession of counseling, and a unified identity. They also significantly affected the direction of the future of professional counseling. Clearly, a series of historic actions were taken by the 2015–2016 ACA Governing Council related to accreditation, portability, professional advocacy, and nondiscrimination advocacy that have deeply affected the profession and influenced emerging trends. It is from this frame that we write this chapter.

Given that the counseling profession emerged from a union of multiple professional organizations, its history is rich with balancing solidarity with a respect for the diversity of counselors and practice settings (Evans, Duffey, Erford, & Gladding, 2013). Nevertheless, while leaders and organizations in the counseling profession worked toward increasing collaboration and unity, other helping professions, related organizations, and national policymakers sought to define the counseling profession and codify restrictions on counseling practice and credentialing (National Board for Certified Counselors [NBCC], n.d.; U.S. Department of Defense, 2014).

These efforts, by entities outside the counseling profession, created a sense of urgency in many professional counselors to unite around the profession, especially when state licensure boards and legislators argued for limitations on counselors' scope of practice and reimbursement rates (Council for Accreditation of Counseling and Related Educational Programs [CACREP], 2013). Without a strong, consistent, and clear message about the training, competencies, practice opportunities, and value of professional counseling, these political and economic forces threaten to hinder the continued growth of the profession. As you consider these dynamics, how would you advocate for the counseling profession with peers, family, and the public?

The counseling profession continues to move forward and seeks to actively address important topics related to professional identity, licensure portability, accreditation, and challenges from other professional groups. In addition, clinicians consider issues related to managing and thriving in private practice, counselor supervision, the changing demographics of clients, and how technology affects both counseling and supervision practices. This chapter focuses on these emerging trends in the counseling profession. We invite you to consider how the counseling profession can build on its diverse roots and continue to develop into a progressive, forward-thinking profession that effectively serves people from many walks of life.

Counselor Licensure: Portability and Challenges From Other Professional Groups

Imagine you are independently licensed as a professional counselor in your home state. After 4 years of undergraduate work and 3 years of graduate school, including 700 hours of practica and internship, you graduate with a degree in clinical mental health counseling and apply for a temporary license as a licensed professional counselor intern. This is a designation used in some states for people who complete their graduate training in counseling and are pursuing licensure. You then sit for your NBCC exam and pass it, and over the next 3 years, you complete 3,000 hours of supervised counseling practice. Finally, a decade after beginning your career in higher education and investing in securing it, you reach your hard-won goal of professional status. You establish a private practice and work part time at an outpatient addiction treatment center without any ethical complaints or concerns and with much anticipation and hope for your professional life.

Now, imagine an unforeseen need arises in your family and you feel called to move closer to your family to help. You have invested 10 years into securing your degree and license, and you have worked in independent practice. You feel the confidence of your training and enthusiasm from your experience, and you feel like moving to support your family is the right thing to do. When you move to your new state, the licensing board denies your application for a license. You feel frustrated, scared, and abandoned by your profession. Although you were on several insurance panels in your home state, now you are not eligible to bill for services. You must now advocate with the licensing board and navigate this new system. Clearly, barriers exist that interfere with professional mobility, and several national organizations have developed portability models to address these barriers.

Licensure Portability

Licensure portability is a major issue facing counselors who move to different states (Mellin, Hunt, & Nichols, 2011; Merrill, 2003). Licensing rules and regulations arise at the state level, which creates inconsistency between states with respect to the academic and experiential requirements needed for counselors to obtain their licenses. These differences become problematic when counselors wish to move across state lines. To address these issues, several counseling organizations have developed initiatives to outline portability requirements. The American Association of State Counseling Boards (AASCB; 2015) reported on trends related to requirements for obtaining a counseling license. In general, they found that most states required a 60-hour master's degree from a regionally accredited university coupled with approximately 3,000 hours of post-master's supervised counseling experience. AASCB (2015) recommended the following:

> A fully-licensed counselor, who is licensed at the highest level of licensure available in his or her state, and who is in good standing with his or her licensure board, with no disciplinary record, and who has been in active practice for a minimum of five years post-receipt of licensure, and who has taken and passed the [National Counselor Examination] or the [National Clinical Mental Health Counseling Examination], shall be eligible for licensure in a state to which he or she is establishing residence. The state to which the licensed counselor is moving may require a jurisprudence examination based on the rules and statutes of said state. An applicant who meets these criteria will be accepted for licensure without further review of education, supervision and experiential hours. (para. 10)

In addition, the Association for Counselor Education and Supervision (ACES), NBCC, and the American Mental Health Counselors Association (AMHCA; AASCB, 2015; NBCC, 2015) recommended an alternative reciprocity plan to the AASCB proposal. The NBCC, AMHCA, and ACES portability plan proposed that counselors (a) obtain a clinically focused degree accredited by CACREP, (b) become credentialed as a National Certified Counselor, or (c) meet current state board standards; and (d) document at least 2 years of postlicensure practice to qualify for unrestricted interstate reciprocity. Reflecting on licensure portability, consider Sidebar 12.1.

Sidebar 12.1   Why Is Portability Important to You?

Imagine completing your CACREP-accredited 60-hour mental health counseling degree, finishing your 3,000 hours of postdegree internship, and successfully passing your state licensing exam. Then you work as a counselor for several years in private practice. Now imagine that you have to move, and the state where you are relocating requires 5 years of postlicensure experience and completion of the National Clinical Mental Health Counseling Examination. You have 3 years of postlicensure experience and completed the National Counselor Examination. What are your reactions to these stipulations?

• • •

The ACA Portability Model Plan

Members of the 2015–2016 ACA Governing Council discussed, debated, and passed significant motions related to accreditation, advocacy, and portability. A task force on portability, chaired by ACA former president Robert Smith, reviewed existing portability plans and offered recommendations related to portability to the Governing Council. Smith reported,

> The ACA Task Force on Portability researched the topic of portability, which included an evaluation of state licensure policies, existing portability models, and research literature in this area. . . . The Governing Council agreed that it was important that ACA take leadership on issues, such as portability. We saw this model as visionary, in that it takes current strides in standardization into account, and looks at the long term direction of the profession. We see the ACA Portability Licensure Plan as meeting the needs of practicing counselors moving from one state to another, while protecting the public as put forth by existing licensure laws. (R. Smith, personal communication, June 23, 2016)

He added, "The task force sought feedback from ACA members, members of the Governing Council, and some licensure board members, resulting in a proposed plan which the Governing Council enthusiastically approved" (R. Smith, personal communication, June 23, 2016).

The ACA Counselor Licensure Portability Model
The ACA counselor licensure portability model was adopted by the 2015–2016 ACA Governing Council by an overwhelming majority vote. The model reads as follows:

> A counselor who is licensed at the independent practice level in their home state and who has no disciplinary record shall be eligible for licensure at the independent practice level in any state or U.S. jurisdiction in which they are

seeking residence. The state to which the licensed counselor is moving may require a jurisprudence examination based on the rules and procedures of that state. (ACA, 2017, para. 7)

Following the decision, the Governing Council directed the ACA staff, whose role it is to carry out the policies and procedures of the association, to implement the advocacy process. Advocacy involved clarification, collaboration, and communication among stakeholders. This is important work, and it takes time to accomplish. Nevertheless, in spite of the promising hopes for advocacy, there are risks. As a counselor-in-training, it is important for you to consider how each portability plan may affect your future goals.

Challenges From Other Professional Groups

The vitality of the counseling profession at a national level directly affects your future work, respect, and opportunities to build a productive and solvent career. Keep in mind that as licensing boards modify their statutes and rules to accommodate portability needs, they may open themselves to challenges from other professional groups who may seek to limit counselors' scope of practice (Mellin, 2009). While ACA, its divisions, and its affiliates work to advocate for professional counselors, other professional groups propose policies and legislation to limit counselors' practice options (Jackson & Scheel, 2013b). For example, in 2015 the Kentucky Board of Examiners of Psychology sought to impose legislation that impeded counselors' and other professionals' rights to use various assessment instruments (Fair Access Coalition on Testing, 2015).

Rick Balkin, a professor at the University of Louisville, chair of the 2015–2016 ACA Research and Knowledge Committee, and author of Chapter 4 of this book, testified before the Kentucky Board of Examiners of Psychology and also communicated the following in writing: "Psychologists financially benefit from limiting testing to their profession. This appears self-serving. The Kentucky Psychology Association has proposed a personal agenda disguised as public policy that will significantly impair public health" (R. Balkin, personal communication, August 28, 2015). He added, "By denying counselors lawful access to aspects of their training, Kentucky will not stand out in front nationally, they will stand alone" (R. Balkin, personal communication, August 28, 2015). Balkin also communicated that "counselors and other nonpsychologists have been providing these services for years, and there is no evidence of harm to the public" (R. Balkin, personal communication, August 28, 2015). Finally, Balkin concluded with, "Removing testing rights will limit access to care, and disavowing counselors' legal right to provide assessment would further magnify this disparity and delay important, perhaps lifesaving services to citizens" (R. Balkin, personal communication, August 28, 2015).

As a result of advocacy efforts by ACA, the Kentucky Counseling Association, the Fair Access Coalition on Testing (2015), and other advocates, these restrictions were not codified in Kentucky law.

These recent advocacy efforts underscore the continued need for the counseling profession to advocate for counselors, students (U.S. Department of Veterans Affairs, 2015), and faculty. Although the profession of counseling may share common elements with other helping professions, it has worked diligently over the years to establish itself as a valuable and unique mental health profession focused on human wellness, strength, diversity, and development (Hanna & Bemak, 1997; Spurgeon, 2012).

As we have seen in Kentucky, outside professional groups actively challenge the profession of counseling in various ways, particularly as we gain traction in strengthening our own identity, focus, and role (Goodyear, 2000; Horne, 2013; Palmer, 2013). For example, another challenge to the counseling profession involves professional identity, accreditation, counselor education employment, and licensure. Psychologists trained at the master's degree level often pursue licensure as professional counselors. This is partly because the American Psychological Association endorses doctoral-level training as the minimum academic requirement for licensure as a psychologist (Mellin et al., 2011). When CACREP published standards that specified that counselor education faculty must hold a degree in counselor education after 2013, or alternatively they must have taught in a counselor education program for 1 year (CACREP, 2009; Even & Robinson, 2012), many psychologists and master's-level psychology programs protested this change (Horne, 2013; Palmer, 2013). Jackson and Scheel (2013a) noted that this accreditation change will hamper opportunities for psychologists to teach in counseling programs. Likewise, counseling psychologists asserted that master's-level training in counseling and psychology is similar and that a foundation in psychology undergirds counseling and psychology training (Jackson & Scheel, 2013b). They argued that counselor licensure is generic enough to accommodate a wide range of related professions (Jackson & Scheel, 2013b).

These notions directly counter the decades of hard work of counselors and leaders to establish counseling as a viable and unique profession in its own right (Spurgeon, 2012). The counseling profession is grounded in its own history, approach to human nature, and diversity among practice settings and populations (Hanna & Bemak, 1997). Counselor licensure is the culmination of the profession's development and growth and strengthens the profession's vitality (Morgen, Miller, & Stretch, 2012). The growth of the counseling profession is challenged when other professions seek to dilute or diminish this accomplishment to meet the needs of their constituents (Mellin et al., 2011).

Through the work of advocates, ACA, and its affiliates, the counseling profession developed clear definitions of professional identity, counseling philosophy, and counselor supervision practice (Hanna & Bemak, 1997; Spurgeon, 2012). In addition, the 2015–2016 ACA Governing Council voted to acknowledge CACREP as the accrediting body for counselors. It also voted to continue advocating for all counselors licensed by 2020 regardless of accreditation status. The goal was to move the profession forward by naming CACREP as the profession's accrediting body while ensuring that professional counselors who did not graduate from CACREP programs would not be inadvertently left behind (Duffey, 2016). This is an important policy stance because it standardizes the entry-level training requirements for counselors at the national level. Our efforts toward professionalization are impassioned and ongoing.

Professionalization involves many components, and the next section of this chapter addresses the role of counselor supervision as a professional practice. You have been engaged in supervision as a student, and when you graduate, your next step will be to seek postgraduate supervision to obtain your license. As you consider potential supervisors, we recommend that you consider their professional training, their experience, and how well they relate to you professionally. An effective supervisor will mentor, challenge, and support you through your work with clients. A good supervisor models professionalism, supports your professional identity, and works collaboratively to enhance your counseling practice (Gordon & Luke, 2016).

Counselor Supervision: Roles and Credentials

Supervision is a recognized and valued practice in the counseling profession (Foster, 2012). Various supervision models and theories guide the work of supervisors, and effective supervisory relationships set the foundation for productive supervision (Goldberg, Dixon, & Wolf, 2012). In 1940, ACES began as a division of a group previously known as the National Association for Guidance Supervisors (Elmore, 1985). Throughout the next several decades, counselors and supervisors developed competencies, training models, and expectations for the role of supervision as a key facet of counselor development (Blount & Mullen, 2015).

The Role of Supervision

Supervisors assume many different roles in their practices (Sackett, Lawson, & Burge, 2015). Bernard's discrimination model (Bernard & Luke, 2015) highlights three primary roles in counselor supervision: counselor, teacher, and consultant. Supervisors can act as teachers and instruct you in skill development, administrative procedures, and professional development. Given the interpersonal nature of counseling work, supervisors also attend to relational process in supervision.

When in this role, supervisors counsel you on personal development, strengths, and potential issues in your work with both clients and colleagues (Boston et al., 2011). Finally, supervisors consult with other professionals and offer their guidance and perspectives (Knoff, 1988). Soon you will be working under supervision. What do you imagine being the best supervision experiences for you?

Like counseling theories, supervision models grew from the intersection of practice and scholarship (Borders et al., 2014). Early supervisory theories focused on the psychodynamics between counselors and clients (Carroll, 1996), and the role of the supervisor was analytic in nature. As the profession grew, new theories accounted for the multicultural, educational, and clinical aspects of supervision (Carroll, 1996). Progressive theories of supervision now address the relational, contextual, and developmental aspects of supervision (Duffey, Haberstroh, Ciepcielinski, & Gonzales, 2016; Ladany & Bradley, 2011). In fact, effective supervisory relationships lead to increased counselor competence and performance (Ladany & Bradley, 2011). Therefore, the professionalization of this relational practice benefits you and your supervisor through the development and promulgation of common expectations and credentials (Foster, 2012).

Supervision Training and Credentials

Supervisor training evolved from 1-day trainings to comprehensive doctoral programs focused on counselor education and supervision (Ladany & Bradley, 2011). Many state licensing boards now outline specific educational and experiential requirements for approved supervisors who work with counselor interns (Borders et al., 2014). Moreover, ACES established best practices for counselor supervision that set competency benchmarks for supervisors to attain and manage in their practice (ACES, 2011). Likewise, several states (e.g., Idaho, Michigan, Texas, and Washington) require that approved supervisors also be licensed as professional counselors (Ladany & Bradley, 2011). These efforts toward developing standardized training, credentialing, and best practices in supervision represent ongoing movement toward clarity about the role of supervision in counselor development. As you develop professionally, many occupational opportunities may present themselves. Given that counselors are now licensed in all 50 states and the District of Columbia, full- or part-time private practice is a viable and growing career path (O*NET OnLine, 2016).

Private Practice Settings

Many professional counselors work in private practice offices (Bureau of Labor Statistics, 2015). Once licensed, you can choose to work in a variety of settings. These options range from solo offices to corporate partnerships, to office space shared among independent practitioners (Harrington, 2013). You can focus on educational, rehabilitation, couples and family, addiction, mental health, and other specialized modalities once you are licensed and receive training and supervision in your specialty. I (Thelma) opened a multidisciplinary private practice 26 years ago that includes colleagues from psychiatry, psychology, and professional counseling, and I serve as the business's managing partner. Over the years, we have worked with individuals, couples, and families managing a variety of life events. I have found private practice to be a viable career option for counselors, one that requires clinical skill and expertise in navigating a business. Indeed, in addition to clinical expertise, counselors in practice must also have informed business acumen to support their success (Carney & Jefferson, 2014).

Administration and Management

Related to the business and administrative factors found in private practice, Carney and Jefferson (2014) identified many tasks unique to private practitioners. To be successful in your practice, you must develop marketing strategies, furnish your office, cultivate client referral resources, and establish billing and record-keeping procedures (Harrington, 2013). As your practice grows, you may enjoy the freedom to choose your work hours and setting while experiencing increased creativity and theoretical flexibility (Harrington, 2013). Unlike counselors in agency settings, which may adhere to prescribed theoretical orientations and schedules, private practitioners can chart their own professional paths (Brennan, 2013). You may also establish yourself as a managing partner of a practice, which introduces managerial aspects to your work (Wheeler & Bertram, 2015). In this respect, supervisors may also directly hire and fire counselors and interns under their employment (Stark et al., 2013; Wheeler & Bertram, 2015). These skills draw on business and administrative competencies that may feel uncomfortable for you (Bjornestad, Johnson, Hittner, & Paulson, 2014).

Private Practice Supervision

As you gain more experience, you can grow your practice and work as a supervisor in private practice (Wheeler & Bertram, 2015). Despite the benefits of being self-employed, counselors in private practice reported that they desired more collaboration and support and access to training and supervision resources (Harrington, 2013). The potential for professional isolation can insulate private practitioners and supervisors from needed feedback and consultation (Savic-Jabrow, 2010). This underscores the need for private practitioners to develop a consultation and supervision network to help them navigate complex cases and situations. For many years, I (Thelma) participated in weekly consultation lunch meetings with practitioners in my group practice. In addition to nourishing our relationships and securing case consultation, these meetings and our exchanges gave us each a sense of community and mediated the isolating aspect that private practice employment can bring.

Practitioners and supervisors in solo practice also deal with complicated situations, traumatic loss, and people experiencing mental health and addiction issues. As the number of counselors in private practice grows, these professionals will be exposed to a wide variety of issues and problems and will clearly benefit from strong connections with peers and colleagues (Reese, Young, & Hutchinson, 2013). These connections support counselors' own wellness and serve as a form of self-care. You will most likely work with many challenging situations and may find that relationships can help you deal with the vicarious trauma that can at times ensue.

Changing Client Demographics and Current Issues

National and international tragedies, wars, and changing client needs in a technological and increasingly splintered society will challenge you to think globally about many of your clients' concerns. As counselors work with people escaping natural disasters, war-torn countries, and impoverished living conditions, they attend to their clients' traumatic experiences, potential feelings of dislocation, and ways in which acculturation to mainstream society can create disconnection and foster isolation (Yakushko, Watson, & Thompson, 2008). Veterans can experience issues transitioning back into society after experiencing tours of duty in war-torn countries (Rausch, 2014). Until recently, the Veterans Administration (VA) excluded counselors from its cadre of mental health professionals. Despite a shortage of mental health professionals, counselors faced opposition related to inclusion in both VA and TRICARE legislation (Prosek & Holm, 2014). After much professional advocacy, both the VA and TRICARE authorized counselors entry into the VA system and independent practice status in TRICARE. As counselors work with veterans in the future, they can offer wellness, relational, and systemic perspectives to help them cope with their return to society (Prosek & Holm, 2014).

Working With Veterans

War and combat exact psychological and emotional tolls on many individuals (Carrola & Corbin-Burdick, 2015). Veterans experience heightened risk for suicide, substance use disorders, family conflict, posttraumatic stress disorder (PTSD), homelessness, and financial issues (Ramchand, Rudavsky, Grant, Tanielian, & Jaycox, 2015). The VA developed many resources to work with veterans suffering from PTSD, and the VA and U.S. Department of Defense also offer postdeployment counseling and reintegration services (U.S. Department of Veterans Affairs, 2015). As a professional counselor, you can assist veterans by working from a relational, developmental, and nonpathological perspective (Carrola & Corbin-Burdick, 2015). Some authors argue that pathologizing veterans may result in less than optimal outcomes (Carrola & Corbin-Burdick, 2015). In a recent exposé published by National Public Radio, a veteran disclosed how his psychiatrist failed to listen to him, dismissing his struggles (Mabeus & Van Woerkom, 2015). Professional counselors, using a relational focus, can help clients and families normalize adjustment experiences, consider new perspectives to understand their experiences, and advocate for change (Rausch, 2014).

PTSD

Many veterans return from combat suffering from PTSD (Fulton et al., 2015). An established body of research supports various treatments for PTSD (Bernardy & Friedman, 2015). Medication, exposure therapy, cognitive processing therapy, and eye-movement desensitization and reprocessing reportedly help veterans cope with their PTSD symptoms (U.S. Department of Veterans Affairs, 2015). Counselors can receive training in the various modalities for PTSD work. These efforts, coupled with a focus on developing a respectful, collaborative, and trusting relationship, can lead to positive outcomes for clients (Wampold et al., 2010). Effective counselors also consider familial, social, and developmental contexts unique to veterans and their loved ones (Beder, 2009).

A Counseling Context: The Deployment Cycle

The deployment cycle is a contextual developmental process unique to families and individuals actively serving in the military (Rausch, 2014). It is important for counselors to understand the emotional and relational ramifications of family separation and reintegration. The deployment cycle consists of phases that include predeployment, deployment, sustainment, redeployment, and postdeployment (Padden & Agazio, 2013). Each of these stages of deployment has practical, emotional, and systemic considerations (Padden & Agazio, 2013). As the reality of a future deployment crystallizes for a family, members may feel anger or despair and protest the upcoming loss. Once the service member is deployed, family members learn to function in new ways and then begin to experience the anticipation of the return of their deployed family member (Beder, 2009; Padden & Agazio, 2013). Once reunited, the family adjusts to new patterns of relating, possible combat injuries, and anticipation of future deployments. This cycle is a foundational perspective counselors use to understand military families and veterans' readjustment process.

Child and Family Counseling

Counselors understand the systemic and familial nature of reintegration and consider maladaptive behaviors in the family from this perspective (Lester et al., 2010). Children may express their fears, grief, and anticipation of reunification in ways that may seem maladaptive (Beder, Coe, & Sommer, 2011). However, when counselors realize that families often face the terrifying uncertainties of having a parent deployed to war, or cope with a parent who was wounded or killed in combat, they can help families navigate the loss and grief associated with deployment, death, and injury. Even when a parent is unharmed, the family develops relational patterns during his or her absence (Beder, 2009). Counselors help veterans and their family members reintegrate and adjust to the time apart, discuss hopes for the future, and then address the realization that deployment can occur in the future (Carrola & Corbin-Burdick, 2015).

Working with veterans and families requires that counselors attune themselves to the nuances of the military culture, issues of reintegration and loss, and systems of care in place (Carrola & Corbin-Burdick, 2015). This work requires multicultural counseling competency, training, and appreciation of loss and adjustment (Duffey, 2005, 2015). These factors are also vital in work with immigrants or refugees fleeing their homes for any number of reasons (Nilsson, Schale, & Khamphakdy-Brown, 2011).

Immigrant and Refugee Populations

Like veterans, immigrants escaping violence and war often experience PTSD and feelings of anxiety (Marotta, 2003). They also report a sense of loss, isolation, a desire to return home to loved ones, and employment and financial problems (Villalba, 2009; Williams, 2003; Yakushko, Watson, et al., 2008). Counselors recognize these stressors and work with clients as they negotiate their losses (Cárdenas, Taylor, & Adelman, 1993). As a future counselor, you can help immigrant clients honor their culture and loved ones back home (Nilsson et al., 2011) and capitalize on their desire to succeed academically and vocationally (Yakushko, Backhaus, Watson, Ngaruiya, & Gonzalez, 2008). As you work with clients from different cultures, you can find guidance related to multicultural counseling competencies (Ratts, Singh, Nassar-McMillan, Butler, & McCullough, 2016). And as you develop your clinical and multicultural competencies, you can be a ready resource to advocate for your clients' basic needs and adjustment to their host country. Many people experience stress, anxiety, and fear due to acculturation pressures, prejudices, and isolation (Yakushko, Watson, et al., 2008). Familiar values and routines may clash with their new contexts. Some host countries may seem hostile to newcomers and fearful that refugees harbor malintent. These political and cultural messages resonated throughout the world during the crises brought on by the Syrian war. Given the animosity they may experience in a host country, people and families seeking refuge may also face racism, ethnocentrism, and isolation.

Consider the case of Ben, who is working with a family who recently arrived in the United States after spending 2 years in a refugee camp. Both parents were medical professionals in their home country and now live on limited public assistance and work at minimum-wage jobs. The family faces significant barriers related to language (Yakushko, Watson, et al., 2008), educational opportunities, finances, and career options (Yakushko, Backhaus, et al., 2008). In addition, they experience discrimination and racism regularly. They desperately miss their now destroyed neighborhood and globally dispersed network of good friends. As Ben works with this family, he conceptualizes the enormity of their needs, the role of loss and grief in their lives, their cultural worldview, and how his cultural perspective frames his own work and reactions. As he gains more experience working with disenfranchised groups, he begins to see how positivistic and diagnostic counseling approaches can miss important contextual and cultural factors in his clients' lives (Duffey, 2006/2007; Duffey, Haberstroh, & Trepal, 2016).

The Role of Diagnosis Across Settings

Diagnostic practice in counseling settings is multifaceted. Counselors use diagnoses to conceptualize client needs and directions for intervention. The profession of counseling is characterized by a wellness, developmental, and strengths-based framework. Thus, counselors in all settings work to promote client welfare and counseling success using a variety of diagnostic, relational, and supportive approaches. However, given that counselors work in a myriad of practice settings, such as academic campuses, hospitals, and private practices, the role of diagnosis varies depending on the work setting. For example, whereas one person working in a rehabilitation setting will use the *Diagnostic and Statistical Manual of Mental Disorders* (American Psychiatric Association, 2013) and International Classification of Diseases–10 codes, another person working in a school setting may use developmental theories to conceptualize student issues. Practitioners in agencies and practice settings, particularly those who receive insurance reimbursements, often use the *Diagnostic and Statistical Manual of Mental Disorders* and International Classification of Diseases–10 diagnoses to comply with managed care requirements. These third-party participants in client care clearly delineate the parameters for reimbursement. As a result, licensed counselors who receive reimbursement from insurance companies must reconcile their understanding of the counseling profession's strengths-based focus with a system that requires diagnosis-driven care. This reconciliation is important on a number of levels. It is important for clients, who deserve to be seen holistically while receiving an accurate diagnosis, if needed. It is also important for counselors to uphold their ethical responsibilities while working with systems that require diagnoses for reimbursement.

As you can see, you will be challenged to balance your knowledge and skill in diagnosis with an understanding that a counseling focus is broader, contextually derived, and more relationally driven than objective evaluation alone (Strong, 2015). Counselors work from a wellness and strengths-based philosophy, yet the medical and diagnostic model drives much of modern health care and mental health treatment (Dougherty, 2005).

The Medical Model of Diagnosis

The medical model of diagnosis focuses on resolving identifiable ailments. This model permeates mental health treatment (Dailey, Gill, & Karl, 2014). Diagnosis of illness and dysfunction is central to the medical model. In fact, without establishing a formal diagnosis, medical professionals cannot follow a prescribed course of treatment for a particular disease or disorder. Counselors, in contrast, use diagnostic criteria as one element during their case conceptualization but also consider nonpathological aspects of their clients' lives and circumstances when planning treatment (Duffey, Haberstroh, & Trepal, 2016; Kassirer et al., 2013). Whereas medical professionals treat illness, counseling professionals consider a client's development, context, and culture when conceptualizing issues and the direction of counseling (Duffey & Somody, 2011; Frey, 2013). Many counselors also work in settings in which diagnosis-driven treatment is inappropriate (Jun, 2009). Counselors who work with people who are grieving, coping with career issues, dealing with family problems, or seeking personal growth and development may find diagnosis-driven treatment to be clinically inappropriate. However, clients who suffer from a diagnosable mental disorder do benefit from empowering relationships, a focus on their strengths, and trained counselors who assist them in navigating their complex worlds and relationships (Frey, 2013).

A Contextual Model of Diagnosis

Many counseling, wellness, and mental health models consider how a person's strengths, circumstances, culture, social aspects, and development frame how a counselor conceptualizes his or her situation and issues (Jun, 2009). Wellness and relationally based models do not assume that clients are sick or promote using a prescribed course of treatment monitored and evaluated by a dispassionate professional (Barden, Conley, & Young, 2015). Instead, many of these models place the counseling relationship as central to a client's change, growth, and development (Miller & Rollnick, 2013). Much research has indicated that the relationship and relational competencies of the counselor far outweigh strict adherence to any theoretical model (Duncan, 2010; Wampold et al., 2010). The implication of this research is that when counselors spend time and effort developing their relational capacities and intentionally attend to the relational dynamics in the counseling space (Barden et al., 2015), clients do measurably better across many domains. With this in mind, your focus in initial sessions and assessment activities is not on completing checklists and comparing a person against objective and reductionist criteria. It is instead on understanding, connecting, and charting a course of treatment based on an evolving understanding of the person's situation, relationships, and unique perspectives. Technology, the digital culture, and social networks are contexts in which clients can thrive or struggle. As you work to understand a client's world, exploration into his or her digital life may reveal important information. Furthermore, you can now expand your counseling practice to the electronic realm. Technology is a new innovative and resourceful form of media that offers creative and supportive avenues for connection globally.

Distance Counseling and Supervision

Indeed, the evolution of technology and social media presents distinct challenges and opportunities for both counselors and supervisors. Distance counseling and supervision are not necessarily new concepts. Before the advent of the Internet, clients and counselors often interacted via telephone when face-to-face communication was not possible. However, the rise of the Internet has allowed clients and counselors to interact via text-based formats at little to no cost (Conn, Roberts, & Powell, 2009). Currently, many communities offer broadband and high-speed networking, which allows people to interact through video and audio channels (Afanasyev, Chen, Voelker, & Snoeren, 2010). These opportunities clearly affect how you, your clients, and your supervisor communicate (Barnett, 2011). The Center for Credentialing and Education offers a Distance Credentialed Counselor national certification that attests to your training in the relational, legal, ethical, technological, and clinical aspects of online and distance counseling. Despite national credentialing and guidelines, there are several concerns about (a) the security of online networks, (b) how counselors and supervisors can address nonverbal dynamics, (c) the potential dilution of therapeutic and supervisory relationships due to distance, and (d) the most effective ways to communicate using distance technologies (Haberstroh, Duffey, Evans, Gee, & Trepal, 2007). Much research has investigated these variables, and researchers have generally found that distance technologies can facilitate both counseling and supervisory work with certain adjustments and considerations (Haberstroh & Duffey, 2016; Zeren, 2015). The Internet and social media are powerful platforms that can promote healing and goodwill. Sidebar 12.2 describes a national project to harness the power of social media to honor and document the impact others make on our lives. Who would you honor online?

Legal and Ethical Considerations in Distance Counseling

Distance counseling can take many forms (Holmes & Foster, 2012), and it is a forum available to all counselors regardless of specialty. Counselors who respond to client e-mails, visit with clients on the telephone, use interactive audio and visual technologies, and chat with clients in text-messaging sessions use distance counseling strategies (Haberstroh, Barney, Foster, & Duffey, 2014). More and more, when a client moves away, or when I (Thelma) am not in town for a regular session, clients will ask for a phone session, or they may send me an e-mail giving me an update on their situation. In cases such as these, I seek the guidance of the *ACA Code of Ethics* (ACA, 2014), which addresses the safety, appropriateness, and limitations of the use of technology in professional counseling and informs the way in which counselors communicate with clients when using technology. In a time when social media is emerging as a form of communication worldwide, identifying its appropriate use by counselors is particularly salient.

Despite the standardization of online counseling practice at the national level through ethics codes and standards, state licensure boards vary considerably in the specificity of the direction they provide related to distance counseling. However, licensing boards do not prohibit distance counseling (Haberstroh et al., 2014). Generally speaking,

---

Sidebar 12.2   Whose Name Would Be on Your Impact Project Sign?

One of the signature projects of my (Thelma Duffey's) 2015–2016 Anti-Bullying and Interpersonal Violence Presidential Initiative was the Impact Project. The mission of the Impact Project was to use social media to make a positive impact in the world. For this project, people publicly acknowledged individuals who had made a significant impact in their lives. To recognize and honor these individuals, and to use social media to promote respect and gratitude, people wrote a message on an Impact Project sign, took a picture of it, and then posted it to the social media outlet of their choice. If you made an Impact Project sign, whose name would you write on it and why?

• • •

counselors who provide ethical distance counseling (a) ensure that clients can access and use technology, (b) communicate confidential information through private and encrypted channels, (c) remain sensitive to time zone and cultural differences, (d) outline alternative methods for contact during times of crisis or technological failures, and (e) list local resources for clients (ACA, 2014). With a solid infrastructure in place to provide distance counseling, counselors can investigate and use effective distance communication and counseling strategies. Please review Sidebar 12.3 and consider how you could prevent and respond to issues related to technology in counseling.

Clinical and Relational Strategies in Distance Counseling

In spite of some initial concerns about the effectiveness and viability of online counseling, studies demonstrated that distance counseling helped clients cope with numerous issues (Conn et al., 2009; Holmes & Foster, 2012). Likewise, clients and counselors discovered and reported that counseling relationships could be facilitated online through text-based communication (Stommel & te Molder, 2015). When counseling via text or e-mail, counselors recognize that the pace of the session is slower and more topically focused than face-to-face sessions (Haberstroh, Parr, Bradley, Morgan-Fleming, & Gee, 2008). Also, counselors consider the absence of nonverbal cues and intentionally invite discussion about emotions and reactions that occur during the session (Bathje, Kim, Rau, Bassiouny, & Kim, 2014).

Clients reportedly experienced relief when discussing personal issues online with a counselor (Dowling & Rickwood, 2014). They found that when their counselor stayed focused on their narratives and responded with reflective statements, the sessions promoted growth. However, clients and potential clients recognized that when counselors ventured off track in conversation and interacted using unprofessional language (Haberstroh, 2010), online counseling was ineffective. Video counseling services could mitigate some of

---

Sidebar 12.3   The Role of Technology in Counseling

You have worked hard to develop an online counseling platform. You use encrypted video; you closely follow the *ACA Code of Ethics* (ACA, 2014) in your assessment, informed consent, and billing practices; and you just completed your Distance Credentialed Counselor certification. In your first session with a client, she begins discussing suicidal ideation just as your neighborhood loses power during a thunderstorm. How do you handle this situation?

• • •

these issues (Zeren, 2015). As more communities adopt broadband Internet technology (Patterson, 2015), the potential for clients and counselors to interact through video grows. Video counseling requires the same ethical considerations as text counseling, but counselors and clients can respond to many nonverbal cues in real time, enjoy greater flexibility in the direction of their conversations, and cover more material than in text-based sessions. These findings suggest that online counseling can be a potential forum for clients to interact with an attentive professional counselor and find solutions and connection (Bathje et al., 2014). Like distance counseling, online supervision offers supervisees and supervisors a flexible and convenient medium for professional growth (Conn et al., 2009).

Distance Supervision: An Emerging Practice

Guidelines and ethical standards for the practice of distance supervision are in the formative stages with some states requiring a specific supervision credential or passing an exam in order to provide supervision. Distance supervisors adhere to many of the same privacy, security, and accessibility considerations as online counselors (Conn et al., 2009). Distance supervision provides a format for supervisees and supervisors to access online resources, navigate time and distance barriers, and open up opportunities for collaboration that could not occur in local communities (Olson, Russell, & White, 2001). For example, a counselor could potentially access and consult with a supervisor or expert who lives hundreds of miles away. These informational and communication technologies facilitate greater access and expanded professional networks (Morissette, Bezyak, & Ososkie, 2012).

As with face-to-face supervision practice, the relational foundation of online supervision sets the tone and direction for the supervisory process. Relational strategies for distance supervision include a focus on intentionally communicating warmth and respect online (Conn et al., 2009; Haberstroh & Duffey, 2016; Morissette et al., 2012) and using technology to provide feedback and consultation. One example of the power of language and how warmth and respect may be conveyed online could rest on tone and grammar use. For example, imagine your reaction to each of the following e-mail introductions:

1. Shane: We will meet at 5 pm at my office. Regards, Dr. Bill Smith.
2. Dear Shane, Our first meeting will be at 5 this evening in my office. I look forward to meeting you. Sincerely, Bill.

Although each of the e-mails contains the same content, the tone differs. Supervisors who are aware and respectful of their power intentionally use technological communication to reinforce themes of respect, professionalism, and support for the relationship. Miscommunications and disconnections can occur online and through e-mails (Frey, 2013), and both supervisees and supervisors actively seek out and address these kinds of disconnections. The focus on relationships, diversity, and empowerment in supervision aligns with the stated definition of counseling promoted by ACA. As the counseling profession grows in sophistication and reach, counselors can truly make an impact globally, virtually, and in their communities.

Chapter Summary

This chapter reflects a broad spectrum of emerging counseling issues. We discussed diverse yet professionally related areas of focus in this chapter. Among these were licensure portability, counselor supervision, the dynamics of private practice settings, changing client demographics, immigration, and trauma work with veterans. We also discussed the role of diagnosis across settings and distance counseling and supervision. Each of these areas plays an integral role in contemporary counseling practice.

Professional counselors are securing their place in the larger mental health profession. In part, the profession of counseling distinguishes itself by focusing on strengths, wellness, context, and the power of relationships for addressing mental health concerns. Opportunities for counselors continue to grow. Counselors work in a multitude of settings using various technologies and communication media (d'Ardenne, 2012). As a result, the career outlook for professional counselors is bright (O*NET OnLine, 2016), and the profession has a strong voice at the national level. These successes follow decades of advocacy efforts, national dialogues, and clarification and standardization of credentials (Chang, 2012). We are heartened that the hard work of the ACA leadership over time has culminated in recent historic acts that further define the counseling identity and bring about public awareness of counseling.

As the counseling profession adopts common training and licensing standards, counselors can enjoy increased professional mobility, practice options, and recognition from state and federal lawmakers. Professional leaders and ACA staff continue to clarify the role of the counseling profession among the public. Moreover, recent decisions by the 2015–2016 ACA Governing Council identified CACREP as the profession's accrediting body and developed and approved an ACA counselor licensure portability model. Additional developments in the profession include progressive clinical supervision approaches, which consider the relational, contextual, and developmental aspects of the supervisory relationship. Technology and distance supervision are also relevant to safe and effective practice. Perhaps one of the profession's greatest strengths is the increasing clarity of the ethical and professional standards that guide our work. The counseling profession offers diverse opportunities for you to capitalize on these strengths and to make a notable difference in your community and in the world around you.

Learning Activities

1. You and your classmates take a field trip to your state's capital to advocate for professional counselors. You have a meeting with the representative from your district, who will soon be voting on a bill to expand mental health services in the state. You only have a few minutes to share why professional counselors need to be included as approved mental health providers in the proposed bill. What would you say to her about the training and qualifications of counselors and why counselors should provide mental health services to her constituents?

2. You are a counselor-in-training fulfilling your practicum requirement at a medical hospital. You are part of a treatment team that includes medical and mental health professionals. At the team's weekly staffing meeting, the team leader asks you whether counselors can conduct assessments using standardized instruments. How do you respond?

3. You attend a social gathering and someone tells you he read an article about the *ACA Code of Ethics* (ACA, 2014) and ACA's fight against discrimination in Tennessee. He shares that he does not really understand the issue and asks you to explain. He remarks, "I would never go to see a counselor who would be biased against me." How do you respond?

4. Someone with an interest in becoming a counselor asks you about the educational requirements involved in becoming licensed. She has heard different opinions regarding the importance of counseling program accreditation and wants to hear your opinion. What do you say?

5. You and several classmates continue to meet after you have graduated from your counseling program. One day you are discussing your supervision. One friend reports that his supervisor is great. They touch base for 5 to 10 minutes every other week and chat briefly about his progress. Your other friend shares a different perspective on supervision. She and her supervisor meet weekly and her supervisor provides honest and clear feedback. She reports that although this sometimes feels uncomfortable, it has made her a better counselor. What are your thoughts on supervision? How do you see the role of a supervisor in your professional growth?

Review Questions

1. What are key differences between the three portability models (ACES/NBCC/AMHCA, AASCB, and ACA) related to testing and postlicensure experience requirements?

2. What strategies did counseling advocates utilize to inform the Kentucky Legislature about the right for counselors to use standardized assessment instruments?

3. How does the standardization of training promote the professionalization of counseling?
4. How do relational models differ from medical models in terms of diagnosis and conceptualization of client issues?
5. What are some of the issues that veterans and their families face related to the deployment cycle?
6. What are the ethical, technical, and relational issues to consider when you provide online counseling?

Further Resources

American Counseling Association
    20/20: A Vision for the Future of Counseling
        https://www.counseling.org/knowledge-center/20-20-a-vision-for-the-future-of-counseling
American Counseling Association
    Disaster Mental Health Resources
        https://www.counseling.org/knowledge-center/trauma-disaster
American Counseling Association
    Licensure Requirements
        https://www.counseling.org/knowledge-center/licensure-requirements)
American Counseling Association
    Position on Accreditation
        www.counseling.org/accreditation
Center for Credentialing and Education
    Distance Credentialed Counselor
        www.cce-global.org/dcc
Council for Accreditation of Counseling and Related Educational Programs
        www.cacrep.org
U.S. Department of Veterans Affairs
    National Center for PTSD
        www.ptsd.va.gov

References

Afanasyev, M., Chen, T., Voelker, G., & Snoeren, A. (2010). Usage patterns in an urban WiFi network. *IEEE/ACM Transactions on Networking, 18*, 1359–1372. doi:10.1109/TNET.2010.2040087
American Association of State Counseling Boards. (2015, September 1). *AASCB 5-year plan on license portability.* Retrieved from http://pacounseling.org/aws/PACA/pt/sd/news_article/111077/_PARENT/layout_details/false
American Counseling Association. (2014). *ACA code of ethics.* Alexandria, VA: Author.

American Counseling Association. (2016). *20/20: A vision for the future of counseling*. Retrieved from https://www.counseling.org/knowledge-center/20-20-a-vision-for-the-future-of-counseling

American Counseling Association. (2017). *Initial licensure and licensure portability*. Retrieved from https://www.counseling.org/knowledge-center/licensure-requirements/licensure-policies

American Psychiatric Association. (2013). *Diagnostic and statistical manual of mental disorders* (5th ed.). Washington, DC: Author.

Association for Counselor Education and Supervision. (2011, January 18). *Best practices in clinical supervision*. Retrieved from www.saces.org/Resources/Documents/aces_best_practices.doc

Barden, S., Conley, A., & Young, M. (2015). Integrating health and wellness in mental health counseling: Clinical, educational, and policy implications. *Journal of Mental Health Counseling, 37,* 152–163. doi:10.17744/mehc.37.2.1868134772854247

Barnett, J. (2011). Utilizing technological innovations to enhance psychotherapy supervision, training, and outcomes. *Psychotherapy, 48*(2), 103–108. doi:10.1037/a0023381

Bathje, G., Kim, E., Rau, E., Bassiouny, M., & Kim, T. (2014). Attitudes toward face-to-face and online counseling: Roles of self-concealment, openness to experience, loss of face, stigma, and disclosure expectations among Korean college students. *International Journal for the Advancement of Counselling, 36,* 408–422. doi:10.1007/s10447-014-9215-2

Beder, J. (2009). Social work in the Department of Defense hospital: Impact, role, and interventions. *Military Medicine, 174,* 486–490. doi:10.7205/MILMED-D-03-9908

Beder, J., Coe, R., & Sommer, D. (2011). Women and men who have served in Afghanistan/Iraq: Coming home. *Social Work in Health Care, 50,* 515–526. doi:10.1080/00981389.2011.554279

Bergman, D. (2013). The role of government and lobbying in the creation of a health profession: The legal foundations of counseling. *Journal of Counseling & Development, 91,* 61–67. doi:10.1002/j.1556-6676.2013.00072.x

Bernard, J., & Luke, M. (2015). A content analysis of 10 years of clinical supervision articles in counseling. *Counselor Education and Supervision, 54,* 242–257. doi:10.1002/ceas.12024

Bernardy, N., & Friedman, M. (2015). *Practical guide to PTSD treatment: Pharmacological and psychotherapeutic approaches*. Washington, DC: American Psychological Association. doi:10.1037/14522-000

Bjornestad, A., Johnson, V., Hittner, J., & Paulson, K. (2014). Preparing site supervisors of counselor education students. *Counselor Education and Supervision, 53*(4), 242–253. doi:10.1002/j.1556-6978.2014.00060.x

Blount, A., & Mullen, P. (2015). Development of an integrative wellness model: Supervising counselors-in-training. *The Professional Counselor, 5*(1), 100–113. doi:10.15241/ajb.5.1.100

Borders, D., Glosoff, H., Welfare, L., Hays, D., DeKruyf, L., Fernando, D., & Page, D. (2014). Best practices in clinical supervision: Evolution of a counseling specialty. *The Clinical Supervisor, 33*(1), 26–44. doi:10.1080/07325223.2014.905225

Boston, Q., Vaughn, M., Pitt, J., Soldner, J. L., Turner-Whittaker, T., & Robertson, S. (2011). Promoting multicultural competencies in early career rehabilitation counsellor supervisors. *Australian Journal of Rehabilitation Counselling, 17*(1), 36–45. doi:10.1375/jrc.17.1.36

Brennan, C. (2013). Ensuring ethical practice: Guidelines for mental health counselors in private practice. *Journal of Mental Health Counseling, 35,* 245–261. doi:10.17744/mehc.35.3.9706313j4t313397

Bureau of Labor Statistics. (2015, December). *Occupational Outlook Handbook: Mental health counselors and marriage and family therapists.* Retrieved from www.bls.gov/OOH/community-and-social-service/mental-health-counselors-and-marriage-and-family-therapists.htm#tab-3

Cárdenas, J., Taylor, L., & Adelman, H. S. (1993). Transition support for immigrant students. *Journal of Multicultural Counseling and Development, 21,* 203–210.

Carney, J., & Jefferson, J. (2014). Consultation for mental health counselors: Opportunities and guidelines for private practice. *Journal of Mental Health Counseling, 36,* 302–314. doi:10.17744/mehc.36.4.821133r0414u37v7

Carrola, P., & Corbin-Burdick, M. (2015). Counseling military veterans: Advocating for culturally competent and holistic interventions. *Journal of Mental Health Counseling, 37,* 1–14. doi:10.17744/mehc.37.1.v74514163rv7327

Carroll, M. (1996). *Counselling supervision: Theory, skills and practice.* London, UK: Cassell.

Chang, C. (2012). *Professional counseling excellence through leadership and advocacy.* New York, NY: Routledge. doi:10.4324/9780203829165

Conn, S. R., Roberts, R. L., & Powell, B. M. (2009). Attitudes and satisfaction with a hybrid model of counseling supervision. *Journal of Educational Technology & Society, 12*(2), 298–306.

Council for Accreditation of Counseling and Related Educational Programs. (2009). *2009 standards for accreditation.* Alexandria, VA: Author.

Council for Accreditation of Counseling and Related Educational Programs. (2013, July 13). *CACREP position statement on licensure portability for professional counselors.* Retrieved from www.cacrep.org/wp-content/uploads/2014/02/CACREP-Policy-Position-on-State-Licensure-adopted-7.13.pdf

d'Ardenne, P. (2012). *Counselling in transcultural settings: Priorities for a restless world.* London, UK: Sage.

Dailey, S. F., Gill, C. S., Karl, S. L., & Bario Minton, C. A. (2014). DSM-5 *learning companion for counselors*. Alexandria, VA: American Counseling Association.

Dougherty, J. L. (2005). Ethics in case conceptualization and diagnosis: Incorporating a medical model into the developmental counseling tradition. *Counseling and Values, 49*(2), 132–140.

Dowling, M., & Rickwood, D. (2014). Investigating individual online synchronous chat counselling processes and treatment outcomes for young people. *Advances in Mental Health, 12*(3), 216–224. do i:10.1080/18374905.2014.11081899

Duffey, T. (2005). *Creative interventions in grief and loss therapy: When the music stops, a dream dies*. New York, NY: Haworth Press.

Duffey, T. (2006/2007). Promoting relational competencies in counselor education through creativity and relational-cultural theory. *Journal of Creativity in Mental Health, 2*, 47–60. doi:10.1300/J456v02n01_05

Duffey, T. (2015). Divorce and other issues in family therapy. In D. Capuzzi & M. Stauffer (Eds.), *Foundations of couples, marriage, and family counseling* (pp. 449–482). Hoboken, NJ: Wiley.

Duffey, T. (2016, June). Know your impact. *Counseling Today, 58*(12), 5.

Duffey, T., Haberstroh, S., Ciepcielinski, E., & Gonzales, C. (2016). Relational-cultural theory and supervision: Evaluating developmental relational counseling. *Journal of Counseling & Development, 94*, 405–414. doi:10.1002/jcad.12099

Duffey, T., Haberstroh, S., & Trepal, H. (2016). Creative approaches in counseling and psychotherapy. In D. Capuzzi & M. Stauffer (Eds.), *Counseling and psychotherapy: Theories and interventions* (pp. 445–468). Alexandria, VA: American Counseling Association.

Duffey, T., & Somody, C. (2011). The role of relational-cultural theory in mental health counseling. *Journal of Mental Health Counseling, 33*, 223–242. doi:10.17744/mehc.33.3.c10410226u275647

Duncan, B. L. (2010). *The heart and soul of change: Delivering what works in therapy* (2nd ed.). Washington, DC: American Psychological Association.

Elmore, T. M. (1985). The era of ACES: Tradition, transformation, and the possible dream. *Journal of Counseling & Development, 63*, 411–415. doi:10.1002/j.1556-6676.1985.tb02821.x

Evans, M., Duffey, T., Erford, B. T., & Gladding, S. T. (2013). Counseling in the United States. In T. Hohenshil, N. Amundson, & S. Niles (Eds.). *Counseling around the world: An international handbook* (pp. 323–334). Alexandria, VA: American Counseling Association.

Even, T. A., & Robinson, C. (2012). The impact of CACREP accreditation: A multiway frequency analysis of ethics violations and sanctions. *Journal of Counseling & Development, 91*, 26–34. doi:10.1002/j.1556-6676.2013.00067.x

Fair Access Coalition on Testing. (2015, October 22). *Kentucky Psychology Board withdraws restrictive testing rules* [Press release]. Retrieved from www.fairaccess.org/extras/fairaccess/pdfs/FACT_Press_Release_on_KY_Test_Rules_10-15-1.pdf

Foster, L. H. (2012). Professional counselor credentialing and program accreditation in the United States: A historical review. *Journal for International Counselor Education, 4,* 42–56.

Frey, L. L. (2013). Relational-cultural therapy: Theory, research, and application to counseling competencies. *Professional Psychology: Research and Practice, 44*(3), 177–185. doi:10.1037/a0033121

Fulton, J. J., Calhoun, P. S., Wagner, H. R., Schry, A. R., Hair, L. P., Feeling, N., & Beckham, J. C. (2015). The prevalence of posttraumatic stress disorder in Operation Enduring Freedom/Operation Iraqi Freedom (OEF/OIF) veterans: A meta-analysis. *Journal of Anxiety Disorders, 31,* 98–107. doi:10.1016/j.janxdis.2015.02.003

Goldberg, R., Dixon, A., & Wolf, C. P. (2012). Facilitating effective triadic counseling supervision: An adapted model for an underutilized supervision approach. *The Clinical Supervisor, 31*(1), 42–60. doi:10.1080/07325223.2012.670077

Goodyear, R. K. (2000). An unwarranted escalation of counselor-counseling psychologist professional conflict: Comments on Weinrach, Lustig, Chan, and Thomas (1998). *Journal of Counseling & Development, 78,* 103–106. doi:10.1002/j.1556-6676.2000.tb02566.x

Gordon, C., & Luke, M. (2016). "We are in the room to serve our clients": We and professional identity socialization in e-mail supervision of counselors-in-training. *Journal of Language and Social Psychology, 35*(1), 56–75. doi:10.1177/0261927X15575577

Haberstroh, S. (2010). College counselors' use of informal language online: Student perceptions of expertness, trustworthiness, and attractiveness. *Cyberpsychology, Behavior, and Social Networking, 13,* 455–459. doi:10.1089/cyber.2009.0280

Haberstroh, S., Barney, L., Foster, N., & Duffey, T. (2014). The ethical and legal practice of online counseling and psychotherapy: A review of mental health professions. *Journal of Technology in Human Services, 32*(3), 149–157. doi:10.1080/15228835.2013.872074

Haberstroh, S., & Duffey, T. (2016). Establishing and navigating relationships in online supervision. In T. Rousmaniere & E. Renfro-Michel (Eds.), *Using technology to enhance clinical supervision* (pp. 87–102). Alexandria, VA: American Counseling Association.

Haberstroh, S., Duffey, T., Evans, M., Gee, R., & Trepal, H. (2007). The experience of online counseling. *Journal of Mental Health Counseling, 29*(3), 269–282.

Haberstroh, S., Parr, G., Bradley, L., Morgan-Fleming, B., & Gee, R. (2008). Facilitating online counseling: Perspectives from counselors in training. *Journal of Counseling & Development, 86,* 460–470. doi:10.1002/j.1556-6678.2008.tb00534.x

Hanna, F. J., & Bemak, F. (1997). The quest for identity in the counseling profession. *Counselor Education and Supervision, 36,* 194–206. doi:10.1002/j.1556-6978.1997.tb00386.x

Harrington, J. (2013). Contemporary issues in private practice: Spotlight on the self-employed mental health counselor. *Journal of Mental Health Counseling, 35,* 189–197. doi:10.17744/mehc.35.3.8742717176154187

Holmes, C., & Foster, V. (2012). A preliminary comparison study of online and face-to-face counseling: Client perceptions of three factors. *Journal of Technology in Human Services, 30*(1), 14–31. doi:10.1080/15228835.2012.662848

Horne, A. M. (2013). Looking to the future—The role of master's programs in counseling psychology: A response to "Quality of Master's Education: A Concern for Counseling Psychology?" *The Counseling Psychologist, 41,* 710–716. doi:10.1177/0011000012473165

Jackson, M. A., & Scheel, M. J. (2013a). Integrating master's education in counseling psychology for quality, viability, and value added. *The Counseling Psychologist, 41,* 717–723.

Jackson, M. A., & Scheel, M. J. (2013b). Quality of master's education: A concern for counseling psychology? *The Counseling Psychologist, 41,* 669–699. doi:10.1177/0011000011434644

Jun, H. (2009). *Social justice, multicultural counseling, and practice: Beyond a conventional approach.* Thousand Oaks, CA: Sage.

Kaplan, D. M., Tarvydas, V. M., & Gladding, S. T. (2014). 20/20: A vision for the future of counseling: The new consensus definition of counseling. *Journal of Counseling & Development, 92,* 366–372.

Kassirer, S., Delaney, N., Goldstein, L., Taylor, M., Dobmeier, R., & Hernández, T. (2013). Scope of practice impact on employability in New York State: Director and counselor views. *Journal of Mental Health Counseling, 35,* 360–376. doi:10.17744/mehc.35.4.2kt620333064707

Knoff, H. M. (1988). Clinical supervision, consultation, and counseling: A comparative analysis for supervisors and other educational leaders. *Journal of Curriculum and Supervision, 3*(3), 240–252.

Ladany, N., & Bradley, L. J. (2011). *Counselor supervision* (4th ed.). Florence, KY: Taylor & Francis. doi:10.4324/9780203877630

Lester, P., Peterson, K., Reeves, J., Knauss, L., Glover, D., Mogil, C., & Beardslee, W. (2010). The long war and parental combat deployment: Effects on military children and at-home spouses. *Journal of the American Academy of Child & Adolescent Psychiatry, 49*(4), 310–320. doi:10.1097/00004583-201004000-00006

Mabeus, C., & Van Woerkom, B. (2015, October 28). *Missed treatment: Soldiers with mental health issues dismissed for "misconduct."* Retrieved from www.npr.org/2015/10/28/451146230/missed-treatment-soldiers-with-mental-health-issues-dismissed-for-misconduct

Marotta, S. A. (2003). Unflinching empathy: Counselors and tortured refugees. *Journal of Counseling & Development, 81,* 111–114.

Mascari, J. B., & Webber, J. M. (2006). Salting the slippery slope: What licensing violations tell us about preventing dangerous ethical situations. In G. R. Walz, J. Bleuer, & R. K. Yep (Eds.), *VISTAS: Compelling perspectives on counseling, 2006* (pp. 165–168). Alexandria, VA: American Counseling Association.

Mascari, B., & Webber, J. (2013). CACREP accreditation: A solution to licensure portability and counselor identity problems. *Journal of Counseling & Development, 91,* 15–25. doi:10.1002/j.1556-6676.2013.00066.x

Mellin, E. A. (2009). Unpacking interdisciplinary collaboration in expanded school mental health: A conceptual model for developing the evidence base. *Advances in School Mental Health Promotion, 2,* 4–14.

Mellin, E. A., Hunt, B., & Nichols, L. M. (2011). Counselor professional identity: Findings and implications for counseling and interprofessional collaboration. *Journal of Counseling & Development, 89,* 140–147. doi:10.1002/j.1556-6678.2011.tb00071.x

Merrill, T. S. (2003). Licensure anachronisms: Is it time for a change? *Professional Psychology: Research & Practice, 34,* 459–462. doi:10.1037/0735-7028.34.5.459

Meyers, L. (2016, July). License to deny services. *Counseling Today, 59*(1), 24–31.

Miller, W. R., & Rollnick, S. (2013). *Motivational interviewing: Helping people change* (3rd ed.). New York, NY: Guilford Press.

Morgen, K., Miller, G., & Stretch, L. S. (2012). Addiction counseling licensure issues for licensed professional counselors. *The Professional Counselor, 2*(1), 58–65.

Morissette, S., Bezyak, J. L., & Ososkie, J. N. (2012). A closer look at distance-based supervisory relationships in master's level rehabilitation counseling programs. *Journal of Applied Rehabilitation Counseling, 43*(2), 3–7.

National Board for Certified Counselors. (2015). *AMHCA-ACES-NBCC portability standards for counselors.* Retrieved from www.nbcc.org/assets/eblast/AMHCA-ACES-NBCC_Portability_Plan.pdf

National Board for Certified Counselors. (n.d.). *TRICARE.* Retrieved from www.nbcc.org/GovtAffairs/TRICARE

Nilsson, J. E., Schale, C. L., & Khamphakdy-Brown, S. (2011). Facilitating trainees' multicultural development and social justice advocacy through a refugee/immigrant mental health program. *Journal of Counseling & Development, 89,* 413–422. doi:10.1002/j.1556-6676.2011.tb02838.x

O*NET OnLine. (2016). *Summary report for: 21-1014.00—Mental health counselors.* Retrieved from www.onetonline.org/link/summary/21-1014.00

Olson, M. M., Russell, C. S., & White, M. B. (2001). Technological implications for clinical supervision and practice. *The Clinical Supervisor, 20*(2), 201–215.

Padden, D., & Agazio, J. (2013). Caring for military families across the deployment cycle. *Journal of Emergency Nursing, 39,* 562–569. doi:10.1016/j.jen.2013.08.004

Palmer, L. K. (2013). Legitimizing and reclaiming master's training and education in counseling psychology: An urgent concern. *The Counseling Psychologist, 41,* 700–609. doi:10.1177/0011000012473164

Patterson, S. M. (2015). *With Internet connection reaching new heights, ITU looks to the IoT.* Retrieved from www.networkworld.com/article/3008495/internet-of-things/with-internet-connection-reaching-new-heights-itu-looks-to-the-iot.html

Prosek, E., & Holm, J. (2014). Counselors and the military: When protocol and ethics conflict. *The Professional Counselor, 4*(2), 93–102. doi:10.15241/eap.4.2.93

Ramchand, R., Rudavsky, R., Grant, S., Tanielian, T., & Jaycox, L. (2015). Prevalence of, risk factors for, and consequences of posttraumatic stress disorder and other mental health problems in military populations deployed to Iraq and Afghanistan. *Current Psychiatry Reports, 17*(5), 1–11. doi:10.1007/s11920-015-0575-z

Ratts, M. J., Singh, A. A., Nassar-McMillan, S. C., Butler, S. K., & McCullough, J. R. (2016). Multicultural and social justice counseling competencies: Guidelines for the counseling profession. *Journal of Multicultural Counseling and Development, 44,* 28–48.

Rausch, M. A. (2014). Contextual career counseling for transitioning military veterans. *Journal of Employment Counseling, 51,* 89–96. doi:10.1002/j.2161-1920.2014.00044.x

Reese, R. F., Young, J. S., & Hutchinson, G. A. (2013). Preparing counselors-in-training for private practice: A course in clinical entrepreneurship. *The Professional Counselor, 3*(1), 23–33.

Sackett, C., Lawson, G., & Burge, P. (2015). Supervisor, counselor-in-training and client perspectives in counseling: A qualitative exploration. *The Professional Counselor, 5*(1), 163–174. doi:10.15241/crs.5.1.163

Savic-Jabrow, P. C. (2010). Where do counsellors in private practice receive their support? A pilot study. *Counselling and Psychotherapy Research, 10*(3), 229–232. doi:10.1080/14733140903469889

Spurgeon, C. (2012). Counselor identity—A national imperative. *Journal of Professional Counseling, Practice, Theory, & Research, 39*(1), 3–16.

Stark, M. D., Nichter, M., Watts, R. E., Slate, J. R., Bruhn, R., & Nelson, J. A. (2013). Texas LPC interns and the cost of supervision. *Journal of Professional Counseling, Practice, Theory, & Research, 40*(1), 25–37.

Stommel, W., & te Molder, H. (2015). Counseling online and over the phone: When preclosing questions fail as a closing device. *Research on Language and Social Interaction, 48*(3), 281–300. doi:10.1080/08351813.2015.1058605

Strong, T. (2015). Diagnoses, relational processes and resourceful dialogs: Tensions for families and family therapy. *Family Process, 54,* 518–532. doi:10.1111/famp.12140

U.S. Department of Defense. (2014). TRICARE certified mental health counselors: Final rule. *Federal Register, 79*(137), 41636–41642. Retrieved from www.gpo.gov/fdsys/pkg/FR-2014-07-17/pdf/2014-16702.pdf

U.S. Department of Veterans Affairs. (2015). *PTSD: National center for PTSD.* Retrieved from www.ptsd.va.gov/public/PTSD-overview/reintegration/help-for-veterans-with-ptsd.asp

Villalba, J. A. (2009). Addressing immigrant and refugee issues in multicultural counselor education. *Journal of Professional Counseling, Practice, Theory, & Research,* 37(1), 1–12.

Wampold, B. E., Imel, Z. E., Laska, K. M., Benish, S., Miller, S. D., Flückiger, C., ... Budge, S. (2010). Determining what works in the treatment of PTSD. *Clinical Psychology Review, 30,* 923–933. doi:10.1016/j.cpr.2010.06.005

Wheeler, A. M., & Bertram, B. (2015). *The counselor and the law: A guide to legal and ethical practice* (7th ed.). Alexandria, VA: American Counseling Association.

Williams, F. C. (2003). Concerns of newly arrived immigrant students: Implications for school counselors. *Professional School Counseling, 7,* 9–14.

Yakushko, O., Backhaus, A., Watson, M., Ngaruiya, K., & Gonzalez, J. (2008). Career development concerns of recent immigrants and refugees. *Journal of Career Development, 34*(4), 362–396. doi:10.1177/0894845308316292

Yakushko, O., Watson, M., & Thompson, S. (2008). Stress and coping in the lives of recent immigrants and refugees: Considerations for counseling. *International Journal for the Advancement of Counselling, 30*(3), 167–178. doi:10.1007/s10447-008-9054-0

Zeren, S. G. (2015). Face-to-face and online counseling: Client problems and satisfaction. *Egitim Ve Bilim, 40*(182), 127–141.

Chapter 13

Personal and Professional Counselor Identity Development

Craig S. Cashwell and W. Bradley McKibben

Learning Objectives

1. Understand various aspects of personal and professional development.
2. Characterize the critical factors in counselor identity development.
3. Evaluate your own developmental progress to date and important developmental markers that remain.
4. Understand the integration of personal and professional development.

• • •

What does it mean for you to develop an identity as a professional counselor? One of the most scholarly developmental theorists, Erik Erikson, argued that identity formation occurs as we establish a self-image that evolves out of social interaction (Erikson, 1994). In that vein, your identity as a professional counselor will evolve out of how you come to understand yourself through the ongoing developmental process of gaining knowledge and skills as a professional counselor. This developmental process largely occurs through your interactions not only with course content but also with professors, supervisors, peers, and clients. In this chapter, we briefly discuss the global process through which counselor development occurs, although each individual has his or her own unique developmental experience in ways far too nuanced to capture in one chapter. In that spirit, what we present here is a broad framework for counselor development.

If you are early in your training, you may be more focused on establishing your professional identity as a counselor by developing your skills, understanding theory, and learning about current issues in the field. Researchers who have examined counselor identity development, however, have found that it is the integration of personal and professional identity that serves as a hallmark of counselor identity development (Moss, Gibson, & Dollarhide, 2014). Accordingly, we examine both personal and professional development in this chapter and attempt to highlight how the two are inextricably interwoven throughout your lifelong journey as a professional counselor. Perhaps this point—that development as a professional counselor is a lifelong commitment to learning, skill development, and self-reflection—is the single most important point we make in this chapter. Although development may look quite different in various seasons of your career, it is indeed a commitment to a lifelong developmental journey.

What Does It Mean to Be a Professional Counselor?

Throughout this chapter, we use the term *professional counselor* to refer to a licensed and credentialed counselor trained minimally at the master's level with a degree in counseling. We use this term with great intention and encourage you to describe yourself in this way as well. Unfortunately, the term *counselor* is not a well-protected term legally, so the term *professional* is important for distinguishing yourself from others who call themselves counselors (such as sales counselors or attorneys). In all likelihood, you will meet professional counselors who define themselves as a *therapist* or *psychotherapist,* but these generic terms do not accurately tell the public who you are as a professional. In fact, we argue that it is an act of professional advocacy to always call yourself a *professional counselor*, as this most accurately describes who you are!

On a related note, self-identifying as a professional counselor gives primacy to your identity as a counselor. When counselors self-identify first by their specialization (e.g., school counseling, clinical mental health counseling, college counseling, addictions counseling), this serves to fragment the counseling profession and weaken advocacy efforts, particularly when these subspecialties work at cross-purposes. As noted by Sweeney (1995), "No single specialty has the equivalent influence and strength that comes from the united effort called professionalization . . . one should know that the saying 'united we stand, divided we fall' is more than just a slogan" (p. 117). If you wish, you can provide information on your work setting or population of interest by saying, "I am a professional counselor in an elementary school" or "I am a professional counselor who specializes in addictions." Being intentional about how you identify yourself to the public and to consumers is an important act of advocacy.

What is it then that makes professional counselors unique from others in the mental health service delivery system? We want to emphasize that we hold other mental health professions, including psychology, social work, marriage and family therapy, and psychiatry, in the highest regard. All are necessary in the continuum of services needed by people facing challenging mental health issues and crises. That is, our stance throughout this chapter is that counseling as a profession is neither better nor worse than any other mental health profession. What is critical, however, is to recognize the unique niche held by professional counselors in the world of mental health service delivery.

As highlighted in Sidebar 13.1, it has long been argued that what makes professional counselors unique in the world of mental health services is a focus on wellness, development, and prevention. If you are a professional counselor working in a more clinical setting, you may need to understand the language of the medical model (i.e., there is something wrong with the client that needs to be fixed; to do this, the expert must first diagnose the problem and prescribe a treatment). If you are a professional counselor working in a school setting, you may need to speak the language of teachers and administrators (who say "student"

Sidebar 13.1   Voice From the Field

"To me, being a professional counselor is a deeply personal endeavor that calls forth my most human instincts while abiding by professional standards and best practices of the profession. As the son and grandson of educators and ministers, serving others through knowledge sharing, advocacy, and encouragement has been in my proverbial DNA. Professional counseling was a natural extension of my being, a refinement of my desires to find the best in others and encourage them to experience wellness in all parts of their lives. Although my personhood impacts my practice, I have also grown by being challenged by supervisors and current research that enable me to see beyond myself. I am proud to be a part of this community of professionals who make me a better practitioner and a better person."

—Michael D. Brubaker, PhD
Associate Professor
University of Cincinnati

• • •

rather than "client" and who emphasize academic achievement). At the same time, as a professional counselor, the lens through which you see a client is different. Professional counselors view clients first as people (as opposed to symptoms or diagnoses) who have a developmental story that informs their current struggles and successes. This triumvirate focus on wellness, development, and prevention is more than theoretical; researchers have supported the fact that professional counselors operate from this focus (Mellin, Hunt, & Nichols, 2011).

Although your preferred work setting may require you to provide formal diagnoses for clients—and in fact we argue that counselors need a working familiarity with the *Diagnostic and Statistical Manual of Mental Disorders, Fifth Edition* (American Psychiatric Association, 2013)—this does not mean that you abandon your counseling roots. If you reduce a client to a cluster of symptoms that constitute a clinical diagnosis, the best that you can hope for is symptom reduction. If, however, you operate from a wellness paradigm that does not simply settle for symptom reduction, you have the potential to foster optimal development and functioning for clients. In fact, wellness, development, and prevention are the key cornerstones of the counseling profession (Myers, 1992).

When possible, professional counselors provide services broadly to society to block the onset of symptoms (primary prevention; e.g., teaching students about mental health hygiene) or target people at increased risk for developing symptoms (secondary intervention; e.g., running a grief loss support group) as an early intervention. Even when professional counselors are working with clients who have already developed symptoms (tertiary prevention; e.g., individual counseling with a client struggling with depression), their training encourages them to see with different eyes. Sidebar 13.2, which gives the perspective of a practicing professional counselor, highlights this point.

Sidebar 13.2   Voice From the Field

"I believe being a professional counselor means accepting the honor of being a person who sees. People's stories are sacred spaces, sometimes only revealed in this relationship of trust and safety. After working with many mental health providers from various educational disciplines, I am struck by the distinction that most professional counselors have a greater ability to see themselves and what they bring into the counseling room. Within this shared awareness, the amazing work of healing begins to grow. Having both the ability and flexibility to notice—to see and celebrate victories as they show up, even when they are different from our brilliant treatment plans. That is for me the heart of being a professional counselor."

—Anita Faulkner, MS, LPCS

• • •

Along with emphasizing prevention and a strengths-based focus, counselors recognize that each client is a product of his or her developmental experiences. Thus, to fully join with the client and truly be able to empathize, it is necessary to hear and strive to fully understand the client's developmental narrative. For example, so-called borderline personality features may simply be a product of unprocessed trauma (MacIntosh, Godbout, & Dubash, 2015). Consider the importance of this alternative lens for a moment. One lens labels the client with a personality disorder characterized by extreme reactions, labile mood swings, and impulsive and dangerous behaviors, whereas the other recognizes with compassion that the individual has experienced severe trauma and that the current behaviors, however bizarre, can only be understood through the developmental lens of the trauma that he or she has experienced (Herman, Perry, & van der Kolk, 1989).

Developing a Personal Identity

Among the many aspects of your personal identity that will be important in your development as a professional counselor, three that are particularly salient to highlight are self-awareness, realistic expectations, and self-care.

Self-Awareness

"Know thyself" is a maxim that dates back to the teachings of Greek philosophers, with the words found inscribed at the temple of Apollo at Delphi. Although there is much content for you as a developing counselor to learn in the classroom and supervision, this learning will have limited impact on your counseling work without a process of self-examination and emerging self-awareness (Pompeo & Levitt, 2014; Skovholt & Ronnestad, 1992). When asked what surprises them most about graduate school, students often respond that they are surprised by the amount of self-reflection they are invited to do and at times how difficult this is. One thing that makes this difficult is that as a student you wrestle with your own self-awareness, particularly awareness of your limitations, in an environment rife with external evaluations. This extensive evaluation may at times leave you feeling vulnerable and unsure how much to disclose to fellow students, supervisors, or professors about your struggles. We compare our internal experience, particularly our self-doubts, with what we observe in others, who seem to be more confident than we feel.

Self-doubt and a vocal inner critic are among the most normal experiences of graduate students. The journey to becoming a professional counselor is not a path of mastery but a path of development, of stumbling, of learning from those stumbles, of seeing our own struggles mirrored in the lives of the clients we see, and of uncovering yet another piece of our own unfinished business.

This emerges from readings, lectures, course discussions, role plays, and client contact. Many counselors-in-training have previously been in their own counseling, yet graduate school awakens a longing for even deeper self-awareness, and they return to counseling. For others, graduate school brings an initial awareness of family-of-origin issues and other unresolved psychological struggles that lead them to pursue their own counseling (see Sidebar 13.3).

For the record, we do not support mandated counseling for all students. We believe, in general, that students should pursue their own counseling when they are ready, on their own time, and that in most cases, this should be an autonomous decision made by the student (the exception being a student deemed impaired by the faculty). At the same time, we often hear students who are resistant to being in the other chair. For our purposes here, we argue simply that the best counselors are the ones who have done, are doing, and will continue to do their own work to optimize their wellness and wholeness.

Idealism to Realism

One transformational task of developing counselors is to move from an idealistic stance to one that is more realistic (Moss et al., 2014). Many, if not most, people are drawn to the counseling profession with a somewhat naïve perspective of what it will mean to help other people as a professional counselor. Although there may be many facets to this naiveté, three that are common are (a) assuming that clients will be ready to change, (b) failing to understand how issues such as

---

Sidebar 13.3   Self-Reflection

Consider the following scenario. You might journal and/or discuss your reflections with classmates. Assume that a favorite professor in your program walked into class and announced a new policy in your counseling program that required all students to undergo at least 10 sessions of counseling at the university counseling center.

What is your initial reaction to this? (Include thoughts, feelings, and any actions you would take.)

Do you have some clarity about what you would focus on in your counseling?

Do you believe it is in the purview of the program to make this a requirement?

What are the upsides of requiring counseling?

What are the downsides?

• • •

perfectionism and self-efficacy affect development and growth, and (c) idealizing what relationships with clients will be like.

Often, students begin their studies with the belief that clients will present in counseling ready to change and with no ambivalence or fear of changing. As practicum and internship experiences begin, however, students realize (often quickly) that ambivalence often arises from a fear of change, leading a client who is earnestly asking for help to resist every effort on the counselor's behalf to facilitate change (Bugental & Bugental, 1984). Counselors early in their development are particularly prone to taking this personally and to responding by either being overly self-critical or being critical of the client and labeling him or her as *resistant* rather than honoring the fear that naturally emerges for most around making substantial changes in life. On a related note, the ethical principle of autonomy suggests that clients have the right to choose whether they want to change (Kitchener & Anderson, 2011), a fact that is difficult for many counselors early in their development to fully grasp and embrace.

Somewhat related to this is that many students struggle with self-efficacy and perfectionism in ways that make it difficult for them to enter into genuine dialogue with both supervisors and clients (Ganske, Gnilka, Ashby, & Rice, 2015), which can limit their development and counseling effectiveness. When a client's fear of change interacts with a beginning counselor's own self-efficacy and perfectionistic tendencies, and when the beginning counselor fails to see and understand this interaction, the results can be debilitating. Furthermore, students who are struggling with self-efficacy and perfectionism may be less inclined to be open with supervisors and peers with these struggles (Ganske et al., 2015), which further impedes their development.

Finally, counselors-in-training often are naïve about the relational challenges of working as a professional counselor, thinking that relationships with clients will be positive and easy. Although this is the case with many clients, some clients present in counseling with life struggles that emerge in part out of their social and interpersonal style. For other clients, historical factors, such as institutional racism, may provide a backdrop for their hesitancy to fully engage in counseling. In such cases, it can be challenging to form a therapeutic working alliance between counselor and client. This is normal, and experienced professional counselors understand that building a healthy therapeutic relationship will take time with some clients. In fact, for some clients, establishing a positive working alliance may ultimately be the core aspect of their progress in counseling. For counselors-in-training with limited experience, however, these challenging relationships can interact with low counselor self-efficacy or perfectionistic tendencies, leaving them impatient and frustrated with the client. Often, this is communicated to the client either overtly or covertly, reinforcing their expectations for a negative relationship.

In sum, one important aspect of counselor development is movement toward having realistic expectations of the client, the self, and the counseling process. Clinical supervision and consultation are vital aspects to support the student in establishing realistic expectations.

Self-Care

Given the complexities of counselor personal development discussed to this point, it is not surprising that Moss et al. (2014) found that a transformational task for counselors was moving from burnout to rejuvenation. Simply stated, well counselors are better able to promote optimal wellness among clients (Witmer & Young, 1996). When carried to an extreme level, the absence of wellness can lead to counselor impairment and harm to clients (Lawson, Venart, Hazler, & Kottler, 2007). Thus, the importance of establishing a clear pattern of self-care cannot be emphasized enough. What better time to begin practicing self-care than as a student? Although self-care behaviors vary by individual, common activities include varying work responsibilities, using positive self-talk, balancing personal and professional lives, spending time with family, turning to spiritual beliefs, maintaining a professional identity (discussed below) and values, reading literature to maintain currency, and maintaining a sense of humor (Lawson & Myers, 2011). Personal self-care activities such as engaging in aerobic activity, taking time off work when needed, engaging in spiritual practices, and building relationships with noncounselors also may be important.

Developing a Professional Identity

Licensure and Credentialing

In addition to building your personal identity as a professional counselor, there are a variety of ways in which you can develop your professional identity. One way is to pursue licensure as a counselor in your state. A state counseling license essentially is permission from a state to provide professional counseling services (National Board for Certified Counselors [NBCC], 2016). All 50 states have licensure laws that detail the requirements necessary to become licensed. Although the names and requirements for licensure vary by state, there are some commonalities, such as earning a master's degree in counseling, passing a licensing exam, and completing a minimum number of supervised hours of post-master's counseling practice. The American Counseling Association (ACA) provides a list of all 50 state counseling boards on its website (www.counseling.org), along with contact information and the name of the license. Note that states vary in what they call a *licensed professional counselor,* which underscores the importance of what we mentioned earlier: How you describe yourself professionally to others matters and is a form of advocacy.

Another way to develop professionally is to obtain professional certification. Whereas a state license is granted by a state government as permission to practice counseling, certification is granted by a professional counseling organization. Although certification does not grant you permission to practice counseling in a given state, it does show that you have met professional standards or have obtained expertise in a counseling specialty or technique. NBCC is one professional organization that provides counselors with several certification opportunities. One of the most common, the National Certified Counselor (NCC) certification, demonstrates that a counselor has met national counseling standards (NBCC, 2016). We recommend that you explore the NCC certification as you prepare to graduate. One requirement to obtain an NCC certification is passing the National Counselor Examination (NCE), which is administered by NBCC. Some states also use the NCE as the state licensing exam; thus, you may be able to pursue state licensure and national certification by successfully passing the NCE.

Professional Organizations

Another way to develop professionally as a counselor is to join and get involved in professional organizations. Students and professionals can join ACA, which is the flagship organization for professional counseling, and some states have state-level branches of ACA (e.g., the North Carolina Counseling Association is a state-level branch of ACA). ACA also has 20 divisions focused more specifically on certain interests and practices. If you are a professional counselor working in schools, for example, you may wish to join the American School Counselor Association (ASCA). If you are interested in working with children, you may wish to join the Association for Child and Adolescent Counseling, the Association for Creativity in Counseling, the International Association of Marriage and Family Counselors, or all three! A unique counseling organization is Chi Sigma Iota (CSI), an international honor society specifically for professional counselors. CSI was designed to support counselors-in-training, practitioners, and educators with resources to achieve excellence in the field and to recognize the achievement of excellence. Joining CSI provides access to a wealth of professional development resources (e.g., webinars, essay contests, counseling resources) and opportunities to get involved at the chapter and national levels.

ACA and most of its divisions host annual conferences that offer opportunities to attend presentations on current issues and techniques, to learn from preeminent counseling scholars, to network with other counselors and share ideas, and to learn how you can advocate for clients and for the counseling profession. State-level organizations may also host conferences in your state. At each ACA conference, CSI hosts CSI Day, which is filled with workshops and resources for CSI members.

Many professional organizations also publish journals and newsletters to keep members informed about current issues and events. Other services provided by professional organizations may include education opportunities (e.g., workshops and webinars), information sharing, increased visibility and recognition (e.g., networking, advertising), and advocacy for counselors and clients (Darcy & Abed-Faghri, 2013). All of these benefits can enhance your professional counselor identity by connecting you to the profession and enhancing your knowledge and activity in the field.

Knowledge of History

Professional counseling has a rich history, and it is important for you to learn about where counselors come from to understand how counselors are similar to and distinct from other helping professionals. Indeed, CSI's *Principles and Practices of Leadership Excellence* (CSI Academy of Leaders, 1999) underscore the importance of preserving and understanding history to guide future decision making. Several chapters in this book have briefly recounted the history of counseling as a unified profession and how specialties have evolved in the field. Although a thorough investigation into the history and professional evolution of counseling is beyond the scope of this chapter—and, really, this book—there are many ways in which you can learn about our history. For example, ACA (2016b) and CSI (2016) have information about their respective organizations' history posted on their websites. Sweeney (2012) provided a comprehensive review of counseling history in *Professional Counseling Excellence Through Leadership and Advocacy* (Chang, Barrio Minton, Dixon, Myers, & Sweeney, 2012). In addition, Lawson (2016) chronicled how professional counseling developed as a distinct discipline from psychology and the implications this has had, and continues to have, on counselors' efforts to work toward licensure portability and parity with other mental health providers. Finally, getting involved in service and leadership in professional organizations is a great way to learn about our history from leaders in the field. By learning and understanding our history, you can further enhance your professional identity by discerning how we provide services to our clients from a uniquely counselor approach as well as how we work together with other helping professionals and community members to optimize service delivery.

Service and Leadership

You can develop your professional identity by getting involved in service and leadership opportunities. The vast majority of professional organizations depend on volunteers who serve on committees, panels, and task forces and in formal leadership roles (e.g., president, secretary). For example, ACA has 17 committees, subcommittees, and panels as well as two task forces at the time of this writing (ACA, 2016c). One committee, the Graduate Student Committee, is composed of students and is designed specifically to represent students' interests in the organization (ACA, 2016c). On a somewhat related note, initiation into CSI frequently occurs during training, and CSI offers a wide variety of resources and benefits to students specifically. Service and leadership in a professional organization is not only vital to an organization's success in achieving its mission and goals but also a great way for you to invest in your professional development. Service and leadership allow you to develop new interpersonal, leadership, and advocacy skills or to extend and refine existing skills. You can also benefit from mentorship from more experienced counseling leaders who can help you grow personally and professionally (Black & Magnuson, 2005; Borders & Cashwell, 2014; Luke & Goodrich, 2010; McKibben, Umstead, & Borders, 2017; Portman & Garrett, 2005). Finally, professional counselors may find rewarding opportunities to serve in their local communities in various civic and religious groups. This has a secondary gain of educating the broader public about the work of professional counselors.

Professional Advocacy

An extension of service and leadership is advocacy for clients and for the profession (McKibben et al., 2017). Indeed, to know the history of counseling is to know that counselors evolved as advocates for wellness, holism, and development across the life span in a variety of contexts (e.g., schools, career centers, community mental health). Counselors are often taught to be agents of social change for clients and the environments in which our clients live, but, as highlighted in Sidebar 13.4, we also must advocate for ourselves as professionals and the skills that we have to offer our clients (Myers, Sweeney, &

Sidebar 13.4 Voice From the Field

"A professional counselor is best exemplified by being a steward of the counselor education profession. That is, one has received formal training in counselor education and supervision and utilizes his or her counseling, teaching, and research skills to promote the dignity and worth of all human beings. Being a professional counselor requires one to be a fearless voice for the oppressed and for those that have temporarily lost their ability to cope with life."

—Carla R. Adkison-Bradley
Professor
Western Michigan University

• • •

White, 2002). Professional advocacy is necessary because the public—including clients, insurance companies, legislators, and professionals with whom counselors may work—does not always understand who counselors are, the skills we provide, and how our training and philosophy are distinct from those of other helping professionals. This, in turn, can limit clients' access to counseling services. Ultimately, the burden of clarifying our professional identity for the public lies with us, and we do this by advocating.

Many counseling organizations advocate for the profession by advancing practice and policy and by engaging in political advocacy. For example, NBCC, ACA, and the American Mental Health Counselors Association (AMHCA) have long advocated for increased hiring of counselors by the U.S. Department of Veterans Affairs, thereby increasing veterans' access to mental health services. They have done so largely by clarifying who counselors are and how they can meet veterans' needs. ASCA (2012) provided the *ASCA National Model* to clarify the roles of professional counselors working in schools throughout the United States. Finally, the Council for Accreditation of Counseling and Related Educational Programs (CACREP; 2016) provides a uniform set of minimum education and training standards for all graduates of accredited counselor education programs. These standards are a critical component of professional advocacy because they establish how counselors are educated and prepared for practice. Recently, the Association for Counselor Education and Supervision, AMHCA, and NBCC jointly endorsed a licensure portability plan that clarified a professional counselor identity for the purposes of uniform state licensure laws. Note that this portability plan identifies graduation from a CACREP-accredited counseling program as one pathway to licensure (NBCC, 2015).

Counseling organizations have a variety of groups and committees that offer information on issues facing the profession and provide an opportunity to get involved in advocacy. For example, ACA has a Government Affairs department that monitors legislation affecting counseling and takes action as necessary to strengthen our field (ACA, 2016a). Similarly, AMHCA has an Advancement of Clinical Practice Committee and a Public Policy and Legislation Committee. ASCA maintains a legislative affairs page on its website to keep members informed of issues and events affecting professional counselors in schools (ASCA, 2016). These are just a few examples!

That said, you do not have to be on an organizational committee to engage in professional advocacy. Each time you correctly explain to others who a counselor is and what a counselor does, you are advocating for the profession via education. The ability to concisely yet comprehensively describe your professional identity is perhaps the most important form of professional advocacy. One way that you can develop this skill is to develop a personal model of counseling.

A Personal Model of Counseling

A central component of your growth as a counselor is to develop a personal working model of counseling, which refers to how you comprehend and process the human experience and how you understand your role as a counselor. It can be quite overwhelming, if not impossible, to figure out why people do the things they do! In your counselor education program, you are exposed to theories of personality and human behavior; therapeutic models that structure the counseling process; ways to assess behaviors, thoughts, feelings, and values; and counseling skills that aid in working with clients in diverse settings. As overwhelming as it can be to make sense of the human experience and your role as a counselor, it can be equally challenging to integrate all of the information you learn in your counseling program into a personal model of counseling. If you find yourself overwhelmed by all of this information, do not worry! We are always developing as counselors, and as you gain experience and fluency with what you are learning in your counselor education program, you will be able to more comprehensively mold a model of counseling that fits you and your style.

When you first begin as a counselor-in-training, you likely have not yet developed a knowledge base for understanding clients' needs (Strasser & Gruber, 2015), but you do have a wealth of personal experience that has guided you through life to this point (Spruill & Benshoff, 2000; Wagner & Hill, 2015). You may be pursuing a career in professional counseling because you are a good listener or because you have a strong desire to help others. The first step you can take in developing a personal counseling model is to examine your strengths and abilities, your personal experiences, and your growing areas as you learn new information about what it means to be a professional counselor (Skovholt & Ronnestad, 1992; see Sidebar 13.5).

As you progress through your counselor education program, you will complete practica and internships in which you work with clients under close supervision. Your supervisors are an important resource in helping you navigate counseling practice for the first time, and they

---

Sidebar 13.5   Self-Reflection

As you work to build a personal model of counseling, consider the following questions:

How do the values of counseling align, or not, with your personal values?
What counseling skills seem to come naturally to you?
Which are more difficult and why?
When you learn about theories, which ones stand out to you?
Why is it that you are drawn to certain theories and not to others?

• • •

can help you mold your personal counseling model. With a supervisor, you can discuss many things, including what may or may not be happening with clients, what your clients may need from you, how to prevent or intervene in crises, how you can tend to your wellness as a counselor, and where your strengths and growing edges are. As you integrate feedback from your supervisor, you are developing your personal model of counseling.

In sum, evolving from a very basic understanding of counseling to a complex, flexible model of counseling takes time and effort. By working through the feedback you receive, trusting the growth process, embracing the multitude of emotions involved in the growth process, taking comfort in yourself and in others, and seeking out and gaining experience (Wagner & Hill, 2015), you are contributing to your own professional and personal growth. It is important to learn new information, to hear feedback from others, and to self-reflect openly and nondefensively. Counselors learn and grow by looking within as much as looking outward at others. Even the most skilled and experienced counselors reflect on who they are and how this affects how they view others and the counseling process (Skovholt, Jennings, & Mullenbach, 2004). In the end, you may very well find yourself thinking more complexly about yourself and your clients (Granello, 2002, 2010; Welfare & Borders, 2010), holding a stronger professional identity, being more self-aware, and feeling more confident and competent.

The Integration of Personal and Professional Identity

Although we have separated personal and professional identities for clarity in this chapter, one hallmark of counselor development is the integration of the two (Moss et al., 2014), with more experienced counselors reaching a level of congruence between their professional and personal selves, recognizing how their own life experiences shape their work as professional counselors. Although professional counselors must maintain a healthy boundary between their professional work and their personal lives as part of their self-care plan to avoid burnout and compassion fatigue, with experience and ongoing mentoring, you will grow to think of yourself as a professional counselor rather than thinking of counseling as what you do.

Chapter Summary

As noted in Sidebar 13.6, professional counselors affirm the dignity and respect of all persons and work to optimize wellness and potential for all. By intentionally developing both personally and professionally as a counselor, you are growing to join a noble profession. As with other aspects of development, it will not be linear. There will be

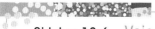

Sidebar 13.6 Voice From the Field

"I am proud to be a part of a community of competent professionals with a common philosophy and values related to helping others optimize their well-being across the life span. We work from a strengths-based perspective using methods that affirm dignity and respect for all. As a consequence, we are strong advocates for the realization of a healthy society as well as a vibrant profession."

—Tom Sweeney
Executive Director, Emeritus
CSI International

• • •

good days and bad days. There will be days where you think you nailed it in your counseling work and other days when you question whether you have what it takes to be a professional counselor. Seek help and support from other more senior members of our profession and recognize that identity development never ends. You will spend the remainder of your career continuing to evolve personally and professionally to optimize your impact as a professional counselor.

Learning Activities

1. Review the websites for CACREP, CSI, NBCC, and ACA. How does each promote counselor identity? If you were hired as a consultant, how would you encourage each organization to strengthen the promotion of a counselor identity using its Web presence?
2. Using the information provided in this chapter as a guideline, develop a prioritized list of two or three tasks that would promote your own identity development. Consult with a mentor or peer about your tasks. What obstacles might prevent you from moving forward? How can you overcome these barriers?
3. Review the websites of two to four state licensing boards for professional counseling in the United States. List the similarities and differences that you notice in the licensure requirements among the states. What would it take for the states you researched to have a portable license? How would you explain this to legislators in those states?
4. List three or four self-care strategies that are feasible and effective for you. For each strategy, describe a concrete plan (e.g., when, where, how, how often, with whom) for how you can implement the self-care strategy in your personal and/or professional life. Share your self-care plan with someone who will hold you accountable, and check in with him or her as you implement the strategies.

Review Questions

1. What does it mean to be a professional counselor?
2. How do self-awareness, moving from idealism to realism, and self-care factor into developing a personal identity as a counselor?
3. What are effective strategies for developing a professional identity as a counselor?
4. How does one integrate one's personal and professional identities as a counselor?

Further Resources

American Counseling Association
www.counseling.org
American Counseling Association Advocacy Competencies
https://www.counseling.org/docs/default-source/
competencies/advocacy_competencies.pdf?sfvrsn=9
Chi Sigma Iota, Counseling Academic and Professional Honor Society International
www.csi-net.org
Council for Accreditation of Counseling and Related Educational Programs
www.cacrep.org
National Board for Certified Counselors
www.nbcc.org

References

American Counseling Association. (2016a). *Government affairs.* Retrieved from https://www.counseling.org/government-affairs/public-policy

American Counseling Association. (2016b). *Our history.* Retrieved from www.counseling.org/about-us/about-aca/our-history

American Counseling Association. (2016c). *2017-2018 ACA committees.* Retrieved from https://www.counseling.org/about-us/leadership/committees

American Psychiatric Association. (2013). *Diagnostic and statistical manual of mental disorders* (5th ed.). Washington, DC: Author.

American School Counselor Association. (2012). *The ASCA national model: A framework for school counseling programs* (3rd ed.). Alexandria, VA: Author.

American School Counselor Association. (2016). *Legislative affairs.* Retrieved from https://www.schoolcounselor.org/school-counselors-members/legislative-affairs

Black, L. L., & Magnuson, S. (2005). Women of spirit: Leaders in the counseling profession. *Journal of Counseling & Development, 83,* 337–342.

Borders, L. D., & Cashwell, C. S. (2014). Nicholas A. Vacc: A legacy of professional leadership and mentoring. *Journal of Counseling & Development, 92,* 347–354.

Bugental, J. F. T., & Bugental, E. K. (1984). A fate worse than death: The fear of changing. *Psychotherapy, 21,* 543–549.

Chang, C. Y., Barrio Minton, C. A., Dixon, A. L., Myers, J. E., & Sweeney, T. J. (Eds.). (2012). *Professional counseling excellence through leadership and advocacy.* New York, NY: Taylor & Francis.

Chi Sigma Iota. (2016). *History of CSI.* Retrieved from www.csi-net.org/?page=History

Chi Sigma Iota Academy of Leaders. (1999). *Principles and practices of leadership excellence.* Retrieved from www.csi-net.org/?page=Leadership_Practices

Council for Accreditation of Counseling and Related Educational Programs. (2016). *2016 CACREP standards.* Retrieved from www.cacrep.org/for-programs/2016-cacrep-standards/

Darcy, M. G., & Abed-Faghri, N. M. (2013). The relationship between counselors and their state professional association: Exploring counselor professional identity. *The Professional Counselor, 3,* 152–160.

Erikson, E. (1994). *Identity and the life cycle.* New York, NY: Norton.

Ganske, K. H., Gnilka, P. B., Ashby, J. S., & Rice, K. G. (2015). The relationship between counseling trainee perfectionism and the working alliance with supervisor and client. *Journal of Counseling & Development, 93,* 14–24.

Granello, D. H. (2002). Assessing the cognitive development of counseling students: Changes in epistemological assumptions. *Counselor Education and Supervision, 41,* 279–293.

Granello, D. H. (2010). Cognitive complexity among practicing counselors: How thinking changes with experience. *Journal of Counseling & Development, 88,* 92–100.

Herman, J. L., Perry, C., & van der Kolk, B. A. (1989). Childhood trauma in borderline personality disorder. *American Journal of Psychiatry, 146,* 490–495.

Kitchener, K. S., & Anderson, S. K. (2011). *Foundations of ethical practice, research, and training in psychology and counseling* (2nd ed.). New York, NY: Routledge.

Lawson, G. (2016). On being a profession: A historical perspective on counselor licensure and accreditation. *Journal of Counselor Leadership and Advocacy, 3,* 71–84.

Lawson, G., & Myers, J. E. (2011). Wellness, professional quality of life, and career-sustaining behaviors: What keeps us well? *Journal of Counseling & Development, 89,* 163–171.

Lawson, G., Venart, E., Hazler, R. J., & Kottler, J. A. (2007). Toward a culture of counselor wellness. *Journal of Humanistic Counseling, Education and Development, 46,* 5–19.

Luke, M., & Goodrich, K. M. (2010). Chi Sigma Iota leadership and professional identity development in early career counselors. *Counselor Education and Supervision, 50,* 56–78.

MacIntosh, H. B., Godbout, N., & Dubash, N. (2015). Borderline personality disorder: Disorder of trauma or personality, a review of the empirical literature. *Canadian Psychology, 56,* 227–241.

McKibben, W. B., Umstead, L. K., & Borders, L. D. (2017). Identifying dynamics of counseling leadership: A content analysis study. *Journal of Counseling & Development, 95,* 92–102.

Mellin, E. A., Hunt, B., & Nichols, L. M. (2011). Counselor professional identity: Findings and implications for counseling and interprofessional collaboration. *Journal of Counseling & Development, 89,* 140–147.

Moss, J. M., Gibson, D. M., & Dollarhide, C. T. (2014). Professional identity development: A grounded theory of transformational tasks of counselors. *Journal of Counseling & Development, 92,* 3–12.

Myers, J. E. (1992). Wellness, prevention, development: The cornerstone of the profession. *Journal of Counseling & Development, 71,* 136–139.

Myers, J. E., Sweeney, T. J., & White, V. E. (2002). Advocacy for counseling and counselors: A professional imperative. *Journal of Counseling & Development, 80,* 394–402.

National Board for Certified Counselors. (2015). *AMHCA-ACES-NBCC portability standards for counselors.* Retrieved from www.nbcc.org/assets/eblast/AMHCA-ACES-NBCC_Portability_Plan.pdf

National Board for Certified Counselors. (2016). *Certification.* Retrieved from www.nbcc.org/Certification

Pompeo, A. M., & Levitt, D. H. (2014). A path of counselor self-awareness. *Counseling and Values, 59,* 80–94.

Portman, T. A. A., & Garrett, M. T. (2005). Beloved women: Nurturing the sacred fire of leadership from an American Indian perspective. *Journal of Counseling & Development, 83,* 284–291.

Skovholt, T. M., Jennings, L., & Mullenbach, M. (2004). Portrait of the master therapist: Developmental model of the highly functioning self. In T. M. Skovholt & L. Jennings (Eds.), *Master therapists: Exploring expertise in therapy and counseling* (pp. 125–146). Boston, MA: Allyn & Bacon.

Skovholt, T., & Ronnestad, M. (1992). Themes in therapist and counselor development. *Journal of Counseling & Development, 70,* 505–515.

Spruill, D. A., & Benshoff, J. M. (2000). Helping beginning counselors develop a personal theory of counseling. *Counselor Education and Supervision, 40,* 70–80.

Strasser, J., & Gruber, H. (2015). Learning processes in the professional development of mental health counselors: Knowledge restructuring and illness script formation. *Advances in Health Sciences Education, 20,* 515–530.

Sweeney, T. J. (1995). Accreditation, credentialing, professionalization: The role of specialties. *Journal of Counseling & Development, 74,* 117–125.

Sweeney, T. J. (2012). Leadership for the counseling profession. In C. Y. Chang, C. A. Barrio Minton, A. L. Dixon, J. E. Myers, & T. J. Sweeney (Eds.), *Professional counseling excellence through leadership and advocacy* (pp. 3–20). New York, NY: Taylor & Francis.

Wagner, H. H., & Hill, N. R. (2015). Becoming counselors through growth and learning: The entry transition process. *Counselor Education and Supervision, 54,* 189–202.

Welfare, L. E., & Borders, L. D. (2010). Counselor cognitions: General and domain-specific complexity. *Counselor Education and Supervision, 49,* 162–178.

Witmer, J. M., & Young, M. E. (1996). Preventing counselor impairment: A wellness approach. *Journal of Humanistic Education and Development, 34,* 141–155.

Index

Tables are indicated by "t" following the page numbers.

(Continued)

(Continued)

Discontinuous vs. continuous
development, 38
Discrimination
addiction and, 121
in career counseling, 150
clinical mental health counseling
and, 171, 177
human development and, 37,
39–40, 49–50
immigrant and refugee populations,
323–324
in professional counseling, 312
racial microaggressions, 49
Discrimination model of supervision,
18, 318–319
Dissociation and living with an addict, 115
Distance counseling and supervision,
15, 22–23, 276, 326–329
Distance Credentialed Counselor
certification, 326
Divergent evidence, 102
Diversity, 33–35. *See also* Multicultural
considerations
in addictions counseling, 121–123
in clinical mental health counseling,
173
in college counseling and student
affairs, 224, 226–227, 230
in couples and family counseling,
252, 259, 261
in school counseling, 295–296, 301,
303
Divorce, 267
Dollarhide, C. T., 91, 95
Domestic violence
addiction and, 116–117
in couples and family counseling, 261
Dopamine, 128
Double bind, 254
Downing, N. E., 48
Dream analysis, 41
Dreikurs, Rudolf, 252, 253
Drug abuse. *See* Addictions counseling
Drug Abuse Resistance Education
(DARE), 113
Drug education, 113
DrugRehab.us, 116
DSM–5 *(Diagnostic and Statistical
Manual of Mental Disorders, 5th ed.)*,
124, 168, 324–325, 344
Dual disorders treatment, 205–206
Duan, C., 68
Duffey, Thelma, 311–312, 320, 327
Dynamic theories of career counseling,
145–146

Dysfunctionality and functionality in
relationships, 263, 267–268

E

Ecological systems theory of human
development, 46–47
Ecstasy (drug), 114
Effect size, 94–95, 103
EFT (Emotion-focused therapy),
269–270
Egan, G., 72–73
Ego, 41
Elementary and Secondary Education
Act (1965), 286
Ellis, Albert, 70–71
Ellis, C. M., 68
Emotional regulation skills, 77–78
Emotion-focused therapy (EFT),
269–270
Empathy, 67–68, 71, 265
*Empirical Research Studies Supporting the
Value of School Counseling* (ASCA), 300
Encouragers, 73
Engel, George, 112
Epstein, J. L., 300–301
Epston, David, 254, 265
Erford, B. T., 66, 75
Erickson, Milton, 264
Erikson, Erik, 40, 42, 341
Erikson's psychosocial stages, 42, 42t
ESSA (Every Student Succeeds Act,
2015), 286
Ethics. *See also* Professional counseling
and ethical practice
in college counseling and student
affairs, 228t, 236–239, 236t
in couples and family counseling,
270–271
in distance counseling, 327–328
in professional counseling, 13–16
in rehabilitation counseling, 189
Evaluation. *See* Research and assessment
in counseling
Every Student Succeeds Act (ESSA,
2015), 286
Exception finding questions, 267
Existential therapy, 6
Exosystem, 46–47
Experiential family therapy, 265
Experimental research, 92–93
Expert witness testimony, 174–175
Exposure therapy, 322
Eye-movement desensitization therapy,
322

professional advocacy, 342–343,
351–352
professional identity, developing,
348–354
professional organizations, 349–350
self-awareness, 345–346
self-care, 348
service and leadership, 350–351
wellness model and, 343–345
Identity development theories, 47–49,
228t
Imitation, 43
Immigrant and refugee populations,
323–324
Incongruency, 260
Indiana State Board of Psychology,
176–177
Indirect student services, 294–295
Individual counseling, 66–74. *See also*
Group counseling; Helping relationships
for addiction, 118
basic counseling skills for, 72–74
counseling process and, 66–67
effective helping and, 67–69
listening skills and, 73–74
personal characteristics and self-care
and, 69–70
resistance vs. reluctance, 71–72
therapeutic alliance and, 70–72
Individuals with Disabilities Education
Act (1990), 207, 292
Informed consent, 14, 81, 234, 328
In loco parentis, 222, 239
Insurance and payment issues, 117–119,
121, 123, 276
Integrated developmental model of
supervision, 18–19
Integrated health care, 167–168
Integrative approaches to college counseling and student affairs, 240
Internal consistency, 101
Internal structure evidence, 102
International Association of Addictions
and Offender Counselors, 120
International Association of Marriage
and Family Counselors (IAMFC),
274–275, 349
International Association of Rehabilitation
Professionals, 191
International Classification of Diseases–10,
324
International Classification of Functioning, Disability, and Health (ICF), 194
Interpersonal communication, 77
Interpersonal relationships, 52

Interpersonal violence, 49, 259, 261,
312
Interpretation. *See* Research and assessment in counseling
Intersectionality, 34, 38–40, 51
Intrapersonal communication, 77
Ivey, A. E., 32, 72–73
Ivey, M. B., 72–73

J

Jackson, Don, 254
Jackson, M. A., 317
Jacobs, E. E., 77, 79
JBLI (Juhnke–Balkin Life Balance
Inventory), 98, 100–101
Jed Foundation, 235
Jefferson, J., 320
Jensen, M. A. C., 76
Job analysis research methods, 195
Johnson, Phillip D., 170
Johnson, Sue, 269–270
Journal of Mental Health Counseling,
168
Juhnke, G. A., 98
Juhnke–Balkin Life Balance Inventory
(JBLI), 98, 100–101
Jung, Carl, 42, 126
Justice in counseling, 14
Just Say No campaign, 113

K

Kaslow, F., 254
Kelly, S. M., 68
Kendrick, Kristi, 290
Kentucky Board of Examiners of Psychology, 177, 316–317
Kimbrough, S., 91
Knowledge-validation research methods,
195–196
Koob, G. F., 128
Kottler, J. A., 70, 71
Kraatz, R., 68
Krumboltz, John, 146–147

L

Lancaster, C., 91
Landon, Trenton, 185
Laszloffy, T. A., 259
Latinas/Latinos, addictions counseling
for, 122
Lawson, G., 350
Leahy, Michael J., 185, 195

(Continued)

Y